ART AND SCIENCE OF MANAGING PUBLIC RISKS

ART AND SCIENCE OF MANAGING PUBLIC RISKS

V S Ramamurthy
Dinesh K Srivastava
Shailesh Nayak
National Institute of Advanced Studies, Bengaluru, India

World Scientific

NEW JERSEY • LONDON • SINGAPORE • BEIJING • SHANGHAI • HONG KONG • TAIPEI • CHENNAI • TOKYO

Published by

World Scientific Publishing Co. Pte. Ltd.
5 Toh Tuck Link, Singapore 596224
USA office: 27 Warren Street, Suite 401-402, Hackensack, NJ 07601
UK office: 57 Shelton Street, Covent Garden, London WC2H 9HE

British Library Cataloguing-in-Publication Data
A catalogue record for this book is available from the British Library.

ART AND SCIENCE OF MANAGING PUBLIC RISKS

ISBN 978-981-125-402-4 (hardcover)
ISBN 978-981-125-439-0 (paperback)
ISBN 978-981-125-403-1 (ebook for institutions)
ISBN 978-981-125-404-8 (ebook for individuals)

For any available supplementary material, please visit
https://www.worldscientific.com/worldscibooks/10.1142/12770#t=suppl

Typeset by Stallion Press
Email: enquiries@stallionpress.com

We dedicate this monograph to
the future generations
with apologies for
not leaving behind a safer world.

Foreword

Stanley Miller and Harold Urey from the University of Chicago performed their famous experiment in 1952, which demonstrated that the conditions believed to have been prevailing in the upper reaches of Earth's atmosphere led to the synthesis of more complex organic compounds like amino acids from simple inorganic precursors. This was a brilliant confirmation of the concept of abiogenesis put forward by the British-Indian biologist J. B. Haldane in 1929.

This experiment excited Richard Feynman, who wrote his poem, *A Universe of Atoms, An Atom in The Universe*, which he read during his address at the National Academy of Sciences, USA, in 1955 and which most beautifully sums up the unique position occupied by man, with his conscious mind, made of atoms and his curiosity to understand the formation, constituents, and working of the Universe. The sheer beauty of the poem forces us to recall the early millions of years of the Earth's existence, when waves after waves of mountains of molecules, energized by the Sun, crashed on seashores, producing a white surf in unison on a dead planet till deep in the sea all molecules repeated patterns of each other and made complex new molecules, which grew in size and complexity, and made DNA, proteins, and living things, and performed an intricate dance of creation till man, made of

"... atoms with consciousness,

matter with curiosity,

stands at the sea,

wonders at wondering:

a universe of atoms

an atom in the universe."

This journey of man starting from inert inorganic molecules is the most fascinating journey ever, the details of which are still emerging. The journey of *Homo sapiens* has been anything but perilous, and many of his cousins, e.g., Neanderthals, *Homo erectus*, and *Homo Denisovan*, fell on the wayside as they could not adjust to the evolving conditions on the Earth, much like the Pandavas, falling on the wayside one by one, as they moved up into the Himalayas, leaving Yudhishthira alone to continue his journey.

By now, it is generally felt that *Homo sapiens* had the advantage of superior vocalization that helped them form larger groups, which are so much better at facing dangers and solving problems. They have, in the process, conquered land, sea, and airspace, and have started venturing beyond our planet. They have learnt to live under the harshest conditions even in the remotest part of the world. And they have multiplied, starting perhaps from a few tens of thousands to more than 7 billion now. This number is likely to touch 10 or 11 billion by 2050. Yet, we should not forget that despite our fascination and sustained effort, we have not found any other celestial body with signs of life so far. This tells us how precious life is and why we should do all that we can to preserve it in all its wondrous variety.

However, our planet has paid a very heavy price for harbouring "intelligent" life. Millions of flora and fauna species have gone extinct. The land, the water, and the air have become polluted. The use of fossil fuels has been loading tens of billions of tonnes of carbon dioxide and other greenhouse gases in the atmosphere every year, which is threatening to push Earth into a hot bath. The ice in the Arctic,

Antarctica, and Greenland is melting, glaciers across the world are receding, and the sea levels are rising. The frequency and intensity of cyclones and storms are rising across the globe. Droughts and floods are more severe, more frequent, and prolonged. Deforestation is changing the climate and the patterns of rainfall and snowfall. It is affecting the agriculture which provided enough for mankind over millennia and even more tragically, it is bringing man into conflict with wild animals, which animals are invariably losing. In the process, man is contracting zoonotic diseases. And the requirement of providing a decent life to the masses and to make profits have caused and continue to cause industrial disasters one after the other.

In this monograph, the authors, V. S. Ramamurthy, Dinesh. K. Srivastava, and Shailesh Nayak, use their vast experience and expertise to discuss the public risks faced by mankind, during its eventful journey to the present, and likely to be faced in future. Starting from the asteroid impact, which wiped out the dinosaurs 66 million years ago and cleared the stage for mammals to evolve, they proceed to discuss earthquakes, volcanic eruptions, tsunamis, cyclones, tornadoes, landslides, floods, and droughts, and even invasion of swarms of locusts. A brief historical introduction to major natural disasters is followed by the scientific understanding of the causes and discussions of how we can be better prepared to face these challenges.

Next, they proceed to describe infectious diseases, including plague, smallpox, cholera, polio, tuberculosis, malaria, and dengue, and discuss the heroic efforts of scientists to find cures and vaccines for many of these — some of which like smallpox and polio are eliminated, and many others are well understood, and on the road to complete elimination, with international collaboration, cooperation, and heroic efforts of healthcare workers — often in the face of an illiterate, ignorant, or even hostile population, negotiating very difficult terrain to reach remote areas.

The authors move on to discuss tragic industrial disasters and illustrate them using two tragic accidents, Bhopal Gas Tragedy and Deepwater Horizon Oil Spill, and some dam bursts. The first one brought untold misery, painful deaths, and life-long suffering to a large number of people and the corporation responsible for it got off lightly, while in the second case, a firm administration allowed an efficient cleanup and fair compensation to the victims.

The pollution of water bodies, with a detailed example of Ganga and efforts to clean it, is discussed next. The pollution due to municipal waste, medical waste, plastics, and e-waste are discussed along with methods to combat these. Next, they describe the notion of safe planetary boundaries, which are close to being breached beyond sustainability unless immediate action is taken on all fronts. And finally, the authors turn to risks from emerging technologies, which are in urgent need to be investigated and settled to be able to derive maximum benefits from them and use them for man's welfare.

Fortunately, governments across the world have now resolved to combat climate change, our most urgent crisis, after dilly-dallying, procrastinating, and denying it for decades and delaying actions for remedy, which only aggravated the matter further. The issue of epidemics and pandemics has revealed gaps in the preparedness of global healthcare infrastructure to meet such challenges. The issue of pollution has revealed the immediate need of involving everyone in handling the segregation of municipal waste and plastic waste and enforcing strict measures for handling them. It is known that many rich countries are exporting their waste to third world nations, which is a gross injustice, inhuman and cruel, to say the least.

The authors make it clear that the application of science is the primary means we have at our disposal to solve the mess in which humanity finds itself, and the solutions will invariably require open and persistent international collaborations. No nation can remain unaffected and isolated from infectious diseases, effects of climate change, large-scale industrial disasters, and massive pollution.

This will require that governments and the people across the world work unitedly. International collaboration has paid great dividends in putting up tsunami and cyclone warning systems in the Pacific and the Indian Ocean and has been saving large-scale casualties for quite some time.

For decades, the only organization which was available for a quick mobilization to handle large-scale disasters, be it floods, cyclones, earthquakes, tsunamis, dam bursts, etc., was the army of the country. The establishment of the National Disaster Response Force by the Government of India has filled this gap.

Even the sceptics and naysayers were forced to admit the vulnerability of mankind to a highly infectious virus, which has ravaged families, communities, economies, industries, education, entertainment, travel, and livelihood of masses across the world in the last 18 months or so. On the one hand, it brought into focus the enormous positive forces when societies, nations, and indeed the entire world cooperated to combat the SARS-Cov-2 virus, most notably in the sequencing and production of vaccines in a record time. On the other hand, it has also revealed the helplessness of poor nations who have limited or no access to vaccines, while the rich nations have apportioned enough doses to vaccinate their entire population several times over. This highly undesirable and inequitable situation is very unfortunate and can lead to serious consequences. There are also lessons in it for future challenges, such as climate change and its impacts on lives and economies.

This monograph brings forth the urgent need to include risk communication to our population from early childhood, so that in case of any unfortunate incident, our affected masses, whose wholehearted participation is a must for most steps to succeed, can be a help and not a burden and hindrance. In addition to accessible and affordable technologies, policies, regulations and laws, awareness creation and participation of individuals will play compelling roles. In the final analysis, a long-term resolution of the conflict between the modern concepts of sustainability and development will most likely require a strong commitment to global collaboration, together with a deep understanding of the need for curbing mindless consumption among the richest nations without sacrificing the legitimate aspirations of development elsewhere.

The monograph is written in a lucid style with excellent illustrations and with the inclusion of discussion of some of the quaint ideas due to lack of scientific knowledge and of heroic efforts by scientists and medical practitioners from across the world to make it safe for men to live and prosper. I personally like the analogy of Govardhan with science drawn by the authors for meeting all the past, present, and future risks to mankind and to our planet, for we do not have any other recourse. There is no planet B!

I congratulate the authors for bringing this important and oft-neglected issue to the fore in a forceful and clear manner and for raising the level of public discourse. I hope that the book becomes a source of valuable information for common people, young students, and officials alike.

Ashutosh Sharma
Former Secretary, Department of Science and Technology
Government of India, New Delhi

Preface

The years 2020 and 2021 will hold a unique place in our lives. The global pandemic, COVID-19, has turned our lives upside down. For more than a year, with no vaccines or drugs to protect us from the infection, we had no alternative but to live with the risk hanging on our heads like the proverbial sword of Damocles. By the first week of October 2021, the virus has already infected more than 235 million people in more than 220 countries and claimed over 4.8 million lives worldwide. In India alone, the number of infections is already close to 34 million and it has claimed nearly 0.45 million lives. Our lifestyles have changed, at the professional level, at the social level, and even at the personal level. Fortunately, several vaccines are now available and perhaps in a few months from now, the pandemic may even be gone and become a part of history.

Pandemics like COVID-19 have always been a part of human existence since time immemorial. Prior to the nineteenth century, in the absence of any means to combat the infection, every one of the pandemics took its own course. Only when most of the population acquired infection-induced immunity against the disease, commonly referred to as herd immunity, did the pandemic weaken and gradually disappear. It is not surprising that pandemics were invariably seen as acts of God. It is only in the last two centuries that we have seen the development of vaccines and drugs to combat some of the deadliest infectious diseases, such as smallpox and plague.

What struck us most as bizarre during the entire COVID-19 episode was the wide spectrum in the *perception* of people across the world not only about the risk posed by COVID-19 infection but also about the steps being taken to combat the infection.

For example, one witnessed a rather unexpected and sometimes widespread resistance to COVID Appropriate Behaviour (wearing a mask, observing social distancing, washing of hands frequently and avoiding touching nose, mouth, and eyes unnecessarily). This happened in spite of ample evidence that COVID Appropriate Behaviour limits the spread of infection considerably and has become mandatory in most countries. Yet, a small but vocal group of people have continued to refuse to follow these norms since they consider this as an infringement of their freedom and constitutional rights. It was even more surprising to see such resistance to COVID Appropriate Behaviour in some countries where even traffic rules are readily complied with.

A cause of even greater concern has been vaccine hesitancy, which refers to the reluctance to get vaccinated or even refusal to get vaccinated despite the availability of vaccines. Reasons for the hesitancy range from concerns about the safety and "purity" of vaccination to confidence or a "bravado" that "nothing will happen to me". Thus, Brazil, with a population of a little more than 200 million, ranks third in COVID cases globally, next only to the USA and India. It is fourth in the number of vaccine doses administered. It is indeed surprising to know that the President of Brazil not only chose not to get vaccinated but defied the New York vaccination rule for visitors to attend the Session of the UN General Assembly in September 2021. Closer home, we were surprised and aghast to hear a very senior and reputed advocate, tweeting that "the healthy and the young have hardly any chance of serious effects or dying due to COVID-19. They have a higher chance of dying due to vaccines".

The next cause for concern and worry is narrow political, religious, and cultural interests interfering with the pandemic management efforts. We have already seen political colour being attached to wearing masks in some countries. With more and more countries across the world opting for democratic forms of governance, political interests cannot be avoided. Religious and cultural sentiments against vaccinations are also well known. One may recall the resistance to the polio vaccine in some countries, which actually hampered global efforts to eradicate polio. In the case of a pandemic, one cannot afford to let narrow interests derail the efforts to combat the pandemic. We wonder: When shall the realization that "no one is safe unless everyone is safe" dawn upon these people?

Pandemics are textbook examples of what we call *public risks* — everyone is vulnerable to the risk, and everyone holds the key for containing the risk. Our experience with COVID-19 has brought out very clearly the importance of risk awareness creation among the public to the fore. In the absence of authentic and scientifically validated information, rumours, superstitions, and unverified claims inundate the public discourse, causing irreparable damage.

Pandemics are not the only public risks that humanity faces. Natural calamities such as cyclones, earthquakes, and industrial disasters also contribute to the spectrum of public risks that humans are exposed to. The fast-changing technologies of the twenty first century have also made humanity vulnerable to a completely new set of known and unknown public risks. The present monograph is an attempt to discuss public risks, what they are, how we have handled them in the past and how we prepare ourselves to face the emerging ones.

All three authors have emotional connections to the theme of the monograph.

V.S.R. and S.N., as heads of government departments, mandated to operate observational networks for weather and seismic information and to issue timely warnings of extreme weather events to the government and the public, had seen during their tenure several major natural disasters that the country faced, including the 1999 Orissa Super Cyclone, the 2001 Bhuj earthquake and the 2004 tsunami, the 2013 Phailin cyclone, and the 2019 Fani cyclone.

According to official estimates, the 1999 Orissa Super Cyclone resulted in the death of nearly 10,000 people and displaced several times more. The Bhuj earthquake killed between 13,800 and 20,000 people and injured another 167,000 people. The 2004 tsunami resulted in more than 10,000 casualties with another 5,000 people missing when it struck the southern coast of India and the Andaman and the Nicobar Islands. Following a major modernization of the weather monitoring, modelling capabilities and effective disaster warning systems, the 2013 cyclone Phailin and the 2019 cyclone Fani recorded far fewer fatalities than the Orissa Super Cyclone. S.N. was also responsible to put in place a state-of-the-art Tsunami Early Warning Centre, with a unique capability to analyze seismic and sea-level data, compute earthquake parameters, select the best possible scenario, generate, and disseminate hazard advisory through the web- and location-based services to all stakeholders in near-real time without any manual intervention. This is the only system in the Indian Ocean region that considers both tsunamigenic sources, i.e., the Makran Coast in the Arabian Sea and the Sumatra subduction zone. This centre is now the Regional Tsunami Watch Provider and contributes to the Indian Ocean Tsunami Warning System (IOTWS) and provides tsunami advisory for all Indian Ocean countries. S.N. was also deeply involved in coastal zone management and urban flood management strategies using remote sensing and geographic information system technologies.

D.K.S., during his tenure as Director of the Variable Energy Cyclotron Centre, Kolkata, had a close encounter with public perceptions when he had the responsibility of installing a new cyclotron in Kolkata to produce radioisotopes for medical purposes. Following the Fukushima reactor accident, considerable apprehensions against nuclear facilities close to human habitats were raised across the country and these included the new cyclotron facility in Kolkata. D.K.S. had an uphill task of convincing people that the apprehensions against the facility were ill placed. (The facility did not have a signboard for a long time to ensure that the site did not attract undue public attention.) The facility is fully functional now. D.K.S. has also been closely watching similar ill-placed public concerns on several mega-science projects, such as the Large Hadron Collider in Geneva, Thirty-Metre Optical Telescope in Mauna Kea Observatory in Hawaii, and India-based Neutrino Observatory in Tamil Nadu. While the Large Hadron Collider is making excellent contributions to research in high energy physics and led to the discovery of the Higgs boson following an effective communication campaign, the

India-based Neutrino Observatory (INO) project and the Thirty Metre Telescope (TMT) project are stalled till now. D.K.S. is highly committed to public risk communications to ensure that the public perceptions of such mega-science projects are realistic and are not emotional.

Writing this monograph was an emotional experience for all of us. Our feelings were best summarized in the Facebook post of one of the authors (D.K.S.).

"When we discussed natural disasters like earthquakes, volcanic eruptions, landslides, floods, tsunamis, droughts... I felt helpless.

When we discussed epidemics and pandemics like plague, smallpox, cholera, tuberculosis, malaria, dengue, polio, and COVID-19, I felt fragile but was comforted by Science.

However, when we discussed industrial disasters like the Bhopal Gas Tragedy and the Deepwater Horizon Oil Spill and mining disasters, I saw the duplicity of Multinationals as well as the weakness of the Government of India and the firmness of the US Government in dealing with the offenders, I felt slighted.

When we discussed pollution, I was furious, especially while writing about water bodies."

Risk assessment and management as a field of research evolved several decades ago and a number of research articles including review articles already exist. We have immensely benefited from past literature on the subject though we don't explicitly acknowledge them individually. This monograph is written for the benefit of readers who are not experts on risks but who have to face risks, specifically public risks, in their day-to-day life.

We have also benefited immensely from feedback on the draft manuscript received from several persons. We would specifically like to thank Richa Joshi, Dr Vidhya Ramakrishnan, Mehul Srivastava, and Devesh Kumar Srivastava for their critical comments. We are especially grateful to Prof D. Suba Chandran, Dean, Conflict and Security Studies, and his students Avishka Ashok, Sukanya Bali, Vaishnavi Iyer, Rashmi Ramesh, Akriti Sharma, and Lokendra Sharma, National Institute of Advanced Studies, and Profs. Madhumati Deshpande, N. Manoharan, and Shreya Upadhyay of

Christ University, Bengaluru for a careful reading of an early draft of this monograph and for making several valuable suggestions. We are also grateful to our spouses, Mrs Raji Ramamurthy, Mrs Rekha Srivastava, and Mrs Priti Nayak for bearing with us while we struggled with the collection of facts, checking and rechecking them, being obsessed with making the discussion intelligible to any enlightened common person and young students. We have also benefited immensely from the writings of many authors, not all of whom we have included in the references. We thank them and all those whose compilation of data and illustrations we benefited from. V.S.R. and D.K.S. are grateful for the support received from the National Institute of Advanced Studies, Bengaluru.

V. S. Ramamurthy, Dinesh K. Srivastava, Shailesh Nayak
National Institute of Advanced Studies
Bengaluru, India
November 2021

About the Authors

V. S. Ramamurthy (born 1942) is a well-known Indian nuclear scientist with a broad range of contributions from basic research to science administration. He is currently an Emeritus Professor at the National Institute of Advanced Studies in Bangalore.

Ramamurthy started his career in Bhabha Atomic Research Centre, Mumbai in the year 1963. He made important research contributions in the areas of nuclear fission, medium energy heavy-ion reactions, statistical and thermodynamic properties of nuclei and low energy accelerator applications. During the period 1995–2006, Ramamurthy was fully involved in science promotion in India as the Secretary to the Government of India, Department of Science & Technology (DST), New Delhi. He was also the Chairman of the International Atomic Energy Agency (IAEA) Standing Advisory Group on Nuclear Applications for nearly a decade. Other important assignments held by him include Director, Institute of Physics, Bhubaneswar (1989–1995), Department of Atomic Energy (DAE) Homi Bhabha Chair Professor at the Inter-University Accelerator Centre, New Delhi (2006–2010), Chairman, Recruitment and Assessment Board, Council of Scientific and Industrial Research, New Delhi (2006–2010), and Director, National Institute of Advanced Studies, Bengaluru (2009–2014). After retirement from service, Ramamurthy has also been actively involved in human resource development in all its aspects. In recognition of his services to the growth of science and technology in the country, Ramamurthy was awarded the Padma Bhushan by the Government of India in 2005.

A book on *Climate Change and Energy Options for a Sustainable Future* by Dinesh Kumar Srivastava and V. S. Ramamurthy was published by World Scientific in early 2021.

Dinesh Kumar Srivastava (born 1952) is presently Homi Bhabha Chair Professor at the National Institute of Advanced Studies, Bengaluru. At present, he is working on energy, environment, climate change and science outreach along with a continuation of his research on quark–gluon plasma.

He obtained his graduation from Allahabad University in 1970 and joined the Training School of the Bhabha Atomic Research Centre, Mumbai. He started working at the Variable Energy Cyclotron Project of Bhabha Atomic Research Centre in 1971 and retired as the Director and Distinguished Scientist at the Variable Energy Cyclotron Centre, Kolkata in 2016. Later, he continued there as the Department of Atomic Energy (DAE) Raja Ramanna Fellow until 2019.

He is a Fellow of the National Academy of Sciences, India and the Indian National Science Academy. He holds an Honorary Professorship at Amity University since 2019 and was an Emeritus Professor of Homi Bhabha National Institute.

He was awarded the Indian Nuclear Society's award for "Outstanding Contribution to Teaching of Nuclear Sciences". Srivastava was given the Outstanding Referee Award by the American Physical Society (APS) in 2009. He was honoured with the Lifetime Achievement Award by Chitkara University in 2012. He was also awarded the Homi Bhabha Lecturer Award by the Indian Physics Association and Institute of Physics UK in 2016. He has delivered Sir C. V. Raman Memorial Award Lecture at Calcutta University and Prof Abdus Salam Memorial Award Lecture at Jamia Milia Islamia, New Delhi.

He is serving as an Editorial Board Member of Pramana, Scientific Reports, and Physics (MDPI) Journals. He served as a Member of the Editorial Board of Physical Review C, from January 1, 2010, to December 31, 2012. He was President of the Indian Physical Society during 2014–2021.

Srivastava has worked at several prestigious labs and universities abroad, including KfK (now KIT) Karlsruhe, GSI Darmstadt, Lawrence Berkeley National Laboratory Berkeley, Brookhaven National Laboratory Upton New York, University of Minnesota, Duke University, McGill University, University of Cape Town, Bielefeld University, and the University of Frankfurt.

His research interests include electromagnetic probes of quark–gluon plasma (QGP), relativistic hydrodynamics, production, and propagation of charm quarks in QGP, and transverse flow. Earlier, he made important contributions in the theoretical understanding of elastic, inelastic, and break-up reactions of light nuclei. Srivastava has published more than 170 papers and delivered more than 400 talks, seminars, and colloquia. He is an author of two collections of short stories and more recently two books of children's literature in science.

A book on *Climate Change and Energy Options for a Sustainable Future* by Dinesh Kumar Srivastava and V. S. Ramamurthy was published by World Scientific in early 2021.

Shailesh Nayak is currently the Director of the National Institute of Advanced Studies, Bengaluru, Chancellor of the TERI School of Advanced Studies, Delhi, Editor-in-Chief of the *Journal of the Indian Society of Remote Sensing* and Life Trustee of India International Centre. He obtained his PhD degree in Geology from the M. S. University of Baroda in 1980. He was a "Distinguished Scientist" in the Ministry of Earth Sciences and President, International Geological Congress during 2015–2017. He served as the Secretary, Ministry of Earth Sciences, Government of India, during August 2008–2015, and provided leadership for programs related to earth system sciences. He has been credited with launching many research programs related to monsoon, air quality, seismology, triggered earthquakes, coastal vulnerability, solid earth, climate change, polar science, ocean minerals, etc.

He had set up the state-of-the-art tsunami warning system for the Indian Ocean in 2007 in just 2 years, which has been providing tsunami advisories to the Indian Ocean rim countries. He pioneered in the development of algorithms and methodologies for the application of remote sensing to the coastal and marine environment and generated a baseline database of the Indian coast and developed services for fishery and ocean state forecast. The generation of detailed information on the Indian coast has influenced the development of policy for zoning of coastal zone for regulating coastal activities.

Nayak is a Fellow of the Indian Academy of Sciences, Bengaluru, the Indian National Science Academy, New Delhi, the National Academy of Sciences, India, Allahabad, the International Society of Photogrammetry & Remote Sensing (ISPRS), and Academician of the International Academy of Astronautics (IAA). He has been awarded Honorary Degree of Doctor of Science by Andhra University in 2011, Assam University in 2013, and Amity University in 2015. He was conferred the prestigious ISC Vikram Sarabhai Memorial Award 2012, and Bhaskara Award for 2009 for his outstanding contributions in remote sensing and GIS. He has published about 200 papers in peer-reviewed journals.

Contents

List of Figures

List of Tables

Chapter 1

Prologue

Oxford English Dictionary defines risk as "the possibility of something bad happening at some time in the future". Loss of life has always been the biggest risk to human beings. Our earliest ancestors, the hominins, who in course of time evolved into Homo erectus, Neanderthals, and Homo sapiens, had to face the risk posed by predators, poisonous insects, large animals, life-threatening diseases, and natural disasters. The fire was yet another risk that the early humans had to face. Once humans learnt to control fire, there was no looking back. They soon learnt that fire — while posing a risk — also gave them warmth and light, and made their food tasty and long-lasting while protecting them from predators. Our civilization started taking shape as humans assembled around fire and communities formed. It is now believed that the cultural adaptations by transfer of accumulated knowledge to changing environments by humans were a lot more efficient than the natural selection utilized by most of the other species till now. While the loss of life and loss of livelihood have always remained the most dreaded risks faced by human beings, in today's context, loss of wealth, loss of reputation, and a whole variety of other risks have also been added to the list of risks faced by human beings. Zero risk options do not exist in life. Therefore, conscious risk-taking has also evolved as a part of human culture.

Risk perception is the judgement that people make about the severity of a risk. Risk being a possibility rather than a forecast, risk perception is highly individualistic, varying from person to person, from place to place, and from time to time. Like pleasure and pain, risk has to be experienced. A child has to learn that it hurts to touch a hot vessel only by personal experience, even though he may be constantly warned about it by his/her parents. Unfortunately, personal experiences, however extensive they may be, cover only a minuscule of risks one faces in one's lifetime. Sharing of experiences through risk communication plays a very important role in moulding individual risk perceptions. Risk perception being highly individualistic, risk communication between two individuals whose risk perceptions may or may not coincide is also challenging.

Risk acceptance is even more complex. We are all used to a cost–benefit analysis in most of our day-to-day decisions. When the decision also involves a risk, a cost–benefit–risk analysis becomes important. All of us make such decisions in our lives almost daily. The issue becomes more complex if costs, benefits, and risks are not all financial or are spread over long periods of time. It is not surprising that risk acceptance is also highly individualistic. Even the same individual may not accept the same risk at different times.

Risks associated with such day-to-day mundane practices like violation of traffic rules usually tend to be ignored, even though India loses up to 150,000 lives per year and the world loses 1.3 million lives per year to traffic accidents. Even well-known life-threatening risks such as those associated with chewing tobacco or cigarette smoking — which kills about 5 million persons per year across the world — tend to get ignored because the habits are "self-satisfying" (because the habits tend to give a "certain high" or a "kick" to the practitioners and satisfy a craving). In the case of adventure sports like bungee jumping, the benefits are psychological, and the risks are willingly accepted though they are extreme. There are also other circumstances when risks are knowingly accepted, as, for example, when associated with career options or commitment to a cause. History is replete with instances of individuals who have taken extreme risks, even making the supreme sacrifice of their own lives, for a cause dear to them.

Sometimes, it is argued: Why should anyone opt for a risky choice at all? Why can't we make only safe choices? At the outset, we all know that there is nothing that is absolutely safe. Also, risk perceptions can change with time. Not taking the risk at the right time also carries its own risk. We give some illustrative examples in the following sections.

1.1 Relative Risks

A 6-month pregnant lady was advised by her doctor to take an X-ray scan of the baby in the womb since the doctor had some doubts. The lady, well aware of the ill effects of the radiation on the baby in the womb, hesitated to take the scan. The doctor said, "I have some doubts and if you take the scan, my doubts will be cleared and I can assure you that you will have a safe delivery and if there is a problem, I have time to get prepared for the problem. If you do not take the scan now, we run the risk of discovering a problem at the time of delivery and I may not be able to help at the last moment." The lady agreed to take the risk of X-ray exposure to the child in the womb and avoid the risk of a last-minute problem. She had a safe delivery.

1.2 Calculated Risks

This is a story of a Parkinson disease patient. Doctors attending on him suggested that he goes in for a newly emerging intervention — stem cell therapy. His relatives consulted some well-known experts, who were unanimous that the intervention suggested by the doctors had not been scientifically validated. But the doctors advised to "forget about scientific validation, check with people who have tried it and decide". Yes, some people have tried and benefitted from the therapy. In some cases, the intervention had not been as effective as expected. In some cases, the intervention was indeed counterproductive. Now, how does one make the final decision? The stakes are high, the benefits could be substantial, but the risks are also high. The relatives decided to take the risk and the patient did benefit from the intervention.

1.3 Risk of Not Taking a Risk at the Right Time

Sometimes, "not taking a risk at the right time" may also become a risk. One government officer received a communication from his office administration that being more than 50 years of age, he should go for a medical check-up even if he doesn't have a pre-existing problem. He chose the best hospital in town and submitted himself for a check-up. Lo and behold, the cardiologist detected a block and suggested immediate bypass surgery. Panicked by this sudden discovery, the person asked for a second opinion. The second cardiologist suggested that if indeed he was hesitant to go in for bypass surgery, he could opt for a stent that involved a much less level of intervention. He then went to his family physician for yet another piece of advice. Considering that he had no complaints or symptoms of any kind, the doctor suggested that he should go in for some simple medication and possible lifestyle changes. The cardiologists were indeed unhappy and told him that when he would actually get a symptom and come to the hospital, it might be too late. The officer, totally confused, started consulting his friends and relatives who only confused him more. One thing was emerging clearly. The cardiologists may have had a vested interest in suggesting a surgical intervention. The physician may have had a vested interest in suggesting medicines and lifestyle changes. There was a clear need for someone who had no vested interests and could offer unbiased advice. Who better than an astrologer? The officer started going from one astrologer to another for advice and in the meantime, his health deteriorated, and he died not because of any problem in his heart but because of mental stress.

In all the above cases, the costs, benefits, and risks are confined to an individual or a small and well-defined group like a family.

1.4 Public Risks

When the costs, benefits, and risks are not limited to an individual or a small and well-defined group like a family but involve a large number of stakeholders, such as shareholders in a corporate entity, risk perception and risk acceptance are complex and may involve not only financial and technical but also social issues. Changing consumer preferences, business competition, financial crunch, disruptions in supply chain, etc. are some of the well-known corporate risks for which the companies may not be fully ready. The COVID-19 pandemic has added one more corporate risk, a forced lockdown for reasons beyond control as in the case of restaurants, theatres, shopping malls, etc. Corporate risks have been studied in detail and strategies evolved to manage the risks.

In fact, corporate risk management has been a subject of focussed research for a long time. Rigorous mathematical and statistical methods used to assess corporate risks have indeed evolved as an independent branch of mathematics, the actuarial sciences. Insurance is a time-tested method of protecting companies against unexpected risks. Insurance is also offered to cover loss of life though it provides a financial shield only to the dependents.

When the costs, benefits, and risks involve the public at large, risk perception and risk acceptance are indeed very complex and may involve not only financial and technical but also social, cultural, ethical, and moral issues. Very often, the population that bears the risks, the population that bears the costs, and the population that enjoy the benefits may not be the same. In such cases, it is almost not only impossible to have a consensus but also impossible to do a cost–benefit analysis.

It is usually the government that has to put in place the necessary systems to balance public costs, public good, and public risks. Very often the governments have a hard time justifying the investments in risk preparedness since the risks are futuristic. We shall discuss a few illustrative examples later.

What happens when we do not know the reasons for a natural disaster or the spread of unknown diseases? It is well known that when a natural disaster or an unknown disease strikes, wild speculations, preconceived notions, unfounded fears, conspiracy theories, and superstitions dominate the public discourse and public behaviour till their physical origins become clear. The oft-quoted Pavamana Sukta ("purifying mantra") of Brihadaranyaka Upanishad (1.3.28) invokes the prayer:

"असतो मा सद्गमय ।

तमसो मा ज्योतिर्गमय ।

मृत्योर्माऽमृतं गमय ॥"

which translates to the following: "From falsehood lead me to truth. From darkness lead me to light. From death lead me to immortality". This testifies to the importance of truth in lighting our paths.

Thus, for example, for centuries, tuberculosis was believed to be associated with poetic and artistic qualities in sufferers, and it was called "the romantic disease". The absence of a cure for tuberculosis gave rise to several superstitions. For example, it was believed in Europe that it could be cured by a touch of royals; the Kings of England and France continued to "touch" such patients for centuries. Since many relatives of those succumbing to tuberculosis also contracted the disease, it was also believed that people dying of tuberculosis became "vampires" and "returned to take their relatives" with them. In India, diseases like cholera and smallpox were believed to be averted by offering prayers and sacrifices to some goddesses, and regular festivals were observed for this.

In the following chapters, starting with a discussion of some of the public risks that humanity has faced in the past, is facing now, and is likely to face in the coming decades, we shall address how the governments across the world have functioned as the custodians of public good and managed disasters and public risks. Unlike managing disasters, managing risks involves considerable effort in mapping out the risks and managing public perceptions of the risks. The crucial role played by risk communication in moulding public perceptions of the risks will also be highlighted.

Chapter 2

Extreme Natural Events

Extreme natural events like floods, droughts, cyclones, earthquakes, tsunami, and volcanic eruptions have always been an integral part of the earth system — the planet Earth and its atmosphere (see, e.g., Ref. [1]). These cannot be stopped though some of them can be predicted. Human habitation often converts these extreme natural events into disasters, leading to loss of lives and property. Some of these natural disasters have even changed the course of history, wiping out cities, and in some cases, even civilizations. Humanity had no alternative but to learn to live with them. The strategy across the world has been to be better prepared for the disaster — better prepared to minimize loss of life and property and better prepared for prompt rescue and relief operations.

To understand and appreciate how fragile life on Earth is, let us spend a few minutes on the formation of our solar system (see Fig. 2.1). It is believed to have been initiated about 4.5 billion years ago when the interstellar dust in the region occupied by it was flattened by a shockwave from a supernova explosion far away. The large disc thus formed harnessed the gravitational energy to create the Sun, which appropriated about 99% of the mass, leaving the rest to form planets, moons, asteroids, minor planets, and comets. The very high density and temperature in the interior of the Sun triggered nuclear fusion which has continued to supply us heat and light ever since and is expected to continue to do so for about 5 billion years more before it runs out of its hydrogen supply and transforms into a red giant and swallows the inner planets, the Mercury, Venus, and

Fig. 2.1 An artist's impression of the solar system (Not to scale, Credit: NASA)

Earth. As the heat radiated by the Sun was (and remains) strong, the inner planets closest to the Sun, Mercury, Venus, Earth, and Mars, are composed of rocks and metals and have a gaseous atmosphere. Other planets are basically gas and ice giants. Earth is the only planet in the solar system which has water in liquid form and oxygen, nitrogen, and carbon dioxide in gaseous form. These are essential for life. While the possibility of life on planets other than the Earth and in the Universe at large has fascinated mankind for a long time, so far, we have no evidence for the same.

It is believed that life on Earth appeared about 3.5–4 billion years ago as simple, single-cell organisms and has been evolving since then. Over a period, the first multicellular organisms evolved, and after that, Earth's biodiversity greatly increased. *Homo sapiens* ("wise man"), the species to which all modern human beings belong, is one of the several species grouped into the genus *Homo*, but it is the only one that is not yet extinct. They evolved just about 300,000 years ago. The extinction of Neanderthals and *Homo erectus*, their close "cousins", who spread to occupy a large part of the Old World, is a fascinating subject. All the studies point to one fact: they could not adapt to changing climate and face the attendant risks.

2.1 Asteroid Impact

One of the earliest catastrophic natural events that took place on the face of the Earth was an asteroid strike, nearly 66 million years ago when a 10–15 km large asteroid hit the Earth at a speed of about 64,000 km/h and wiped out nearly 80% of the dinosaurs, both avian and non-avian. Nothing could have prepared the dinosaurs, who had ruled the planet Earth for close to 180 million years, for this disaster. Model calculations have estimated that the collision may have had an energy equivalent to 100 trillion tonnes of TNT. The impact must have penetrated Earth's crust to a depth of several kilometres (some estimates even suggest that it could have reached Earth's core!) which led to the formation of a crater having a diameter of 185 km and a depth of 20 km at Chicxulub in the Gulf of Mexico. It is estimated that the impact must have vaporized thousands of cubic kilometres of rock and set off several catastrophic events in quick succession with disastrous effects (see Fig. 2.2).

The debris must have shot out of the Earth's atmosphere and then fallen back over a vast area as balls of fire, a rain of burning meteorites, several minutes later. A few seconds after impact the blast of radiation must have roasted trees, grass, and all living creatures and they must have burst into flames for up to 1,000 km around the site of the impact. The impact must have led to an earthquake having a magnitude of at least 10.1 and produced a gigantic tsunami with waves as high as 300 m, which must have travelled around the oceans of the Earth. Some authors have estimated this height to be up to 900 m. A blast of wind at a speed of about 1,000 km/h, with a shattering roar, must have followed, levelling everything in its way. The ash and soot must have travelled around the Earth and effectively blocked out the Sun for several years, killing the vegetation, herbivores, and carnivores in succession. The rains, which followed, must have been very acidic, and the ozone layer protecting the Earth must have been destroyed. Even the carbon footprint of the impact must have been huge, releasing an

Fig. 2.2 An asteroid slams into Earth: An artist's impression (Credit: Don Davis, JPL, NASA [2])

estimated 10,000 billion tonnes of carbon dioxide, 100 billion tonnes of carbon monoxide, and another 100 billion tonnes of methane [3].

This impact also paved the way for the emergence of mammals. There are suggestions that, had the asteroid hit the Earth a few minutes later, it would have landed in the deep sea instead of the shallow sea (near solid earth), and would have caused much less damage to the dinosaur world. This would have had far-reaching consequences for the emergence of *Homo sapiens*, and perhaps the history of our planet would have been very different!

On June 30, 1908, an explosion, variously estimated to have a power of 10–30 megatons of TNT equivalent, took place at a very sparsely populated part of Siberia near the Tunguska River. It flattened nearly 80 million trees spread over 2,150 km^2 and killed thousands of reindeer and perhaps three men. It has been suggested that the explosion was due to the "air burst" of a stony meteorite having a size of about 50–60 m, travelling at a speed of about 50,000 km/h, which disintegrated 5–10 km above the surface of the Earth. Eyewitness accounts talked of a bright column of bluish light, bright as the Sun, and hearing a loud explosion followed by a shock wave that damaged windows hundreds of kilometres away. The airwave and the explosion were felt over vast areas of Europe, and the latter was recorded by seismic stations, to be equivalent to an earthquake of magnitude 5. This so-called "Tunguska event" remained a fascinating and intriguing subject of study for decades till detailed numerical simulations closely reproduced the effects and helped put the details together. June 30 is now celebrated as Asteroid Day across the world.

We add that there is always a possibility of a large asteroid hitting the Earth even today. However, now scientists are confident that they can closely monitor their approach much before they reach the Earth, and they can use modern technological tools such as a rocket fired at them blowing them into small pieces or from their surface changing their trajectory. Space crafts from several countries have already made landings on or had intentional collisions with asteroids, following the first such landing on the asteroid named Eros by the United States of America on February 12, 2001.

2.2 Volcanoes and Earthquakes

As presently known, life on Earth is confined to a thin layer of solid earth, a thin layer of the atmosphere, and ocean waters. Humans have been on Earth for only 6 million years over which period they have evolved, created civilizations, and become the humans of today. All the while, the earth under their feet has not been a benign solid mass. Humanity has often faced the wrath of Mother Earth in the form of volcanoes and earthquakes. To understand what causes volcanic activity and earthquakes, we need to recall what we know about the structure of the Earth, the formation of its continents, and the theory of tectonic plates and their motion. We now know that the Earth is a nearly spherical mass having a crust which is of varying thicknesses of up to 100 km, a mantle about 2,800 km thick, a liquid

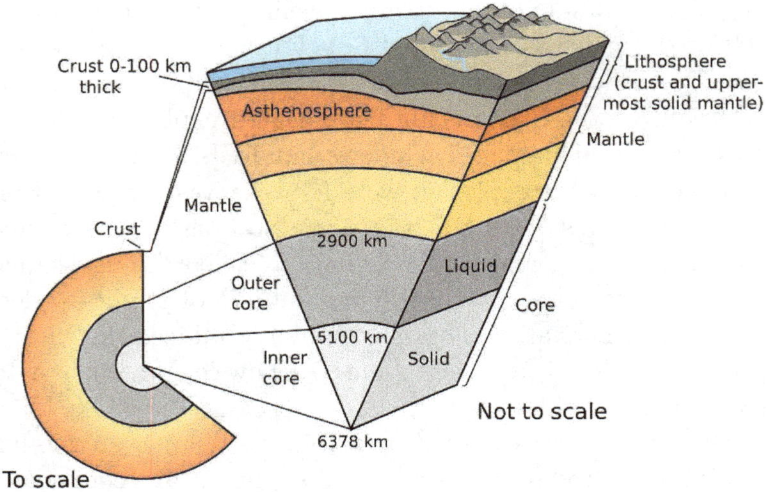

Fig. 2.3 A cross-section of Earth with the subsurface layers [4]

outer core about 2,200 km thick, and a solid central core having a radius of about 1,280 km (see Fig. 2.3).

The inner core is mostly solid iron at a temperature of about 5,200°C. The outer core is a molten liquid consisting of iron and nickel at a temperature of 4,500–5,500°C. The crust of the Earth is made of solid rocks and minerals. The mantle also consists mostly of rocks and minerals; however, it is punctuated with areas of semi-solid magma rather frequently. The coupled layer of crust and uppermost mantle is called the lithosphere. As we proceed towards the centre of the Earth, the temperature rises by about 25° for every kilometre. The primary source of the heat is radioactive decay of elements, such as thorium and uranium. Some of the leftover primordial heat and heat released from the cooling of the core also contribute to it.

2.2.1 *Tectonic plates*

It is now believed that the entire landmass of the Earth was spread across the equator and surrounded by a superocean about 335 million years ago. The landmass has been given the name Pangaea or Pangea, and the superocean is now called Panthalassa. It started breaking

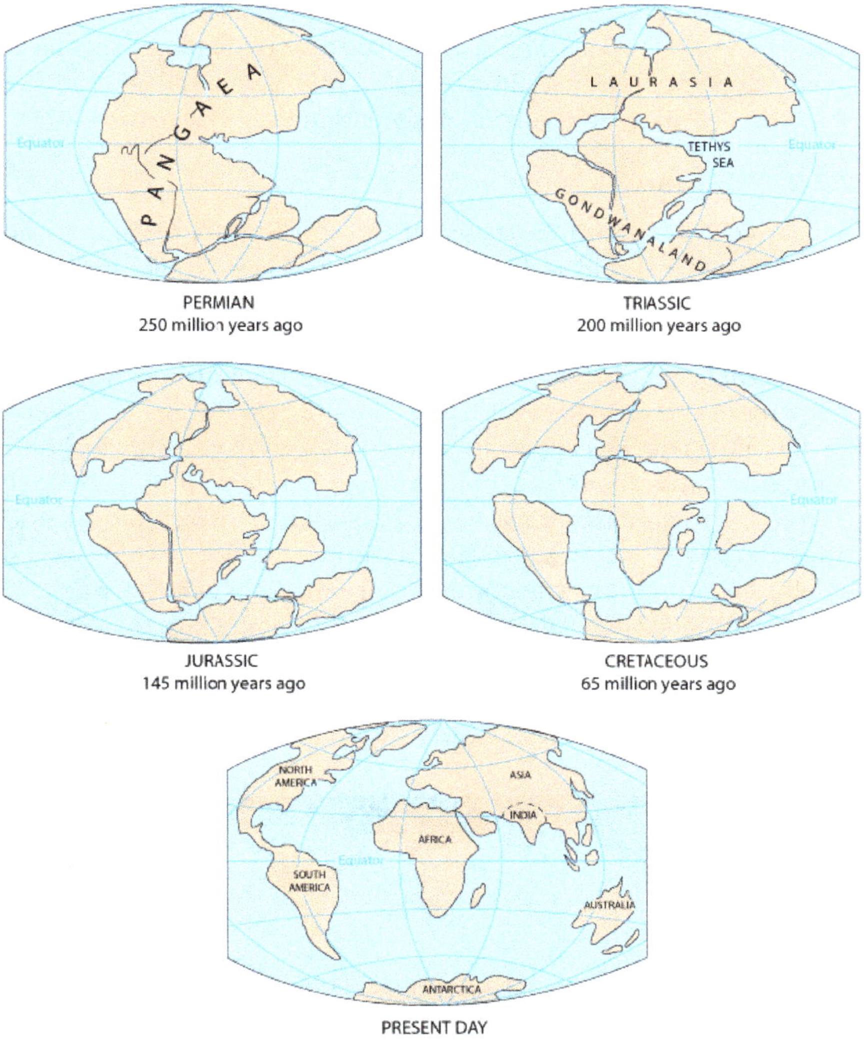

Fig. 2.4 Pangaea, Laurasia, Gondwana Land, and the present [5]

up about 175 million years ago into two landmasses, Laurasia, and Gondwana Land. The Gondwana Land itself broke up into continents of South America, Africa, India, Australia, and Antarctica, which drifted apart to their present locations (see Fig. 2.4).

Thus, the Earth's crust is not a single, unbroken layer like the shell of an egg. It is made of sections called tectonic plates that sit on top of the slowly flowing and moving mantle. The Earth system thus has been continuously evolving and continues to evolve even now.

2.2.2 *Volcanoes*

A volcano is a rupture in the crust of the Earth, throwing out hot lava, volcanic ash, and gases. Volcanoes have played a very important role in shaping the surface of our planet, creating mountains as well as craters. Rivers of lava spread out and with the passage of time, rains, heat, cold, and wind released the nutrients trapped into the stony rocks and created fertile soil to support vegetation, so essential for life on earth. Volcanoes are found on every continent, including Antarctica, and about 1,500 of them are believed to be potentially active. They can have explosive eruptions when viscous molten rock traps the gases, building pressure until it is released explosively, or by effusive eruptions, which are more common, when the magma is less viscous, allowing the gas to escape and the magma to flow down the slopes of the volcano. Most of the volcanoes and earthquakes in the world take place along the boundaries of Earth's tectonic plates, which continually shift and collide with one another (see Fig. 2.5).

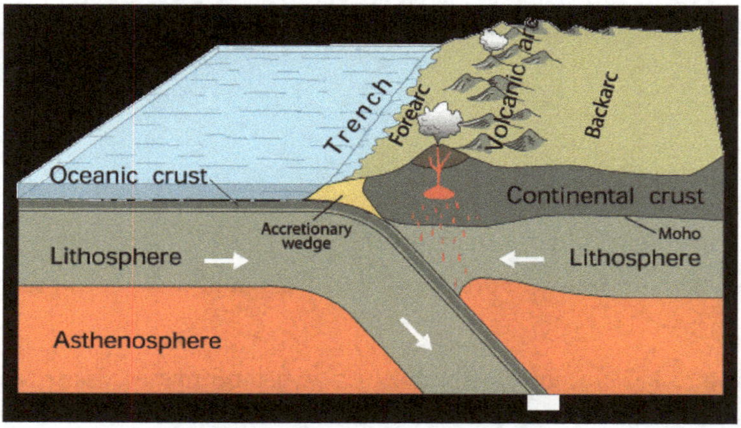

Fig. 2.5 An oceanic plate sliding beneath the continental plate (Credit: USGS [6])

2.2.3 *Pacific ring of fire*

The circum-Pacific Ring of Fire is one such area where the Pacific Plate meets many surrounding tectonic plates. The Ring of Fire is the most seismically and volcanically active zone in the world, even though the volcanic eruptions along the Ring are not geologically connected. Some volcanoes, like the Hawaii volcanic chain, are formed by hot spot volcanism, where a zone of magmatic activity — or a hot spot — in the middle of a tectonic plate can push up through the crust to form a volcano (see Fig. 2.6).

Volcanic eruptions produce flowing lava, and avalanches of hot rocks, toxic gases, and ash which may attain speeds of up to 700 km/h. An event like this wiped out the people of Pompeii and

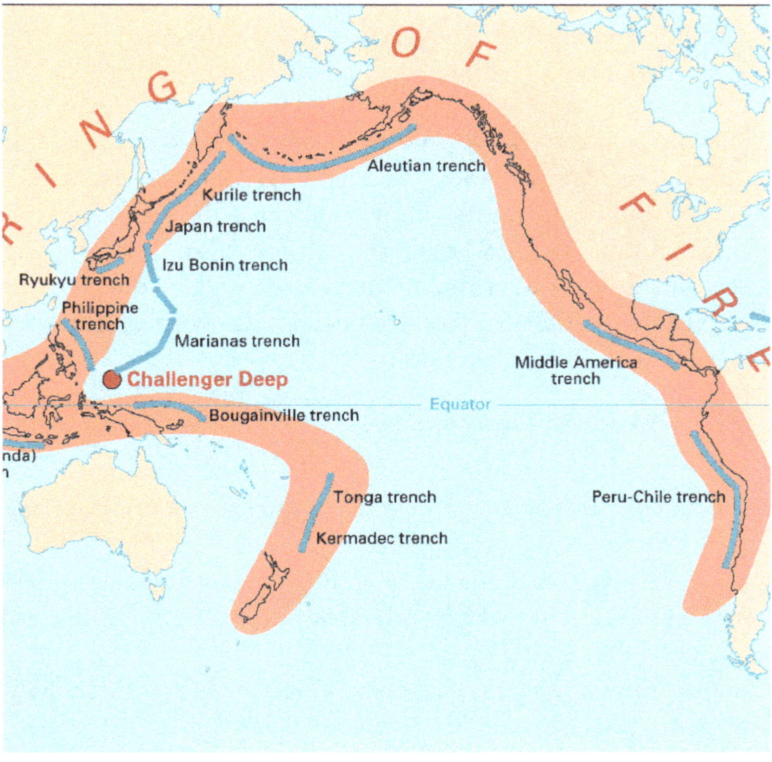

Fig. 2.6 Ring of fire [7]

Herculaneum after Mount Vesuvius erupted in A.D. 79. In addition, volcanic mudflows, called lahars, which are waves of mud and debris, race down the slopes of the volcano and bury entire towns. The volcanic ash is made of sharp fragments of rocks and volcanic glass each less than 2 mm across and dangerous when inhaled. It accumulates easily on rooftops, for example, and structures collapse under their weight. It also enters machinery and equipment and incapacitates them. The ash-laden gas clouds associated with an explosive eruption may contain suffocating or poisonous gases such as carbon dioxide, carbon monoxide, hydrogen sulphide, and sulphur dioxide and can kill vegetation, animals, and people by suffocation.

Fortunately, several warning signals precede volcanic eruptions, which include several small earthquakes, swelling or bulging of the volcano's sides, drying up of vegetation around the upper slopes, increase in temperatures, and change in colour of hot springs, lakes, and wells near the site, drying up of neighbouring lakes and ponds, landslides and rockfalls from the summit area which is not attributable to heavy rains, and increased emission of gases from its old and new vents. However, none of these signs necessarily mean that an eruption is imminent, but they can help scientists evaluate the state of the volcano. Modern methods using several sensors close to and inside the crater of the volcano allow the scientists to continuously monitor the volcanoes and take preparatory steps to minimize loss of life and property.

2.2.4 *Volcanoes of Iceland*

Iceland, located on the Mid-Atlantic Ridge tectonic plate boundary and over a hot spot, is a witness to frequent — once in every 4–5 years — volcanic activity. It has about 30 active volcanic systems. Its location over a hot spot makes it an ideal place for the exploitation of geothermal energy which provides up to 90% of its heating requirements, etc. (see Fig. 2.7).

The deadliest volcanic eruption of Iceland's recent history was in 1783–84, called Skaftáreldar (fires of Skaftá). The eruption killed about one-fourth of the population. The deaths were not caused by

Fig. 2.7 Eruption of the Fagradalsfjall volcano, March 19, 2021 [8]

lava flow, but because of climate change and illnesses of the livestock in the following years due to glass in the ash which stuck to the grass and poisonous gases.

The eruption of April 2010 at Eyjafjallajökull volcano is better known for grounding air traffic for 6 days in Europe as the skies were covered with clouds of smoke which reduced visibility and inconvenienced about 10 million travellers. Domestic animals which had spent the winter indoors had to continue to stay indoors and continue with dry fodder, as the grass was covered with toxic ash and microscopic glass, which when swallowed along with grass would have killed them. The glass particles, if smaller than 10 μm in size, can penetrate deep into the lungs.

On March 19, 2021, another volcano in Iceland, the Fagradalsfjall, also erupted after lying dormant for 800 years. The latest on the list is a volcano on Spain's Canary Island of La Palma on September 19, 2021.

2.2.5 *Earthquakes*

When the tectonic plates move, they sometimes grind against each other, sometimes push into each other to build mountain ranges, and sometimes — when they move towards each other — one plate is pushed underneath the other in a process called subduction. The world's largest earthquakes and volcanoes occur in these zones of subduction (see Fig. 2.8).

As the tectonic plates move relative to each other, they get stuck at their edges due to friction. As a result of this, a huge amount of stress builds up over long periods of time. Eventually, there comes a point when all the accumulated stress is suddenly released: rocks break, and huge sections of the Earth's crust are cracked and displaced. These result in waves of energy called seismic waves that radiate out in all directions. The point on the Earth below which this happens is called epicentre, while the point deep inside the Earth where this rapture takes place is called hypocentre. In the process when a part dips and slips, it is called a normal fault (see Fig. 2.9).

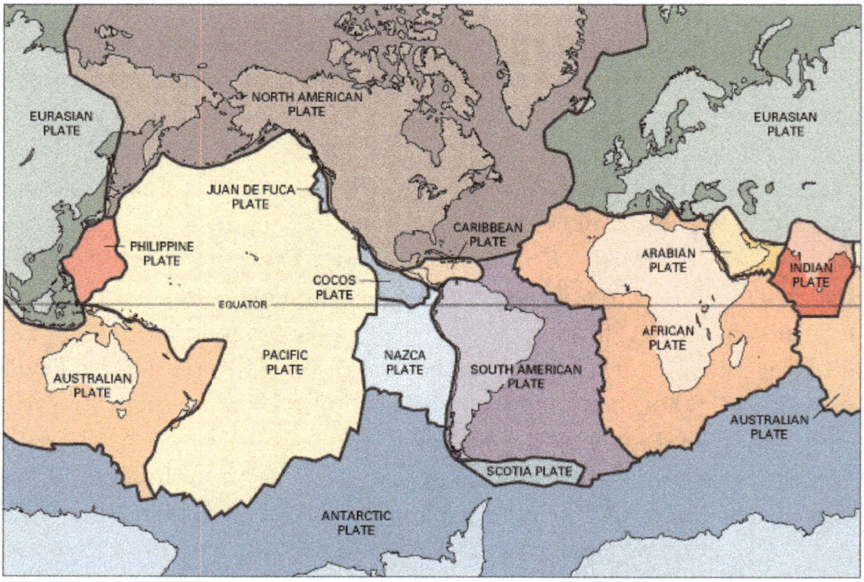

Fig. 2.8 Tectonic plates of the Earth [9]

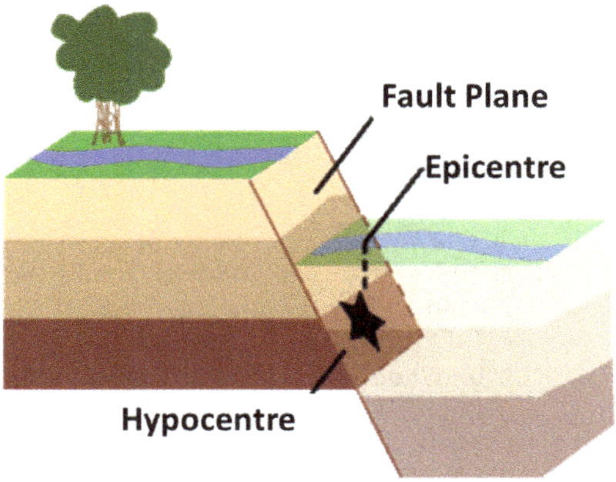

Fig. 2.9 Normal fault (Dip-Slip) [10]

When a part moves up against the other, it is called a reverse fault. And finally, when a part slides along the other part, we call it a strike-slip fault. Earthquakes are preceded by foreshocks and followed by aftershocks, which can occur over hours or even days.

2.2.6 *Some severe earthquakes around the world*

Unlike volcanoes, earthquakes have no reliable precursors. However, the general areas of their likely occurrence can be identified with reasonable success. The magnitude of earthquakes is popularly given in the Richter scale, where a level N of the earthquake is 10 times more intense than the one having level $N-1$. The magnitude, amount of energy released (31.7 times for successive whole number levels), and the effects are given in Table 2.1. Several other scales have also been suggested since then, out of which moment magnitude (Mw) is more frequently used and is more accurate for large magnitude earthquakes and provides an estimate of earthquake size that is valid over the complete range of magnitude.

We recall that China has been maintaining accurate records of earthquakes since 1177 BC. The location, date, and magnitude of the 20 most intense earthquakes in the twentieth century and later can be seen in Ref. [11]. We discuss some of the historically significant

Table 2.1 The magnitude of earthquakes on a Richter scale

Richter Magnitude	Amount of TNT	Result
0–1	0.6–20 kg	We cannot feel it
2	600 kg	The smallest earthquake which we can feel
3	20,000 kg	Felt by people near the epicentre
4	600,000 kg	Damage around the epicentre
5	20 million kg	Damage to weak buildings around the epicentre
6	600 million kg	Great damage around the epicentre
7	20 billion kg	Serious damage; can be detected all over the world
8	600 billion kg	Cause death and major destruction
9	20 trillion kg	Rare but would cause unbelievable damage

earthquakes in the following, as they had profound effects on society and on the study of earthquakes.

The Shaanxi province earthquake of January 23, 1556, in Northern China with an estimated magnitude of 8, is believed to be the deadliest earthquake ever recorded. It reduced an area of about 1,000 km^2 to rubble and 830,000 people were killed as their cave homes collapsed. The records reveal that even though the quake lasted only for a few seconds, it levelled mountains, altered the path of rivers, caused massive flooding, and ignited fires that burned for days. One important outcome of this tragedy was that as most of the people had been killed by falling buildings, it was decided to replace the stone buildings with those made of softer, more earthquake-resistant materials, such as bamboo and wood.

The 1976 Tangshan earthquake, also known as the Great Tangshan Earthquake, was a magnitude 7.6 earthquake that occurred on July 28, 1976, at 3:42 AM in the morning. In minutes, 85% of the buildings in Tangshan collapsed or became unusable, all services failed, and most of the highway and railway bridges collapsed or were seriously damaged. At least 242,000 people died (some estimates have suggested a casualty three times higher), making this the third (or possibly second) deadliest earthquake in recorded history.

A similar tragedy had fortunately been averted during the February 4, 1975, Haicheng earthquake, about 400 km northeast of Tangshan, as it was preceded by an extended series of significant foreshocks, leading the authorities to order an evacuation. It is believed that the death of at least 150,000 persons was averted due to the evacuation, limiting the casualties to about 2,000 and injured to 27,000, even though thousands of buildings collapsed, making it a solitary example in the history, where evacuation of the population before an earthquake was ever done reducing human casualties dramatically.

The 1960 Valdivia earthquake (or the Great Chilean Earthquake) on May 22, 1960, estimated to have a moment magnitude scale between 9.4 and 9.6, was the most powerful earthquake ever recorded. It lasted for approximately 10 min and led to tsunamis which affected Southern Chile, Hawaii, Japan, the Philippines, Eastern New Zealand, South-East Australia, and the Aleutian Island in Alaska. The tsunami reaching Hilo in Hawaii 10,000 km away produced 10-m-high waves and devastated it. Chile lies in the region where the Nazca plate meets the South America plate, which is converging at a rate of 71 mm/year, triggering frequent earthquakes. Since the beginning of the twentieth century, Mw 8.2 earthquakes have occurred in 1906, 1943, and 1960, and an Mw 8.0 earthquake occurred in 1985.

Haiti was hit by an earthquake having a moment magnitude of Mw 7.0, on January 12, 2010, with catastrophic consequences. It was followed by as many as 53 aftershocks of magnitude 4.5 or more and reduced the city of Port-au-Prince to rubble, rendering more than 1 million homeless and killing up to 316,000 persons according to the Haitian Government and about half according to other sources. It was hit by an Mw 7.2 earthquake on August 14, 2021, which killed about 2,100 persons.

Southern California is yet another earthquake country that is caused by the movement of the Pacific and North American plates past each other at a rate of about 50 mm per year. As a result of this, it experiences thousands of smaller earthquakes every year, most of which are not even felt by people.

An accurate prediction of an earthquake should provide the date and time, location, and magnitude of the earthquake. This has not been possible so far. Even the string of foreshocks and the unusual behaviour of animals, e.g., cows and horses looking restless and agitated, rats appearing "drunk", chicken refusing to enter their coops, and geese frequently taking to flight, reported before the 1975 Haicheng (China) earthquake discussed above were not witnessed at the next large earthquake in China. Soil radon emission, sudden change in subsoil water levels, soil temperature changes, and many other precursors have also been suggested, but with no success in earthquake prediction.

2.2.7 *Earthquakes in the Himalayas*

The formation of the lofty Himalayas is one of the most dramatic and visible demonstrations of the tectonic plate movements. The Himalayas covering about 2,900 km along the border between India and Tibet began to form between 40 and 50 million years ago when India, born out of the break-up of Gondwana Land around the South Pole, was driven by plate movement, arrived at its present location, and collided with Eurasia. The two continental landmasses, arising from an earlier break-up of the gigantic landmass of Pangaea, have about the same rock density, and one plate could not be subducted under the other. The pressure of the impinging plates was thus released by thrusting skyward, contorting the collision zone, and forming the jagged Himalayan peaks. The Himalayan range and the Tibetan Plateau to the north have risen very rapidly. In just 50 million years, peaks such as Mount Everest has risen to heights of close to 9 km. The impinging of the two landmasses is yet to end and the Himalayas continue to rise, more than 1 cm a year. India continues to creep northwards a few centimetres every year (see Fig. 2.10).

We have discussed this in detail since a serious consequence of these processes is a deadly "domino effect": tremendous stress builds up within the Earth's crust, which is relieved periodically by earthquakes along the numerous faults that scar the landscape. Some of the world's most destructive earthquakes in history are related

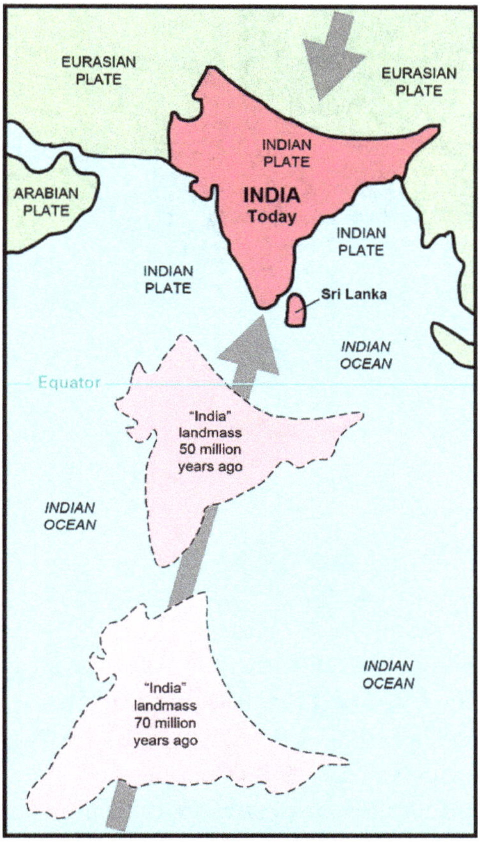

Fig. 2.10 Collision of India and Eurasia and birth of the Himalaya [12]

to continuing tectonic processes that began some 50 million years ago when the Indian and Eurasian continents first met. These will continue to keep the Himalayas very fragile and prone to mighty earthquakes. As a result, great earthquakes have occurred repeatedly in the past in the Himalayas and will continue to do so in the future. We do not know precisely when and where they will occur, but we know that the push of the Indian plate generates enormous stress, and earthquakes are the most "efficient" way to release this stress. It has been suggested that in the last 500 years, there have not been enough big earthquakes (of magnitude 8 and above) to ease

Fig. 2.11 Nepal (or Gorkha) earthquake, April 25, 2015 [13]

the accumulated strain in large sections of the Himalayan arc, and thus earthquakes of magnitude 8.2–8.7 can occur at any time.

The Nepal earthquake of April 25, 2015, also called the Gorkha earthquake, is one of the most studied Himalayan earthquakes ever, as it occurred when we had facilities with accurate GPS data of the rupture and its effects (see Fig. 2.11). It had a moment magnitude of Mw 7.8 and killed nearly 9,000 people and injured some 22,000. In the Kathmandu valley, it destroyed buildings and infrastructure, reducing several historical temples and monasteries — many of them UNESCO World Heritage sites — to rubble. It also triggered an avalanche on Mount Everest, killing 21 people. Another avalanche in the Langtang valley wiped out the village of Langtang, killing 243 people. It even shifted Kathmandu to the south by 1.5 m.

On January 15, 1934, an earthquake in Nepal–Bihar (Mw 8.4) border killed an estimated 7,253 people in Bihar alone (see Fig. 2.12). In Nepal, the death toll exceeded 8,500. It created 75 m long and 3 m wide fissures in Bihar, which vented sand. Wells filled up with sand or dried up. The soft sediment of the Gangetic plain liquefied. The force of the earthquake knocked off the top 7 m from the historical Kesariya Stupa in Bihar's East Champaran district. It also toppled the original spire of St. Paul's Cathedral in Kolkata. The destruction was so

Fig. 2.12 15 January 1934 Bihar–Nepal earthquake [15] and visit of Mahatma Gandhi [16]

complete that the news could reach Calcutta only the next day. The railway tracks buckled, twisted, or were tossed aside. Bridges and culverts collapsed, and the telegraph and telephone networks were destroyed. Most houses were destroyed, and towns and villages were flattened. The districts of Bhagalpur, Champaran, Darbhanga, and Muzaffarpur suffered the most severely [14].

August 15, 1950, earthquake in Tibet–Assam (Mw 8.6) was one of the strongest known on Earth and remains the largest intracontinental earthquake ever recorded. The earthquake was also notable for the loud noises produced by the quake and reported throughout the region (see Fig. 2.13).

It caused landslides on such a large scale that several of the Brahmaputra's tributaries were dammed by landslides and ran dry for days. When the dams burst, Prime Minister Jawaharlal Nehru described in a radio broadcast that year, "They (the waters) came down with a rush and a roar, a high wall of water sweeping down and flooding large areas and washing away villages and fields and gardens. These rivers have changed their colour and carried some sulphurous and other material which spread a horrible smell for some distance around them. The fish in them died. The remains of villages,

Fig. 2.13 Assam–Tibet earthquake, August 15, 1950 [17]

animals, including cattle and elephants and large quantities of timber floated down these raging waters. Paddy fields were destroyed, stocks of grains were washed away, and some tea gardens also suffered great damage." It occurred in the evening, and it was only the sparse population of the region at the time that prevented higher casualties (see Table 2.2).

2.2.8 *Some of the deadly earthquakes in India*

We give a list of the 10 worst earthquakes in India in recent times before proceeding to discuss some of the worst ones.

The Bhuj earthquake on January 26, 2001, in the Kutch region of Gujarat, India, was very tragic as it took place right in the middle of celebrations for Republic Day, and students had reached schools for the celebrations holding flags, and sweets were being distributed. It killed about 20,000 people, injured another 167,000, and destroyed or damaged nearly 1 million buildings. Hundreds of villages were flattened, and many historical forts, palaces, and temples were severely damaged. In Ahmedabad, 50 multistoried buildings collapsed, killing hundreds of people. It took about 6 months of rigorous relief efforts from all sections of society to mitigate the sufferings of the people to some extent.

Table 2.2 Some of the most powerful earthquakes in India

Sr. No.	Place	Deaths	Date	Magnitude	Epicentre
1	Indian Ocean	More than 283,106	December 26, 2004	9.1–9.3	West coast of Sumatra, Indonesia
2	Kashmir	130,000	October 8, 2005	7.6	Muzaffarabad, Pakistan-administered Kashmir
3	Bihar and Nepal	More than 30,000	January 15, 1934	8.7	South of Mount Everest
4	Gujarat	20,000	January 26, 2001	7.7	Kutch, Gujarat
5	Kangra	More than 20,000	April 4, 1905	7.8	Himalayas
6	Latur	More than 9,748	September 30, 1993	6.4	Killari, Latur, Maharashtra
7	Assam	1,526	August 15, 1950	8.6	Arunachal Pradesh
8	Assam	1,500	June 12, 1897	8.1	The exact location is not known
9	Uttarkashi	More than 1,000	October 20, 1991	6.8	Garhwal, Uttarakhand
10	Koynanagar	180	December 11, 1967	6.5	Maharashtra

The Latur earthquake on September 30, 1993, in Maharashtra remains one of the most fatal natural disasters that Maharashtra has ever faced. It killed about 10,000 persons and injured 30,000 across 52 villages. The death toll was high as the earthquake struck when people were asleep. Though the magnitude recorded was 6.4, the destruction that it caused was massive as the earthquake's hypocentre was just around 10 km deep — relatively shallow — allowing shock waves to cause more damage. As the location does not lie on a plate boundary, the cause of the intraplate earthquake is still debated. Now, Latur and adjoining areas are well developed.

Koynanagar, in Maharashtra, is one of the most seismically active areas in the country, and as many as 20 known earthquakes have taken place there, the latest one being on April 14, 2014. The most severe one took place in 1967 with affected areas extending to 25 km and casualties of 180 and 1,500 injured. There are strong suggestions that some of these could have been triggered by a reservoir there. We shall discuss this in detail under triggered earthquakes.

Earthquake zonation helps us to plan our building and other infrastructure to minimize the damages. We conclude this discussion by giving the earthquake zones of India:

- **Zone 5 — Very High-Risk Area:** 11% of land area in India is considered as high risk. The states that fall in this zone are Arunachal Pradesh, Assam, Nagaland, Mizoram, Meghalaya, Tripura, Central Kashmir, Central Himalayas, Northern Bihar, Rann of Kutch, and Andaman and Nicobar Islands.
- **Zone 4 — High-Risk Zone:** 18% of land area, including some parts of Jammu and Kashmir, Uttarakhand, Delhi, Gujarat, Bihar, West Bengal, Koynanagar in Maharashtra, and the whole of Sikkim, lie in this zone.
- **Zone 3 — Moderate Risk Zone:** 30% of land area, including some parts of Haryana, Punjab, Rajasthan, Gujarat, Maharashtra, Telangana, Andhra Pradesh, Uttar Pradesh, Jharkhand, West Bengal, Odisha, Madhya Pradesh, Bihar, Karnataka, Tamil Nadu, and the whole of Dadra and Nagar Haveli, Goa, and Kerala, fall under this risk zone.
- **Zone 2 — Low-risk Zone:** 41% of land area is considered as low risk (see Fig. 2.14).

2.3 Tsunamis

Tsunamis are large ocean waves that are usually triggered by an undersea earthquake, a volcanic explosion, glacier calving, or submarine landslides. These are often a train of waves, one wave following the other. We have earlier seen that gigantic tsunami waves are believed to have been formed after the asteroid impact 66 million years ago near Mexico. It is likely that the Mausala Parva of the Mahabharata records a massive tsunami triggered by either an underwater volcanic activity or a major earthquake centred at

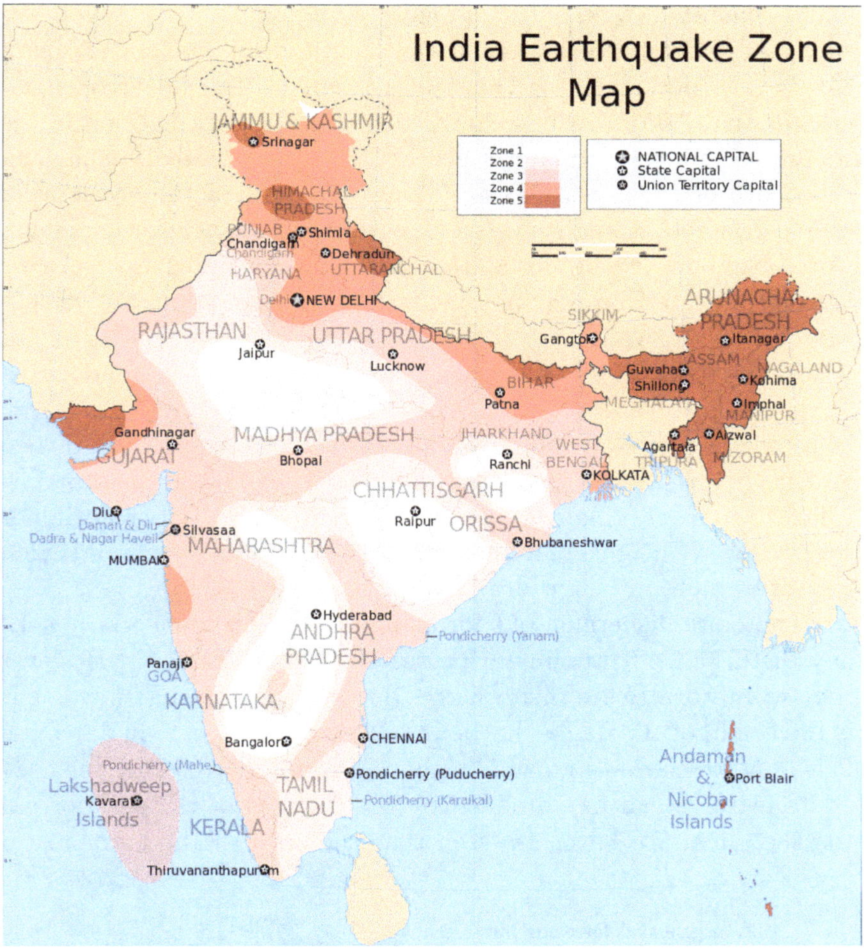

Fig. 2.14 Earthquake zone map of India [18]

Makran Coast (in present-day Pakistan). Dholavira, a major Indus Valley Civilization site, has massive, 14–18-m-thick walls, possibly as a protection against tsunamis.

In the case of normal tidal waves, which are caused by the forces of the Moon and the Sun upon the tides as well as the wind as it moves over the water, water flows in circles. However, in the case of a tsunami, water flows straight. This makes tsunamis devastating.

Wind-generated waves usually have a period (time between two successive waves) of 5–20 s and a wavelength of 100–200 m. A tsunami can have a period in the range of 10 min to 2 h and wavelengths greater than 500 km. The velocity of tsunami waves is given by the square root of the product of acceleration due to gravity times and the depth of the ocean. Thus, taking the value of the acceleration due to gravity ($9.81\,\mathrm{m/s^2}$) we can see that the velocity of the tsunami would be about 220 m/s or 800 km/h, for the region where the ocean is 5,000 m deep. However, in a modest 10-m-deep ocean, the velocity would drop to 35 km/h.

As the tsunami leaves the deep waters of the open sea and arrives at the shallow waters near the coast, it undergoes a transformation as the faster waves arriving from deeper seas "pile up" behind these and its height grows while maintaining its "strength" in a process called "shoaling". Thus, a tsunami remains nearly imperceptible at sea, with wave heights of a fraction of a metre, but grows to be several metres or more in height near the coast (see Fig. 2.15).

Therefore, fishermen out for fishing in the deep sea will not feel any disturbance if a tsunami passes their boats or ships. However, they will return to see their villages devastated by a huge wave. This is the origin of the name "harbour (*tsu*) waves (*nami*)" in Japanese. It is easy to see that tsunami height will vary greatly along the coast as its features can be amplified by the features of the seafloor and the shoreline. We have also seen that the crest of the tsunami can

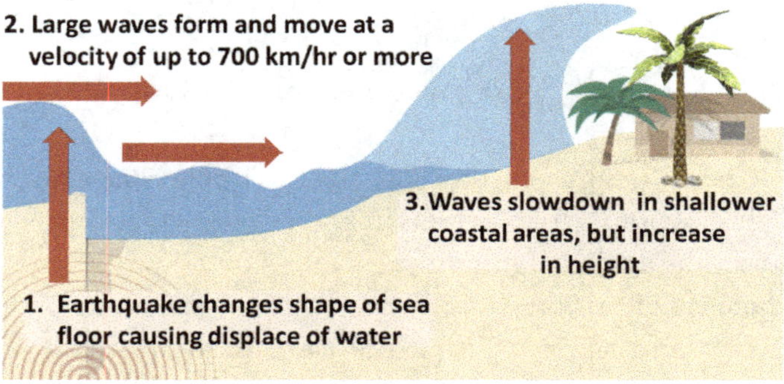

Fig. 2.15 Development of tsunami [19]

be several metres high ("run-up") as they reach the shore. This may happen, for example, when the tsunami is caused by an undersea volcano, which pours out huge quantities of rocks and lava, displacing the water or a landslide which generates huge waves as in the case of Vajont Dam in Italy.

Sometimes, however, the crest of the wave is not the first to arrive. This generally happens when the tsunami has its origin in an oceanic earthquake that takes place due to sinking or subsidence of land. This causes the water column to drop down at the site of the earthquake. In this case, instead of extremely high levels of water, the first sign of a tsunami is what appears to be an unusually low low-tide, which is called "drop-down" as the trough of the tsunami wave reaches the coast first. This serves as a very useful warning, as the water recedes from the shore, exposing the seafloor and leaving the fish behind.

2.3.1 *Some major tsunami events*

Even though almost all oceans have witnessed tsunamis, most of them (80–85%) occur in the Pacific Ocean. The Pacific Ocean, after all, covers more than one-third of the surface of the Earth and is surrounded by the "Ring of Fire" with chains of mountains, deep-ocean trenches, and arcs of islands (see Fig. 2.6), where most earthquakes occur. Destructive tsunamis have also been generated in the Atlantic and Indian Oceans, the Mediterranean Sea, and even within smaller bodies of water, like the Sea of Marmara, in Turkey, though not as frequently.

2.3.2 *The 1755 Great Lisbon earthquake and tsunami*

The Great Lisbon earthquake occurred on November 1, 1755. It has been estimated that the earthquake had a magnitude of 8.5–9.0 on the moment magnitude scale, with an epicentre in the Atlantic Ocean about 200 km from Cape St. Vincent. The earthquake was felt all over Europe and Africa. Morocco was severely affected with a loss of about 10,000 persons. It was followed by a tsunami, with waves as high as 6–30 m, which even reached England, the Caribbean, and Brazil. The earthquake started a fire, which along with the tsunami destroyed Lisbon and its palaces, churches, libraries, valuable archives, works of art, museums, and living quarters. The earthquake was one of the most destructive and deadly earthquakes in Lisbon's history and killed more than a third of the entire population of the Portuguese capital. Tens of thousands of its inhabitants who survived the earthquake were killed by the tsunami, which accounted for most of the approximately 70,000 deaths in Portugal, Spain, and Morocco.

The Lisbon earthquake was the first to be studied scientifically for its effects on a large area. For this reason, it is often called the "slap that led to the birth of modern seismology and earthquake engineering".

2.3.3 *The 2004 Sumatra earthquake and tsunami, Indonesia*

The tsunami caused by the 9.1 magnitude earthquake off the coast of Sumatra on December 26, 2004, was the deadliest tsunami in recorded history, as it killed about 280,000 persons across 14 countries. The undersea earthquake had its hypocentre at a depth of 30 km, and the fault zone that caused the tsunami was roughly 1,300 km long. It vertically displaced the seafloor by several metres along that length. The ensuing tsunami was as high as 50 m and reached 5 km inland near Meubolah, Sumatra (see Fig. 2.16). This tsunami is also one of the most widely recorded and studied [20, 21].

The largest number of fatalities was reported from Aceh (Indonesia), Sri Lanka, Tamil Nadu (India), and Khao Lak (Thailand). In addition to the heavy toll on human lives, property, and infrastructure, the tsunami had an enormous environmental impact. Severe damage was inflicted on ecosystems such as mangroves, coral reefs, forests, coastal wetlands, vegetation, sand dunes and rock formations, animal and plant biodiversity, and groundwater.

The tsunami brought out heart-breaking stories of devastation, enormous efforts of the international community for humanitarian help, and accounts of deep insight by ancient tribes, and even some animals. Thus, it was reported that in Sri Lanka wild elephants

Fig. 2.16 South-West Suburb of Aceh, Sumatra [20]

moved to higher areas just before the tsunami. The earthquake pushed up the Andaman Island by 1.2–1.8 m, exposed and destroyed the exquisite coral reefs and pushed down the Nicobar Island by almost 4.6 m, causing extensive damage, killing many inhabitants, and destroying property, agricultural fields, and plantations. There were widespread apprehensions that the Onge tribes of the Andaman Islands would be badly affected by the tsunami. However, oral traditions developed from previous earthquakes helped the aboriginal tribes escape the tsunami by moving to higher ground and suffering very few casualties. The folklore of the Onges talks of "huge shaking of ground followed by the high wall of water".

The island of Simeulue in Indonesia is very close to the epicentre. Yet, it suffered no casualties, as the inhabitants ran to inland hills after the initial shaking and before the tsunami struck, based on the folk memories of the earthquake and tsunami in 1907.

A particularly impressive incident involved a 10-year-old British tourist named Tilly Smith, at the Maikhao Beach in north Phuket City, Thailand. From her lessons on tsunami in geography, she recognized the warning signs of the receding sea and along with her parents warned others on the beach, which was evacuated safely. Similarly, John Chroston, a teacher from Scotland, also recognized the signs at Kamala Bay north of Phuket and took a busload of vacationers and locals to safety on higher ground. We will return to this incident when we discuss the importance of risk communication in reducing the impact of the event.

The tsunami attracted international efforts led by India in setting up a state-of-the-art tsunami warning system for the Indian Ocean.

2.3.4 *The 2011 Fukushima disaster*

The 2011 earthquake off the Pacific coast of Tohoku, also known as the Great East Japan Earthquake, was a magnitude 9.0 undersea earthquake off the coast of Japan that occurred on March 11, 2011. It was the world's fourth largest earthquake since 1900 and the largest in Japan since modern instrumental recordings began 130 years ago. The earthquake triggered powerful tsunami waves that reached heights of up to 40.5 m and at some places travelled up to 10 km inland. The tsunami obliterated tens of thousands of buildings. It devoured almost anything in its path and caused widespread devastation, with an official count of around 20,000 people confirmed to be killed/missing. In addition, the tsunami precipitated multiple hydrogen explosions and a nuclear meltdown at the Fukushima-I Nuclear Power Plant, which led to freezing and rethinking nuclear energy by many countries. Around 340,000 persons from an area of about 20 km around the site were evacuated. The World Bank's estimated economic cost was 235 billion USD, making it the costliest natural disaster in history. The radioactive decontamination of the area may take years.

2.4 Floods

Almost all civilizations, viz., Indians, Persians, Babylonians, Syrians, Native Americans, Polynesians, the Celts of Britain, and the Maoris of New Zealand have legends of Great Floods which are sometimes believed to be a tribal memory of events as the last Ice Age ended about 10,000–12,000 years ago. The essential requirement of water for drinking and irrigation also led to settlements coming up near rivers from ancient times across the world, which also makes them vulnerable to floods in case of excessive rains.

The yearly flooding of the Nile due to monsoon has been an important natural cycle in Egypt since ancient times, which supported an abundant agriculture-based civilization, as long as the people effectively managed the floodwaters using bunds, and dykes, at several levels. These floods were called "Gift of the Nile". Thus, when the water receded, a very thin, evenly spread layer of black mud was left behind. In fact, the ancient name for Egypt was "Kemet", which means "Black Land". As the floods receded, farmers immediately planted their crops, never needing fertilizers because the soil deposited by the flood was so rich. Once this arrangement stopped as dykes decayed and were destroyed, the civilization withered. Now, the Aswan Dam on the Nile provides year-round water for irrigation in a controlled manner. Modern Aerial Imaging of the Nile Basin now provides more detailed imagery of the topography and understanding of annual floods.

There are suggestions that the Indus Valley Civilization witnessed a long and devastating drought followed by devastating floods which led to the abandonment of the settlements along the banks of the Indus and Saraswati rivers, ending an urban civilization that had flourished.

Heavy rainfall is the most common cause of floods. Heavy rainfall in a short span of time or a cloud burst (where hot moist air rises and loads existing clouds with excessive moisture, which is released suddenly over a small area (see Fig. 2.17) can lead to flash floods. Heavy siltation of the riverbed reduces the water-carrying capacity of the rivers and the streams leading to flooding. Large-scale deforestation in the catchment areas of the rivers is considered to be a major cause of floods.

In urban areas, blocked drains are the primary cause of floods. The severe flooding of Mumbai on July 26, 2005, which killed more than 1,000 persons, was caused by near-complete blockage of the Mithi river due to encroachments, and very heavy rains, coinciding

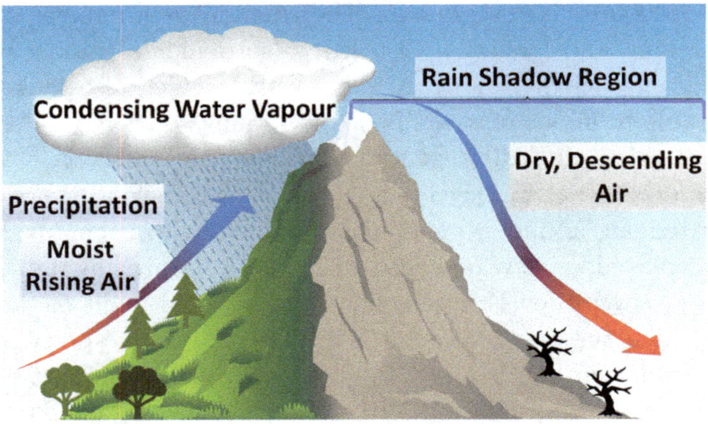

Fig. 2.17 Conditions for a cloud burst [22]

with high tides. A similar case occurred in Chennai when it received one of the heaviest rainfalls in the previous 100 years in 2015. These affected the Coromandel Coast region of the South Indian states of Tamil Nadu and Andhra Pradesh, killing more than 500 people and displacing over 1.8 million people. The damages and losses were estimated to be at 200 billion rupees (about 2.7 billion USD) or more. In the case of Chennai, the flood was blamed on unregulated construction and the usurpation of lakes, ponds, and other water bodies for high-rise buildings without consideration for water flow.

In hilly areas, landslides blocking the flow of streams and rivers can cause floods and, in June 2013, several days of heavy rain triggered flash floods and landslides in the state of Uttarakhand. This happened during the busy tourist season, a month before the normal beginning of the monsoon, catching many by surprise. An estimated 5,000 or more people were killed and nearly 1 million were affected by the disaster. The flooding also caused more than 3.8 billion USD in economic losses. As the floodwaters rushed down the rivers, one saw buildings, mostly constructed illegally, close to and even in the middle of the river collapsing like a pack of cards. The floods also caused serious damage to about 30 dams, some of which were already in operation while the others were under construction.

Natural hazards like earthquakes, cyclones, and encroachment of riverbanks and water bodies can also cause flooding. Apart from the loss of life and property, recurrent floods adversely affect agricultural operations. Ganga, Yamuna, Kosi, Brahmaputra, and their tributaries flood regularly, causing havoc almost every year. It is very likely that, with the onset of global warming and climate change, the frequency and ferocity of such events will increase.

In 2008, the Kosi River — sometimes called the "Sorrow of Bihar" — burst through its embankment, sending the full force of the river pouring into the state of Bihar and neighbouring Nepal. It is estimated that 3.3 million people were affected by the floods, 222,000 homes were destroyed, 527 people and 19,323 animals were killed. Reconstruction costs were estimated to be around 1.2 billion USD.

We recall some of the devastating floods in history in the following to illustrate the enormous damage to life and property and see what causes them and how, if at all, they could be averted.

The 6,300-km-long Yangtze River is the third longest river in the world. Its drainage basin covers one-fifth of the land area of China and is home to nearly one-third of the country's population. The river has shaped the history, culture, and economy of China by providing water for irrigation, sanitation, transportation, industry, and helping in carving out boundaries and in wars. It experienced major floods in 1931, 1954, and 1998. The floodplains of the river have tens of millions of people living in them and these areas naturally get flooded every year. These are habitable because of extensive dykes on the river, also due to the construction of the Three Gorges Dam which holds the flow of water from the Yangtze River's upstream and prevents it from rushing into the downstream branches. However, as mentioned earlier, floods large enough to overflow the dykes have happened several times in the past.

The flood of 1931 covered more than 77,700 km^2, killed more than 300,000 people, and left 40 million more homeless. Some sources put the loss of life as 4–5 million. An earlier flood in 1911 had killed around 100,000 people and caused severe property loss. In 1935, another flood had hit the Yangtze River. It killed more than 150,000 people and destroyed everything that the residents of the valley had

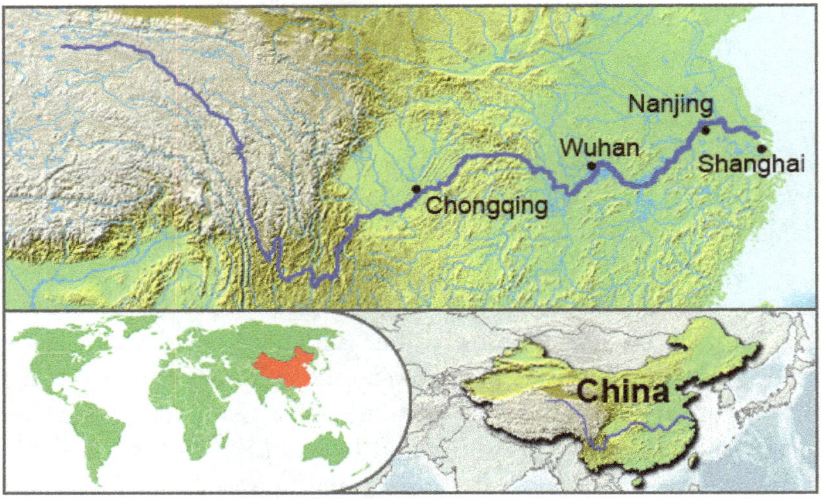

Fig. 2.18 The basin of Yangtze River [23]

ever possessed. Subsequently, more effective levees were built, but the floods of 1954 and 1998 were still highly destructive and killed some 30,000 and 3,650 people, respectively (see Fig. 2.18).

China has had a particularly long and terrible history of flooding. In the last 2,000 years, the Yangtze River flooded more than 1,000 times. But it is the Hwang Ho or "Yellow River" that has been responsible for China's most catastrophic floods and was given the name "China's Sorrow".

Much of the problem stems from the high silt content of this river, which is as high as 60% by weight in lower reaches. Millions of tonnes of yellow mud choke the channel, as it proceeds on its journey and causes the river to overflow and change course. In its lower reaches, the riverbed has actually become higher than the level of the surrounding countryside, and water is held in by dykes of ever-increasing height, some of which reach a height of 10 m or more.

A catastrophic flood in the Yellow River in China in 1911 killed more than 900,000 people (some reports say 2 million) and rendered more than 2 million people homeless by submerging more than 50,000 km^2 of land, destroying agriculture and commerce. The estimates of the death toll in the flood of 1931 range from 150,000 to 4 million.

The Yellow River flood of 1938 was, on the other hand, one of the largest acts of environmental warfare. The then Nationalist Government of China decided to halt the Japanese forces during the Second Sino-Japanese War by destroying the dykes of the Yellow River. Unfortunately, several provinces were flooded, without causing any inconvenience to the invading army, and at least around 800,000 people were killed.

The Netherlands has had a long history of a series of floods, as the country is originally formed by three large estuaries of the Rhine, the Meuse, and the Scheldt River, and their other tributaries. The 1212 CE North Sea flood may not be the worst flood ever occurred in the country, but it killed around 60,000 people. The "First St. Marcellus flood" occurred in 1219 AD, along the coast of West Friesland and Groningen province of The Netherlands, causing immense damage to property and killing 36,000 people. A high tide, a severe European windstorm, and low pressure led to a rise of water level by more than 5.6 m above mean sea level in the North Sea, causing St. Lucia Flood in The Netherlands and North Germany in December 1287 and killing 80,000 people. St. Felix Flood in November 1530 washed away most of the land of the Netherlands and killed more than 120,000 people. The submerged areas, including large parts of Flanders, Zeeland, and Reimerswaal cities, turned into salt marsh areas.

The Lower Mississippi River experienced very extensive floods following extremely heavy rains in 1927. Several states including Missouri, Illinois, Kansas, Tennessee, Kentucky, Arkansas, Louisiana, Mississippi, Oklahoma, and Texas were severely affected. The span of the flooded river extended to 130 km. More than 70,000 km^2 of farmland was inundated under 9 m of water, about 500 people were killed, and 700,000 people were rendered homeless. More than 200,000 African Americans were displaced from their homes along the Lower Mississippi River. They spent long periods in relief camps, and many migrated to northern and mid-western states instead of returning to rural agricultural areas. The estimated loss was about 930 billion USD.

To prevent future floods, the US Government built the longest levee system and floodways in the world. It improved the navigability of the river and prevented floods. This dramatic development spurred millions of Americans to move onto the floodplain, where the soil was fertile and the property was cheap. However, this has resulted in the loss of much of the river's bordering wetlands to agriculture and construction. In 1993, the rising waters of the river broke a large part of the privately constructed levees and flooded vast areas, and ignited debates about the loss of trees, grasses, deep roots, and wetlands, which used to absorb floodwaters after seasons of intense snow and rain.

Bangladesh encounters regular floods due to its geographical settings. The flood in 1974, however, remains the worst flood ever recorded due to monsoons, which killed more than 30,000 and rendered countless seriously ill. Bangladesh is especially vulnerable to floods as it is watered by a total of 57 transboundary rivers coming down to it: 54 from India and 3 from Myanmar. It is situated at the bottom of the mighty Ganges, Brahmaputra, and the Meghna river system, and nearly a quarter of Bangladesh is less than 2.1 m (7 feet) above sea level. Moreover, climate change is causing heavy rains over short periods, increased frequency, intensity, and recurrence of floods, flash floods, and monsoon floods, which in turn lead to intrusion of salinity along the coast, scarcity of potable water, coastal erosion, loss of crops, and riverbank erosions. It is estimated that if the sea level rises by just 0.9 m (3 feet), one-fifth of the land area of the country will be under seawater and require tens of millions of people to move away from their present dwellings. All these problems are also being faced by the people of India living in the Sundarbans and neighbourhood.

2.5 Landslides

Landslides denote the movement of a mass of rock, debris, or earth down a slope, which could be in the form of a fall, a topple, a slide, a spread, or a flow under the influence of gravity. These occur in slopes on the verge of movement due to rainfall, snowmelt, earthquakes, volcanic activity, change in water level, disturbance by human activity (e.g., blasting of rocks using dynamite), or a combination of such factors. Earthquakes can also induce underwater landslides and may even lead to a tsunami. Landslides load rivers, block roads and highways, and bury people alive. Worldwide, landslides cause thousands of casualties and monetary losses amounting to billions of USD annually. These describe a wide variety of processes that result in the downward and outward movement of slope-forming materials including rock, soil, artificial fill, or a combination of these, which involve movement of the material by falling, toppling, sliding, spreading, or flowing [24].

India, unfortunately, is not a stranger to landslides, and every monsoon season ushers in floods and landslides. One of the severe natural disasters that India has experienced in recent times was when the township of Kedarnath Temple in Uttarakhand was hit by a massive landslide involving debris avalanche on June 16 and 17, 2013, following incessant rains. As mentioned earlier, it killed about 6,000 people and affected nearly 3 million local persons and more than 100,000 pilgrims and tourists. More than 8,000 km of motorable road, 200 bridges, and 30 hydro-power projects were affected, and it caused distress across more than 5,000 villages in the hills and 30 urban clusters [25].

Even though officials blamed Nature for the disaster, many environmentalists and scientists believe that relentless and thoughtless human intervention in the Himalayan Mountain ecosystem had made it extremely fragile and prone to disaster. It has also been suggested that unchecked tourism in the region had led to the rapid growth of hotels, roads, and shops throughout the region by completely ignoring the environmental laws and with a complete disregard to the demands of the ecosystem. The mushrooming of hydroelectric dams in Uttarakhand was also blamed for the environmental damage. It has been argued that the phenomenon of regular landslides in the Himalayas can be effectively managed only by developing a scientific understanding of the fragile ecology of the tectonically active and geologically vulnerable and the physically abused and technologically neglected mountain–river systems [25].

In the following, we give examples of some of the major landslide disasters across the world in recent history [26], caused by earthquakes, volcanic eruptions, and rains. We have already discussed how a landslide into the Vajont Dam caused a catastrophic disaster.

The 8.5-magnitude Haiyuan Earthquake in Ningxia, China in December 1920 was the second deadliest earthquake of the twentieth century. It generated a series of 675 major loess landslides, causing massive destruction. It killed more than 100,000 people, buried entire villages, and severely damaged an area of approximately 20,000 km^2.

The sudden eruption of a dormant volcano, the Nevado del Ruiz in Tolima, Colombia, on November 13, 1985, wreaked havoc on the nearby villages and towns and killed as many as 23,000 people. A pyroclastic flow from the crater of the volcano melted the glaciers in the mountain and sent deadly lahars, saturated with mud, ice, snow, and volcanic debris, which rushed down the mountain at killer speeds towards the residential areas directly below it. The lahars soon engulfed the town of Armero, killing thousands there and in Chinchiná.

It is hoped that the technological breakthroughs in weather forecasting, timely early warning, high-resolution hazard and vulnerability mapping and management of big data for swift decision-making can greatly reduce casualties resulting from these disasters through timely action.

2.6 Droughts and Forest Fires

A drought is an event of prolonged shortages in the water supply either due to below-average precipitation or reduced streamflow or depleted groundwater. A drought can last for months or years. It can very adversely affect not only the agricultural operations and therefore the economy but also the biodiversity in the region, increasing the chances of bushfires. A study of tree rings has revealed that droughts are a recurring feature in most parts of the world. The thickness of tree rings decreases in the years of lower availability

Fig. 2.19 The thickness of tree rings are records of droughts over its life

of water. Global warming and climate change are making them more frequent and intense, like the floods, as mentioned earlier. Droughts often lead to forest fires, thus compounding the disasters (see Fig. 2.19).

Droughts are often categorized as meteorological when there are long gaps in normal rainfall, agricultural when there is insufficient moisture in the soil for agriculture following scanty rains, hydrological when the subsurface water supply becomes scarce due to scanty rainfall and drying-up of streams, lakes, and rivers, for example, due to construction of dams or diversion of the river water, and socioeconomic when all the above affect the lives of people at individual and collective levels (see Fig. 2.20).

India has had a long history of droughts. During the recent period of 1870–2018, there were 26 major droughts, when all India summer monsoon rainfall was found to be lesser than the mean rainfall for the country. The most severe meteorological droughts were in the years 1876, 1899, 1918, 1965, and 2000, while the five worst hydrological droughts occurred in the years 1876, 1899, 1918,

Fig. 2.20 A drought-stricken agricultural land [27]

1965, and 2000. The drought of 1899 is classified as meteorological as well as hydrological and was the most severe documented drought India has ever experienced to date. Droughts and monsoons of India are intensively and extensively studied subjects as they affect the overall food production and well-being of its people.

El Niño — Southern Oscillation is an irregularly periodic variation in wind and sea surface temperatures over the tropical eastern Pacific Ocean, affecting the climate of much of the tropics and subtropics. When the temperatures are higher than normal, the conditions are called El Niño, and when they are lower, the conditions are called La Niña. There are indications that El Niño Southern Oscillation modulates Indian monsoon, with less than normal rain during El Niño phases and more than normal rain during La Niña phases. Evidence is also emerging that Indian Ocean Dipole, the irregular oscillation of sea surface temperatures, in which the western Indian Ocean becomes alternately warmer (termed as the positive phase) and then colder (termed as the negative phase) than the eastern part of the ocean, also strongly affects the rains in India. Thus, the positive phase sees greater-than-average sea-surface temperatures and greater precipitation in the western Indian Ocean region.

The associated cooling of waters in the eastern Indian Ocean tends to cause droughts in adjacent land areas of Indonesia and Australia. Its negative phase brings about the opposite conditions, with warmer water and greater precipitation in the eastern Indian Ocean, and cooler and drier conditions in the west.

Famines caused by drought are believed to have killed more than 60 million people over the course of the eighteenth, nineteenth, and early twentieth centuries in India. However, more intensive recent studies have invariably revealed that the deaths could have been averted by providing relief to the populace as food grain was available in other parts of the country. The 1943 famine in Bengal, which killed 4–6 million people, was the last catastrophic famine in India. There is evidence to suggest that food grains were actively stopped from being transported to Bengal by the colonial government [28].

After the independence, India has fairly successfully tackled subsequent droughts, e.g., Bihar drought (1966–1967), Maharashtra drought (1972), West Bengal drought (1979–80), and Maharashtra drought (2013) by rushing relief, including sending drinking water and fodder for animals from other parts of the country. This gave rise to the oft-quoted remark that "famines do not take place in democratic nations".

Droughts are a recurrent and often devastating feature of sub-Saharan Africa. Climate and the availability of water in the Middle East have undergone a vast change over the last several millennia and remain to be understood in detail.

Another disastrous consequence of droughts is a forest fire, as the trees dry up for lack of water. The 2019–2020 fire in Australia burned down 46 million acres of forest and killed several billion wild animals, several of them found only in Australia. Fortunately, the human toll was limited to about 34, as the population density in that region is very low, even though the environmental impact was substantial with the emission of almost 400 million tonnes of carbon dioxide, which may take decades to be reabsorbed by the forest when it recovers. Year after year, forest fires burn larger and larger swathes of forests in California. In 2020, this amounted to more than 4 million acres of forests.

2.7 Locusts

While on the subject of floods and droughts, we would like to digress a little and discuss another disaster — the locust menace. While it is not in the same category of natural disasters like floods or droughts, it is intimately connected to extreme weather conditions — a long drought followed by heavy rains. Locusts have been around since ancient times, multiplying and vanishing in irregular booms and bursts. Locusts in general are solitary. During dry spells, these are forced together in the patchy areas of land with remaining vegetation. The crowding releases serotonin in their central nervous systems that makes locusts more sociable and spurs behavioural changes, such as rapid movements, increased self-grooming, and a more varied appetite within hours of crowding. This switch to the gregarious state also includes physical changes, such as a larger brain and shorter legs. The large brain perhaps helps them in more complex information processing. The offsprings of gregarious locusts develop smaller femurs, which provides them increased endurance. Their hops are shorter, but then they use less energy to cover the same distance. When rains return, producing moist soil and abundant green plants, environmental conditions are right to create a locust storm. They reproduce rapidly and move as a group rapidly in search of more food (see Figs. 2.21 and 2.22).

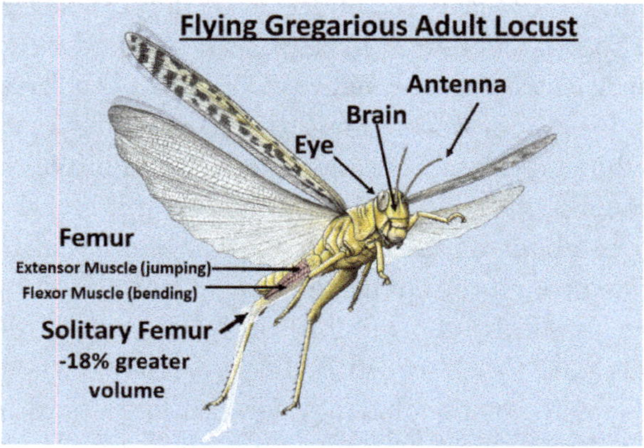

Fig. 2.21 Flying gregarious locust [29]

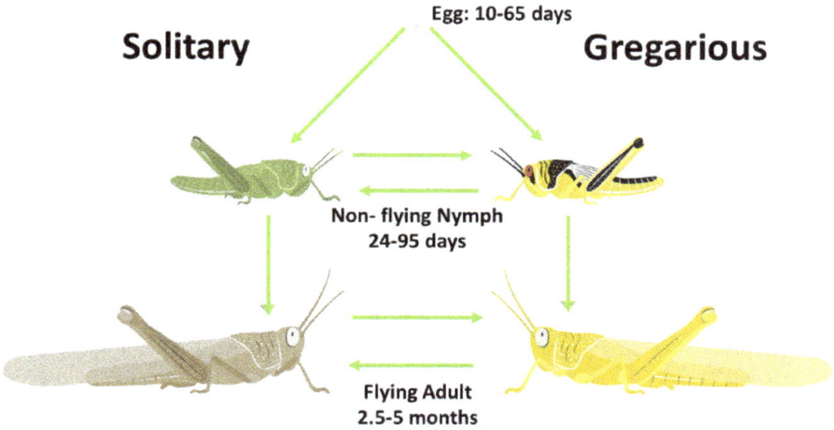

Fig. 2.22 Life of a desert locust [29]

Even though not very common, a major "plague" begins when swarms, often travelling 50–100 km a day, develop over multiple regions and merge. Locust swarms fly with the wind at roughly the speed of the wind. Locusts can cover from 100 to 200 km in a day and fly at a height of up to about 2,000 m above sea level (the temperature becomes too cold at higher altitudes). Thus, swarms can neither cross tall mountain ranges such as the Atlas Mountain range in Africa, the Hindu Kush, or the Himalayas nor venture into the rainforests of Africa or into Central Europe.

When locusts swarm like this, they ravage agriculture devouring practically anything in sight. Imagine a polyphagous swarm of 50 billion flying insects, covering an area of 850 km^2, where each insect eats 2 g of crops per day, every day as it moves. It will strip the land of 100,000 tonnes of vegetation every day (see Fig. 2.23).

History is replete with references to swarms of locusts from ancient times. Kautilya talked of extending every possible help to people by the administration during the "plague" of locusts in his Arthashastra. The Mahabharata, the Bible, and the Quran have references to swarms of locusts.

Due to their impact on the agriculture and food security of poorer nations, the Food and Agriculture Organisation (FAO) of the United

Fig. 2.23 A swarm of locusts [30]

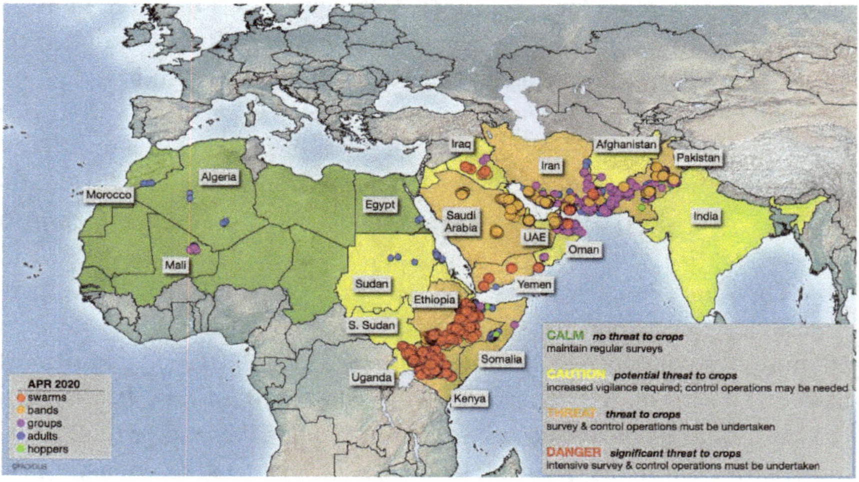

Fig. 2.24 A typical locust warning by FAO

Nations monitors their emergence and issues warnings at regular intervals. One such warning, issued at the beginning of 2020, which impacted India and Pakistan, is given in Fig. 2.24 as an illustrative example.

Locust Warning Organization of India was established in 1939, with its headquarters in New Delhi and a branch in Karachi. It is now incorporated into the Directorate of Plant Protection, Quarantine, and Storage. India and Pakistan routinely cooperate in tackling the menace. The Government of India has a detailed Contingency Plan for Desert Locust Invasions and Upsurges [30], which it updates regularly with feedback from FAO.

2.7.1 *Control of locusts*

As mentioned earlier, solitary locusts are harmless and need no special attention. When the gregarious swarms are on the move, insecticides are often sprayed on them using helicopters or drones. The pests can also be doused with chemicals using hand pumps and land vehicles. By using these methods, the swarms can be targeted and killed in a relatively short time. Up to 97% or more of the pests must be killed, else they recover and develop into a swarm again. For smaller swarms, using flamethrowers, smoke, and beating metallic plates are also tried. Of course, if one can locate their breeding grounds, one can plough the area and destroy the eggs. One may also dig a 60-cm-wide and 60-cm-deep ditch around that place for the flightless nymphs to get trapped (see Fig. 2.25).

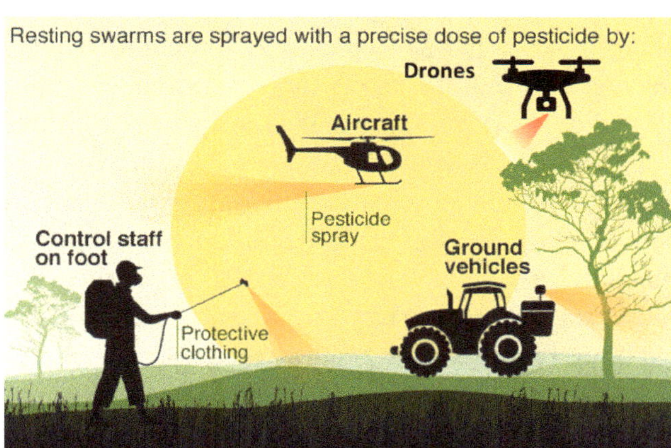

Fig. 2.25 Control of locusts [19]

Farmers in Africa have, for centuries, depended on birds such as Glareola, starlings, and ibis to alert them about the impending emergence of locusts and to keep them under control, as they appear at the time of their breeding and follow them. Several biopesticides are now available to control locusts. As locusts are also eaten by many, care should be taken not to consume the ones exposed to pesticides.

Australia has been using satellites to locate large locust swarms. Satellite imaging can also locate sites in isolated and difficult terrains, which may hold moist earth which locusts use for laying eggs [31]. It has been mentioned that solitary locusts become gregarious when rains follow a prolonged drought or when rains fall on deserts leading to a large growth of vegetation. The climate change resulting in prolonged droughts and heavy rains is also leading to the frequent emergence of locust swarms.

Locusts can sense weather in advance. As the wind flows from regions of high pressure (hot and dry) to those with low pressure (cold and with rains and vegetation), so do the locusts. This is a useful indicator to follow and destroy them before their numbers assume alarming proportions. Locusts at the hopper stage are still destructive. Once they get their wings, they would fly several tens of kilometres an hour and get more difficult to control. Thus, the hopper stage is the best period to spray, i.e., after hatching but before growing wings. Nevertheless, we should remember that the use of insecticides has harmful effects on the ecosystem and more research is required to find safer chemicals. It is unfortunate that developing countries that are most adversely affected by locusts also lack the financial resources and the scientific know-how to do this effectively. We add that a study has found that male locusts apply a particular scent to the females they have mated with to make them unattractive to other male locusts. Scientists are hoping that this scent can be synthesized and applied to a general locust population. This will break down their production and eliminate them without harming the environment.

Even though a particularly menacing outbreak of locusts may affect only a few per cent of the total production of food of the world, the local effect — especially on small farmers whose entire crop is destroyed — is overwhelming.

2.8 Cyclones

A cyclone is a general term for a weather system in which winds rotate inwardly to an area of low atmospheric pressure. These are violent storms that originate over oceans in tropical areas and move over to the coastal areas, bringing about large-scale destruction caused by strong winds, very heavy rainfall, and storm surges. Tropical cyclones form over warm ocean waters near the equator as warm, moist air over the oceans rises upward from near the surface, resulting in an area of lower air pressure below. Air from the surrounding areas with higher air pressure moves into the low-pressure area. This new cool air becomes warm and moist, and rises. The cycle continues. As the warmed, moist air rises and cools, the water in the air forms clouds. For a cyclone to form, the sea surface temperature must be 27°C or more up to a depth of about 50 m. The rotation of the Earth on its spin generates a Coriolis force because of which the storms that form on the south of the equator spin clockwise, while those that form on the north of the equator spin anti-clockwise. Cyclones are also called typhoons when they occur in the north-western Pacific Ocean and hurricanes when they form over the Atlantic Ocean or the eastern north Pacific Ocean. In the south Pacific or the Indian Ocean, people generally call these disturbances cyclones (see Fig. 2.26).

The tropical cyclones usually weaken when they hit land because they are no longer being fed by the energy from the warm ocean waters. However, they often move far inland, dumping many centimetres of rain and causing lots of wind damage (see Table 2.3) before they die out.

Cyclones are divided into categories based on the strength of the winds. The wind speeds in a cyclone can reach over 250 km/h and cause considerable damage.

Details of most of the ancient cyclone disasters are lost to history. However, estimates of the number of fatalities and collateral damage

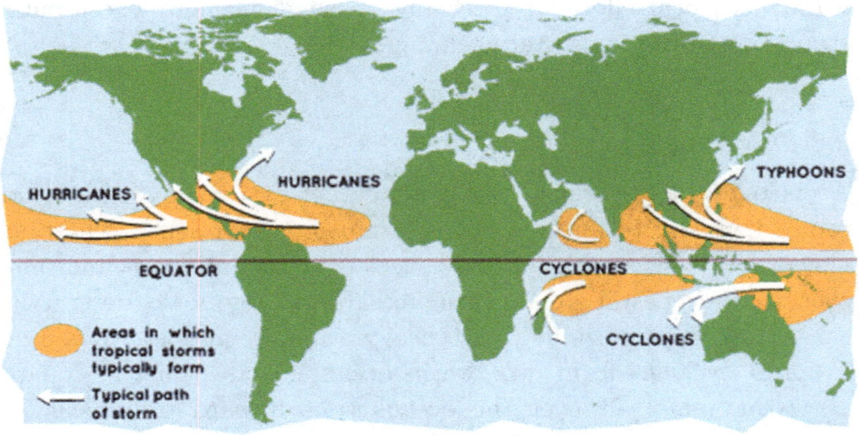

Fig. 2.26 Cyclones, typhoons, or hurricanes [32]

Table 2.3 Categories of cyclones

Cyclone Category	Wind-speed in km/h	Damage
1	120–150	Minimal
2	150–180	Moderate
3	180–210	Extensive
4	210–250	Extreme
5	250 and above	Catastrophic

to the properties linked to recent disasters are available from diverse sources. The Bay of Bengal is a favourable breeding ground for tropical cyclones, and the north Indian Ocean rim countries are the worst sufferers of cyclonic casualties in the world. In general, around four cyclones of varying intensities form over the Bay of Bengal per year and one per year over the Arabian Sea. There are indications that the number of cyclones per year may be increasing over the Arabian Sea due to global warming and climate change. The complex role of the increasing amount of water vapour in the air due to increased heating of the oceans and the land aggravating and abetting extreme weather events is now under intense study. Cyclones in the north Indian Ocean tend to form between April and December, which is called the cyclone season. It normally peaks between May and November.

The 1737 Hooghly River cyclone, also known as the Calcutta Cyclone, is considered to be one of the deadliest natural disasters recorded in history. The cyclone made landfall just south of Calcutta in the Delta of the Ganges, created a storm surge as high as 9–12 m, and emptied 38 cm of rain within 6 h. The cyclone devastated the city of Calcutta, destroying most buildings and structures made from wood and having straw roofs. Many existing brick structures were also damaged to a point beyond repair. The cyclone led to the deaths of 300,000–350,000 people, and many domestic and wild animals, including crocodiles. It is also estimated that villagers in East Bengal also suffered extensive damage and were killed in large numbers. The cyclone is believed to have destroyed 20,000 vessels.

The 1970 Bhola cyclone was a category 4 tropical cyclone that hit what is now Bangladesh on November 12–13, 1970. According to the National Oceanic and Atmospheric Administration's Hurricane Research Division, the storm's strongest wind speeds measured 205 km/h. Ahead of its landfall, a 10.7-m storm surge washed over the low-lying islands bordering the Bay of Bengal, causing widespread flooding. The storm surge, combined with a lack of evacuation, resulted in a massive death toll estimated at 300,000–500,000 people and 86 billion USD in damages. The Bhola cyclone is considered the deadliest tropical cyclone on record. The then government of Pakistan was criticized for not taking adequate precautions and for not providing proper information to the people, and finally, for not providing speedy and adequate relief. It has been suggested that this may also have fuelled the resentment of the people against the rulers, which hastened the break-up of the country.

On April 29, 1991, a devastating category 5 super cyclone, BOB 01, hit Bangladesh, killing more than 138,000 people and causing damage amounting to more than 1.5 billion USD. The winds reached a peak speed of 260 km/h. The cyclone, further, whipped up a 6-m-high storm surge. Although there had been ample warning of the coming storm and shelter provisions had been built in the aftermath of the deadly 1970 storm, not enough people took advantage of these havens before the 1991 storm and decided to wait out the cyclone in their mud and straw huts. Some islands were entirely swamped. Thousands of people were washed out to sea and drowned during the 9-h storm.

On October 29, 1999, a category 5 super cyclone slammed into Odisha. It whipped up winds reaching 260 km/h and raised a 5–6 m storm surge, which travelled up to 35 km inland, inundating villages and towns. It also caused torrential rains. The result was an unimagined death toll and damage. Nearly 10,000 people died, 350,000 houses were destroyed, more than 200,000 animals were killed, and 2.5 million people were marooned. Most large trees in the path of the cyclone were destroyed. The infrastructure was so badly affected that the state went out of contact with the rest of the world for almost a day. Warning about the cyclone was sounded at least 2 days before its landfall. Some efforts were made to evacuate people from harm's way. There were two major challenges: the unwillingness among people to part with their life belongings and the inadequate number of cyclone shelters. The presumption that the two inland cities, Bhubaneswar and Cuttack, would not be affected turned out to be a fatal miscalculation.

The cyclone spurred the extensive establishment of well-equipped cyclone shelters in West Bengal, Odisha, and Andhra Pradesh, a robust and extremely reliable cyclone prediction system, and training of the government officials in handling cyclones. These measures went on to save lives in cyclones that struck in the following years.

The Amphan was a category 5 and catastrophic tropical cyclone that caused widespread damage in Eastern India, specifically West Bengal and in Bangladesh in May 2020, with an estimated damage of over 15 billion USD and more than 200 fatalities (see Fig. 2.27). It was the fourth super cyclone that hit West Bengal and Kolkata since 1582, after 1737, 1833, and 1942, as well as one of the strongest storms to impact the area. The greatly reduced number of fatalities was due to the accurate and timely predictions for the intensity, timing, and track of the cyclone and extensive measures taken by the authorities to evacuate people and shelter them even while combating the COVID-19 pandemic.

Fig. 2.27 The category 5 super cyclone Amphan over the Bay of Bengal (May 18, 2020, NASA [33])

In August 2005, when Hurricane Katrina hit Louisiana, Mississippi, Florida, and Alabama, about 1,200 died and tens of thousands of people were forced to seek refuge in the Superdome which descended into chaos and became a symbol of the city's unpreparedness. The damage was estimated at 125 billion USD.

Typhoon Haiyan (2013) was a category 5 super cyclone and one of the largest and strongest typhoons that swept through the Philippines. It had winds that reached 310 km per hour. The fatalities were estimated at 6,352, while 1,771 persons were reported missing.

It caused damages worth about 3 billion USD and affected regions of Micronesia, the Philippines, South China, Vietnam, Taiwan, and Palau.

Before closing this section, we add that the frequency and ferocity of cyclonic storms are increasing with the increasing global warming. This will severely affect the livelihood of fishermen, who would be unable to venture into the sea for extended periods.

2.9 Tornadoes

A tornado is a rapidly rotating column of air extending downward from a thunderstorm to the ground. The most violent tornadoes, with wind speeds of up to 500 km/h, are capable of tremendous destruction. Tornadoes form in regions of the atmosphere that have abundant warm and moist air near the surface with drier air above and a change in wind speed and wind direction with height above the ground (see Fig. 2.28).

Fig. 2.28 A Tornado near Manitoba, 2007 [34]

Tornadoes are most frequent in the USA and Tornado Alley is a loosely defined area of Texas, Louisiana, Arkansas, Oklahoma, Kansas, South Dakota, Iowa, and Nebraska, where these occur. Tornado survival skills are extensively imparted to citizens of these regions.

2.10 Discussions

Figure 2.29 shows a plot of deaths due to all natural disasters globally during the last 50 years. One can see that over the past decade, approximately 60,000 people died each year on average from natural disasters, representing about 0.1% of global deaths. However, in many years, the number of deaths can be very low, while there can be a devastating impact of shock events, e.g., the 1983–85 famine and drought in Ethiopia; the 2004 Indian Ocean earthquake and tsunami; Cyclone Nargis which struck Myanmar in 2008; and the 2010 Port-au-Prince earthquake in Haiti. Each one of these events pushed global

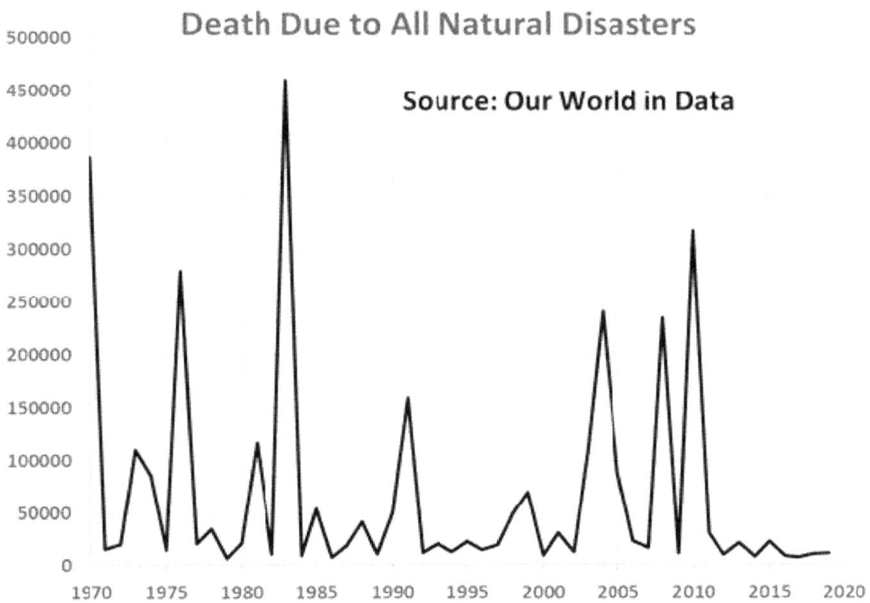

Fig. 2.29 Death due to all natural disasters during the last 50 years [35]

disaster deaths to over 200,000 in these years. Historically, droughts and floods were the most fatal disaster events. Deaths from these events, however, are very low in recent years due to precautions based on accurate weather predictions. Earthquakes tend to be the most deadly events presently [35].

One can also see that in the early-to-mid twentieth century, the annual death toll from disasters was high, often reaching over 1 million per year. In recent decades, there has been a substantial decline in loss of lives. In most years, fewer than 20,000 deaths have been recorded, and in the most recent decade, this has often been less than 10,000. Even in peak years with high-impact events, the death toll has not exceeded 500,000 since the mid-1960s.

This decline is even more impressive when we consider the rate of population growth over this period. If we correct for population — showing this data in terms of death rates (measured per 100,000 people) — we see an even greater decline over the past century.

We do know that low-frequency, high-impact events such as earthquakes and tsunamis are not preventable, but a loss of human lives can be minimized by adopting safety measures, such as building code in the case of earthquakes and predictions and evacuations in the case of tsunamis. The world has seen a significant reduction in disaster deaths through earlier prediction, more resilient infrastructure, emergency preparedness, and response systems (see Fig. 2.30).

The Indian subcontinent has the unique distinction of having vulnerabilities to almost all natural disasters described above. India is a peninsular country with a long coastline, hugged by the Arabian Sea in the west, the Bay of Bengal in the east, and the Indian Ocean in the south. India experiences two monsoons every year, the south-west monsoon from June to September and the north-east monsoon from October to December, bringing in copious rainfall across the country and catering to our freshwater needs. The monsoons also bring in extreme weather events such as floods, droughts, and cyclones, often resulting in loss of life, loss of livelihood, and loss of property. The Himalayan region is known to be a highly active seismic zone. We add that several areas in the Himalayas are also prone to the disaster of avalanches, following heavy snowfalls, which

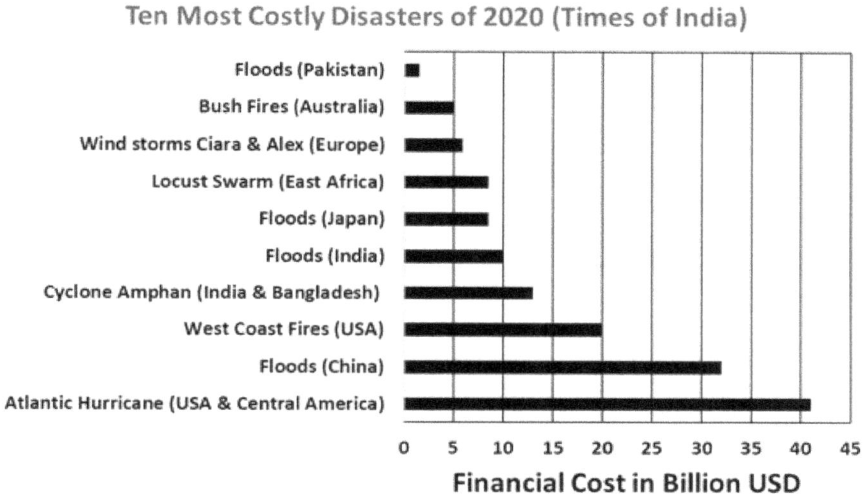

Fig. 2.30 Financial cost of top 10 natural disasters in 2020

cause severe hardships including loss of life and property and which are also very hard to predict.

As will be discussed in later chapters, India has put in place a variety of disaster management strategies to minimize the loss of lives and property resulting from these disasters. Considerable emphasis is also laid on risk communication to the public at large.

References

[1] A. Kapur, *Vulnerable India: A Geographical Study of Disasters*, Sage Publications, New Delhi, India (2010).
[2] http://www.jpl.nasa.gov/releases/98/yucatan.html.
[3] R. Smith, https://www.nationalgeographic.com/animals/article/what-happened-day-dinosaurs-died-chicxulub-drilling-asteroid-science; https://www.nhm.ac.uk/discover/how-an-asteroid-caused-extinction-of-dinosaurs.html.
[4] https://www.usgs.gov/media/images/earth-cross-section.
[5] https://pubs.usgs.gov/gip/dynamic/historical.html.
[6] https://www.usgs.gov/news/earthword-subduction.
[7] https://www.usgs.gov/media/images/ring-fire.
[8] https://commons.wikimedia.org/wiki/File:Geldingadalagos.jpg.

[9] https://www.usgs.gov/media/images/tectonic-plates-earth.
[10] See e.g., https://www.usgs.gov/natural-hazards/earthquake-hazards/science/science-earthquakes?qt-science_center_objects=0#qt-science_center_objects for details.
[11] https://www.usgs.gov/natural-hazards/earthquake-hazards/science/20-largest-earthquakes-world?qt-science_center_objects=0#qt-science_center_object.
[12] https://pubs.usgs.gov/gip/dynamic/himalaya.html.
[13] https://en.wikipedia.org/wiki/April_2015_Nepal_earthquake.
[14] M. S. Krishnan, The North Bihar Earthquake of the 15th January, 1934, *Curr. Sci.* **2**, 323–326 (1934).
[15] https://munger.nic.in/gallery/1934-earthquake-glimpse/.
[16] https://en.wikipedia.org/wiki/1934_Nepal%E2%80%93India_earthquake.
[17] A. Sharma and F. Zaman, The Great Assam Earthquake of 1950: A Historical Review, *Senhri J. Multidiscip. Stud.* **4**, 1–10 (2019). archives.assam.gov.in.
[18] https://en.wikipedia.org/wiki/Earthquake_zones_of_India.
[19] Adapted from bbc.com.
[20] https://en.wikipedia.org/wiki/2004_Indian_Ocean_earthquake_and_tsunami.
[21] See also https://www.usgs.gov/centers/pcmsc/science/tsunami-generation-2004-m91-sumatra-andaman-earthquake?qt-science_center_objects=0#qt-science_center_objects.
[22] Adapted from Enclopediaca Britannica.
[23] https://en.wikipedia.org/wiki/Yangtze.
[24] See e.g., D. J. Varnes, Slope movement types and processes, in R. L. Schuster and R. J. Krizek (Eds.) Landslides — Analysis and Control: National Research Council, Washington, D.C., Transportation Research Board, Special Report 176, pp. 11–33 (1978), https://pubs.usgs.gov/fs/2004/3072/pdf/fs2004-3072.pdf.
[25] R. K. Bhandari, Dark clouds of disaster over Uttarakhand and the silver lining, *Curr. Sci.* **112**(1), 29–30 (2017).
[26] https://www.worldatlas.com/articles/deadliest-landslides-in-recorded-history.html.
[27] M. Erskine, unsplash.com.
[28] M. Mukerjee, *Churchill's Secret War: The British Empire and the Ravaging of India during World War II* Basic Books, New York, (2010).
[29] Adapted from National Geographic: https://www.nationalgeographic.com/magazine/2020/02/how-to-set-off-a-plague-of-locusts-interactive.

[30] http://ppqs.gov.in/sites/default/files/contingency_plan_0.pdf.
[31] A. V. Latchininsky, Locusts and remote sensing: a review, *J. Appl. Rem. Sens.* **7**, 075099 (2013).
[32] https://spaceplace.nasa.gov/hurricanes/en/.
[33] https://en.wikipedia.org/wiki/Cyclone_Amphan.
[34] https://en.wikipedia.org/wiki/Tornado; https://www.noaa.gov/education/resource-collections/weather-atmosphere/tornadoes.
[35] https://ourworldindata.org/natural-disasters.

Chapter 3

Infectious Diseases

Infectious diseases have always been a part of human existence since the hunter–gatherer days, but the shift to agrarian life about 10,000 years ago created communities that were more vulnerable to the rapid spread of these diseases within a short time, commonly referred to as epidemics. Plague, smallpox, malaria, influenza, and several other diseases first appeared during this period. The more "civilized" humans became, building cities and forging trade routes to connect with other cities in different parts of the world, the more prevalent epidemics became. When an epidemic spreads beyond a country's borders, the disease officially becomes a pandemic. Prior to the twentieth century, every one of the pandemics in history took its own course in the absence of any means to combat the infection. Only when most of the population acquired infection-induced immunity against the disease, commonly referred to as herd immunity, did the pandemic weaken and gradually disappear. It is not surprising that epidemics and pandemics were invariably seen as acts of God. We may add that in many societies, there are folk traditions or folk memories about some of the diseases and their possible cures. The origin of these is lost in the mists of time, and these may or may not be scientifically valid, or these may be just superstitions without any ground. However, if these are effective, it must be investigated to identify the operative component of the treatment. Recall that Tu Youyou (born 1930) won the Nobel Prize in medicine in 2015 for identifying artemisinin, a cure for malaria from plants mentioned in ancient Chinese medical texts. Closer home, medicinal properties of turmeric (*Curcuma longa*), neem (*Azadirachta indica*), etc., popular in the Indian tradition of medicines, have now been closely studied. It is also heartening to note many treatments in Ayurveda are being scrutinized using modern scientific procedures.

The nineteenth and twentieth centuries were watershed years in the field of human healthcare. New discoveries in drugs and pharmaceuticals, vaccines, and diagnostic tools to combat diseases have considerably strengthened our ability to counter diseases of any kind including some of the well-known infectious diseases. We have already seen total eradication of some of the communicable diseases, such as smallpox. In the following, we discuss man's encounter with some well-known pandemics of the past, his heroic efforts in combating these, and his onward march not only towards the complete eradication of the known diseases but also emerging new ones. The role of public support and the government's efforts in mobilizing public support through effective risk communication will be dealt with in a later chapter in the monograph.

3.1 Plague

Plague is a severe infectious disease with a high mortality rate if left untreated. It is transmitted by the bite of infected fleas, direct contact with infected tissues, or inhalation of infected respiratory droplets. The first plague pandemic in recorded history was the Plague of Justinian, as it came to be known after Emperor Justinian-I who held the throne of Byzantium in the year 540 CE. It is said to have originated in Northern Egypt and transmitted to Constantinople through black rats that travelled on the grain consignments from North Africa [1]. The pandemic had a free run in the absence of any drugs or targeted efforts to contain the infection. Over 50 years or so, it spread to the Mediterranean and Persia, and resulted in the loss of at least 25 million human lives. Understandably, the pandemic also resulted in the fall of the Byzantine Empire.

The plague reappeared several times afterwards, most notably, the disastrous "Black Death" in Europe in the fourteenth century (the Second Plague) and the "Third Plague" of the nineteenth century.

The "Black Death" that occurred in Afro-Eurasia from 1346 CE to 1353 CE was perhaps the deadliest plague pandemic recorded in human history. It is reported to have resulted in the deaths of about 75–200 million people in Eurasia and North Africa, peaking in Europe from 1347 CE to 1351 CE. It created religious, social, and economic upheavals, with profound effects on the course of European history, as it reduced the population by 30–60%. The pandemic originated in either Central Asia or East Asia, but its first definitive appearance in Europe was in October 1347, when 12 ships from the Black Sea docked at the Sicilian port of Messina. These ships were carrying people from the Genoese trading port of Kaffa (now Feodosiya) in Crimea, who were fleeing from the attack of an army led by Mongol ruler Janibeg. When people gathered on the docks, they witnessed a horrifying scene. Most sailors were dead, and those still alive were gravely ill and covered in black boils that were oozing blood and pus. Sicilian authorities hastily ordered the fleet of "death ships" out of the harbour, but it was too late, and the plague spread across Europe. From Kaffa, Genoese ships carried the epidemic westward to the Mediterranean ports of Constantinople, Messina, and Genoa, and then the disease quickly spread across Europe. At that time, no one knew what caused the disease, how it spread, and what was the cure. "Many people fled the cities for the countryside, but even there they could not escape the disease: It affected cows, sheep, goats, pigs, and chickens, as well as people [2]." Many people believed that the Black Death was a kind of divine punishment — retribution for sins against God. The plague never really ended, and it returned several times on a larger or smaller scale. However, the officials were able to keep its spread slow by keeping arriving sailors in isolation until it became clear that they were not infected. The sailors were held on their ships for 40 days, or a *quarantine*, thus leading to the origin of the term "quarantine". As we have seen during the recent COVID-19 episode, quarantine continues to be useful as an effective tool to contain the spread of infectious diseases even today.

The "Third Plague" during 1894–1905 was one of the turning points in the history of the plague. The plague originated in China's Yunnan and Guangxi Provinces, spread to Hong Kong in 1894, and then to other locations in East Asia and the Pacific rim-Macao in 1895, Taiwan in 1896, India in 1896–1898, San Francisco in 1899, and Australia in 1900–1903. India suffered the most. By the time the plague subsided, it had killed 22 million people across the world.

3.1.1 *The playout in Hong Kong*

The plague in Hong Kong has been studied and even more importantly documented in detail [3]. The first confirmed case of plague in Hong Kong was noted on May 8, 1894, and by May 10, 20 patients having plague were identified at a traditional Chinese hospital. The colonial officials recommended the following sanitary measures: drain of every house was to be cleaned and disinfected, the house of every patient was to be disinfected, the clothes of the infected and their family members were to be disinfected, and patients were not to gather at the Chinese hospital under any circumstances. A ship, which had been converted to a quarantine ship was moved from the coast to the centre of the harbour. A restriction on the movement of people was also suggested. By May 12, against the opposition from the locals, patients were moved to the quarantine ship, and additional quarantine houses were established. On May 23, the colonial authorities mobilized 300 light infantry soldiers and started a house-to-house inspection to impose a forced quarantine. It was essential for finding new patients and the dead to isolate the infected or bury the dead and to clean and disinfect contaminated areas. On May 31, the authorities revised the legislation to demolish or close inappropriate housing facilities (see Fig. 3.1).

The plague outbreak in Hong Kong also led to the introduction of Western medicine into the Hong Kong society and induced the colonial authorities to strengthen the prevention and control of the plague epidemic. The colonial authorities were obviously viewing China as a hygienically "backward" country that continued to incubate a "medieval" disease and believed that the preventive measures taken by them were rational and reasonable. The person in charge (James Alfred Lowson) believed the disease occurred due to the dirty and overcrowded environment and focused on drainage, lighting, ventilation, and human waste in Chinese residences. He even believed

Fig. 3.1 British troops destroying the refuse from infected houses [4]

that the plague was not contagious. He continued to insist that plague patients could only be detected by symptoms, and prevention of the spread of the disease was to be achieved only by wiping out dirty living conditions, incineration of the clothes and furniture of patients, demolition of residences, and the imposition of quarantine. It is not surprising that the Chinese were regarding the measures as violent and destructive, a conflict between colonialism and nationalism and a confrontation between the Eastern and Western medicine. They refused to transfer patients to the quarantine ship as they didn't believe that the plague could be treated by the Western medicine. The measures by the authorities faced strong resistance from the local

Chinese population who didn't cooperate with the authorities. It should also be mentioned that understanding the source of infection and how it spread was far from complete during these years.

3.1.2 *The playout in Poona*

As the epidemic was having a free dance in Hong Kong, it soon spread to Bombay (now called Mumbai) and then on to Poona (now called Pune). On October 2, 1896, two passengers from Bombay, alighting at Poona railway station, were found to be infected with plague by a medical officer, who was stationed there to keep an eye on persons with symptoms of the plague and send them to a shed erected for them. By December, the city was witnessing local transmission and the disease was spreading rapidly in densely populated areas. By February 1897, there were 308 known cases of plague with 271 deaths. It was estimated that 15,000–20,000 people had fled the city and settled on the outskirts. On February 10, 1897, Walter Charles Rand, an Oxford-educated officer of the Indian Civil Service, was appointed as an Assistant Collector and Chairman of the Poona Plague Committee. He examined the records and concluded that "Poona had become a very dangerous plague centre". Surgeon Captain WWO Beveridge, who had had "considerable" experience of the Plague in Hong Kong, arrived to assist in fighting the epidemic. He expressed the opinion that the help of soldiers would be desirable in Poona too, especially to search for sufferers from the plague, their removal to suitable hospitals, and the disinfection of plague-infected houses, as in Hong Kong. It was also felt that the help of the soldiers was needed because they were disciplined, they could be relied upon to be thorough and honest in their inspection, and above all no reliable Indian agency was available. Poona's population at that time was 161,000. A house-to-house search for infected patients and suspects was started but was met with intense resistance among the people for taking out the plague-infected family members to the hospital. The families even hid the patients in lofts, cupboards, and gardens to prevent the authorities from taking them for isolation. Special hospitals for Hindu, Muslim, and Parsi communities were established, while the Europeans had a hospital of their own. Similarly, four segregation camps were set up for family members and other contacts of the plague patients to be kept under observation. Following the Hong Kong model, the policy envisaged an active search of the localities in the city with the help of the soldiers accompanied by natives for plague-infected patients (or their dead bodies) and taking them to the hospitals (or cremating the bodies under medical supervision). The houses where patients were found were cleaned, fumigated, dug up (to destroy rats), and lime washed. The search parties usually had three British soldiers, one Indian official, one medical officer, and one lady, to examine women in purdah. Surprise checks were conducted to avoid evasive actions. They searched 218,214 houses (each house was searched 11 times during the operation) and found 338 plague cases and 64 corpses in about 2 months. It was reported that British soldiers were also employed to make sure that no one from the infected area entered Pune or plague suspects never left the city or tried to smuggle out the dead bodies to escape testing by the authorities [5]. The British maintained that there were very few complaints against the conduct of the soldiers — both British and Indian — and there were only six cases of violation of discipline by soldiers, which involved stealing cash, pocketing goods, and receiving money from the locals. The local population, however, took the entire exercise as a reign of terror. The complainants talked of the destruction of property during searches, digging up of the floor, putting litres of disinfectant in the nooks and corners of the houses, breaking open the doors, and taking away "perfectly healthy" persons, including neighbours and passers-by to the isolation camps. There were also complaints that "all the females are compelled to come out of their houses and stand before the public gaze in the open street where they will be subjected to inspection by soldiers. Some soldiers were also said to have behaved 'disgracefully with native ladies'." The examination of bubonic plague involved checking the armpits and groins. It is now believed that the regulations and measures as they were imposed in Poona were the most stringent among all the cities afflicted by the pandemic. In fact, the Lieutenant-Governor of the North-Western Provinces had observed: "If the plague regulations had been enforced in any city of these provinces in the way in which ... they were ... enforced in Poona, there would have been bloodshed here."

During all this, Bal Gangadhar Tilak (1856–1920), a nationalist, teacher, and activist for India's independence, wrote in *Mahratta*, his English newspaper: "Plague is more merciful to us than its human prototypes now reigning the city. The tyranny of the Plague Committee and its chosen instruments is yet too brutal to allow respectable people to breathe at ease." His commentaries in *Kesari*, the Marathi newspaper, were even more scathing. On June 22, 1897, the Chapekar brothers — Damodar (27), Balkrishna (24), and Vasudev (17 or 18) — shot Rand and Lieutenant Charles Ayerst. Ayerst died immediately and Rand succumbed to his injuries on July 3. He had prepared a report on his efforts on containing the plague but died before it could be submitted (see Fig. 3.2).

All the while plague mortality continued to rise and reached its peak between 1903 and 1907, exceeding the levels of the late 1890s by 12-fold, and proved far more lethal in Punjab. The epidemic was to last for well over two decades and kill about 10 million Indians between 1896 and 1918, as it ravaged one city after the other. Yet, neither plague policy nor plague riots in Punjab appear to have displayed the zeal or acquired the political prominence they achieved in the province of Bombay [7].

Fig. 3.2 The Chapekar Brothers — Damodar (27), Balkrishna (24), and Vasudev (17 or 18) [6]

3.1.3 *The legal fallout of the Rand–Ayerst assassination*

Bal Gangadhar Tilak, as indicated earlier, had been publishing the Marathi newspaper, *Kesari*, since the 1880s. On June 15, 1897, he published two articles. The first one was written in "the name of Chhatrapati Shivaji", lamenting the fact that "relentless death moves about spreading epidemics of diseases in India" and that "opportunities are availed of in railway carriages, and women are dragged by the hand", which was a possible allusion to plague inspections at railway stations. The second article published in his own name heaped praise on Shivaji for killing Afzal Khan, a General of the Adilshahi Army, and cited Lord Krishna's teachings to Arjuna in Shrimad Bhagavad Gita. As mentioned earlier, the plague commissioner of Pune, W. C. Rand, and his army escort, Lieutenant Ayerst, were killed by the Chapekar Brothers, who were arrested, tried, and hanged. Tilak was arrested on July 27, 1897, on charges of sedition and tried at the Bombay High Court in September. Advocate General Basil Lang, appearing for the colonial rulers, told the jury that it was up to them to decide what effect Tilak's words had "at a time when much excitement and distress existed" because of the famine and the measures undertaken by the government to prevent the spread of the plague. Justice Arthur Strachey told the jury to remember that "a man was free to strongly condemn the government's attempts to suppress the plague". However, it was sedition, he continued, for a journalist to make his readers hate the government. He further added that if a person commented on government measures in "violent and bitter" language, such that "ignorant people at a time of great public excitement" would "become indisposed to obey and support the Government", it amounted to sedition. Tilak was convicted and sentenced to 18 months in prison.

Gopal Krishna Gokhale (1866–1915), a prominent political leader of the period, visited England to appear before the Welby Commission and gave an interview to *The Manchester Guardian* (now *The Guardian*) on July 2, 1897. In the interview, he levelled serious accusations against the British soldiers, including "violation of two women, one of whom is said to have committed suicide rather than to survive her shame". The Bombay Presidency Government challenged Gokhale to prove them. After his return to India, Gokhale tried his best to gather evidence from the persons who had written to him, but nobody was willing to come forward, especially in the light of the severe crackdown in Pune following Rand's assassination, including the sedition case against Tilak. Unable to substantiate these claims, Gokhale published an "unqualified apology" to British soldiers, which was published by *The Manchester Guardian* and *The Times of India* on August 4, 1897. In Britain, a speech was only considered seditious if it encouraged listeners to violently revolt against the government from 1832 onwards. In the Bombay High Court, on the other hand, Justice Strachey said that sedition means the "absence of affection" towards the government, i.e., even making listeners hate the government was enough to be considered seditious. Many freedom fighters of India were to be jailed based on these rulings. Even though the Federal Court of India tried to change the sedition law to those applied in Britain, during the Second World War, it was turned down by the Privy Council, London. It was only in 1962 that the Supreme Court of India finally declared that sedition means inciting violence, public disorder, or a disturbance of the public peace, which is how sedition is still understood today.

We can only imagine the immense consolidation of the efforts and positive force in the fight against the plague that could have resulted, had the authorities co-opted Lokmanya Tilak and Gokhale, and used their immense popularity and formidable influence to communicate the risks of plague, how it spread, and how it could be controlled.

3.1.4 *Science in the war against plague*

It had long been noticed that unusual deaths among rats preceded outbreaks of plague among humans. This link was again noted in the outbreaks in Hong Kong and India, and the Japanese physician Ogata Masanori described the epidemic in Formosa as "rat pest". He also showed that rat fleas carried the plague bacillus. The following year Paul-Louis Simond, a French researcher sent by the Pasteur

Institute to India, announced the results of experiments, demonstrating that Oriental rat fleas (*Xenopsylla cheopis*) carried the plague bacillus between rats. It was further definitively demonstrated that rat fleas infected humans and transmitted plague through their bites. It is now known that the bacillus travels from person to person through the air (pneumonic form) as well as through the bite of infected fleas and rats (bubonic and septicemic forms). The plague bacillus was isolated in Hong Kong in 1894 by Alexandre Yersin (1863–1943) and Kitasato Shibasaburō (1852–1931), and their work laid the foundation on which vaccines and treatments were developed. Kitasato Shibasaburō and Alexandre Yersin arrived in Hong Kong in June and soon succeeded in isolating the plague bacillus. Yersin, in a breakthrough, succeeded in separating a plague bacillus from a lymph gland, while Kitasato had isolated it from the blood and internal organs taken from a dead body provided to him. While Yersin was experimenting with routes of infection in various sources, such as mice, flies, and soil, Paul-Louis Simond confirmed that bubonic plague was caused through rat fleas in 1898. Yersin named the new bacillus *Pasteurella pestis*, after his mentor, Louis Pasteur, but in 1970, the bacterium was renamed as *Yersinia pestis* in honour of Yersin himself.

Working in Mumbai, Waldemar Mordechai Wolff Haffkine built on these discoveries and developed a vaccine by 1897 for plague, inoculating about 4 million and saving a much larger number. The epidemic also laid to rest the so-called "miasma theory" which blamed such diseases on "bad air" and provided a firm confirmation for the "germ theory" for the disease proposed by Louis Pasteur, Joseph Lister, and Robert Koch in the 1880s. We also now know that focusing only on house-to-house inspections and forced quarantine or isolation without encouraging people to wear masks and social distancing exposed everyone to the dangers of infection and resulted in poor quarantine effectiveness.

It is also heartening to note that the plague episode led to the establishment of more bacteriological laboratories, testing facilities, and most importantly several modern hospitals with proper examination and treatment facilities and proper isolation wards. Beginning in the 1930s, sulfa drugs and then antibiotics such as streptomycin gave doctors a very effective means of attacking the plague bacillus directly.

3.1.5 *The 1994 Surat plague*

Surat is a well-known commercial city in the state of Gujarat. Located on the banks of the Tapti River, Surat experienced in August 1994 a breakout of pneumonic plague. It is believed that the plague had its origin in the 1993 Latur earthquake when most homes were abandoned with food grains inside. It led to the destabilization of the population of domestic and wild rats (in which the plague is endemic, i.e., regularly found). Thus, the transmission of the plague progressed from wild rats to domestic rats to people. Reports of fleas following excessive deaths of rats came from the neighbouring district of Beed, which were followed by reports of deaths by suspected bubonic plague. It was followed by flooding in Surat. The open sewers of Surat put the bodies of many dead rats on the streets. Soon after this, the festival of Ganesh Chaturthi created large crowds, accelerating the spread of the pneumonic plague. Confusion was created by the misidentification of over 6,000 cases of ordinary fever as a plague by the authorities. There are reports that villagers in Rajasthan tried to exterminate rats. This may have led to more cases as fleas would have to abandon their rat hosts for humans. The pneumonic plague spreads rapidly compared to the bubonic plague and the plague in Surat caused widespread panic. It prompted a large-scale purchase of surgical masks and the medicine tetracycline. More than 300,000 people fled from the city. The pneumonic plague quickly spread to five states and the national capital Delhi. There were more than 1,000 suspected cases and the disease killed over 50 people across the country. The Government, however, recovered fast and controlled the spread by identifying cases and providing antibiotics quickly. In between, the cargo was fumigated, ports were cleared of rats, and insecticides were spread over vast areas. Flights to India were cancelled and some planes from India were fumigated at airports. Many flights from India to the nearby Gulf region were suspended. Some countries also put a hold on imports from India. The loss was estimated at more than 8 billion INR. The city implemented massive infrastructure improvements, tearing down slums, covering sewers, constructing public pay toilets, and implementing fines for littering. It also improved its plans for emergency travel advisories and fired some corrupt officials and disciplined ineffective city workers, including street sweepers. By 1996, the city was judged the cleanest in India [8].

The 1994 Surat plague is considered a classic case of how a lack of coordination among government bodies can lead to panic and enable the spread of diseases. It also tells how decisive steps implemented with clarity can quickly bring the situation under control, especially if the necessary medication is known and easily available.

3.1.6 *Waldemar Mordechai Wolff Haffkine*

The story of the plague will remain incomplete if we do not use this opportunity to recall the single-minded devotion, dedication, and perseverance of Haffkine and the travails, triumphs, and turmoil in his life (see Fig. 3.3).

Fig. 3.3 Waldemar Mordechai Wolff Haffkine [9]

Waldemar Mordechai Wolff Haffkine (March 15, 1860–October 26, 1930) was born in Ukraine in the then Russian Empire and received his graduation in zoology from the University of Odessa in 1884. He was barred from taking up a professorship there as he was a Jew. In 1888, Haffkine left his home country and, after a short-lived teaching job in Geneva, went to Paris. He took up a position in the library at the Louis Pasteur Institute, which was the leading centre of research in bacteriology in the world. In his free time, he experimented in the bacteriology lab. While working there, he developed a vaccine against cholera which he first tested on guinea pigs, rabbits, and pigeons, and then finally upon himself and several volunteers. He was looking for a large human population to test his vaccine when in 1893, he met Lord Frederick Dufferin, who was a former Viceroy of India and the then ambassador of Britain in France. Lord Dufferin advised him to go to Bengal, where cholera was rife. Initially, people resisted his attempt to vaccinate them, but to allay their fears, he publicly inoculated himself. He also collaborated with Indian medical professionals to help him with the process. This led to long queues of people from morning till evening for inoculation. He was invited by owners of tea gardens where he successfully inoculated several tens of thousands of workers. He was planning to further improve his vaccine but was forced to return to England to recuperate as he contracted malaria.

By 1896, the plague had reached Bombay, and the Governor of Bombay invited Haffkine to develop a vaccine against it. By December 1896, working from a room and a corridor in Parel, he had developed and tested his vaccine on rabbits. On January 10, 1897, he publicly vaccinated himself. He recovered after getting a severe fever for several days. The vaccine was tested on prisoners of Byculla Jail, where the plague had spread and after its successful demonstration, it was used extensively across the country. His vaccine saved millions from painful death.

In March 1902, in the village of Mulkowal in Punjab, 19 people died from tetanus after being inoculated with Haffkine's vaccine. The contamination was traced back to a particular bottle, prepared earlier in the Parel laboratory. A commission of inquiry appointed by the

Government concluded that the use of heat instead of carbolic acid by Haffkine to speed up production, could have caused this accident though this was a safe and time-tested method in use at the Pasteur Institute but not known to the British. Haffkine lost his job as the Director of the Plague Lab and was placed on leave from the Indian Civil Service in 1903. However, his vaccine continued to remain at the forefront of combating the plague which was raging across the country.

Four years later, the Indian Government published the full inquiry, from which W.J. Simpson, a professor at King's College, London, traced the contamination to a dropped forceps by an assistant, during the process of preparing the vaccine, which he continued to use without sterilizing. Prof Simpson was joined by Nobel Laureate, Sir Ronald Ross, in his campaigns to exonerate Haffkine and finally, in November 1907, Haffkine was exonerated. However, he was debarred from carrying out any trials and forced to do only theoretical research. He retired in 1914 from the Indian Civil Service and lived alone and died in 1930 in Lausanne, Switzerland. In 1925, five years before his death, the Indian Government renamed the Parel laboratory "The Haffkine Institute", and the name remains to this day.

3.1.7 *Lessons from the history of tackling plague*

One of the best analyses of the plague epidemic appears in the famous allegorical novel, *The Plague* (*La Peste*), by Nobel Laureate Albert Camus. Towards the end of the book, the narrator states that he tried to present an objective view of the events. He reflects on the epidemic and declares that he wrote the chronicle "to simply say what we learn in the midst of plagues: there are more things to admire in men than to despise". It is worthwhile recalling some of the events discussed in the novel, very briefly — as they are relevant for our narrative [10]:

> "In the town of Oran, thousands of rats, initially unnoticed by the populace, begin to die in the streets, leading to hysteria. Authorities respond by collecting and cremating the rats, without realizing that the collection itself was the catalyst for the spread of the bubonic plague. Dr Bernard Rieux (the main character)

examines death from fever and concludes that it is due to the plague. He, along with a colleague, approaches fellow doctors and town authorities about their theory but is eventually dismissed based on one death. However, more deaths quickly ensue, and it becomes apparent that there is an epidemic. Authorities are slow to accept that the situation is serious and quibble over the appropriate action to take. As the death toll begins to rise, homes are quarantined; corpses and burials are strictly supervised, the town is sealed, and an outbreak of plague is officially declared. The town is sealed, town gates are shut, rail travel is prohibited, and all mail service is suspended. The use of telephone lines is restricted only to 'urgent' calls, leaving short telegrams as the only means of communicating with friends or family outside the town. The separation depresses the spirit of the townspeople, who begin to feel isolated. People try to escape the town, and some are shot by armed sentries. Authorities declare martial law and impose a curfew to curb violence and looting. Funerals are conducted with speed, without any ceremony, and concern for the feelings of the families of the deceased. The inhabitants become despondent and waste away emotionally as well as physically. As the plague retreats and gates are opened people rejoice and meet their loved ones."

Almost every aspect of the above story has been enacted again and again, in pandemic after pandemic, in country after country, and over millennia. The first and the second epidemics of plague were marked by a complete lack of understanding of the underlying causes. Thus, the entire conduct of society was driven by superstition and unscientific procedures. The third epidemic took place at a time when the germ theory was taking shape, modern means of investigation and medicines were emerging, and the importance of hygiene had been realized. There is no doubt that colonial authorities, who handled the plague in Hong Kong and India, were not trusted by the natives. We definitely feel that effective risk communication by authorities about the seriousness of the epidemic and the procedures that were being adopted to control the same could have resulted in more enthusiastic support for their efforts, but this could have been done only by persons whom the population trusted. Finally, there is no alternative to speedily finding effective cures, using scientific methods, and making it available to the masses quickly. This can only happen in an atmosphere of open discussion and sharing of information and knowledge across the world. We must not forget that it must have taken an enormous time and effort for persons associated with the Louis Pasteur Institute to travel to Hong Kong and India, work among the dying, and identify the plague bacillus, the route of transmission of plague, and to develop the vaccine. To win the trust of the people, Haffkine used to publicly administer the vaccine to himself. Earlier, while working with the vaccine for cholera, he had gone to the slums of Calcutta with Indian doctors, thus very effectively countering the distrust of colonial authorities. *With the advantage of hindsight, it looks that, had the colonial authorities of Poona (now Pune) taken the elders of the society into confidence and taken their help in widespread communication of risks of the plague involved and advantages of preventive steps being taken, the outcome would have been much less traumatic.* As an aside, there is also a very important message — prejudices invariably push us down.

3.2 Smallpox

Smallpox is another communicable disease that is known to have ravaged humanity for thousands of years. Smallpox-like rashes found on three mummies from the third century BCE suggest that the disease may have existed in ancient Egypt. Chinese records from the fourth century CE describe a disease that resembles smallpox. Records of smallpox in India from the seventh century CE and Asia Minor (the Asian part of modern Turkey) from the tenth century CE have also been found. The risk of death after contracting the disease was about 30%, with higher rates among babies. Often, those who survived had extensive scarring of their skin, and some were left blind. It is also generally accepted [11] that smallpox spread across the world due to the mobility of people and merchandise.

Closer home, isolation and quarantine for the patients suffering from smallpox and social distancing from the family to which the patient belonged was practised for centuries. The residences with such cases used to hang neem (*Azadirachta indica*) leaves on their doors to warn visitors to keep their distance. Water in which neem leaves were boiled — which we now know is antiseptic — was also used to wash the eruptions.

It has been estimated that in eighteenth-century Europe, 400,000 people died from smallpox per year and that up to one-third of cases of blindness were caused by smallpox. It killed one in 10 children in Sweden and France, and one in seven children in Russia during the same period. It is further estimated to have killed up to 300 million people in the twentieth century and around 500 million people in the last 100 years before it was eradicated (see Fig. 3.4).

Smallpox had two main forms: variola major and variola minor. The two forms showed similar lesions. The disease followed a milder course in variola minor, which had a case fatality rate of less than 1%. The fatality rate of variola major was around 30%. There are two rare forms of smallpox: haemorrhagic and malignant. In the former, invariably fatal case, the rash was accompanied by haemorrhage into the mucous membranes and the skin. Malignant smallpox was characterized by lesions that did not develop to the pustular stage but remained soft and flat. It was almost invariably fatal. In addition, a form called "*variola sine eruptione*" (smallpox without rash) was

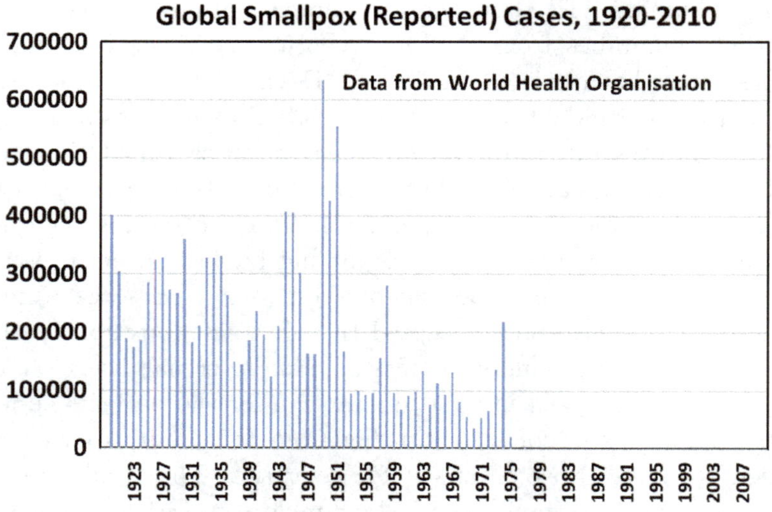

Fig. 3.4 Reported cases of smallpox [12, 13]

seen generally in vaccinated persons. This form was marked by a fever that occurred after the usual incubation period and could be confirmed only by antibody studies or, rarely, by viral culture.

Smallpox was highly contagious. Transmission occurred through inhalation of airborne variola virus, usually, droplets, expressed from the oral, nasal, or pharyngeal mucosa of an infected person. It was transmitted from one person to another primarily through prolonged face-to-face contact with an infected person, usually within about 2 m, but could also be spread through direct contact with infected body fluids or contaminated objects such as bedding or clothing [14]. It is painful to recall that smallpox was also used as a biological weapon. As early as the fourteenth century, Tartar (or Tatar) forces are believed to have catapulted the corpses of smallpox victims into besieged towns to weaken and destroy entrapped defenders. There are speculations that the fifteenth-century Spanish conquistador Francisco Pizarro offered the Incas gifts of cloth possibly laden with smallpox during his conquest of Peru, which spread smallpox through the native population, who had no defence against it. During the French and American Indian Wars (1754–1767), soldiers under the Commander of Fort Pitt distributed blankets that had been used by smallpox patients with the intent of initiating outbreaks among American Indians. An epidemic indeed occurred, killing more than 50% of infected tribes [15].

3.2.1 *Science in our war against smallpox: Development of vaccine for smallpox*

A procedure, now called variolation, was practised in India and China for centuries. While the Chinese preferred to introduce pulverized dried smallpox scabs or pustule fluid by blowing it into the nose of persons, Indians also used a lancet or needle to introduce it under the skin of individuals. This used to induce a milder form of the disease which ultimately made the person immune to smallpox. However, it led to death in 2–3% of the cases. It was still much less compared to the mortality rate of over 30% in the case of smallpox. Occasionally, it also led to other complications like hepatitis. Variolation was never risk-free. Not only could the patient die from the procedure, but

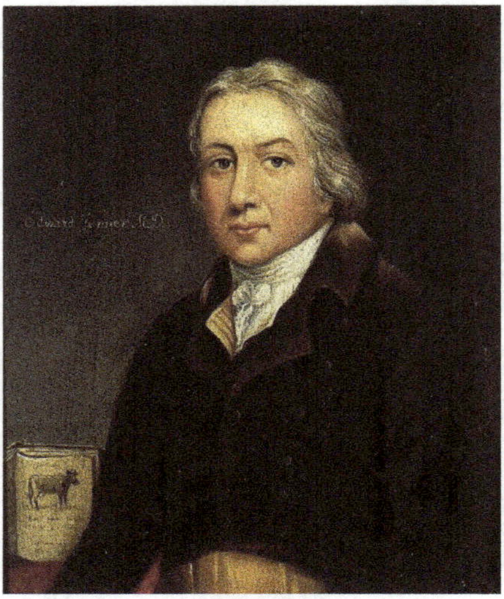

Fig. 3.5 Edward Jenner (May 17, 1749–January 26, 1823)

the mild form of the disease which the patient contracted could spread, causing an epidemic. In 1717, Lady Mary Wortley Montagu, the wife of the British ambassador, learned about variolation in Constantinople (Istanbul) and introduced it in Europe.

Edward Jenner was an English physician and scientist, born in Berkeley, Gloucestershire, where he had his medical practice (see Fig. 3.5). He pioneered the concept of vaccines, including creation of the smallpox vaccine, the *world's first vaccine.* He knew that in English literature and poetry milkmaids are celebrated for their creamy complexion, "as pretty as a milkmaid" being the common refrain. He postulated that by being exposed to a bovine form of the disease, cowpox, milkmaids were protected from the much more lethal smallpox.

Thus, when a milkmaid Sarah Nelmes was exposed to cowpox from her cow named Blossom and got cowpox sores (see Fig. 3.6), Dr Jenner took material from a cowpox sore on Nelmes's hand and inoculated it into the arms of his gardener's 9-year-old son James Phipps. James was mildly sick and recovered. Later, Jenner exposed James several times to the variola virus, but he never

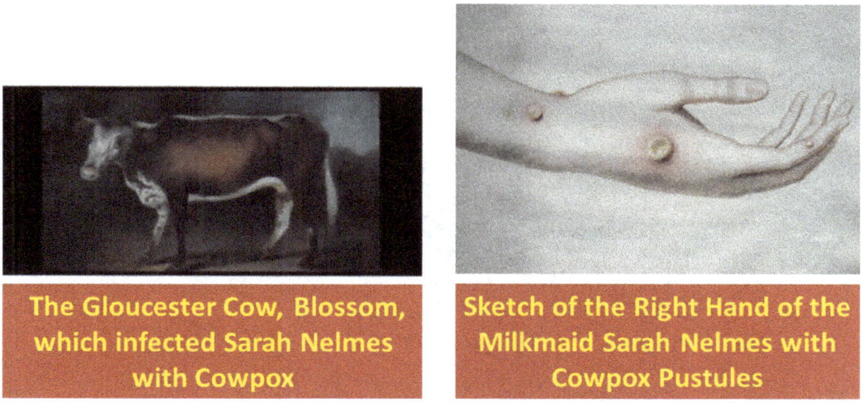
The Gloucester Cow, Blossom, which infected Sarah Nelmes with Cowpox
Sketch of the Right Hand of the Milkmaid Sarah Nelmes with Cowpox Pustules

Fig. 3.6 An illustration of Cowpox Pustules from the first edition of Edward Jenner's *An inquiry into the cause and effects of the variolae vaccinae*

developed smallpox. He submitted a paper to the Royal Society in 1797 describing his experiment, but the paper was rejected. Jenner experimented on several other children, including his own 11-month-old son. In 1801, Jenner published his treatise "On the Origin of the Vaccine Inoculation", in which he summarized his discoveries and expressed hope that "the annihilation of smallpox, the most dreadful scourge of the human species, must be the final result of this practice [16]." In the same work, he introduced the term "vaccine", taken from "*vacca*" for a cow in Latin.

Jenner's idea was widely ridiculed and opposed in the beginning. Religious leaders said that it was immoral to stop a disease that God has created and that it was repulsive and ungodly to inoculate someone with material from an animal. Some critics went on to spread rumours that children upon vaccination developed features and habits of a bull or a cow and maidens "started going out in search of bulls". A satirical cartoon of 1802 showed people who had been vaccinated sprouting cow's heads (see Fig. 3.7).

However, the obvious advantages of vaccination and the protection it provided became clear by the day, and vaccination soon became widespread. At some point in the 1800s, the virus used to make the smallpox vaccine was changed from cowpox to vaccinia

The Cow-Pock — or — the Wonderful Effects of the New Inoculation! — vide. the Publications of ye Anti-Vaccine Society

Fig. 3.7 The cow pock or the wonderful effect of the new inoculation [17]

virus, which is a pox virus, similar to smallpox, but less harmful. It was already realized that as smallpox had no other host than humans, no carriers like mosquitoes for malaria, and spread only from personal contact, it was possible to eradicate it from the world, which was ultimately done.

3.2.2 *Eradication of smallpox*

The World Health Organisation (WHO) initiated a plan to eradicate the world of smallpox in 1959. Unfortunately, the effort suffered from lack of funds, personnel, and commitment from countries, as well as a shortage of vaccine donations. Smallpox was still widespread in 1966, causing regular outbreaks in multiple countries across South America, Africa, and Asia.

Renewed efforts were started in 1967. By then, smallpox had already been eradicated from North America (1952) and Europe (1953), leaving South America, Asia, and Africa (smallpox was never widespread in Australia) involved in mass vaccinations and surveillance to track and contain outbreaks.

The campaign succeeded in eradicating smallpox from South America (1971), Asia (1975), and finally Africa (1977).

As smallpox only travels from person to person, the strategy adopted was to break the chain of spread by tracking smallpox cases and vaccinating everyone in a geographic circle of 2.5 km. The Smallpox Eradication Programme team members also used to visit every house, public meeting area, school, and healer within 8 km of the infected person to ensure that the illness did not spread. The resolve of the WHO team, against difficult conditions, should be put on record here. By the mid-1970s, Ethiopia, which was having a bloody rift, was also one of the last smallpox holdouts. The vaccinators had to use a helicopter. One helicopter was blown up, and one was captured for ransom. The last case of smallpox ever recorded was on October 26, 1977, in neighbouring Somalia.

Almost two centuries after Edward Jenner had expressed the hope of eradicating smallpox by vaccination, the WHO declared the world free from smallpox on May 8, 1980 (see Fig. 3.8). It is the only disease of man which we have succeeded in eradicating. Eradication of smallpox is considered the biggest achievement in international public health.

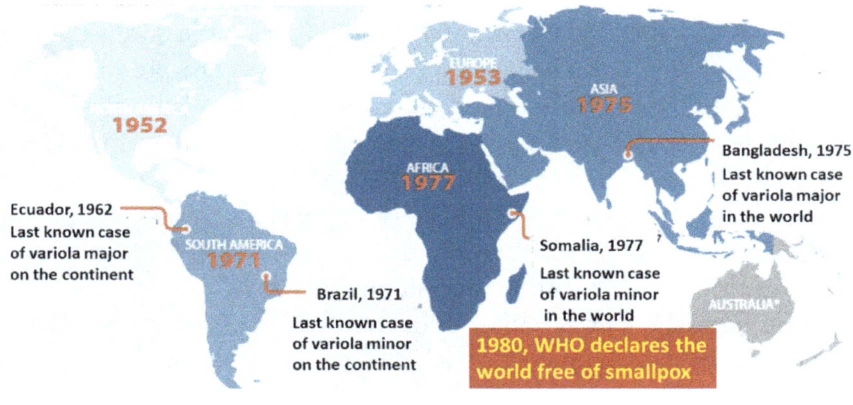

Fig. 3.8 Eradication of smallpox (Adapted from CDC [18])

No effective treatment has ever been found for the smallpox infection. Ongoing research on a possible cure is now handicapped as there are no cases of smallpox to test their treatments.

3.3 Malaria

Malaria is a life-threatening disease caused by parasites that are transmitted to people through the bites of infected female *Anopheles* mosquitoes. *Anopheles* mosquitoes lay their eggs in water, which hatch into larvae, eventually emerging as adult mosquitoes. The female mosquitoes seek a high-protein blood meal to nurture their eggs. Bites by infected female mosquitoes transmit the parasites to humans. Research on the development of a vaccine for malaria has been going on for quite some time. In a major breakthrough, the first vaccine for malaria, "RST, S", having the brand name, Mosquirix, was approved for use among children by the WHO, in October 2021, as we write this. Malaria treatment using antimalarial drugs is marked by a constant struggle between evolving drug-resistant parasites and the search for new drug formulations. The focus of the malaria eradication programme has therefore been to eliminate stagnant water bodies where the mosquitoes could lay their eggs and kill the larvae by using pesticides like dichlorodiphenyltrichloroethane (DDT). Originally synthesized in 1874, DDT was rediscovered in 1939 as a new insecticide. The 1948 Nobel Prize in Physiology and Medicine was in fact awarded to Paul Hermann Muller for his discovery of the high efficiency of DDT as a contact poison against several arthropods. For the next 30 years, DDT was extensively used across the globe as a "wonder" pesticide in our war against vector diseases, in particular malaria. The WHO's anti-malaria campaign of the fifties and sixties relied heavily on DDT.

The great reduction in vector diseases using DDT did not come without its environmental and human costs. Not only did DDT contaminate the water bodies and harm the ecosystem, but it also even entered the human food chain and is considered a possible carcinogen. Ultimately, the US Government imposed a ban on the use of DDT in 1973 and piloted a worldwide ban on its use.

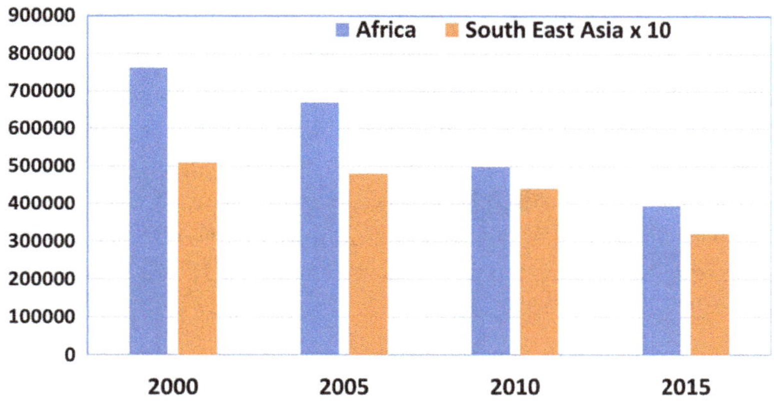

Fig. 3.9 Deaths due to malaria in Africa and South-East Asia

Incidentally, even today there is a section of people who believe that the governments have overreacted to the ill effects of DDT and compromised malaria eradication. India is one country that is still manufacturing DDT and is opposing a worldwide ban on DDT.

According to the WHO, there are 300–500 million malaria cases annually. Ninety per cent of these cases are in Africa (see Fig. 3.9). Estimates from WHO also suggest that there are 700,000 to 2.7 million deaths annually across the globe due to malaria. More than 75% of these involve African children and expectant mothers. In South-East Asia, about 1.2 billion people living in 11 countries are at risk of contracting malaria, most of whom live in India. Till recently, of about 2.5 million cases of malaria in this region, India accounted for about 76% of the cases. Eastern Mediterranean, Western Pacific, and the Americas are also at risk of malaria. The World Malaria Report, released on November 30, 2020, suggests that there were 229 million cases of malaria in 2019 and 409,000 deaths. Africa accounted for 94% of all cases of malaria and deaths. Children under 5 years of age are the most vulnerable group affected by malaria; in 2019, they accounted for 67% (274,000) of all malaria deaths worldwide.

India's experience in combating vector-borne diseases like malaria and dengue needs a special mention. In 1947, when India became independent, it was estimated to have 75 million malaria cases in a population of 330 million. During the eradication era in the late 1950s and early 1960s, which was built around spraying DDT and coordinated by WHO, a spectacular achievement was witnessed on the malaria eradication front. The number of cases reported in 1964 was just about 100,000. The discontinuation of the use of DDT due to health concerns, without taking alternative effective measures, led to a reversal and malaria staged a comeback. It reached 6.4 million cases in 1976 (see Fig. 3.10).

Seventy per cent of cases of malaria in India occur in five states: Odisha (36%), Chhattisgarh (12%), Jharkhand (9%), Madhya Pradesh (9%) and Maharashtra (5%). The high-risk populations dwell mainly in forest, hilly, tribal, and conflict-affected areas, which makes it difficult to control malaria. The awareness of methods of malaria prevention is also low in the tribal population. The WHO has expressed apprehensions that a considerable number of cases in these areas may not have been reported.

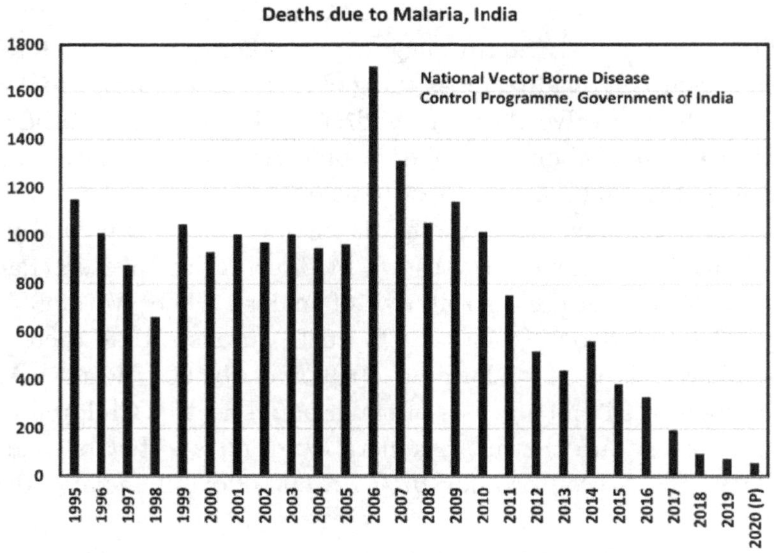

Fig. 3.10 Deaths due to malaria in India

3.3.1 *Sir Ronald Ross and malaria*

The credit for the discovery of the malaria parasite and its transmission by the female *Anopheles* mosquito goes to Sir Ronald Ross, who first identified it on August 20, 1897, while working at a military hospital in Secunderabad. The memory of this momentous discovery is kept alive by celebrating August 20 as World Mosquito Day. Soon afterwards, working at Calcutta and performing experiments under controlled conditions using birds, he identified the mechanism of transmission. He received the Nobel Prize in Medicine in 1902. Till then, malaria (which stands for "bad air") was supposed to be caused by "miasma" and rotting vegetation.

Sir Ronald Ross was not only a Nobel Prize-winning scientist, but he was also a mathematician, epidemiologist, sanitarian, editor, novelist, dramatist, poet, an amateur musician, composer, and artist (see Fig. 3.11). His formulation of the mathematical model for the propagation of malaria remains valid and has now been developed

Fig. 3.11 Sir Ronald Ross (May 13, 1857, Almora–September 16, 1932, London) [19]

to a high degree of sophistication and proved extremely effective in studies of the spread of vector-borne diseases.

Ross's life is a study in passion, determination, and perseverance in the face of administrative apathy, bordering hostility (he called it "administrative barbarism") and even ridicule. He received essentially no help for his work and most of the expenditures, including the hiring of assistants, were paid by him from his own salary. He was transferred frequently, at times against his passionate pleas, as he was on the verge of a breakthrough, and posted at different times in Madras, Burma, Baluchistan, Andaman Islands, Bangalore, Secunderabad, and Calcutta.

Ross's excitement and passion for finding the root cause of malaria can be gauged by the poem he wrote to his colleague and mentor Patrick Mason of his momentous discovery on August 22, 1897:

"This day relenting God
Hath placed within my hand
A wondrous thing; and God
Be praised. At his command,
Seeking his secret deeds
With tears and toiling breath,
I find thy cunning seeds,
O million-murdering Death.
I know this little thing
A myriad men will save,
O Death, where is thy sting?
Thy victory, O Grave?"

Earlier, he had written to Mason at the end of May 1896: "The belief is growing on me that the disease is communicated by the bite

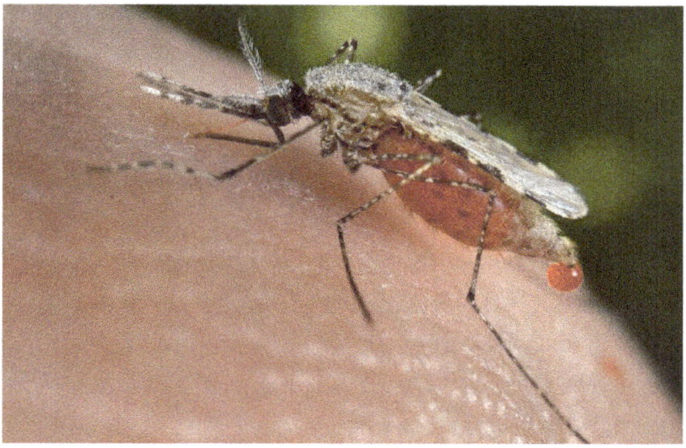

Fig. 3.12 ***Anopheles*** **mosquito [20]**

of the mosquito... She always injects a small quantity of fluid with her bite — what if the parasites get into the system in this manner."

His paper titled "On Some Peculiar Pigmented Cells Found in Two Mosquitoes Fed on Malarial Blood", describing his discovery, was published in the *British Medical Journal* on December 18, 1897. He called the malaria-carrying mosquitoes "dappled mosquitoes", which we now call (female) *Anopheles* mosquitoes (see Fig. 3.12).

Ross has had extensive correspondence with Patrick Mason, which is now considered among the best literary writings in the genre of scientific correspondence. His book *Prevention of Malaria* highlights the sanitary measures which can be taken to eliminate malaria [21].

The biological significance of his work lies in three areas: basic research, malaria transmission/epidemiology, and the identification of what is perhaps the most vulnerable stage in the parasite life cycle for effective intervention.

The excitement of Ronald Ross did not subside after he had identified the vector for malaria and its habits. He was excited and thrilled at the possibility of controlling this misfortune for millions by controlling the breeding of the mosquito vector. He had already proved that malaria was related more to the stagnant water in the pots, tubs, and tanks scattered around human dwellings where its vector bred in millions than to the marshes and pools as was believed until then. His discovery provided a natural explanation for the increase in cases during the rainy seasons and that subsoil drainage, practised for centuries, helped in controlling it. His work suggested that it was enough to clear the breeding sites to control malaria and mosquitoes.

Ross attempted to eradicate malaria from England by forming "mosquito brigades" to eliminate mosquito larvae from stagnant pools and marshes. His attempts at achieving this in Free Town, Sierra Leone, however, did not provide a permanent solution, perhaps as he underestimated the problem and had limited funds to use oil to cover ponds for the killing of the larva of mosquitoes. However, his suggestions were successfully implemented in Cuba, Greece, Mauritius, Spain, and various battlefronts during the First World War.

At the end of 1902, Ross was asked to save Ismailia, the city that was built as a base for the construction of the Suez Canal. It was gravely threatened by malaria for a long time. Ross led a sanitation drive so successful that by the following year, no mosquito nets were needed and by 1904, a whole year had passed without a single reported case of malaria in Ismailia.

Ronald Ross wrote his sanitary axiom in 1910: "Widespread diseases ... cause much pain, poverty, sorrow, expense and loss of prosperity ... and the rule is to grudge spending a hundred pounds for a disease which costs thousands ..." [Therefore] "for economic reasons alone, governments are justified in spending for the prevention of [malaria] a sum of money equal to the loss which the diseases inflict on the people [21]."

It is a pity that even though the prevention of malaria is straightforward, half-hearted efforts, which were not sustained, have continued to allow the breeding of mosquitoes that are also becoming resistant to various insecticides. Even after more than a century of Ronald Ross's painstaking efforts at the control of malaria, the "administrative apathy" towards malaria control programmes continues for "inexplicable" reasons, as Ross put it [22].

3.3.2 *The Panama Canal: An engineering miracle made possible by preventing malaria*

The Panama Canal, connecting the Atlantic Ocean with the Pacific Ocean, is an artificial 82-km waterway. It is one of the largest and most difficult engineering projects ever undertaken and helped reduce the time for travel between the two oceans. Prior to its construction, the ships had to undertake a lengthy and hazardous Cape Horn route around the southernmost tip of South America via the Drake Passage or Strait of Magellan. The alternative was the even less popular route through the Arctic Archipelago and the Bering Strait.

And it was almost not made. During 1881–1889, the French, after spending 287 million USD and losing about 22,000 men to disease and accidents, abandoned the project.

The United States of America started its construction anew in 1904, completing it in about 10 years. The foundation for this success — in addition to improvements in the plans — was a near elimination of deaths due to malaria, achieved by Colonel William C. Gorgas of US Army, who was appointed as the Chief Sanitation Officer of the Canal Project in 1904, following recommendations of Sir Ronald Ross (see Fig. 3.13).

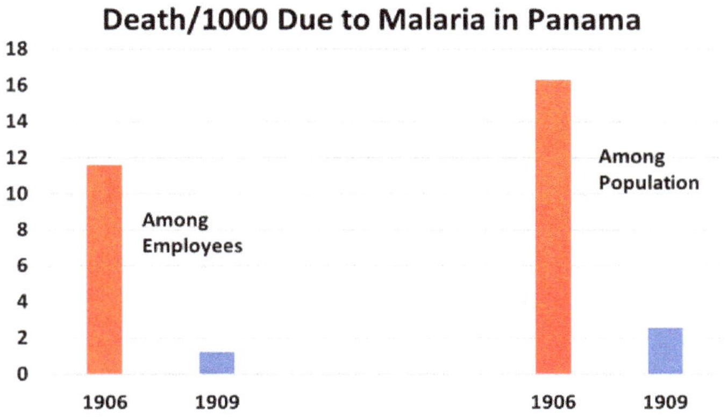

Fig. 3.13 Reducing deaths in Panama after introduction of malaria prevention measures

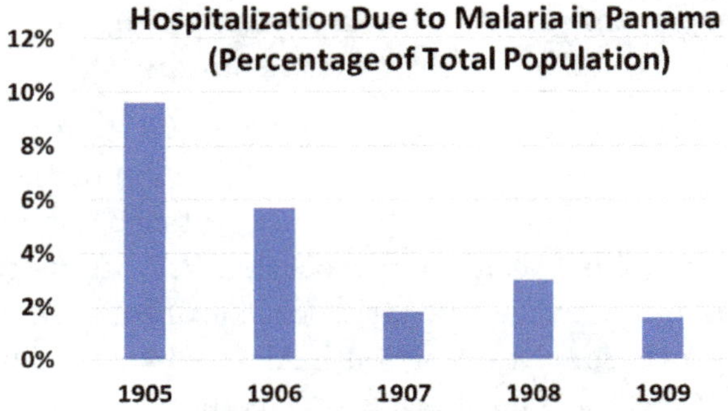

Fig. 3.14 Reducing hospitalizations in Panama after introduction of malaria prevention measures

The Isthmus of Panama provided an ideal breeding ground for mosquitoes. The average day temperature stays close to 30°C, while the night temperature stays close to 25°C throughout the year. It has a rainy season lasting for 9 months and the interior of the Isthmus is a 68-km-deep tropical forest. The population of about 80,000 lived within a kilometre of a railway line laid down earlier. Malaria was so abundant that it was estimated that one-sixth of the population was suffering from its attacks each week (see Fig. 3.14).

Colonel Gorgas implemented the following [23]:

(i) *Drainage*: All pools within 200 m of all villages and 100 m of all individual houses were drained. Subsoil drainage was provided, leading to open ditches, which were kept free from obstructions.
(ii) *Bush and grass cutting*: All bush and grass were cut and maintained at less than 30-cm high within 200 m of villages and 100 m of individual houses. It was believed that mosquitoes would not cross open areas over 100 m.
(iii) *Oiling*: When drainage was not possible along the grassy edges of ponds and swamps, oil was added to kill mosquito larvae.
(iv) *Larviciding*: When oiling was not sufficient, larviciding was done using a larvicide mixture of carbolic acid, resin, and caustic soda, which was spread in great quantities.
(v) *Prophylactic quinine*: Quinine was provided freely to all workers every day.

(vi) *Screening*: All buildings were screened against mosquitoes.
(vii) *Killing adult mosquitoes*: Noting that the mosquitoes usually stayed in the tent or the house after feeding, these were collected, examined, and eliminated. This proved very effective.

With these measures in place, the construction of the Panama Canal — the miracle of the early twentieth century — was completed. It also was a great demonstration of malaria control based on an integrated mosquito control programme. Yellow fever, another disease caused by mosquito bites, was eliminated as well.

3.3.3 *Recent developments in combating malaria*

In 1955, the WHO commenced a programme to eradicate malaria in countries with low to moderate transmission rates worldwide. As we have seen earlier, it relied largely on DDT for mosquito control and rapid diagnosis and treatment to reduce transmission. The programme eliminated the disease in "North America, Europe, the former Soviet Union", and in "Taiwan, much of the Caribbean, the Balkans, parts of northern Africa, the northern region of Australia, and a large swath of the South Pacific" and dramatically reduced mortality in Sri Lanka and India.

However, failure to sustain the programme, increasing mosquito tolerance to DDT, and increasing parasite tolerance led to a resurgence. In many areas, early successes partially or completely reversed, and in some cases, rates of transmission increased.

With global climate change, the potential for the reappearance of malaria in countries where it was previously eradicated is rising. *Anopheles* mosquitoes are in fact still present in those areas, including in Europe. There is also a growing resistance to the cheap, most used antimalarial medicines, which is a cause of worry.

Deforestation in Africa and Amazon is also believed to create conditions for the breeding of mosquitoes and the rise in malaria. Deforestation increases the incidents of malaria because it creates several favourable conditions for the *Anopheles* mosquito. The reasons are as follows:

- As pools of water get exposed to sunlight, the temperature increases, which provides an ideal breeding ground for mosquitoes.
- Deforestation creates ditches and puddles, which are more likely to pool less acidic water. This helps in the development of *Anopheles* larvae.
- When trees are felled and their stumps are left standing, it leads to a formation of "tree bowls", which accumulates water.

Ronald Ross had already noted that *Anopheles* mosquitoes lay their eggs in water, which hatch into larvae, eventually emerging as adult mosquitoes. Now, we know that the female mosquitoes seek a blood meal to nurture their eggs. Each species of *Anopheles* mosquito has its own preferred aquatic habitat, for example, some prefer small, shallow collections of freshwater, such as puddles and hoof prints, which are abundant during the rainy season in tropical countries.

Transmission is more intense in places where the mosquito lifespan is longer (so that the parasite has time to complete its development inside the mosquito) and where it prefers to bite humans rather than other animals. The long lifespan and strong human-biting habit of the African vector species is the main reason why approximately 90% of the world's malaria cases are in Africa.

Human immunity is another important factor, especially among adults in areas of moderate or intense transmission conditions. Partial immunity is developed over years of exposure, and while it never provides complete protection, it does reduce the risk that malaria infection will cause severe disease. For this reason, most malaria deaths in Africa occur in young children, whereas in areas with less transmission and low immunity, all age groups are at risk [24].

Vector control measures depend on vector species, mosquito biology, epidemiological context, cost, and acceptability by populations. The main current measures are focused on the reduction of the contact between mosquitoes and humans, the destruction of larvae by environmental management and the use of larvicides, or mosquito larvae predators, and the destruction of adult mosquitoes by indoor residual spraying and insecticide-treated bed nets. A release of sterilized mosquitoes is also being tried.

Insecticide-treated nets reduce contact between mosquitoes and humans by providing both a physical barrier and an insecticidal effect. Population-wide protection can result from the killing of mosquitoes on a large scale by extensive usage of such nets within a community.

Resistance to antimalarial medicines is a recurring problem. Resistance of *P. falciparum* malaria parasites to previous generations of medicines, such as chloroquine and sulfadoxine–pyrimethamine, became widespread in the 1950s and 1960s, which affected malaria control efforts and reversed gains in child survival.

Protecting the efficacy of antimalarial medicines is critical to malaria control and elimination. Regular monitoring of drug efficacy is needed to inform treatment policies in malaria-endemic countries and to ensure early detection of, and response to, drug resistance.

The first and the only vaccine called "RTS, S/AS01 (RTS, S)" (Mosquirix) has been shown to significantly reduce malaria, even life-threatening severe malaria, in young African children. It acts against *P. falciparum*, the deadliest malaria parasite globally and the most prevalent in Africa. As mentioned earlier, this was approved for use among children by the WHO in October 2021 and may revolutionize man's crusade against malaria.

The WHO Global Technical Strategy for malaria 2016–2030 aims to achieve the following:

- reduce malaria case incidence by at least 90% by 2030,
- reduce malaria mortality rates by at least 90% by 2030,
- eliminate malaria in at least 35 countries by 2030,
- prevent a resurgence of malaria in all countries that are malaria-free.

In 2016, the Government of India developed a National Framework for Malaria Elimination (2016–2030) and a National Strategic Plan, in line with the above strategy of WHO, with the aim of eliminating malaria in all districts, including low and medium transmission districts by 2022. It is also planned to ensure that districts having the highest transmission are covered by a pre-elimination and elimination programme by 2022.

The goals of the National Framework for Malaria Elimination (2016–2030) are as follows:

- Eliminate malaria (i.e., zero indigenous cases) throughout the entire country by 2030,
- Maintain malaria-free status in areas where malaria transmission has been interrupted,
- Prevent the reintroduction of malaria.

We have all the necessary scientific knowledge and tools to eliminate malaria for good. Only political will, active support and participation of the community, and necessary resources and sustained efforts are needed to eliminate this ancient scourge for good.

3.4 Dengue

Dengue used to be known by different names in different parts of the world. The origin of the term "dengue" is generally traced to the Swahili word for the disease *ka dinga pepo* (or *ka denga pepo*). The Spanish started using the term "dengue" in 1800. The earliest records of dengue are from 992 CE in China. They called the disease, "water poison", and noted that it was associated with flying insects. The term "dengue" has now been universally adopted (see Fig. 3.15).

By now, it is established that dengue is transmitted by the bite of an infected *Aedes* species (*Ae. aegypti* or *Ae. albopictus*) mosquito.

Fig. 3.15 Dengue spreading mosquitoes [25]

They are also called Tiger Mosquitoes of Asia. These mosquitoes also spread Zika, chikungunya, and yellow fever. Four kinds of dengue serotypes, DENV-1, DENV-2, DENV-3, and DENV-4, are now known. An exposure to DENV-1, for example, gives lifelong immunity to dengue serotype, DENV-1, but one may still get it from the other three. Thus, the same person can get infected four times. There is clinical evidence that expectant mothers can pass on their dengue infection to the unborn. While many dengue infections produce only mild illness, where people may not even know that they have been infected, it can cause an acute flu-like illness. Occasionally, this develops into a potentially lethal complication, called severe dengue, leading to complications associated with severe bleeding, organ impairment, and/or plasma leakage. Severe dengue is a leading cause of serious illness and death in some Asian and Latin American countries.

The incidence of dengue has grown dramatically around the world in recent decades. A vast majority of cases are asymptomatic or mild and self-managed, and hence the actual numbers of dengue cases are under-reported. Many cases are also misdiagnosed (see Fig. 3.16).

Model estimates [26] suggest up to 390 million dengue virus infections per year, of which 96 million cases manifest clinically

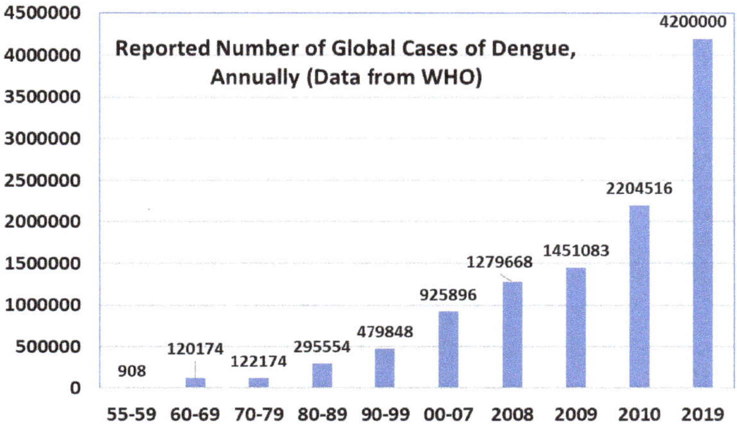

Fig. 3.16 Annually reported global cases of dengue

(with some severity of disease). A study on the prevalence of dengue estimates that 3.9 billion people are at risk of infection with dengue viruses. Despite the risk of infection existing in 129 countries, 70% of the actual burden is in Asia.

WHO informs that in 2020, dengue continued to affect several countries, with reports of increases in the numbers of cases in Bangladesh, Brazil, Cook Islands, Ecuador, India, Indonesia, Maldives, Mauritania, Mayotte (Fr), Nepal, Singapore, Sri Lanka, Sudan, Thailand, Timor-Leste, and Yemen [27].

The reported number of cases in India has risen sharply [28, 29] (see Fig. 3.17).

Fortunately, the fatalities are still somewhat low, though worrisome (see Fig. 3.18).

3.4.1 *Prevention and eradication of dengue*

As mentioned earlier, the *Aedes aegypti* mosquito is considered the primary vector of dengue. It lives in urban habitats and breeds mostly in man-made containers. It is a daytime feeder; its peak biting periods are early in the morning and in the evening before sunset. Female *Aedes aegypti* frequently feeds multiple times between each egg-laying period. Once a female has laid her eggs, these eggs can remain viable for several months and will hatch when they are in contact with water.

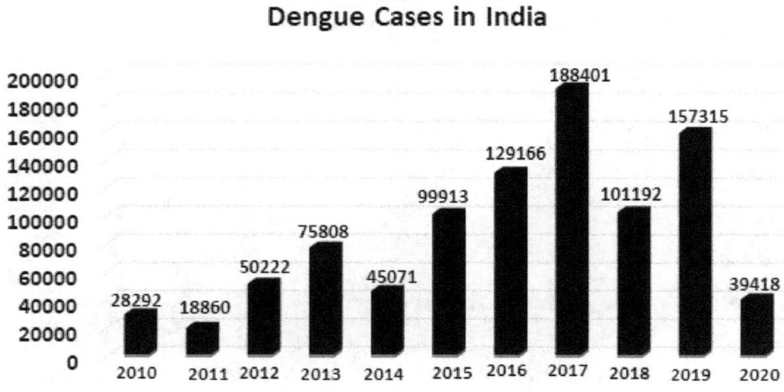

Fig. 3.17 Rise of reported cases of dengue in India [28, 29]

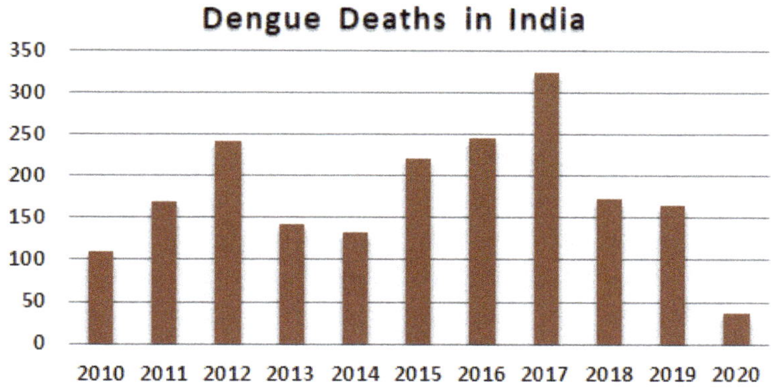

Fig. 3.18 Reported number of deaths due to dengue in India [28, 29]

Aedes albopictus, a secondary dengue vector in Asia, has spread largely due to the international trade in used tyres (a breeding habitat) and other goods (e.g., lucky bamboo). It is highly adaptive and has evolved to tolerate colder conditions both as an egg and as an adult.

There is no specific treatment for dengue fever. It is recommended to avoid ibuprofen and aspirin against fever and body ache, as it can lead to thinning of blood and cause complications as dengue can lead to haemorrhage. However, we would like to mention the identification of a compound JNJ-A07 reported in October 2021, which has been found to effectively disarm dengue, stopping it from replicating and preventing the disease in cell culture and mice, though its effect on humans remains to be seen.

The first dengue vaccine, Dengvaxia® (CYD-TDV) developed by Sanofi Pasteur, was licensed in December 2015 and has now been approved by regulatory authorities in several countries. The vaccine is to be given to people, in the age group of 9–45 years, who have had at least one dengue infection previously. However, as it carries an increased risk of severe dengue in those who experience their first natural dengue infection after vaccination, caution is required before vaccination.

At present, the main method to control or prevent the transmission of the dengue virus is to combat the mosquito vectors. It is important to prevent mosquitoes from accessing egg-laying habitats by disposing of solid waste properly and removing artificial man-made habitats that can hold water. It has been suggested that we cover, empty, and clean domestic water containers regularly and apply appropriate insecticides to outdoor water containers. Since these mosquitoes continue to bite throughout the day, personal household protection measures, such as window screens, repellents, insecticide-treated materials, coils, and vaporizers need to be implemented rigorously. It is also advised to wear clothing that minimizes skin exposure to mosquitoes.

Globalization, trade, travel, demographic trends, and warming temperatures are associated with the recent spread of the primary vectors *Aedes aegypti* and *Aedes albopictus* and of dengue. Several models project that new geographic areas along the fringe of current geographic ranges for *Aedes* will become environmentally suitable for the mosquito's life cycle and dengue transmission. Unplanned urban growth, inadequate housing, water, and waste management are continuing to provide an ideal ecology for the mosquito to proliferate. It is very important that we rapidly improve living standards and public health capacity in resource-poor tropical and subtropical countries.

We remarked in the beginning that the *Aedes* species of mosquitoes also spread Zika, chikungunya, and yellow fever. Thus, any effort to prevent dengue by eradicating the breeding of these mosquitoes will also greatly help us in our fight against these diseases as well.

3.5 Cholera

Cholera is yet another infectious disease that has been threatening humanity for a long time. It can cause acute diarrhoea following ingestion of food or water contaminated with the bacterium *Vibrio cholerae*, leading to dehydration and even death if untreated. Though descriptions of cholera are found as early as the fifth century BCE in Sanskrit texts, many outbreaks have occurred even over the last 200 years with millions of deaths. Cholera remains a global threat to public health and an indicator of inequity and lack of social development. A major milestone in our efforts to combat cholera is the development of modern oral rehydration salt (ORS) solution. Today, ORS is a part of the standard tool kit in our fight against cholera. It has been estimated that each year, there are about 1.3–4.0 million cases of cholera worldwide. Up to 80% of the cases are successfully treated with oral rehydration solution (ORS). Provision of safe water and sanitation is critical to control the transmission of cholera as with many other waterborne diseases. In 2017, the WHO launched a global strategy on cholera control with a target to reduce cholera deaths by 90%.

Cholera is endemic in the Ganges delta and over the last two centuries, it escaped six times to result in pandemics. The rapid modernization associated with the Industrial Revolution of the mid-nineteenth century propelled the spread of the disease from its ancient homeland around the Ganges delta.

The following discussion closely follows the discussion in Ref. [30].

The **First Cholera Pandemic (1817–1823)** started in 1817 in Jessore (now in Bangladesh). It spread throughout India by 1820 and then to China, Indonesia, Iraq, Turkey, Eastern Africa and the Mediterranean. It is believed to have killed 8,750,000 Indians, about 10,000 British troops, and several hundred thousand in Indonesia. By 1823, it subsided everywhere except for its home base of Bengal. The **Second Cholera Pandemic (1829–1837)** started in 1829 and reached Europe (including England, Germany, Poland, Hungary, Russia, and Finland) and the Americas (including Canada, modern USA, Mexico, and Cuba), being carried along shipping lines. The **Third Cholera Pandemic (1846–1860)** caused about a million deaths in Russia, over 15,000 deaths in Mecca, more than 50,000 deaths in England and Wales, over 236,000 deaths in Spain, about 200,000 deaths in Mexico, and about 26,000 deaths in Puerto Rico. Sadly, no reliable number of deaths of Indians is found in the literature. While a scientific understanding of the disease had not yet taken root, one major medical development was the intravenous saline drip, which continues to save lives to this day.

The third pandemic was notable for the discovery by John Snow (see later) from London that cholera was caused by contamination of drinking water with the water from the sewage, even though it was to take several years before this was admitted by civic administration and necessary steps for providing sewage treatment and supply of safe drinking water was taken. A sad outcome was the grossly unjust conclusion in the USA that cholera was associated with African Americans, while the fact was that they often lived along the waterways along which the disease travelled due to shipping and which had poor sanitation and hardly any provisions for safe drinking water.

The **Fourth Cholera Pandemic (1863–1875)** again started from the delta of the Ganges and travelled with Islamic pilgrims to Mecca where it claimed between 30,000 and 90,000 lives. It travelled to the Middle East and was carried to Russia, Europe, Africa, and North America, in each case spreading from port cities and along inland waterways. The disease claimed 70,000 lives in Zanzibar, 90,000 lives in Russia, 165,000 lives in the Austrian Empire, 115,000 lives in Germany, and 30,000 lives in Belgium, 113,000 lives in Italy, 80,000 lives in Algeria, and about 50,000 Americans. The **Fifth Cholera Pandemic (1881–1896)** consumed 250,000 lives in Europe, at least 50,000 in the Americas, 267,890 lives in Russia, 90,000 lives in Japan, over 60,000 lives in Persia, and more than 58,000 lives in Egypt. This was perhaps the last serious outbreak of cholera in Europe as the cities quickly improved their sanitation and water supplies. During this period, the germ theory for cholera was firmly established, with Robert Koch from Germany isolating the bacterium responsible for cholera and Waldemar Haffkine developing his vaccine for cholera, which he used to great success in Calcutta (see later).

The **Sixth Cholera Pandemic (1899–1923)** hit India hard. More than 800,000 Indians lost their lives. Europe, having improved its sanitation and water supply extensively, remained mostly untouched. The Ottoman Empire suffered greatly. Russia suffered greatly due to disruptions caused by revolution and war, and lost more than 500,000 lives to cholera. The Philippines lost more than

200,000 lives. This was also a period when immigrants and travellers were blamed for carrying the disease with them. Thus, Italians blamed the Jews and the Gypsies, the British in India blamed the "dirty natives", and the Americans blamed the arrivals from the Philippines.

Deaths in India during the first three pandemics of the nineteenth century are estimated to have exceeded 15 million people while another 23 million are reported to have died during the next three pandemics. We are now having the **Seventh Pandemic of Cholera** and it has been going on since 1961. According to WHO, it is the longest running pandemic. It started in Sulawesi Archipelago (Celebes, Indonesia) and spread to much of Asia in the 1960s. Cholera infects approximately 2.9 million people every year and kills 95,000.

3.5.1 *How does cholera spread?*

The credit for discovering the cause of the spread of cholera goes to the British doctor John Snow. Even though Dr Snow, an obstetrician with an interest in many aspects of medical science, had long believed that water contaminated by sewage was the cause of cholera and had written a paper about it in 1849, he was not able to convince his colleagues (see Fig. 3.19).

Cholera reached England in 1831. Between 1831 and 1854, when the epidemic lasted, tens of thousands of people were killed due to cholera. Until the mid-1800s, people in England did not have access to safe running water or modern toilets. Town wells and communal pumps were used to get the water needed for drinking, cooking, and washing. Septic systems were quite primitive. Most homes and businesses dumped untreated sewage and animal waste directly into the Thames River or into open pits called "cesspools". Water companies mostly filled water bottles directly from the Thames and supplied them to pubs, breweries, and restaurants. In August of 1854, Soho, a suburb of London, was hit hard by a terrible outbreak of cholera, killing more than 500 persons within 10 days. Dr Snow put fatalities on a map of London and found that most of these deaths were within 250 feet (about 76 m) of a particular pump that supplied water to the area. He suspected that the water there was

Fig. 3.19 John Snow (March 15, 1813–June 16, 1858) [31]

contaminated by sewage water. He also observed that the area served by the "contaminated" pump had a rate of mortality 14 times higher than for the areas served by "cleaner" pumps or wells. He further investigated the history of several patients to confirm his suspicion of contamination. He persuaded the authorities to disable the pump. The cases stopped.

John Snow's work was a major event in the history of public health and geography, and he is considered the father of the science of epidemiology.

In 1883, the German physician, Robert Koch (see later), took the search for the cause of cholera a step further when he isolated the bacterium *V. cholerae*, the "poison" Snow contended caused cholera, while working in India. He also determined that cholera is not contagious from person to person but is spread only through unsanitary water or food supply sources, a major victory for Snow's theory. Robert Koch had also isolated the bacterium for tuberculosis and anthrax. Unknown to Koch, the Italian physician Filippo Pacini (see Fig. 3.20) had already discovered the comma-shaped

Fig. 3.20 Filippo Pacini (May 25, 1812–July 9, 1883) [32]

bacillus, using a microscope, which he described as a *Vibrio* and noted its connection with cholera. He published a paper in 1854 entitled, "Microscopical Observations and Pathological Deductions on Cholera" in which he described the organism, but his work was not well known and well publicized till after his death, as most physicians of his period still believed in the "miasma" theory of diseases. The Catalan scientist Joaquim Balcells i Pascual also discovered the cholera bacterium in 1854.

Now, we know that cholera is an acute diarrhoeal infection caused by ingestion of food or water contaminated with the bacterium *V. cholerae*. This bacterium flourishes in warm water and is transmitted through the intake of contaminated food and water. There are many serogroups of *V. cholerae*, but only two — O1 and O139 — cause outbreaks. *Vibrio cholerae* O1 has been responsible for all recent outbreaks. Based on phenotypic and genotypic characteristics, *V. cholerae* O1 is subdivided into two biotypes: classical and El Tor.

Vibrio cholerae O139 was first identified in Bangladesh in 1992. It caused outbreaks in the past but recently has only been identified in sporadic cases. It has never been identified outside Asia. There is no difference in the illness caused by the two serogroups. Presently, *V. cholerae* O1 belonging to the El Tor biotype is the most common serogroup in India, while the frequency of serogroup O139 has declined considerably over the past few years.

Dr Waldemar Haffkine working at Louis Pasteur Institute in Paris made the first cholera vaccine in 1893, travelled to India, and inoculated a very large number of persons in Calcutta before being requested to take up the job of developing a vaccine for plague, which he successfully did, while working in Bombay in 1897, which went on to save millions of lives (see Fig. 3.21).

These days three oral cholera vaccines approved by the WHO are routinely used. These are Dukoral®, Shanchol™, and Euvichol-Plus®. All three vaccines require two doses for full protection. Children in the age group of 2–5 years need three doses. Two doses of Dukoral® (given with a gap of 7 days to 6 weeks) protect against

Fig. 3.21 Waldemar Haffkine giving inoculation against cholera in Calcutta in 1894 (Credit: Wellcome Trust)

cholera for 2 years. Two doses of Shanchol™ and Euvichol-Plus® (given with a gap of 15 days) protect against cholera for 3 years, while one dose provides short-term protection. Shanchol™ and Euvichol-Plus® are the vaccines currently available for mass vaccination campaigns through the Global OCV Stockpile and supported by Gavi, the Vaccine Alliance.

3.5.2 *Oral rehydration solution and oral rehydration therapy*

Oral rehydration solution (ORS) is considered one of the most significant medical treatments invented in the twentieth century. It arose out of an urgent need to manage severe cholera outbreaks spreading among innocent and helpless refugees arriving in numerous refugee camps along India's border at the time of the Bangladesh War in the early 1970s. These camps did not have any access to drinking water and sanitation, and suffered from a severe outbreak of cholera. Everyone, especially children, was dying of diarrhoea and cholera. At one refugee camp in Bangaon on the Indian side of the border, patients were lying on the floor in their vomit and faeces (see Fig. 3.22). There were not enough intravenous saline stations and only a few staff who could handle it.

In these trying and seemingly hopeless conditions, Dr Dilip Mahalanabis of John Hopkins International Centre for Medical Research and Training in Calcutta, who had been sent there to help, decided to use the oral rehydration solution prepared by simply using equal amounts of salt and sugar in water, which could be administered by even untrained personnel. The death rate dropped to 3% from 30% for those who were treated with IV saline. Pamphlets describing how to mix salt and glucose were distributed along the border and information was also broadcast on a clandestine Bangladeshi radio station. It went on to save millions of lives. It was also called Oral Saline in the beginning to arouse the trust of people in its efficacy [34] (see Fig. 3.23).

This was the first large-scale use of oral rehydration solution in a disaster situation. Later, it was used in hundreds of refugee

Fig. 3.22 A refugee camp in Bangaon (India) from East Pakistan (Bangladesh), 1971 [33] (WHO)

camps by the United Nations. The initiative has successfully reduced total diarrhoeal deaths, especially among children under five. It has received recognition from the WHO, and its application was spread worldwide. Each year around 500 million packs of oral rehydration solutions are used in more than 60 developing countries, saving millions of lives around the world.

July 29 is now celebrated as ORS day. ORS is prepared by adding 2.6 g of sodium chloride, 29 g of trisodium citrate dihydrate, 1.5 g of potassium chloride, and 13.5 g of anhydrous glucose to a litre of water and administered orally to the patient as often as possible. ORS with

Fig. 3.23 Dr Dilip Mahalanabis (November 12, 1934–)

zinc (called ORS Jodi in India) has been found to be very effective in cases of acute diarrhoea and dehydration [35].

The combination of electrolytes and glucose simulates water and electrolyte absorption from the gut and therefore prevents or reverses dehydration and replaces lost salts in conditions, such as diarrhoea and vomiting. A very effective substitute can be prepared at home by mixing six level teaspoons of sugar (one teaspoon equals 5 g) and a half level teaspoon of salt to 1 l (five cups) of water and stirring it till the sugar dissolves fully [36].

3.5.3 *Spread of cholera in recent times*

The annual reported cases of cholera along with the rate of mortality is shown in Fig. 3.24. It includes a massive eruption of the epidemic in Yemen in 2017 due to ongoing conflict and extremely poor living conditions in refugee camps. The advent of ORS, antibiotics, and vaccines has kept the death rate low, but the suffering across the world remains completely unacceptable as it can be completely avoided.

Cholera has been eliminated in Europe and North America. The continent-wise spread of cholera is given in Fig. 3.25.

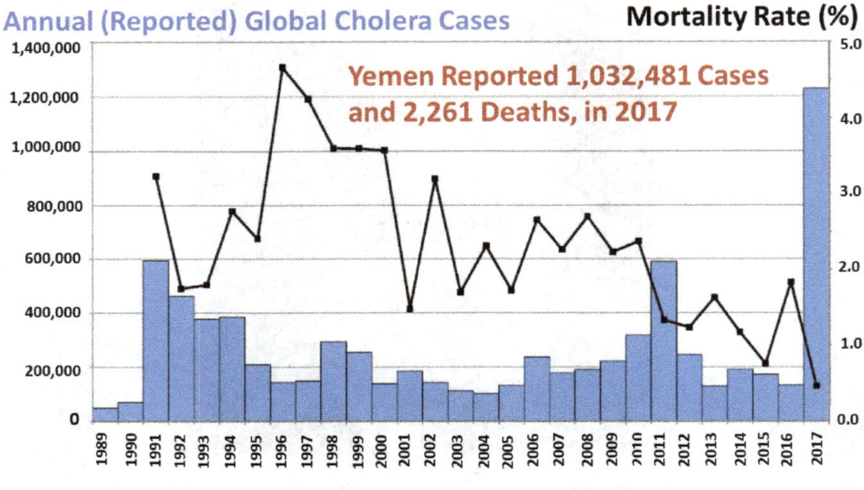

Fig. 3.24 Annual reported cases of cholera globally [36]

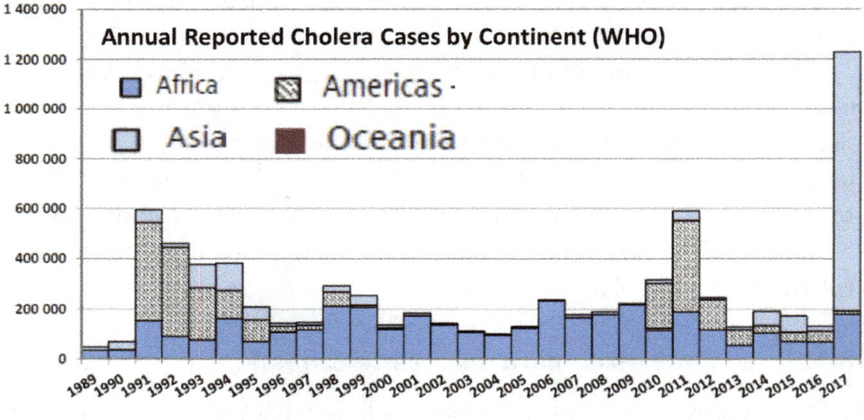

Fig. 3.25 Continent-wise spread of cholera [36]

We see that cholera continues to haunt poor regions of Asia, Africa, and Latin America. The occurrence of cholera in India in recent times is shown in Fig. 3.26, based on data from WHO. We see that the number of cases in recent years is generally small. It is hoped that the current emphasis on ending open defecation, Swachchha Bharat, and Atal Mission for Rejuvenation and Urban

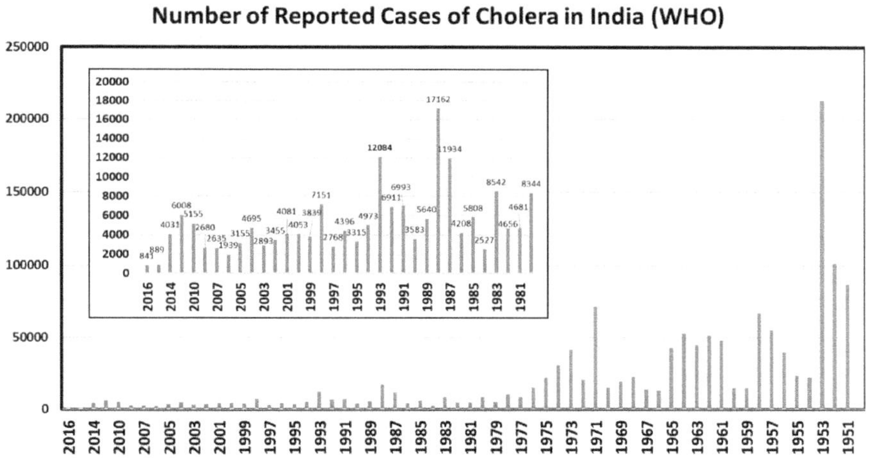

Fig. 3.26 Annual cases of cholera in India (Data from WHO)

Transformation (AMRUT) will go a long way in ending this ancient scourge.

3.5.4 *Combating cholera*

The cause of cholera, its spread, and its cure are fully understood, and thus it is a matter of great concern that it still affects masses, along with other waterborne diseases, such as typhoid and diarrhoea.

We have seen that cholera is caused by intestinal infection with the bacterium, *V. cholerae*, resulting in severe dehydration, shock, and often rapid death. The bacterium *V. cholerae*, including members of the O1 and O139 serogroups that cause cholera, is a natural inhabitant of the aquatic environment, particularly brackish riverine, estuarine, and coastal waters. It can survive for long periods in water and is commonly transmitted by contaminated water or food that has been washed in such water. Thus, cholera is spread through the faecal–oral route, either directly from person to person or indirectly through contaminated water, food, and flies and fomites (i.e., objects like clothing and utensils which can carry infection).

It has been observed that endemic cholera is often associated with tidal seawater intrusions and seasonal climatic patterns. Epidemic cholera, on the other hand, often occurs near waterways when weather conditions are favourable for the growth of the bacteria. such that an interaction between the aquatic environment and faecal–oral spread of cholera has long been held. Persons with cholera infection excrete *V. cholerae* in their stool. Eating vegetables grown with water containing human wastes and eating seafood found in polluted water is also one of the main reasons for the spread of cholera.

Figure 3.27 is from the website of WHO. Such scenes are common in third world countries. No explanations are needed to tell how the populace is exposed to the hazards of waterborne diseases. Cholera is endemic in more than 47 countries across the globe. It is estimated that in Africa, more than 40 million people live in cholera "hotspots" where outbreaks are a regular occurrence.

Climate change, forced migration, prolonged conflict, urbanization, population growth, and poor access to health services are all blamed for the occurrence of cholera. However, we have known for a long time that cholera is the result of the lack of adequate water and sanitation. Let us admit once for all that cholera spreads when

Fig. 3.27 Cholera [37]

people have no choice but to eat food or drink water that contains faeces. More than 2 billion people worldwide drink water from sources contaminated with faeces and 2.4 billion are without basic sanitation facilities.

Vaccines have been touted as a solution for cholera. However, we have seen that the vaccine for cholera gives a respite only for a short period.

Dr Dominique Legros, who leads the WHO cholera team, has observed: "Vaccination will not solve the cholera problem but only buy us some time. Unless we plan mid and long-term water and sanitation interventions, cholera is going to reappear as soon as immunity to the vaccine wanes..."

The WHO has concluded: "Fundamentally, cholera is the result of a lack of investment for adequate water and sanitation infrastructure, maintenance, and governance — all of which are needed to solve the problem. Among refugees, who are particularly vulnerable to cholera outbreaks because of their crowded conditions and poor water, sanitation and hygiene facilities, proper treatment of the disease has made a real difference." Safe drinking water and proper sanitation will not only eliminate cholera but also help us control several other waterborne diseases. The WHO has a plan for "Ending Cholera: A Global Roadmap to 2030". The Government of India has been working closely with WHO on this plan.

3.6 Polio

Polio is an infectious disease that predominantly affects children and can lead to permanent paralysis of various body parts and can ultimately cause death by immobilizing the patient's breathing muscles. An Egyptian stele from the period 1403–1365 BCE showing the Doorkeeper Roma, with one leg thinner and deformed, is generally believed to be the earliest recorded depiction of polio. There are also several paintings from the same period, showing children and grown-ups with deformed limbs (see Fig. 3.28).

We recall that while Ancient Egypt and the Indus Valley Civilizations were contemporaneous, there seems to be no depiction

Fig. 3.28 An Egyptian Stele (1403–1365 BCE) depicting polio [38]

of polio affected persons in the Indus Valley Civilization. Many skeletons from burials have been found. We have not come across any mention of deformations of bone limbs in them. Yet, the Indus Valley settlements were crowded urban settlements. Did it have to do with their very elaborate flush toilets (see later) and wastewater disposal drainage network? We hope that historians and archaeologists can answer this question.

3.6.1 *Polio in modern times*

Till the end of the eighteenth century, occurrences of polio were rather scarce. Only about 30 cases were recorded in Europe in the nineteenth century. Major epidemics of polio took place in Norway and Sweden in 1905 and later in the United States of America. The first known polio outbreak in the USA was in Vermont in 1894. In 1916, New York City experienced the first large epidemic of polio, with over 9,000 cases and 2,343 deaths. The 1916 toll in the USA was 27,000 cases and 6,000 deaths. As children were mostly affected by polio, and no one yet knew its cause, life was disrupted to the point of the ridiculous. Children were not allowed to swim in the summer, and if they did, could not sit around in wet bathing suits, fruits were banned because it was thought the germ might reside in the skins, and a sign was erected outside of New York City that read: "Children under 16 not allowed to enter this town." [39] (see Fig. 3.29).

The situation continued to worsen and in 1952, a record 57,628 cases of polio were reported in the USA, out of which 3,145 died and

Fig. 3.29 A road sign outside New York city [39]

21,269 were left with mild to disabling paralysis. Polio (also called infantile paralysis) was most often associated with children, but it affected teens and grown-ups as well.

It has been mentioned that polio can lead to the death of infected patients when the paralysis immobilizes their breathing muscles. To prevent death by suffocation, an "iron lung" was invented in 1928. Infected patients used to be placed in an airtight tube — with their heads outside — and the machine decreased the pressure inside the box, to induce inhalation, before returning to normal after weeks in an iron lung before their paralytic symptoms faded and independent breathing was achieved once again. In the case of permanent paralysis, on the other hand, patients would be bound to live inside the iron lung for years. The iron lung saved many lives. It is believed to be a precursor of intensive care units (see Fig. 3.30).

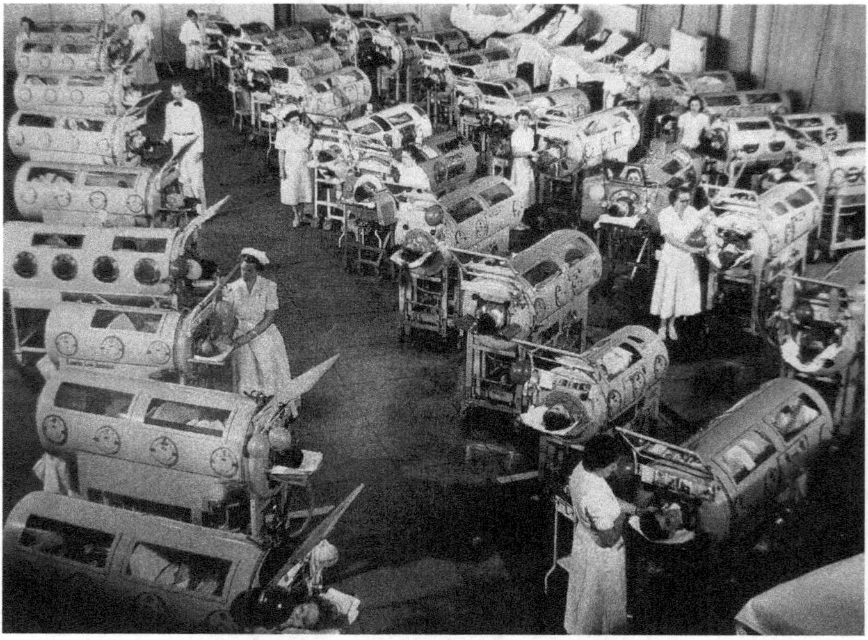

Fig. 3.30 Polio patients in iron lungs during the 1953 epidemic in the USA [40]

3.6.2 *Science in our war against polio: Vaccine for polio*

No cure exists for polio. Jonas Salk developed an inactivated poliovirus vaccine for polio by 1953 (see Fig. 3.31). He tested it on pets, monkeys, himself, and his relatives. It was administered to over a million volunteers and the news of the vaccine's success was made public on April 12, 1955. The polio vaccine, given multiple times, can protect a child for life. Salk refused to patent the vaccine or to seek any profit from it to maximize its global distribution. He is believed to have famously remarked: "There is no patent. Could you patent the Sun?".

This was followed in 1960 by a live attenuated oral vaccine developed by Albert Bruce Sabin (see Fig. 3.32). After trials, Sabin's vaccine was found to be superior and to have a longer-lasting effect. By 1962, it replaced the Salk vaccine. Several more vaccines (including more popular oral ones) are available now.

Universal vaccination allowed some developed countries to eliminate the disease entirely in the 1960s and 1970s. The last cases of wild (naturally occurring) polio in the United States were in 1979

Fig. 3.31 Jonas Salk (October 28, 1914–June 23, 1995) [41]

Fig. 3.32 Albert Sabin (Originally Abram Saperstejn) (1906–1993) [42]

in four states among Amish residents who had refused vaccination. However, the rest of the world continued to face regular outbreaks. It was estimated that in the 1980s, polio was prevalent in 125 countries and the number of paralytic cases was over 350,000 per year.

The "Global Polio Eradication Initiative" was founded by the WHO in collaboration with Rotary International, the Centre for Disease Control, and the United Nations Children's Fund in 1988 to fight the virus's spread and the disease with a global vaccination campaign. The world has made rapid progress against polio since then and by 2016, the number of paralytic cases was reduced by 99.99% with 42 cases worldwide.

As of 2017, the virus remains in circulation in only three countries in the world — Afghanistan, Pakistan, and Nigeria — and it is hoped that the disease will soon be eradicated globally [43] (see Fig. 3.33).

3.6.3 *Polio eradication in India*

The fact that the virus can only survive in humans (and no other animals) makes it possible to completely eradicate the disease from the world. If it were a virus with an animal host such as influenza

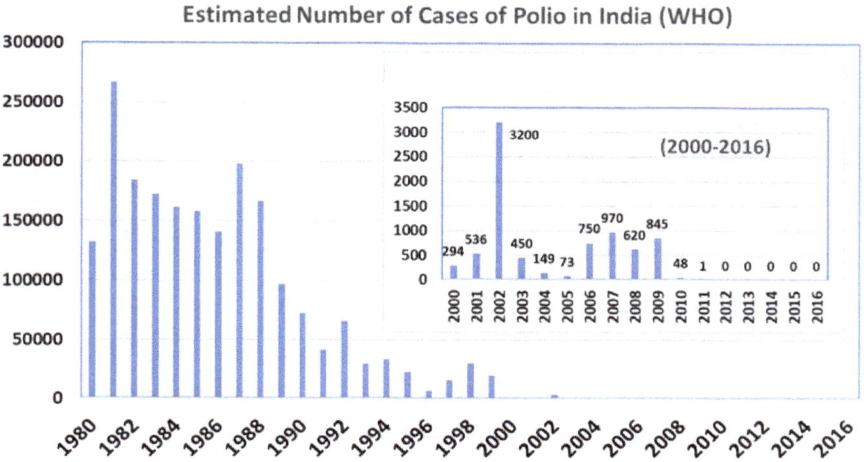

Fig. 3.33 Progress of polio eradication in India (Data from WHO [44])

(birds) or tuberculosis (cows) that occasionally mutates to attack humans, polio could only ever be controlled but not eradicated.

The poliovirus cannot survive for long periods outside of the human body. If the virus cannot find unvaccinated persons to infect, polio will die out.

The National Polio Surveillance Project was launched in India in 1988. It was executed in collaboration with the WHO with the sole objective of making India polio-free. The Government of India launched the "Pulse Polio" immunization campaign 1995–1996. Under this extensive drive, two drops of oral poliovirus vaccine (OPV) were given to all children younger than 5 years of age (see Fig. 3.34). Very active surveillance of acute flaccid paralysis cases resulted in a decrease of their numbers to just 134 in 2003 from 24,000 in 1988. In India, the last reported case was on January 13, 2011. India was officially declared polio-free in 2014.

Eradicating polio in India was a feat of dedication, commitment, and perseverance against difficult conditions. It was not easy, given India's vast population, tropical climate in many parts of the country, hilly terrains and villages scattered far and wide in the vast forested areas, as well as other environmental challenges. One should not

Fig. 3.34 A nation-wide immunization campaign for eradicating polio in India (WHO/2011 [45])

forget that as recently as 2009, India constituted over 60% of all global polio cases.

3.6.4 *Opposition to polio vaccination*

It is important to put on record the challenges faced by the health workers in reaching a stage when we are on the verge of declaring the world free from polio.

One of the biggest obstacles to global polio eradication has been the lack of basic health infrastructure, which makes vaccine distribution and delivery very difficult. We also have devastating effects of civil war and internal strife in some regions. It was always a great challenge to maintain the potency of live (attenuated) vaccines in extremely hot or remote areas. The oral polio vaccine must be kept at 2–8°C for vaccination to be successful.

And then there have been several cases of opposition to vaccination. These mostly arose from distrust and rumours. Thus, there were rumours in the Islamic nations that immunization campaigns were using deliberately contaminated vaccines to sterilize local Muslim populations or to infect them with HIV. In Nigeria, refusal to get vaccinated was considered opposition to western expansionism. The rumours mentioned above added fuel to fire and the Nigerian Supreme Council for Sharia gave a call for a boycott of the polio vaccination. The number of cases in Nigeria rose by a factor of five.

In Afghanistan and Pakistan, the Taliban issued fatwas against polio vaccination due to fears that the vaccine contained contraceptives. As a result, Pakistan had the largest number of polio cases (198) in the world in 2011. Muslims were not alone in opposing the vaccination for fear of it containing contraceptives, the Roman Catholic clergy of Kenya gave a similar call on the same grounds. We have already pointed out that Amish community members in the USA refused vaccination.

The polio eradication drive in Afghanistan and Pakistan also suffered when it was found that a doctor had organized to collect blood samples from a door-to-door campaign in the name of inoculating people against Hepatitis B to be able to perform DNA analysis to confirm the presence of Osama Bin Laden and his family in the town.

Other religious objections voiced included suggestions that it was interfering with God's will or that it used products from "unclean" animals and was "*haram*" or that animals were killed for making the vaccine.

Some communities, sensing that the national governments were emphasizing vaccination, used it as a bargaining chip to raise some political demands or draw attention to things like the construction of roads and schools. Some governments were accused of going slow on vaccination in the regions which were opposed to them, while some were accused of corruption and non-payment of wages to the health workers.

Finally, we should not forget that the efforts of thousands of health workers across the globe spread over decades has led to a situation where more than 18 million, who would otherwise have been paralyzed, can walk today and that no child will have to experience the devastating effects of the disease again.

3.7 Tuberculosis

Tuberculosis (TB) is yet another bacterial disease that mainly affects the lungs and has been around for thousands of years. It finds mention in Rigveda and writings of Indian physicians, Charak and Sushrut. One very early historical evidence for TB in humans comes from Atlit Yam, a city now under the Mediterranean Sea, off the coast of Israel. Archaeologists found TB in the remains of a mother and child buried together about 9,000 years ago. Historical references to TB were also found in a medical papyrus from 1550 BC. Some Egyptian mummies also have evidence of spinal tuberculosis. The name "tuberculosis" was coined by Johann Schonlein in 1834. The tubercle is a diminutive of tuber and comes from the Latin term, *tuberculum*, meaning a small swelling. While conducting autopsies of tuberculosis patients, doctors noticed small, round, firm, and white swellings on the surface or within an organ, most typically the lungs. Because of the colour of these tubercles, the disease was also sometimes referred to as the "White Plague" (see Fig. 3.35).

Fig. 3.35 The sick child by Edward Munch 1885–1886 [46]

It is now believed that about one-third of the world's population is infected with the microbe and each year some 8 million people contract tuberculosis and about 2 million succumb to the infection. It usually spreads through the air from one person to another when a person having active TB in his lungs coughs, spits, sneezes, laughs or even sings and the virus gets into the air. The other person can breathe the air and transport the TB to his lungs, where it begins to grow and even move through the blood. Depending on how the air containing the droplet nuclei moves, such an infection may spread across a wide area. As TB germs released into the air can linger for an extended period in locations with poor air conditioning or ventilation, there have been cases of the disease spreading even when the infected person is no longer present. For the same reason, large cities where many people live and work together in close quarters have high risks of infection. This makes the poor more vulnerable to infection since poverty facilitates transmission of *Mycobacterium tuberculosis* with people living in overcrowded and poorly ventilated homes. Malnutrition, diagnostic delays, and discontinuities in treatment often increase the vulnerability further. It is not surprising that TB is often referred to as a poor man's disease. Having said that, TB does not always spare the rich. The classic case is the story of a rich man contracting the infection from his poor car driver with whom he used to spend hours together in a closed air-conditioned car.

3.7.1 *War on tuberculosis*

The first report that the slow-growing *M. tuberculosis* is the causative agent of the disease was by a German scientist, Robert Koch in 1882 (see Fig. 3.36). Wilhelm Roentgen's discovery of X-rays in 1895 allowed physicians to diagnose and track the progression of the disease. X-ray imaging remained one of the most reliable methods for the diagnosis of TB for quite a long time.

When someone breathes in the TB bacteria, his body's immune system fights the bacteria and may win. In this case, the bacteria are still there but do not make the person sick and no symptoms are seen. The person also does not spread the infection. If the body's immune

Fig. 3.36 Heinrich Hermann Robert Koch (1843–1910) [47]

system of the person who inhaled the bacteria loses the fight, then the infection becomes active, and the person becomes sick. However, depending on the general health condition of the person, the disease can develop quickly or take years. Once the person has an active TB infection, he can spread the infection to others. Untreated active TB can lead to death, but it can be treated, and the person can be completely cured. Unfortunately, latent TB can't be detected but can become active TB at any time. For this reason, TB is also called an opportunistic infection, as it occurs more often or is more severe in people with weakened immune systems than in people with healthy immune systems.

Signs and symptoms of active TB begin gradually and worsen over time. Common signs and symptoms include fevers, chills, a cough that lasts more than 3 weeks, coughing up blood or sputum (phlegm from deep inside the lungs), night sweats, loss of appetite, unexplained weight loss, trouble in breathing, pain in the chest, and weakness.

Active TB mostly lives in people's lungs and is called pulmonary TB. However, it can live anywhere in the body, and in this case, it is

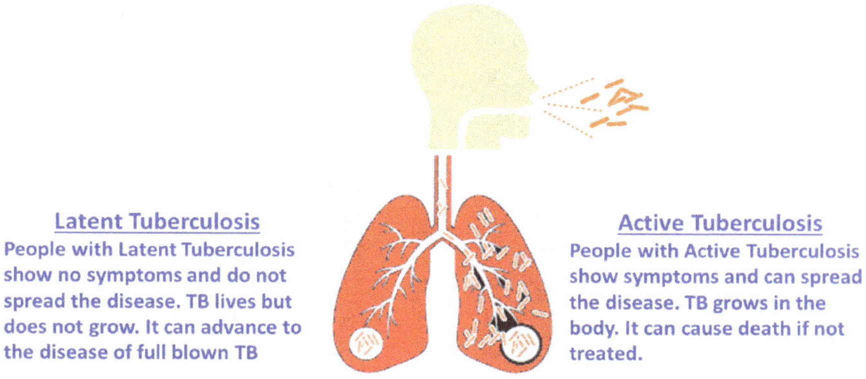

Fig. 3.37 Latent and active tuberculosis

called extrapulmonary TB. It can even live in more than one place at a time, and in this case, it is called disseminated TB (see Fig. 3.37).

Microscopic examination of sputum samples has been the primary method for diagnosis of pulmonary tuberculosis in low- and middle-income countries, which is where nearly 95% of TB cases and 98% of deaths due to TB occur. It is a simple, rapid, and inexpensive technique that is highly specific in areas with a very high prevalence of tuberculosis [48]. Though there are other more reliable and sophisticated methods, sputum smear microscopy alone faces the challenge of making effective TB diagnosis available to populations that need it most but can afford the least.

3.7.2 *Vaccine for tuberculosis*

Bacillus Calmette–Guérin (BCG), a vaccine for immunization against tuberculosis, was first developed by two French scientists, Léon Charles Albert Calmette and Jean-Marie Camille Guérin as early as 1921 (see Fig. 3.38). It is made from a weakened strain of TB bacteria and triggers the immune system to protect against the disease without causing the disease.

The vaccine is 70–80% effective against the most severe forms of TB, such as TB meningitis in children. However, it is less effective in preventing respiratory disease, which is the more common form

Fig. 3.38 Inventors of the BCG vaccine for tuberculosis [49]

of TB in adults. The vaccine remains effective for 10–15 years. In most tuberculosis endemic countries including India, BCG is usually given around birth to prevent severe TB in infants. Several other tuberculosis vaccines are at various stages of development, but BCG is the only vaccine authorized by the WHO.

Two of the most important drugs currently used for the treatment of TB are Isoniazid and Rifampicin. Both Isoniazid and Rifampicin are antibiotics that fight bacteria and are used in combination with other TB medicines. There is also one strain of TB, multidrug-resistant tuberculosis (MDR-TB), that has developed resistance to both Isoniazid and Rifampicin. Some situations that lead to the development of MDR-TB are inadequate treatment, irregular drug administration, or drug administration that is suspended before the course is finished. MDR-TB has recently been increasing globally and is the most critical issue surrounding the global increase of TB today.

Now, even though very effective cures are available, quite often TB patients suffer from social stigma, a daunting and difficult treatment, lack of social support, and lack of motivation to undergo prolonged treatment. This leads to large incidences of patients abandoning the treatment before they are fully cured, which may result in giving them a drug-resistant strain of TB.

3.7.3 *Incidences of tuberculosis*

We have already remarked that one-third of the world's population, or about 2 billion persons, are infected by the bacterium, 8–10 million people contract active tuberculosis every year and about 2 million people die. The introduction of Bacille Calmette–Guerin (BCG) as a vaccine against TB in the last century was a major advance in combating tuberculosis. Even today, BCG remains the only vaccine available against TB. The BCG vaccine, in addition to its specific effects against tuberculosis, is reported to have beneficial non-specific effects on the immune system that protect against a wide range of other infections. The recent emergence of MDR-TB and the HIV-TB "duet" have raised even greater concerns across the globe.

It is unfortunate that so many people continue to die in India (see Fig. 3.39) from this ancient malady, even though very effective medicines are now available. India has had a TB Control Programme since 1962. A countrywide BCG vaccination programme was launched targeting young children. Several district-level TB centres were also set up. However, due to resource constraints, inadequate

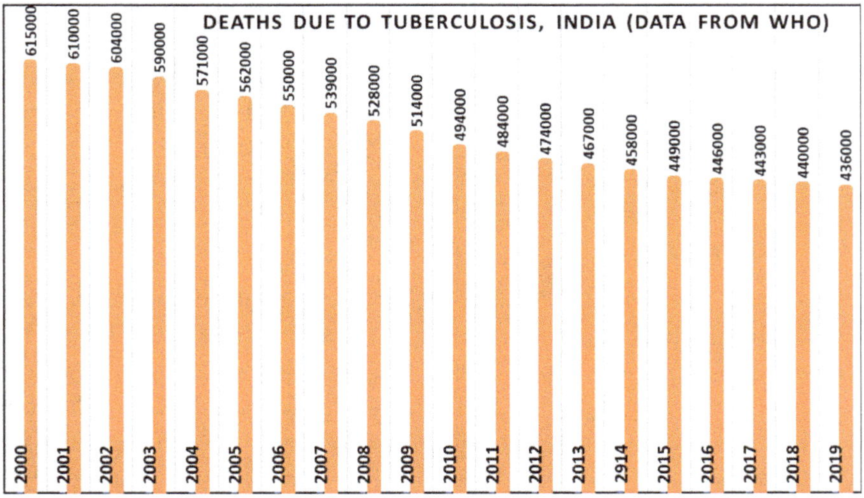

Fig. 3.39 Deaths due to tuberculosis in India (WHO [50])

supply of drugs, and a low rate of completion of treatment which often led to MDR-TB, the program had limited success.

Tuberculosis was the first infectious disease to be declared as a global emergency by WHO in 1993. It was recommended that all countries follow a control strategy, Directly Observed Treatment, Short-course (TB-DOTS). TB-DOTS has five main components: government commitment, case detection by sputum smear microscopy, standardized treatment regimen, drug supply at affordable costs and a standardized recording and reporting system. Following this declaration, the Indian TB control programme was also reviewed by the Government of India, leading to a Revised National Tuberculosis Control Plan. Despite making substantial progress, it was also found that TB was the leading cause of death among patients with HIV/AIDS and cases of MDR-TB were on the rise. DOTS-Plus was recommended by WHO to handle cases of MDR-TB. Following the "End TB by 2025" strategy of WHO, India plans to end TB by 2025, five years ahead of the Sustainable Development Goals set by WHO, basically adopting the WHO "test–treat–prevent–build" strategy. Malnutrition aggravates the severity of the TB infection, and therefore, it is important to provide not only nutritious meals but also supplements of vitamin A, C, and D, and minerals like calcium and iron to the patients. A special drive was also taken up to treat paediatric TB. The strategy also includes extensive health education about cough etiquettes, the importance of well-ventilated housing and other preventive measures.

3.8 Influenza

Influenza, a viral infection that attacks our respiratory system, our nose, throat, and lungs, has been with mankind for centuries. For most people, influenza, also called flu, resolves on its own. However, sometimes flu and its complications can be deadly. This can happen in children under 5 years, especially those less than 6 months old, pregnant women and women soon after giving birth, people older than 65, and people who have chronic illnesses, such as asthma, heart disease, kidney disease, liver disease, and diabetes, and people who are extremely obese. Seasonal influenza is caused by influenza viruses that circulate all over the world. These are broadly categorized as A, B, C, and D types. Out of these, A and B types of viruses circulate and cause seasonal epidemics. Currently, A(H1N1) and A(H3N2) viruses are believed to be active among humans. Type C of the virus is detected occasionally and is mostly mild. Type D mostly affects cattle and is not known to cause illness in humans. Only type A virus is known to have caused pandemics, including the H1N1 pandemic of 2009. The WHO estimates suggest that 3–5 million people across the world have serious cases of illness to influenza every year, which results in 290,000–650,000 respiratory deaths.

3.8.1 *Great Influenza pandemic of 1918–1920*

Even though there are several historical references to diseases that look like influenza, the first convincing record is believed to be from the year 1510, which ravaged North Africa and Europe. Since then, it emerged repeatedly at irregular intervals, though most of the time the fatality was low.

The world suffered the most deadly and ferocious onslaught of an influenza epidemic during the years 1918–1920, which affected 500 million (close to 50% of the world population during that period) and killed 20–50 million people. India was hit particularly hard, with a death toll variously estimated to be between 12 and 17.5 million (5–7% of its population). Mortality among young women of reproductive age was particularly high. The origin of the disease is not yet firmly established, though it was first recorded in Kansas, USA, in early 1918. The American soldiers travelling to Europe to take part in the First World War are believed to have spread it to Europe. About 1 million Indian soldiers had participated in the war as a part of the British Army. As these soldiers returned to India and travelled home, they spread it across the country.

The pandemic was caused by the H1N1 Influenza A virus, as mentioned earlier. However, the microscopes of the period were not powerful enough to see the virus, and the cause of the infection remained unknown. Some medical practitioners believed the illness to be caused by bacterial infections and treated accordingly, occasionally bringing some relief from the resulting complications. Complications included the development of pneumonia or bleeding from the nose, stomach, and intestines. In the absence of antiviral drugs to treat the virus and antibiotics to treat the secondary bacterial infections, medicines like aspirin, quinine, and other traditional medicines were used to bring whatever relief could be provided. Clinical, pathological, bacteriological, and virological studies of the lung tissues of 68 American soldiers who died before and during the epidemic were performed recently and the virus responsible for their deaths has been painstakingly recreated for further study.

A poster published in New Haven, Connecticut, in the *Illustrated Current News*, 1918, showed a nurse with a mask and advised people to follow certain safeguards to prevent influenza:

"Do not take any person's breath. Keep the mouth and teeth clean. Avoid those that cough and sneeze. Don't visit poorly ventilated places. Keep warm, get fresh air and sunshine. Don't use common drinking cups, towels, etc. Cover your mouth when you cough and sneeze. Avoid worry, fear, and fatigue. Stay home if you have a cold. Walk to your work or office. In sick rooms, wear a mask." These precautions when implemented strictly were quite effective in limiting the spread of the infection and have proved to be effective again during the ongoing COVID-19 pandemic. (Till September 2021, the Great Influenza pandemic was the biggest killer in the USA with about 675,000 casualties. COVID-19 casualties have crossed this figure despite the enormous developments in healthcare since the 1920s. This number is still rising. However, the population of the USA and the world was less than one-third of its present value during those days.)

Because of the ongoing World War, most European countries had imposed censorship on the news to avoid mass panic and maintain high morale, and the news of the infection was not widespread. However, Spain was not participating in the War and did not impose censorship on the newspapers, which gave detailed coverage to the mayhem. This led to the coinage of the phrase "Spanish flu" to the infection, which is now considered a misnomer. Several other names were also used, which reflected the prejudice of the people about the supposed origin. Thus, when three Japanese sumo wrestlers on their return from Taiwan succumbed to it, it was given the name "sumo flu" in Japan. It is believed that the censorship hid the extent of the ferocity of the epidemic and hindered the preparations and readiness of the medical fraternity and people to face it.

The epidemic raged in several waves. During the first and milder wave, it affected mostly children under 5 and older people with relatively low mortality. It was followed by a very ferocious and deadly second wave as the virus mutated and mostly killed people in the age group of 20–45 years. It was followed by two milder waves. There have been suggestions that the spread of the infection may have been assisted by the weakened immune systems of the people due to the tension, anxiety, and malnutrition and war, as well as the plague, which had haunted the globe in the preceding years.

3.8.2 *The 2009 influenza pandemic*

In 2009, a strain of the H1N1 influenza A virus mutated and jumped species from swine to humans. A new viral strain is referred to as a novel one. These are significant as most humans, especially younger people, have no natural immunity to defend against it. It is believed to have originated in North America, which spread quickly across the world and led to the death of up to 575,400 persons.

3.8.3 *Vaccines against influenza*

The isolation of the influenza virus around 90 years ago in 1933 very quickly led to the development of the first generation of live attenuated vaccines. As the virus evolves continuously, since 1973, the WHO has issued annual recommendations for the composition of the influenza vaccine based on results from surveillance systems that identify currently circulating strains. The influenza vaccine has thus continuously evolved to match the evolution of influenza viruses. Annual flu vaccination is quite effective against influenza.

3.9 COVID-19

We are in the middle of a global pandemic: COVID-19 (Corona Virus Disease 2019) as we write this. COVID-19 is caused by Severe Acute Respiratory Syndrome, CoronaVirus-2 (SARS-CoV-2). It is an invasive, highly infectious, and virulent disease. Initial symptoms of the infection may include fever, body ache, weakness, dry cough, difficulty in breathing, and loss of smell and taste. It can lead to severe complications in the lungs as well as in other organs, especially in old and infirm, and in people having co-morbidities like diabetes and problems of the heart, and can lead to death. The first case of COVID-19 was identified in Wuhan, China, in December 2019. It soon spread to other countries through travellers from and to China. On 11 March 2020, the WHO made the assessment that COVID-19 can be characterized as a pandemic and issued an interim guidance document [51].

The virus spreads mainly by close contact between an infected person and others. Small droplets containing the virus can spread from an infected person's nose and mouth as they breathe, cough, sneeze, sing, or speak. If the virus gets into the mouth, nose, or eyes of others, they can get infected. It may also spread via contaminated surfaces, although this perhaps is not the main route of transmission. Once this was known, use of mask, covering nose and mouth, maintaining a distance of at least 6 feet (about 2 m) from others (physical or social distancing), washing hands with soap, using sanitizers frequently, and avoiding crowded and closed spaces were advised and have remained the most valuable guard against the spread of the infection (see Fig. 3.40).

To minimize person-to-person contacts, all modes of transport, public and private, had to be curbed. Offices, factories, schools, and colleges had to be closed. Shops, markets, and malls had to be closed. All activities involving the gathering of people such as sporting events, social and religious events, and entertainment events had to be curbed. The impact of these on the citizens was unprecedented. Billions of jobs were lost. Lifestyles changed at the professional level, at the social level, and even at the personal level. With educational

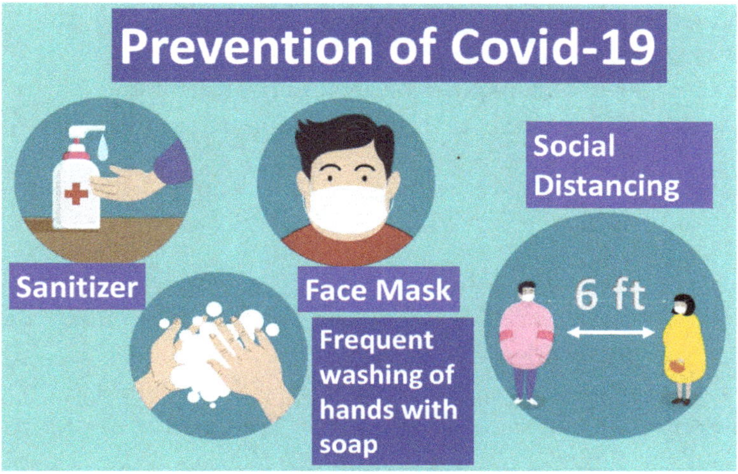

Fig. 3.40 Preventive measures to arrest the spread of COVID-19

institutions remaining closed, education went into the doldrums. National and global economies were impacted in unprecedented ways. The COVID-19 pandemic left nobody untouched, nothing untouched. At the same time, it was also clear right from the beginning that no one was safe unless everyone was safe. A little more than a year after its first appearance in Wuhan, the pandemic had engulfed the entire world barring a few countries and territories, and extinguished more than 2 million lives.

On January 30, 2020, the presence of the COVID-19 virus in India was officially identified. On that day, a medical student who returned to Kerala a week earlier from Wuhan was confirmed to be infected with the COVID-19 virus by the National Institute of Virology, Pune. The need for stringent steps to contain the spread of the virus was obvious. There were many concerns:

1. billion plus population,
2. high population density, particularly, in the metropolitan cities,
3. large rural population,
4. relatively poor public healthcare infrastructure and sanitation facilities,

5. the federal structure of governance,
6. limited resources,
7. large non-resident population including students, and
8. to top it all, absence of drugs and vaccines to combat the pandemic

Some of the early measures that India adopted like many other countries to stem the spread of the infection were as follows:

1. Surveillance at the points of entry.
2. COVID-19 Appropriate Behaviour by all — face masks, personal sanitization, and social distancing.
3. As a preventive measure against the spread of COVID-19, a nationwide lockdown was ordered on March 25, 2020, for 21 days, when the number of confirmed positive cases across the country was only about 500. At the end of the lockdown, it was further extended in phases.
4. In the absence of any vaccines and drugs to fight the pandemic, there was no alternative to COVID Appropriate Behaviour along with active surveillance, contact tracing, and quarantine to slow down and stop transmission of the virus.

The infections reached their maximum in India by September 2020 and started declining thereafter. It was to pick up later during the more ferocious second wave, peaking by the first week of May 2021.

As mentioned earlier, India was not alone in combating the pandemic. COVID-19 had rampaged almost all countries across the world. Figures 3.41–3.44 summarize the global status of the pandemic in the top 10 affected countries. The United States of America seems to be the hardest hit.

The unusually low mortality and mortality per million population in India have been a matter of intense discussion and speculations.

Apart from the loss of lives, the impact of the pandemic on the lives of people — their jobs, their education, even their entertainment — has not been any less traumatic. According to the International Labour Organization, the COVID-19 pandemic and the resulting lockdown caused, across the world, more than 100 million

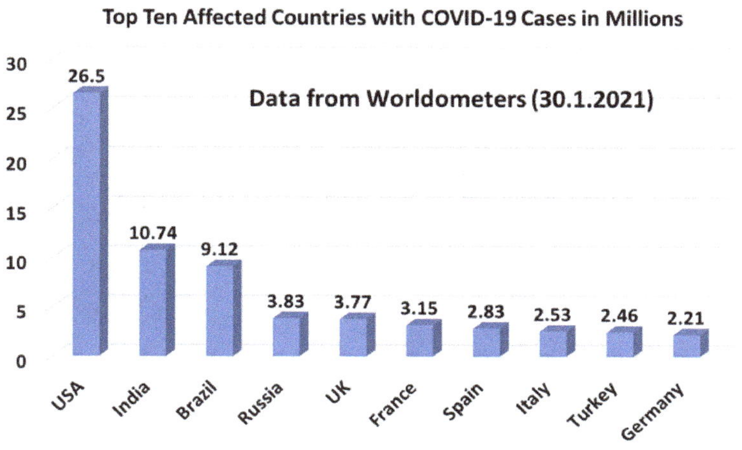

Fig. 3.41 Number of COVID-19 cases in top 10 affected countries

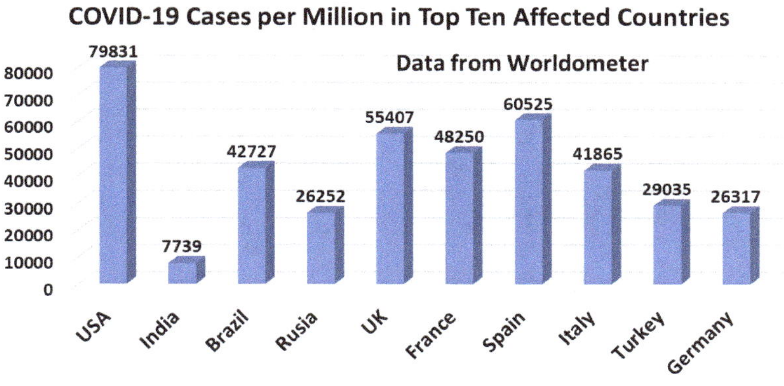

Fig. 3.42 COVID-19 cases per million in top 10 affected countries

people to lose their jobs during the year 2020. Hundreds of millions of people across the world are forced to work from home. The number of working hours lost in 2020 was even more, nearly equivalent to 255 million full-time jobs. Undoubtedly, the ongoing crisis has disrupted labour markets around the world at an unprecedented scale.

In India alone, it is estimated that 122 million people lost their livelihood, with more than 75% from the unorganized sector. In India,

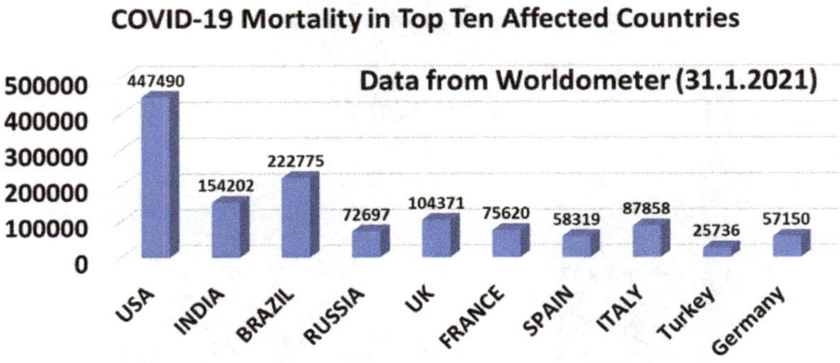

Fig. 3.43 COVID-19 mortality in top 10 affected countries

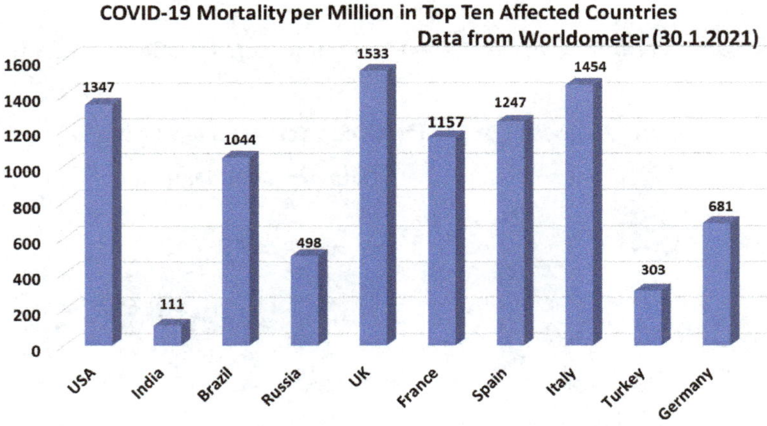

Fig. 3.44 COVID-19 mortality per million in top 10 affected countries

when lockdown started millions of daily wage earners lost their jobs overnight and as no transport was available, men, women, and children trekked thousands of kilometres along highways and railway lines to reach home, many losing their life to exhaustion, disease, and accidents. It remains one of the saddest spectacles to emerge from this episode.

More than one billion students have been forced to stay home and take online lessons. Online classes have put an enormous strain on the students, on the teachers, and on the parents. Gadgets like personal computers, smartphones, internet connectivity, and even power to run these couldn't be taken for granted to the weaker sections of the population both in urban and rural India. Thus, the opportunity for education, which allows the poor to be able to improve their lot, was denied to them. During this period, only extreme determination could keep them going. The psychological strain on all sections of society, especially young children, has been enormous.

Only a massive distribution of aid by way of free rations and small cash allowances by the Government of India, philanthropic organizations, and individuals could keep large-scale suffering at bay.

3.9.1 *Development of vaccines for COVID-19*

We have already seen that in the case of several past infectious diseases, the most effective weapon against the infections was the availability of vaccines. Vaccine development, however, is a costly and time-consuming process. Since the emergence of COVID-19 in December 2019, more than a dozen vaccines have started to be rolled out thanks to unprecedented financial investments and scientific collaborations. Vaccines go through rigorous testing for safety and effectiveness before they are approved for public use, a process that typically takes a few years. Many stages are involved in the development and production of a vaccine from initial academic research to the hands of the healthcare providers. Keeping in mind the urgency, and the well-known dictum, "Let not the best be the enemy of the good", governments across the world have chosen to short-circuit some of the final approval stages and make the vaccines available for all. The development of so many vaccines for COVID-19, in such a short time, will remain one of the most outstanding achievements of mankind.

Vaccination started in India on January 16, 2021. India initially accorded emergency use authorization to two vaccines, Covishield, manufactured under license in India, and Covaxin, developed and manufactured in India. They have since been joined by other vaccines, Sputnik V and Moderna, to be manufactured under license in India.

The Government had decided that the health professionals and other "COVID Warriors", including police personnel and municipal workers, would be vaccinated first, followed by the elderly and vulnerable population, and thereafter the rest of the population would be vaccinated. While universal vaccination would be most ideal, it is not necessary to contain the infection provided COVID Appropriate Behaviour is also adhered to. Vaccination of a sufficiently large number of people is expected to lead to what is called "herd immunity" [52], which allows unvaccinated people also to stay safe. Adherence to COVID Appropriate Behaviour together with immunization influences the herd immunity considerably.

We take a little diversion here to discuss the story of vaccine development for COVID-19 in India. When India became independent in 1947, it was a net importer of even generic drugs. Even though pharma research and pharma industry in the country were in their infancy, through a strategy mostly based on reverse engineering, India could build a strong industry in generic drugs at affordable costs. When India opened its economy in 1990, India was not only a net exporter of generic drugs but also self-sufficient in several vaccines.

During the late nineties, India also made major investments in vaccine research using modern techniques. Several vaccines at affordable costs like the Hepatitis-B vaccine, Rotavirus vaccine, and combo vaccines came out of India. It is therefore not surprising that in the wake of the COVID-19 pandemic, many Indian academia and industries participated in global efforts to develop suitable vaccines. Two vaccines, Covaxin, developed by Bharat Biotech International Ltd in collaboration with the Indian Council of Medical Research, and Covishield, developed by the Oxford–AstraZeneca and manufactured by Serum Institute of India, Pune, were added to our armour against the COVID-19 pandemic. As we write this, Zydus Cadila's COVID-19 DNA vaccine, developed in partnership with the Department of Biotechnology for adults and children aged 12 and older, becomes the second homegrown vaccine approved in India. We should also mention the vaccines developed by the Pfizer–BioNTech collaboration and Moderna, which deliver mRNA that instructs cells to create SARS-CoV-2's spike protein, which, in turn, stimulates the human body to make antibodies. It is a sobering realization that the mRNA technique, advocated by Katalin Kariko and her colleagues since the 2000s, was not taken seriously by other researchers. Shanker Balasubramanian and his colleagues at the University of Cambridge had earlier developed a technique in the mid-2000s that allows billions of DNA fragments to be imaged and read in parallel, which speeded up sequencing by 10 million times and helped keep track of the mutating virus, almost immediately. It is gratifying to note that both these procedures were honoured with breakthrough prizes.

We should not forget that never before such vaccines have been developed and received approval in such a short time, almost along with those developed in other developed countries such as the USA, UK, Germany, Russia, and China, which is a testimony of our strengths in pharma research and industry. We also add that the vaccines may have to be continuously modified as the virus mutates, and indigenous capabilities are a major strength.

As the world was gearing up to combat the virus with the newly developed vaccines, the virus itself was mutating with some of the strains being more infectious and often more resistant to the vaccines. The world was also witnessing fatigue, both from the point of view of the public at large and the governments resulting in considerable relaxation in the COVID Appropriate Behaviour. There is also a fear that while most of the people in richer countries will get vaccinated, the vulnerable people in poorer states will be left behind and nucleate future waves. Our only hope is that with vaccination which has started in many parts of the world, the situation may be brought under control in a few months, even if the virus is not fully eradicated.

COVID-19 is an ongoing pandemic. The virus is continuously mutating and as mentioned, some mutants are possibly resistant to the vaccines available so far. Even though we shall discuss it again, the availability of the vaccine to poorer nations is extremely low. In several countries, the vaccination is as low as 1% of the population, while some countries have procured enough vaccines to vaccinate their entire population several times over. India, the biggest producer of vaccines, was forced to impose an initial ban on the export and donation of vaccines in the face of opposition to it and a galloping infection. We must realize that the only hope of recovery lies in the vaccination of all the people of the world.

It should be accepted that COVID-19 gave a severe jolt to a complacent world and severely exposed the lack of its preparedness to a pandemic of this nature.

The pandemic has made us realize that our expenditure on building health infrastructure, over the years, has not been sufficient. In the short term, the focus should be on providing hospital beds, drugs, oxygen, ventilators, and vaccines which had to be done on an emergency basis. In the long term, there should be increased focus towards health expenditure for creating basic infrastructure, hospitals with sufficient facilities of oxygen, ventilators, ICUs, etc., primary health centres, and laboratories, as well as having more doctors, nurses, ward staff, lab technicians, etc. It should be planned that primary healthcare is available within a radius of 3 km of all settlements and should have facilities of telemedicine.

Based on the current understanding, the efficacy of current vaccines is likely to last for a maximum of a year. Given this, massive efforts are required to vaccinate 70–80% of the population by the end of 2021 in the country. Such a cycle may have to be repeated for the next few years unless better vaccines are developed and administered.

There is an urgent necessity to improve the prediction system of the geographic spread of the pandemic (peaking and flattening) both spatially and temporally. The reasonably accurate, timely and reliable predictions will improve the response of governments at different levels for identifying vulnerable communities, provisioning of medical facilities, medicine availability, planning travel restrictions, scaling up of hospital operations, lockdowns, curfews, etc. The current models did predict the timing right, but the magnitude was no way near what ultimately happened. Efforts are required to improve these models.

In the long term, an early warning system, such as the one for cyclones, floods, and tsunamis, needs to be developed, so that governments and communities are well prepared to respond to such pandemics.

The pandemic has threatened human security and has seriously affected social systems, i.e., the economy, industry, education, etc.

The knowledge about COVID-19 is improving day by day as compared to early days, fortunately, helped by large investments for the study of COVID-19 and its mutations, as well as technologies to address resultant effects. This support needs to be continued. The government policies and actions should continuously consider the emerging new knowledge and set up a mechanism to adopt such insights through flexibility and innovation. Educating people about COVID-19 and vaccination should be taken on a priority. We shall come to this again in Chapters 7 and 8.

3.9.2 *Some initial mistakes*

Mistakes are believed to have been committed in the initial handling of COVID-19, which may have led to it getting converted to a pandemic from an epidemic in Wuhan. Thus, either because it was not known that it is a highly contagious virus that spreads from person to person, or to avoid a panic, or to control economic loss, isolation of the affected area and persons was delayed in China when it was first identified. The large number of persons travelling across China and between China and the rest of the world due to the Chinese New Year 2020 (January 25) rapidly spread the virus across the world. There are reports that a particular city in Italy, which had a large Chinese population, started the "Hug a Chinese" programme to allay the fears of its people, which may have led to the mayhem caused by the virus.

A real sad episode involved Dr Li Wenliang (34), who raised an alarm about the coronavirus in the early days of the outbreak already towards the end of December 2019. Dr Li was working at the centre of the outbreak in December when he noticed seven cases of a virus that he thought looked like SARS — the virus that had earlier led to a global epidemic in 2003. The patients from Hunan Seafood Market were in quarantine in his hospital. He sent a message to fellow doctors, on a chat group, on December 30, warning them about the outbreak and advising them to wear protective clothing to avoid infection. Three days later police paid him a visit and told him to stop. He returned to work, caught the virus from a patient, and died on February 7, 2020, after being in hospital for 3 weeks.

Fig. 3.45 Dr Li Wenliang (October 12, 1986–February 7, 2020) [53]

Since then, a very large number of health professionals across the world have sacrificed their lives (see Fig. 3.45).

Much later, on January 15, 2021, China had to enforce a strict lockdown in some areas around Beijing and order a crash testing programme covering every one of the 22 million residents of those areas, following a re-emergence of the cases of COVID-19 infection. It is a testimony to the sacrifice of Dr Li Wenliang that on this occasion, the Chinese premier, Li Keqiang, is reported to have remarked as follows: "In the process of infectious disease prevention and control, one of the key points is to seek truth from facts, to openly and transparently release epidemic information and never to allow covering up or underreporting."

Some western observers, especially Amnesty International, were sceptical of the lockdown and called it a violation of human rights. However, as the COVID-19 pandemic worsened, similar measures were enacted around the globe.

The lockdown had mixed responses in some western countries, especially the United States of America, where the President himself

Fig. 3.46 Anti-lockdown protestors in Ohio, April 20, 2019 [54]

kept ridiculing the use of masks and social distancing till he was infected. By then, it was too late. Reports suggest that in some states of the USA, people refused to wear masks and continued to join large gatherings, protesting the measures suggested by the health authorities. Some prominent opponents of the measures, unfortunately, succumbed to the virus. Recently, violent protests opposing the lockdown have been reported from the Netherlands (see Fig. 3.46).

Sweden did not implement any lockdown. It only banned a gathering of more than 50 persons and depended upon its people following social distancing and adapting health measures like frequent washing of hands. The results were mixed. However, one should not forget that Sweden is a relatively thinly populated country of just 10 million people. Western Australia, the largest state of Australia by area, continued with essentially normal life after some early snap lockdowns by sealing its state borders and implementing a strict quarantine on visitors arriving in case of emergency, while the rest of Australia has had frequent lockdowns of varying durations.

In India, Covid Appropriate Behaviour was repeatedly flouted during large election rallies, religious gatherings, and even in social functions involving influential persons. This may have fanned the second wave and may still trigger the third wave, which is feared to hit us, as we write this.

Amid all this, a very rapid pace of vaccination for the vast population is continuing, which is our only hope.

3.9.3 *Doctors and other frontline workers*

This narrative will remain incomplete if we do not highlight the role of the COVID-19 Warriors — the doctors, the paramedical staff, the sanitation workers, the police, the ambulance drivers, and even the persons entrusted with the last rites of the deceased. Long before even the vaccines were available, these warriors were placing the public before themselves (Fig. 3.47). As the pandemic spread and engulfed the hospitals, with no definite drugs to treat it, the

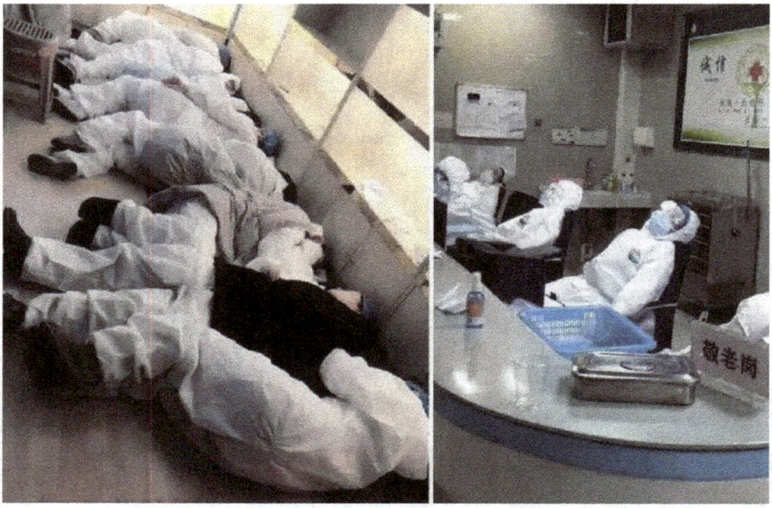

Fig. 3.47 Exhausted nurses and doctors: Battling COVID-19 [55]

outcome for patients remained quite unpredictable. This frustration was coupled with long hours of continuous work by doctors and nurses, many of whom avoided returning home to protect their families. As hospitals ran out of beds, and critical care workers were not enough, many hospitals hurriedly trained specialists like plastic surgeons, and ear, nose, throat specialists to assist them with patient care. Even when the pandemic ebbed, it never left hospitals and this continuous strain — with no end in sight along with the fear of the unknown, unpredictable, and predatory virus — was a great burden for healthcare workers. They also had to wear protective gear for hours at a stretch which is at best most uncomfortable. One can easily imagine their frustration when they see people flouting simple precautions like wearing masks and maintaining social distance, which can at least keep the number of infections down. Many of them made the ultimate sacrifice and we would like to put on record our heartfelt gratitude to them. In fact, every pandemic or disaster invariably puts our medical workers under severe strain.

3.10 Discussions

We must realize that combating pandemics requires robust governance, credible communication, and community engagement for the battle to be won. The response must be aligned with international directives. It should be realized that in the event of a pandemic, governments are required to make several difficult decisions, including decisions about the restriction of the movement of its citizens and allocation of limited resources, by prioritization in favour of those who need it most urgently. This may limit individual freedom. It is hoped that if the actions taken by the government are based on evidence and expert advice and applied equitably, it will meet wholehearted support from people, which plays the most important role in any war on pandemics.

However, this discussion would be grossly inadequate unless we accept that most of the governments across the world have neglected public health, nutrition, education, and civic facilities for too long. These need to be streamlined most urgently.

3.10.1 *Lessons*

Pandemics, like COVID-19, are few and far in between. Are there lessons to be learnt from such pandemics? Pandemics are textbook examples of public risks; everyone is vulnerable to the risk, and everyone is responsible for containing the risk. Who is responsible for protecting the public from the risk? It is usually the government that is seen as responsible for the public good. The government must balance public costs and public good while charting out a strategy to fight the pandemic while putting in place the necessary support systems. As will be discussed later, the government system also has its own disadvantages.

The pandemic brought yet another positive lesson. It proved that if we take a crisis seriously, we can change how we live, almost overnight, in a dramatic manner, globally. It can also encourage governments to apportion huge funds for research and prevention.

It is also important to realize that from plague to smallpox to tuberculosis to COVID-19, international collaboration in health and science has always been blessed with breakthroughs and successes, which would not have taken place, had the countries worked on it alone. Doctors, researchers, engineers, and scientists from all fields of knowledge around the world have worked together tirelessly to confront the coronavirus outbreak with an unprecedented spirit of collaboration.

The first genome of the new virus was published by Chinese and Australian scientists in January 2020. The genetic map was made freely available for access to researchers worldwide. Since then, the virus and its various mutations have been sequenced close to 4,000 times. The much-needed vaccines could not have been made without this valuable knowledge. As a result, researchers, scientists, doctors, and engineers from across the world worked together to confront the virus in a spirit of collaboration. It is known for quite some time [56] that: "There is strength in numbers. We learn more, and faster, together — and the pandemic is underscoring the critical role of international collaboration on the frontiers of science and technology". It has been further argued that we should not retreat into the "world of aggressive competition among states for commercial gain. Not when the global population is so large and interconnected; and not when lifesaving breakthroughs are needed in many places at once". We must add that international collaboration is particularly important considering the gaps in research capabilities within developing countries and the limited ability of many countries to undertake technological horizon-scanning, foresight, and risk assessment.

References

[1] https://en.wikipedia.org/wiki/Plague_of_Justinian.
[2] https://www.history.com/topics/middle-ages/black-death.
[3] Sihn Kyu-hwan, Reorganizing Hospital Space: The 1894 Plague Epidemic in Hong Kong and the Germ Theory, *Korean J. Med. Hist.* **26**, 59–94 (2017).
[4] D. K. Griffith, *Illustrated London News*, July 28, 1894.
[5] https://indianexpress.com/article/research/how-oppressive-containment-measures-during-poona-plague-led-to-assassination-of-british-officer-6450775/.
[6] https://civilaspirant.in/chapekar-brothers/.
[7] R. Chandavarkar, (1992), Plague panic and epidemic politics in India, 1896–1914, in T. Ranger and P. Slack (Eds.), *Epidemics and Ideas: Essays on the Historical Perception of Pestilence* (Past and Present Publications, pp. 203–240). Cambridge: Cambridge University Press.
[8] https://www.montana.edu/historybug/yersiniaessays/godshen.html; https://en.wikipedia.org/wiki/1994_plague_in_India.
[9] https://en.wikipedia.org/wiki/Waldemar_Haffkine.
[10] https://en.wikipedia.org/wiki/The_Plague.
[11] https://www.cdc.gov/smallpox/history/history.html.
[12] https://www.who.int/health-topics/smallpox#tab=tab_1.
[13] A. W. Crosby, Smallpox, in K. F. Kiple (Ed.) *The Cambridge World History of Human Disease* (pp. 1008–1014). Cambridge: Cambridge University (1993).
[14] https://en.wikipedia.org/wiki/Smallpox.
[15] K. Alibek, Smallpox: A disease and a weapon, *Int. J. Infect. Dis.*, **8**S2, S3–S8 (2004); D. A. Anderson *et al.*, Smallpox as a biological weapon, *JAMA* **281**, 2127–2137 (1999); S. Smith, Old tactics, new threat: What is today's risk of smallpox?, *AMA J. Ethics*, Virtual Mentor. **4**(9) (2002).

[16] https://www.cdc.gov/smallpox/index.html.
[17] Spoof by James Gillray (1802), https://en.wikipedia.org/wiki/File:The_cow_pock.jpg.
[18] Adapted from https://blogs.cdc.gov/global/2020/11/20/smallpox-eradication-40th-anniversary/.
[19] https://en.wikipedia.org/wiki/Ronald_Ross.
[20] https://en.wikipedia.org/wiki/Anopheles.
[21] https://www.ebooksread.com/authors-eng/ronald-ross/the-prevention-of-malaria-hci/1-the-prevention-of-malaria-hci.shtml; R. Ross, *The Prevention of Malaria* (pp. 295–296). London: John Murray (1910). See also: R. Ross, *Researches on malaria*, Nobel Lecture (December 12, 1902).
[22] https://www.malariasite.com/ronald-ross/.
[23] https://www.cdc.gov/malaria/about/history/panama_canal.html.
[24] https://www.who.int/news-room/fact-sheets/detail/malaria.
[25] https://www.cdc.gov/dengue/about/index.htm.
[26] S. Bhatt *et al.*, The global distribution and burden of dengue. *Nature* **496**(7446), 504–507 (2013); O. J. Brady *et al.*, Refining the global spatial limits of dengue virus transmission by evidence-based consensus. *PLoS Negl. Trop. Dis.* **6**(8), e1760 (2012).
[27] https://www.who.int/news-room/fact-sheets/detail/dengue-and-severe-dengue.
[28] A. Singh and A. W. Taylor-Robinson, Vector control interventions to prevent dengue: Current situation and strategies for future improvements to management of Aedes in India, *J. Emerg. Infect. Dis.* **2**, 1000123 (2017).
[29] https://www.nvpdcp.gov.in.
[30] https://www.britannica.com/science/cholera/Cholera-through-history; https://en.wikipedia.org/wiki/Cholera_outbreaks_and_pandemics.
[31] https://en.wikipedia.org/wiki/John_Snow.
[32] https://en.wikipedia.org/wiki/Filippo_Pacini.
[33] https://www.who.int/bulletin/volumes/87/2/09-060209/en/; D. Mahalanabis, A. B. Choudhuri, N. G. Bagchi, A. K. Bhattacharya and T. W. Simpson, *Public Health Classic* **1** 105–112 (2012); S. K. Bhattacharya, History of the development of oral rehydration therapy, *Indian J. Public Health* **38**(2) (1994) 39–43.
[34] https://www.who.int/medicines/publications/pharmacopoeia/Oralrehydrationsalts.pdf.
[35] https://www.nhp.gov.in/ors-day_pg.
[36] Weekly epidemiological record, **93**(38), 489–500 (21 September 2018).
[37] https://www.who.int/health-topics/cholera#tab=tab_1.

[38] https://commons.wikimedia.org/wiki/File:Polio_Egyptian_Stele.jpg.
[39] https://amhistory.si.edu/polio/index.htm.
[40] https://en.wikipedia.org/wiki/File:Iron_lungs.JPG.
[41] https://en.wikipedia.org/wiki/Jonas_Salk.
[42] https://en.wikipedia.org/wiki/Albert_Sabin.
[43] https://ourworldindata.org/polio.
[44] See also: https://www.bbc.com/news/world-asia-india-25708715.
[45] https://polioeradication.org/news-post/how-india-eradicated-polio-challenges-and-lessons-learned/.
[46] https://en.wikipedia.org/wiki/The_Sick_Child_(Munch).
[47] https://en.wikipedia.org/wiki/Robert_Koch.
[48] P. Desikan, Sputum smear microscopy in tuberculosis: Is it still relevant?, *Indian J. Med. Res.* **137**(3), 442–444 (2013).
[49] https://en.wikipedia.org/wiki/Albert_Calmette; https://en.wikipedia.org/wiki/Camille_Gu%C3%A9rin.
[50] https://www.who.int/news-room/fact-sheets/detail/tuberculosis.
[51] Engagement readiness and response to coronavirus disease (COVID-19), WHO Interim Guidance, March 19, 2020.
[52] https://en.wikipedia.org/wiki/Herd_immunity.
[53] https://en.wikipedia.org/wiki/Li_Wenliang.
[54] https://en.wikipedia.org/wiki/COVID-19_anti-lockdown_protests_in_the_United_States.
[55] https://www.yeniakit.com.tr/haber/koronavirusu-onlari-da-vurdu-rakamlar-aciklandi-1067298.html.
[56] M. Kituyi, World Economic Forum (May 15, 2020).

Chapter 4

Industrial Accidents

Industrial disasters, by definition, belong to the post-industrial revolution era. The sectors that characterize the present era are energy, transport, manufacturing, and habitat. The ready availability of coal, oil, and natural gas in unprecedented quantities has indeed changed the energy sector. Figure 4.1 shows the global primary energy consumption by source. The increasing role of coal, oil, and natural gas in addressing the global energy needs in the post-industrial revolution era is clearly brought out in the figure. Every form of transport has undergone unprecedented changes. Large-scale

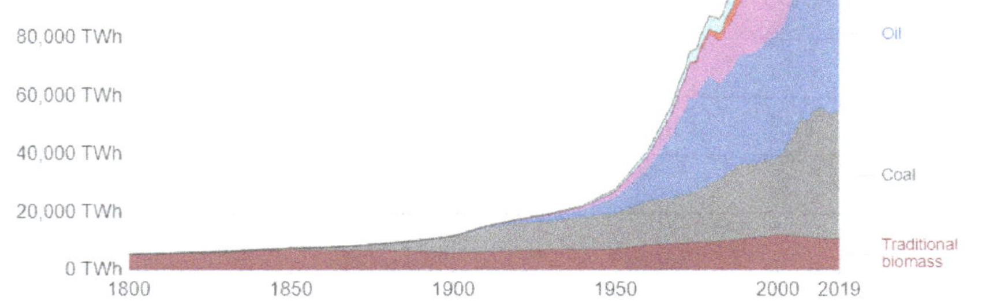

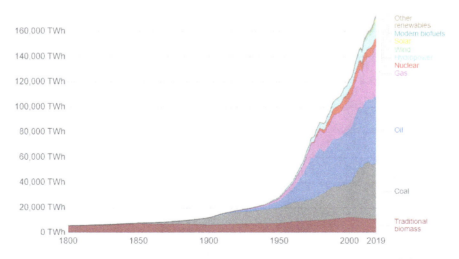

Fig. 4.1 Global primary energy consumption by source [1]

manufacturing is a characteristic of the industrial era. All these sectors have also witnessed accidents, unprecedented in history. Accidents confined within the four walls of the industry are handled internally as part of the professional hazards. However, when the damages go beyond the confines of the industry and affect the public at large, it becomes a public disaster. We shall discuss some typical examples of industrial disasters to illustrate the importance of preparedness for the risks involved and the importance of risk communication to deal with these disasters.

4.1 Coal Mine Accidents

The use of fire distinguishes humans from other animals. While early fuels were primarily wood, charcoal derived from it, straw, and dried dung, coal emerged as the most important primary fuel only in the recent centuries. It will not be an exaggeration to say that the industrial revolution was driven by coal. Even today, coal continues to be the main source of energy globally with the current annual rates of coal mining three to four orders of magnitude greater than the estimated prehistoric annual rates of coal consumption (see Figs. 4.2 and 4.3).

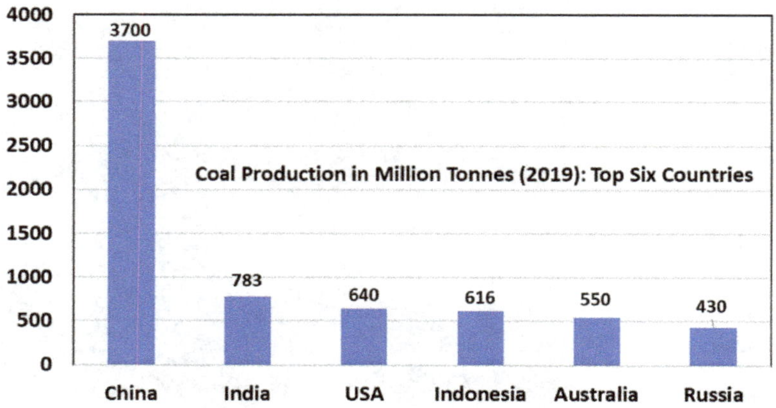

Fig. 4.2 Coal production by top-six coal-producing countries (2019) [2]

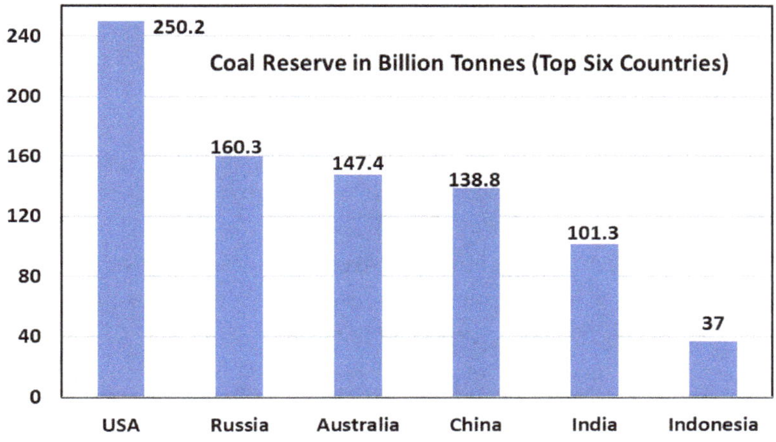

Fig. 4.3 Coal reserves of top six countries [2]

Produced by the compaction and hardening of peat deposits underground over long periods of time, coal has to be mined. However, the mining of coal is a hazardous activity. Mining accidents are quite common during the process of mining coal.

For example, the Benxihu Colliery disaster on April 26, 1942, in China, killed about 1,549 workers and is still considered the worst coal mine accident. It was caused by a fatal explosion of a mixture of coal dust and gas. The ventilation system was shut off and the pit head was sealed by the operator to deprive the underground of oxygen. This in turn resulted in an increase in the carbon monoxide in the mine and was reported to have caused most of the deaths. Nearer home, the Chasnala coal mine accident on December 27, 1975, near Dhanbad killed 375 miners and remains India's deadliest mining accident. It was caused by an explosion that weakened the wall between the mine pit and another abandoned mine above it that was full of water. Among blames and counter-blames, it emerged that possibly the barrier between the two mines had been unsafely thin and that there was inadequate safety equipment. In particular, the mine had no high-pressure pump, and pumps had to be brought in from Russia and Poland to try to pump out the water. By the time the pumps arrived, and all the bodies were recovered over 3 months, most of them had decayed beyond recognition and the persons had to be recognized by the number on the battery lamp. Four mining officials were prosecuted for negligence. By the time the cases were decided at the lower courts 37 years later, two of them had died, and the other two had to pay a fine of INR 5,000 each and a jail term of 1 year. The damages in such coal mine disasters are however confined to the mines and the miners mostly.

Coal-seam fire is yet another fire hazard in coal mine areas. A coal-seam fire is the burning of an underground coal seam or a coal-seam outcrop, ignited by self-heating, lightning, wildfires, etc. (see Fig. 4.4). Coal-seam fire instances date back several million years. Due to thermal insulation and the avoidance of rain/snow extinguishment by the crust, underground coal-seam fires are extremely difficult to control. These are the most persistent fires on earth which can burn for thousands of years.

Considering that the current annual rates of coal mining are three to four orders of magnitude greater than the estimated prehistoric annual rates, it is not surprising that the recent decades have exposed many more fresh coal seams to oxygen, especially while using open cast mining, leading to a proliferation of fires. Some of these can be quite visible on the coalfields. Fires can also erupt in the underground seams, which have large cracks that serve as channels for oxygen to the burning coal. Apart from natural causes

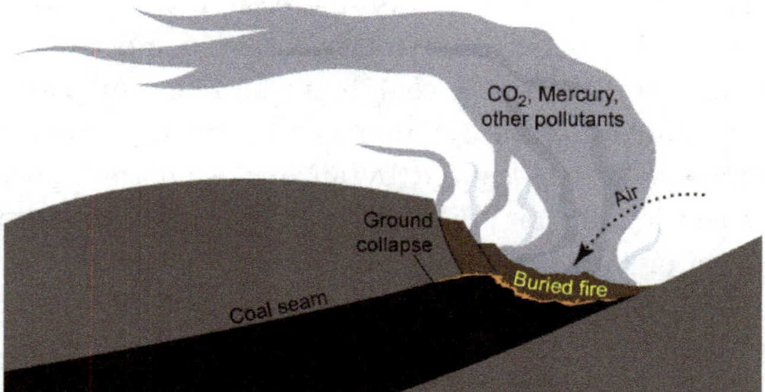

Fig. 4.4 Coal-seam fire [3]

like lightning, human negligence, domestic fires, and lighting fires in abandoned underground mines for heating, etc. can also lead to coal-seam fires. These can generally stop only when the source of the fuel is exhausted. These may also stop when the fire reaches a permanent table of groundwater, or it reaches a depth when the ground can no longer subside and provide an opening or a vent for the carbon dioxide to be released into the atmosphere and fresh air to reach it.

Coal-seam fires have occurred in nearly all parts of the world. One such fire in the Burning Mountain, also known as Mount Wingham or Mount Wingen, has been smouldering (because of limited atmospheric oxygen availability) continuously for the last 6,000 years about 30 m below the surface. It is moving at the rate of about a metre every year towards the south and is believed to have travelled 6.5 km since it started. While the early European settlers in Australia believed it to be volcanic in origin, it has been identified as a coal-seam fire in 1829.

Coal-seam fires also pose a serious health hazard, and they are a cause of concern for the safety of people and property. These release toxic fumes containing carbon mono-oxide, carbon dioxide, sulphur dioxide, mercury, and particulate matter in the atmosphere. These also cause forest fires and lead to subsidence of surface infrastructures, such as homes, buildings, roads, railway tracks, pipelines, electric lines, and bridges.

The measures for controlling coal mine fires include bulldozing, levelling, and covering with soil to prevent the entry of oxygen and to stabilize the land for vegetation. Firefighting generally requires the relocation of a large population, which poses a bigger problem if people have been living there for a long period.

4.1.1 *Coal mine fires in China*

We have seen (Fig. 4.2) that China is the largest coal producer in the world. This keeps bringing more and more fresh seams of coal in contact with oxygen in the air. Thus, China has a serious problem with coal fires. It has been estimated that China loses 10–200 million tonnes of coal to fire every year, and roughly an equivalent amount is made inaccessible to mining annually due to obstruction from the

Fig. 4.5 A surface coal mine fire in Xinjiang, China [3]

fire. China's coal is the best-quality coal in the world. So, when it burns, it is also a great economic loss (see Fig. 4.5).

Besides losses from burned and inaccessible coal, these fires contribute to air pollution and considerably increased levels of greenhouse gas emissions and have thereby become a problem that has gained international attention. The ash and fumes that coal fires spew contain toxins and poisonous gases, including mercury, lead, arsenic carbon monoxide, and sulphur dioxide, which contaminate the air, water, and soil and cause diseases in the population living around the area of the fires.

4.1.2 *Jharia coal mine fire*

Jharia, in Jharkhand, is estimated to have the largest reserve of very good quality coking coal in India (19.4 billion tonnes) [4]. Mining started in Jharia around 1894 and intensified in 1925. The first fire in the mine was noted in 1916. It is believed to have been caused most probably by unsafe and unscientific mining. In 1930, some of the mines collapsed. In those days, coal used to be mined layer by layer, leaving pillars or columns of coal to support the vault. These columns are believed to have collapsed leading to the collapse of the mine. The situation was further aggravated by the 1934 earthquake on the Nepal–Bihar border, having a magnitude of 8.0 on the Richter scale. Several efforts were made to control the fire, with only partial success. By 1938, it was found that there was a raging fire beneath the town with 42 collieries out of 133 on fire. It is estimated that about 40 million tonnes of coal have already been consumed by the fire. It has also been estimated that up to 2 billion tonnes of coal valued at USD 220 billion have been blocked by the fire. The mine fire has led to significant ground subsidence and water and air pollution in local communities, including the city of Jharia (Fig. 4.6). The flames at some of the fires in Jharia occasionally reach a height of 6–18 m and chasms up to 30 m or more deep are reported to have opened suddenly in the middle of a road. Heavy fumes emitted by the fires

Fig. 4.6 A burning coal mine in Jharia [4]

lead to severe health problems such as breathing disorders and skin diseases among the local population.

It has also been suggested that conventionally after open cast mining, areas are supposed to be refilled with sand and water to encourage re-cultivation and prevent accidents. This was perhaps not done properly in Jharia. Thus, exposed coal seams encountered oxygen and ignited. According to Bharat Coking Coal Limited estimates, there are currently 67 fires burning above ground and a huge subterranean fire that never goes out. A recent report suggests that Bharat Coking Coal Limited has recently succeeded in getting control over the Jharia underground fire. The fire, which was spread over 8.9 km^2 during 1994–95, is now confined to only 3.28 km^2.

The authorities have prepared plans to evacuate the people to an area of about 10 km away. But only a few thousand families out of the total 142,000 have moved there — citing lack of means of livelihood and occupation, and inadequate compensation.

Almost all coal-producing countries have coal mine fires though perhaps not of the same ferocity and intensity of fires in north China and Jharia.

4.2 Oil Well and Natural Gas Pipeline Accidents

Apart from coal, oil and natural gas have also evolved as the main fuels of the post-industrial revolution era. Figures 4.7 and 4.8 show the top oil and natural gas producers of the world.

It is also known that offshore oil and gas wells account for nearly 30% of the world production of oil and gas. Offshore wells are also known to be notoriously accident-prone. However, the risks associated with such accidents are in general confined to the persons engaged in the day-to-day operations of the facilities. But there have also been instances when the accidents have a major impact on the public at large and the environment.

An explosion at the BP Deepwater Horizon oil rig took place on April 20, 2010 (Fig. 4.9). It released over 134–206 million gallons (510–780 million litres) of crude oil into the Gulf of Mexico before the well was capped 87 days later on September 19, 2010. The oil

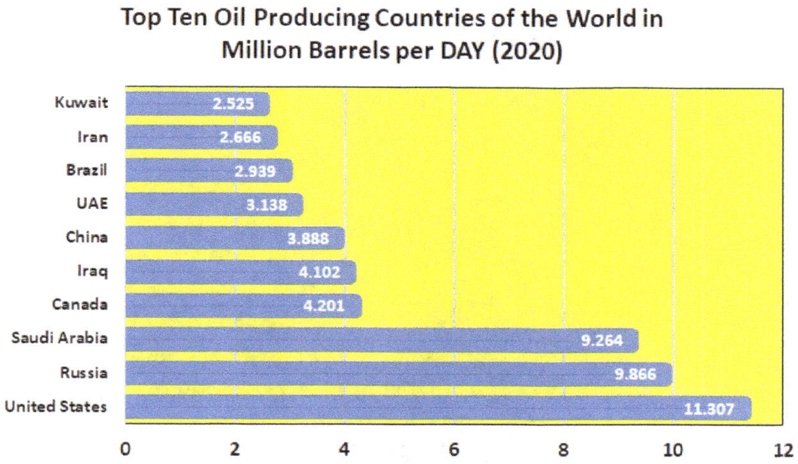

Fig. 4.7 Top 10 oil producers in 2020 [5]

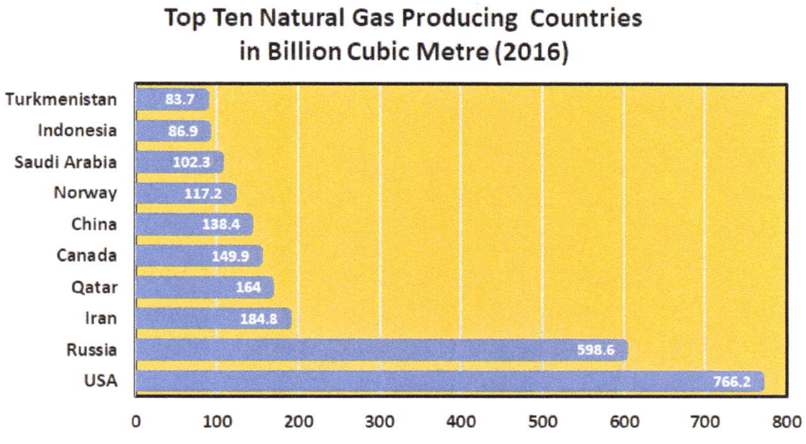

Fig. 4.8 Top 10 natural gas producers in 2016 [6]

well over which the rig was positioned was about 66 km off the coast of Louisiana. It was located on the seabed 1,522 m below the surface of the sea and extended about 5,486 m into the rock. The oil spill covered 68,000–176,100 km^2. It covered more than 2,100 km of the US Gulf Coast in oil. It was the biggest oil spill ever in the US

Fig. 4.9 Deepwater horizon explosion [7]

waters and remains one of the worst environmental disasters in world history.

While 17 rig workers were injured, and 11 workers lost their lives, the oil gushed into one of the planet's most biodiverse marine habitats. An American Geosciences Institute study, as well as others, reported that the spill area hosted 8,332 species, including more than 1,270 species of fish, 604 species of polychaetes, 218 species of birds, 1,456 varieties of molluscs, 1,503 varieties of crustaceans, 4 varieties of rare sea turtles, and 29 species of marine mammals. Thousands of dolphins died within months of the spill, many more were reported to be sick, and the incidence of baby dolphins dying increased considerably. About half of the coral colonies were damaged. A 2017 study estimated that of at least 402,000 sea turtles exposed to oil during the spill, 51% were Kemp's ridley sea turtles, the smallest and most critically endangered species. Up to 1 million birds were estimated to be affected. The livelihood of fishermen, small businesses, and the tourism industry, which depended on the pristine waters and beaches of the Gulf for a livelihood, were also affected. It has been reported that 6 years after the oil spill, the local residents were still suffering from migraines, skin rashes, bloody diarrhoea, bouts of pneumonia, nausea, seizures, muscle cramps, profound depression and anxiety, severe mental fuzziness, and even blackouts (see Fig. 4.10).

Several methods were employed to clean up the oil, which included efforts to contain oil on the surface, dispersal, and removal. Initially, the company employed remotely operated underwater vehicles, 700 workers, 4 aeroplanes, and 32 vessels. On 28 April, the US military joined the cleanup operation and by 29 April, 69 vessels, including skimmers, tugs, barges, and recovery vessels, were in use. By May 4, 2010, the US Coast Guard estimated that 170 vessels and nearly 7,500 personnel were participating, with an additional 2,000 volunteers assisting. In summer 2010, approximately 47,000 people and 7,000 vessels were involved in the response works.

The containment was attempted by deploying many kilometres of containment booms. The booms were used to either corral the

Fig. 4.10 A Brown Pelican covered with oil, Louisiana [7]

oil or to block it from reaching a shrimp/crab/oyster ranch, or a marsh, or mangroves, or other ecologically sensitive areas. Booms extend 0.46–1.22 m above and below the surface of the water but are effective only in calm seas. Ultimately 2,800 km of one-time use sorbent booms (to absorb any remnant of oil like a sponge) and 1,300 km of containment booms were deployed. Skimmer boats were used to remove the oil. Cleanup workers used 5.3 million litres of various chemical dispersants to further break down the oil. This was believed to have helped microbes digest the oil (see Fig. 4.11).

Once the well was capped, the cleanup of the sandy beaches and marshes was attempted. Beaches were mainly cleaned by shifting sand, removing tarballs, and digging out tar mats manually or by using mechanical devices. For marshes, techniques such as vacuum and pumping, low-pressure flush, vegetation cutting, and bioremediation were used.

For years, after the spill injury to fish, turtles, birds, dolphins, and marine animals continued. There are fears that the seabed is

Fig. 4.11 An oil containment boom around new harbor Island, Louisiana [8]

Fig. 4.12 The deepwater horizon oil spill as seen from space [9]

covered with oil and affecting marine life and the food chain. There were reports of cleanup workers falling sick (see Fig. 4.12).

While the initial response of the company was typical of all companies, blaming others for the disaster, in November 2012, the company and the United States Department of Justice settled federal criminal charges, with the company pleading guilty to 11 counts of manslaughter, two misdemeanours, and a felony count of lying to Congress, and paid more than USD 65 billion in criminal and civil penalties, natural resource damages, economic claims, and cleanup costs (see also Ref. [10]).

We add that soon after the spill, President Obama said: "This oil spill is the worst environmental disaster America has ever faced... Make no mistake: we will fight this spill with everything we've got for as long as it takes. We will make BP pay for the damage their company has caused. And we will do whatever's necessary to help the Gulf Coast and its people recover from this tragedy." Interior Secretary Ken Salazar stated: "Our job basically is to keep the boot on the neck of British Petroleum."

4.2.1 *Natural gas pipeline disasters*

While natural gas is often considered a safer fuel to harvest and distribute, an explosion of natural gas did kill nearly 300 children in a school in Texas, USA. The school sat in the middle of a large oil and natural gas field dominated by 10,000 oil derricks, 11 of which stood right on school grounds. The school was routinely using natural gas for its energy needs and as a cost-cutting measure, the school was routinely tapping into the wet-gas lines operated by the oil company that ran near the school. Wet gas is a type of waste gas that is less stable and has more impurities than typical natural gas.

At 3:05 PM on March 18, 1937, a huge and powerful explosion blew the roof off the building and levelled the school. The blast, which came without a warning since natural gas had no smell back then, was felt by people 40 miles away and killed 694 students and 40 teachers instantly; hundreds of injured students were also hauled from the rubble. The exact cause of the spark that ignited the gas was never found, although it is now surmised that the gas could have been ignited by static electricity. As a result of this incident, a *new state law mandating* the usage of mal-odorants in natural gas for commercial and industrial use was put into place. This would provide a warning to anyone in the area of a natural gas leak, and hopefully prevent large casualties such as the ones felt in this explosion [11]. It was also made mandatory to burn the wet gas at the site instead of being piped away.

4.3 Dam Failures

Dams have been built for thousands of years to impound water for diverse purposes such as irrigation, water distribution, and flood control. Dams can also be formed through natural processes such as landslides, glacial moraines, ice, and animal (e.g. otters) activity.

Table 4.1 Countries with the most number of large dams [12]

Country	Number of Dams
China	23,842
United States of America	9,265
India	5,102
Japan	3,116
Brazil	1,392
Korea (Republic of)	1,305
Canada	1,166
South Africa	1,114
Spain	1,082
Turkey	976

Hydroelectricity is the new reason for building dams in the post-industrial revolution era. Presently, hydropower is produced in 150 countries, with the Asia-Pacific region generating almost one-third of the global hydropower. The cost of hydroelectricity is relatively low, making it a competitive source of renewable energy.

The International Commission on Large Dams lists [12] about 40,000 large dams across the world (see, e.g., Table 4.1). Of course, only a small fraction of these are used for the generation of electricity.

China also leads the world in the generation of hydroelectricity (352 GW, 18% of China's overall electricity generation 2018). China plans to add more to this capacity. The Three Gorges Dam is the world's largest dam, with an installed capacity of 22.5 GW. Hydroelectricity is available on demand and can be ramped up and down very fast. Pumped storage is a clean alternative to batteries in the deployment of renewable energies like solar and wind.

Are there risks associated with large dams? Yes, dams can fail. While small earthen dams have the greatest probability to fail due to poor design, poor construction and poor quality of the materials used, the common modes of failure of large dams are as follows:

- extreme runoff into the reservoirs from rain, snowmelt, or an upstream dam failure;

- natural phenomena, such as earthquakes and landslides; a special case is a glacial lake outburst flood where glacial dams (ice-dammed or moraine-dammed) fail leading to a large release of water;
- human error, including poor design and/or poor maintenance.

The numbers of dams given in Table 4.1 emphasize the extent of risk which mankind faces, in case these dams fail.

Let us look at three major dam failures, which have important lessons for the study of risks.

4.3.1 *Banqiao Dam, China*

Banqiao Dam failure took place in 1975 in China. It led to the collapse of 62 dams, including the Banqiao Dam, in Henan, China under the influence of Typhoon Nina, which dumped 1,060 mm within 3 days in the Huai River basin. The dam failure led to a flood that affected a total population of 10.15 million, inundating around 30 cities and counties of 12,000 km^2. The estimated death toll ranged from 26,000 to 240,000. The flood also caused the collapse of 6.8 million houses (see Fig. 4.13).

It remains one of the largest and most destructive dam failures in recent times.

Fig. 4.13 Banqiao dam failure (China, 1975)

4.3.2 *Machchhu dam failure*

Conceived by the Maharaja of Morbi before India got its independence, two dams Machchhu-1 and Machchhu-2 were constructed on the Machchhu river in Gujarat, in 1959 and 1972, respectively. The Machchhu-2 was downstream, with a catchment area of 1,929 km^2. It was an earth-fill dam, and its primary purpose was to impound water. Saurashtra region is a drought-prone area, and the dam was meant to serve as an irrigation scheme and not flood control. The dam had a masonry spillway of 206 m consisting of 18 sluice gates in the river section and earthen embankments on both sides.

Very heavy rains on August 11, 1979, led to a flow of 16,307 m^3/s, three times what the dam was designed for, and led to its collapse. The 762 m of the left embankment and 365 m of the right embankment of the dam collapsed, and within 20 min, low-lying areas of the Morbi industrial town 5 km down the dam were inundated in 4–9-m-high floodwaters (see Fig. 4.14).

The tremendous swirling flow of water struck the town around 3:30 PM, and within 15 min, the low-lying areas were under 6 m of water, which stayed for the next 6 h.

A warning had been sent out through the All-India Radio broadcast around noon instructing people to move to higher ground

Fig. 4.14 The Machchhu-2 dam after failure [13]

because of potential issues at the dam. Approximately 90,000 acre-feet (about 27,000 acre-metres) of water joined the already heavy flow from the river and rushed into the small town of Lilapar (closer to the dam), completely inundating all the buildings in the town. Thankfully, the people of Lilapar had largely heeded the early warning.

On the other hand, few in the much larger town of Morbi, further downstream, gave heed to the warning. Flooding during the monsoon season was not uncommon and many people assumed this flood would not be much different than past floods and failed to grasp the magnitude of the disaster. Because of this, many refused to evacuate or did not evacuate to high enough ground. In Morbi, the flood water destroyed buildings, killed livestock, and took 1,800–25,000 lives. One of the reasons for the large variation in the number is that large mass graves were burned to keep diseases from spreading before proper records or any identification could be completed.

Authorities immediately declared it as an act of God and unforeseeable, and attributed it to the abnormal rainfall of 20 inches which was recorded in 16 h — when that is the normal record for the whole year. Due to difficulties in reaching the city, the relief work could start only on August 13.

A report in a newspaper summed up the situation in the following words: "Considered in perspective the Morbi disaster contains some of the chronic ingredients of everyday inefficiency: a communication system perpetually on the verge of near-collapse, depleted power reserves, virtual lack of organised administration, and an inept bureaucracy that is almost always caught unawares and almost never equipped to mobilise itself quickly enough" [14].

Till the death toll of the 1975 Banqiao Dam failure was declassified in 2005, the Morbi dam failure was listed as the worst dam burst in the Guinness Book of Records.

4.3.3 *Italy's Vajont dam disaster*

The Vajont dam was conceived in the 1920s and eventually built between 1957 and 1960 as a part of an extensive network of dams, powerhouses and tunnels constructed for hydroelectric power generation in Italy. During the first filling, there were differing opinions on whether the reservoir bank along Mount Toc was the site of an ancient rockslide. A local newspaper published an article suggesting that landslides were recurrent near the dam site and increased the likelihood of a disaster. This created a reaction with the public and shortly after, legal action was taken against the newspaper for spreading false news and disturbing the peace. Residents were assured of safety, but they continued to distrust the stability of Mount Toc. Dam construction was completed in September 1960.

On October 9, 1963, during the initial filling, a landslide caused a mega-tsunami in the lake in which 50 million cubic metres of water overtopped the dam in a 250-m-high wave, leading to the complete destruction of several villages and towns and 1,917 deaths. Although the dam itself remained almost intact, and two-thirds of the water was retained behind it, the landslide was much larger than expected and the impact brought massive flooding and destruction to the Piave Valley below [15].

4.3.4 *Dams in The Himalayas*

The Himalayas are much younger and more fragile mountains. Yet, a string of dams has been constructed in the seismologically sensitive zone. The Tehri Dam was constructed in the teeth of opposition by Late Sunder Lal Bahuguna, famous for his "Chipko Movement" (a peaceful agitation, where village women held on to trees to oppose their being felled) for saving the trees and the people of Tehri, whose houses were submerged. The Tehri Dam is in the central Himalayan seismic gap which is a major geologic fault zone. An earthquake with a magnitude of 6.8 had taken place in October 1991, with an epicentre just 53 km from the dam. Officials claim that the complex is designed to withstand an earthquake of magnitude 8.4, but some seismologists say that earthquakes with a magnitude of 8.5 or more could occur in this region. In the case of such a calamity, up to half a million or more people would be in danger. Already, the flow in the Bhagirathi River downstream is considerably reduced and even stops occasionally, leading to ecological issues and religious anxiety as the river develops into the holiest river of India, Ganga, after its confluence with the Alaknanda river.

Before closing this discussion, we add that there are suggestions that global warming and climate change are likely to considerably increase the incidents of severe droughts and excessive rains and the latter will put all the dams in the world under strain.

4.4 Transport and Chemical Industry Accidents

Transport accidents involve road, rail, air, and ship. Increasing speed, increasing capacity, and increasing automation including driverless vehicles are adding to the accident risks. However, the research and developments in accident prevention have also reached unprecedented levels, which are further assisted by detailed computer simulations, making travels safer if preventive maintenance is scrupulously followed. One may cite the example of a thorough check of aeroplanes as well as the alertness of the pilots before a flight is cleared for take-off.

4.4.1 *Road accidents*

The first cars of the world were built in 1886 by Karl Benz. It is estimated that today, over one billion passenger cars traverse the streets and roads of the world. While rigid traffic rules are enforced across many parts of the world, the bulk of the developing part of the world gives a very low priority to the enforcement of traffic rules. As was mentioned earlier, the risks of traffic accidents are accepted as unavoidable. It is also reported that approximately 1.3 million people die each year because of road accidents.

Is road travel safe? Yes, with some risks.

4.4.2 *Train accidents*

Trains have been around for over 200 years. While largely safe, the physical power and sheer weight of trains make train accidents devastating. The 2004 Sri Lanka rail accident following the tsunami is perhaps the largest train disaster in world history by death toll with 1,700 fatalities or more. Closer home, the Bihar train disaster in June 1981 resulted in 500–800 deaths. The accident occurred when the train was travelling on a bridge when the driver suddenly braked causing seven of the nine compartments to plummet into a swelling river.

Is travel by train safe? Yes, with some risks.

4.4.3 *Ship accidents*

Sailboats and ships have been the mainstay of international trade since time immemorial. Travel by sea has always carried an element of risk. The advent of steam engines brought a change in the volume of sea travel, including pleasure travel. While some disasters like the sinking of the Royal Mail Ship Titanic in April 1912 have captured the popular imagination, many others involving a significantly greater loss and life have remained relatively unknown.

The deadliest civilian maritime disaster took place on December 20, 1987. A passenger ferry collided with an oil tanker in the Tablas Strait, south of Manila. An estimated 4,300 people were on board the ferry, far more than the official capacity of the ferry. The collision ignited the 8,800 barrels of oil and gasoline on the oil tanker and both the vessels were quickly engulfed in the blaze. Of the passengers and crew on both the vessels, just 26 people were rescued from the oil-slicked waters.

Is a sea cruise safe? Yes, with some risks.

4.4.4 *Aviation accidents*

Civil aviation is one of the gifts of the twentieth century to humanity. Together with the developments in communication technology, this has shrunk the world into a global village. This has not come without a cost. Despite a very rigorous safety regulation system in place, the aviation industry has witnessed several severe accidents in the past few decades. Thus, in 1985, the Japan Airlines Flight 123 accident led to 520 fatalities, while earlier in 1977, the Tenerife airport disaster involving a collision of two Boeing 747's led to 583 fatalities.

Closer home — Charkhi Dadri mid-air collision — remains the world's deadliest mid-air collision. It occurred on November 12, 1996, and involved a mid-air collision between Saudia Flight 763 and Kazakhstan Airlines Flight 1907 over Charkhi Dadri. All the 349 passengers and crew onboard the two aircraft perished.

Is air travel safe? Yes, but with some risks.

4.4.5 *Chemical industry accidents*

The chemical industry is one of the most vulnerable to accidents. For example, unsafe storage of large amounts (2,750 tonnes) of ammonium nitrate led to a severe explosion in Beirut on August 4, 2020, killing more than 178 people, injuring more than 6,500 people, rendering 300,000 people homeless, and severely damaging critical health infrastructure and medical supplies. This acted as an awakening call for storage of a vast quantity of ammonium nitrate in Chennai and a disaster was averted. Unsafe practices, including employment of child workers, in the fireworks industry in some parts of the country do lead to unfortunate accidents almost every year.

4.5 The Bhopal Gas Disaster

"Of course, it was a multinational that caused this catastrophe. Of course, they will deny causing it. Of course, it was a very poor and powerless population that was hit. Of course, they will not get the support to which they should have the right." — Dr Ingrid Eckerman, Member International Medical Commission on Bhopal gas disaster [16].

The above quote embodies the first reactions of Dr Ingrid Eckerman, upon seeing the images of the Bhopal gas disaster. She was later inducted as a member of the International Medical Commission on Bhopal and authored a well-researched book, *The Bhopal Saga — Causes and Consequences of the World's Largest Industrial Disaster*, which appeared on the twentieth anniversary of the disaster.

On December 3, 1984, human error led to the escape of more than 40 tonnes of toxic gas from the (former) Union Carbide pesticide factory in Bhopal: 574,000 people were exposed to the poison and up to 25,000 of them died. Some 150,000 residents in the region developed chronic health conditions. This remains the *most tragic industrial accident in the history of the world to date.* The numbers that are given here vary according to the authorities of different wings of administration, hospitals, and charitable organizations which stepped forward to try to bring relief to the people of Bhopal.

It had been brought to the notice of the authorities, already in 1975, that the thickly populated slums so close to the chemical plant posed serious environmental hazards (see Fig. 4.15).

Several detailed minute-by-minute accounts of the event leading to the disaster have been reconstructed and reported by various authors [16]. We quote the report by Edward Broughton in the following [18]:

"At 11.00 PM on December 2, 1984, while most of the one million residents of Bhopal slept, an operator at the plant noticed a small leak of methyl isocyanate (MIC) gas and increasing pressure inside a storage tank. The vent-gas scrubber, a safety device designed to neutralize toxic discharge from the MIC system, had been turned off three weeks earlier. Apparently, a faulty valve had allowed one

Fig. 4.15 The Tank No. 610, which leaked (removed from its location during cleanup) [17]

tonne of water for cleaning internal pipes to mix with forty tonnes of MIC. A 30-tonne refrigeration unit that normally served as a safety component to cool the MIC storage tank had been drained of its coolant for use in another part of the plant. Pressure and heat from the vigorous exothermic reaction in the tank continued to build. The gas flare safety system was out of action and had been for three months. At around 1.00 AM, December 3, loud rumbling reverberated around the plant as a safety valve gave way, sending a plume of MIC gas into the early morning air. Within hours, the streets of Bhopal were littered with human corpses and the carcasses of buffaloes, cows, dogs, and birds. An estimated 3,800 people died immediately, mostly in the poor slum colony adjacent to the UCC plant. Local hospitals were soon overwhelmed with the injured, a crisis further compounded by a lack of knowledge of exactly what gas was involved and what its effects were.... Estimates of the number of people killed in the first few days by the plume from the UCC plant run as high as 10,000, with 15,000 to 20,000 premature deaths reportedly occurring in the subsequent two decades. The Indian government reported that more than half a million people were exposed to the gas."

A non-exhaustive list of the problems faced by survivors is given in Tables 4.2 and 4.3 [16], and hundreds of thousands of victims continue to suffer the painful ill effects of the exposure to methyl isocyanate.

Table 4.2 Health effects of the Bhopal methyl isocyanate gas leak exposure, early effects (0–6 months)

Ocular	Chemosis, redness, watering, ulcers, photophobia
Respiratory	Distress, pulmonary oedema, pneumonitis, pneumothorax.
Gastrointestinal	Persistent diarrhoea, anorexia, persistent abdominal pain.
Genetic	Increased chromosomal abnormalities
Psychological	Neuroses, anxiety states, adjustment reactions
Neurobehavioral	Impaired audio and visual memory, impaired vigilance attention and response time, impaired reasoning, and spatial ability, impaired psychomotor coordination

Table 4.3 Health effects of the Bhopal methyl isocyanate gas leak exposure, lafe effects (6 months onwards)

Ocular	Persistent watering, corneal opacities, chronic conjunctivitis
Respiratory	Obstructive and restrictive airway disease and decreased lung function
Reproductive	Increased pregnancy loss, increased infant mortality, decreased placental/fetal weight
Genetic	Increased chromosomal abnormalities
Neurobehavioral	Impaired associate learning, motor speed, precision

It is not surprising that the Bhopal gas tragedy is considered one of the worst industrial disasters. It is also painful to note that the relief and redressal efforts following the disaster were even more disappointing.

In a settlement mediated by the Indian Supreme Court, the company accepted moral responsibility and agreed to pay USD 470 million to the Indian Government to be distributed to claimants as a full and final settlement. The figure was partly based on the disputed claim that only 3,000 people died and 102,000 suffered permanent disabilities. By the end of October 2003, according to the Bhopal Gas Tragedy Relief and Rehabilitation Department, compensation had been awarded to 554,895 people for injuries received and 15,310 survivors of those killed. The average amount to families of the dead was a paltry sum of USD 2,200.

The company discontinued its operations at its Bhopal plant following the disaster. However, it did not clean up the site of the plant completely. The plant continues to leak several toxic chemicals and heavy metals which have now started contaminating local aquifers. Dangerously contaminated water is one more legacy of the company for the people of Bhopal (see Fig. 4.16).

4.5.1 *Lessons from Bhopal*

The Bhopal gas disaster revealed that expanding industrialization in developing countries without strict adherence to modern safety regulations and a culture of safety is bound to have catastrophic

Fig. 4.16 Deteriorating condition of the methyl isocyanate plant, 2008 [19]

consequences. It is essential that international standards and monitoring procedures are evolved and strictly applied to companies performing hazardous activities such as the manufacture of pesticides and similar toxic chemical products. It is also essential that national governments, as well as international monitoring agencies, focus on enforcing a uniform standard of corporate responsibility and accident prevention for advanced industrial nations and the developing world.

It is also important that local governments minimize the risks by not permitting the industrial facilities to be situated within urban areas, and ensure that the land use does not get altered over time and bring a large population near the industry, which is what happened at Bhopal. The industries and the governments should also develop the local medical and civic facilities to minimize hardships in case of a problem.

4.6 Pesticides and Insecticides

It was also expected that India may give serious thought to the abolition of the practice of the large-scale usage of pesticides after

Fig. 4.17 Biomagnification of toxins in food chain [20]

the Bhopal gas tragedy. Perhaps the pressure to feed 1,300 million persons and the rising population has limited India's options. Some studies have estimated that more than 3 million people per year suffer pesticide poisoning and more than 20,000 deaths are caused by this every year.

4.6.1 *The DDT story*

Dichlorodiphenyltrichloroethane (DDT) was developed in the 1940s. It was initially used with great success to combat malaria, typhus, and other insect-borne human diseases. However, many pest species developed resistance to it, forcing one to use larger amounts of it. More importantly, it started poisoning the entire food chain, killing off bugs, worms, birds, fish, and finally mankind [21] (see Fig. 4.17).

DDT was banned in the United States in 1972 and then gradually in most of the western world. The Stockholm Convention adopted in 2004 restricted its use to eliminate mosquitoes. China stopped its production in 2007. The proposal to ban its usage beyond 2020 has been opposed by India, which is the only country still producing it.

4.6.2 *The Endosulfan story*

Endosulfan, a highly toxic pesticide that causes severe health problems, first came to notice in Kerala from its usage in cashew plantations and was banned in Kerala in 2001. A nationwide ban was opposed by politicians with the excuse of loss of jobs, and a complete ban could only be imposed by 2017.

4.6.3 *Asbestos*

Asbestos is a naturally occurring, fibrous material that has been in use for different purposes since prehistoric times. It is now known that exposure to asbestos through inhalation of fibres in the air in the working environment, ambient air in the vicinity of point sources such as factories handling asbestos, or indoor air in housing and buildings containing friable (crumbly) asbestos materials is a health hazard. The World Health Organization estimates that about 125 million people in the world are exposed to asbestos at the workplace. In the year 2004, for example, 107,000 deaths were attributed to exposure to asbestos. Sixty countries have already banned the use of asbestos. Even though the Supreme Court of India banned its use on January 21, 2011, it is still being widely used across India. India was the biggest importer of asbestos valued at USD 181 million in 2019, to be used in cement roofing sheets, cement piping, friction materials, textiles, insulation and even use by railways and armed forces.

4.7 Nuclear Power Plant Accidents

Nuclear power plant accidents similar to those at Chernobyl and Fukushima have ecological consequences covering large areas and involving large populations. These also receive wide coverage and are traditionally investigated in great depth, and enough details are easily available in the literature. We shall cover them only briefly here.

The Chernobyl disaster was caused by a nuclear accident that occurred on April 26, 1986, in the Chernobyl Nuclear Power Plant in Ukraine. The accident started during a safety test to simulate an electrical outage to aid the development of a safety procedure for maintaining the reactor cooling water circulation until the backup electrical generators could provide power. A combination of unstable conditions and reactor design faults caused an uncontrolled chain reaction, resulting in the release of a large amount of energy vaporizing superheated cooling water and a steam explosion rupturing the reactor core. An open-air reactor core fire released considerable airborne radioactive contamination for about 9 days that precipitated onto parts of the USSR and Western Europe [22]. Less than 100 deaths were attributed directly to the accident, while the estimates of people succumbing due to exposure in the later decades are debated. As a result of rising ambient radiation levels off-site, a 10-km radius exclusion zone was created 36 h after the accident. About 49,000 people were evacuated from the area. The exclusion zone was later extended to 30 km when a further 68,000 people were evacuated from the wider area. The initial emergency response, together with later decontamination of the environment, ultimately involved more than 500,000 personnel and cost an estimated USD 68 billion. There has been a marked recovery of the forested area around the site and an increase in wildlife, though it is not certain that the trees and animals are contaminated or sick.

The Fukushima Daiichi Nuclear Power Plant accident was triggered by a powerful earthquake and an ensuing tsunami in March 2011. Eleven reactors at four nuclear power plants were operating in the region at the time of the earthquake and all shut down automatically when the earthquake hit. The reactors proved robust seismically but vulnerable to the tsunami. The 15-m tsunami disabled the on-site backup generators and the heat exchangers for dumping reactor waste heat and decay heat to the sea. Three reactors suffered a core meltdown, while one suffered structural damage following a hydrogen explosion.

Repeated warnings, including one by IAEA, to shift the emergency diesel generators (to power the pumps that would ensure circulation of coolant to remove decay heat after the reactor shutdown) to a higher level were ignored by the operators. Very few lives (just 1) were lost which could be attributed to nuclear radiation, though several were injured due to fire caused by hydrogen blast, while about 19,500 persons lost their lives due to the tsunami. Over 100,000 persons were evacuated from their homes as a preventive measure. It has been estimated that the cleanup may cost USD 470–600 billion and take several decades [22].

Unfortunately, both these accidents have pushed back the deployment of nuclear technology for satisfying our electricity needs, our most potent and green instrument against global warming caused by using fossil fuels [23]. The response of countries across the world to these accidents has also been very diverse. One of the first steps taken by Japan was to revamp the safety systems in the nuclear industry. Based on detailed safety reviews, several reactors were permanently shut down. Recognizing that Japan's geographical constraints do not allow the country to fully make a transition to renewable energies, many reactors were also restarted following safety reviews. Already in 2019, nuclear energy was providing 7.5% of Japan's electricity. By 2030, Japan aspires to achieve 22–24% of its energy from renewables, 20–22% from nuclear and the remaining from fossil fuels. Substantial emphasis is also being laid on energy efficiency. Responses of some countries like Germany were almost panic reactions. Within a few days after the Fukushima disaster, the German Government embarked on an "exit" plan from nuclear energy. Germany is already committed to an exit from hydrocarbons in the next few years. This is not going to come without a cost. The impact of these on the German industries has not been insignificant. India, Russia, China, and South Korea have recognized that nuclear power will remain necessary to plug the gaps left by renewables in the energy mix of the future and are moving forward with their nuclear energy programmes while strengthening their safety and security infrastructures. Countries like the USA and Canada are keeping an "open mind". With very few nuclear reactors under construction in the last several decades or being planned, their nuclear education, research, and industries are indeed losing their leadership positions in nuclear technology.

It is worthwhile mentioning that nuclear accidents similar to those in Chernobyl and Fukushima may not have taken place if internationally accepted safety norms had been followed strictly.

4.8 Discussions

The list of industrial disasters that we have discussed above is nowhere near exhaustive. Our choice is purely based on our personal assessments on whether there are lessons to be learnt from those disasters. Many of them have led to better safety and regulatory norms in those sectors. As we shall see later, the safety of nuclear installations across the world is regularly monitored by independent regulatory agencies. In India, the Atomic Energy Regulatory Board has the mandate to ensure safety and security in nuclear installations. Unfortunately, for other sectors of industry, there are no such structures with focussed mandates. Some industrial disasters are also caused by cost-cutting measures in design and construction, poor training of the operators, and insufficient information to the public. Often no drills are conducted to educate the people who may have started living nearby. The inadequacy of health infrastructure is yet another problem. A casual and lackadaisical attitude of employers can also lead to accidents. In today's environment, security must remain the highest priority to thwart acts of sabotage or terrorism. We have also seen that in the case of disasters like a cyclone or a dam failure, the power and communication infrastructure are the ones that fail first but are the ones that are badly needed for rescue and relief.

It is also felt that a specialized force can be created and trained to manage industrial disasters along the lines of the National Disaster Response Force for rescue and relief in case of natural disasters.

References

[1] OurWorldInData.org/energy.
[2] https://www.nsenergybusiness.com/features/six-largest-coal-producing-countries/.
[3] https://en.wikipedia.org/wiki/Coal-seam_fire.
[4] https://en.wikipedia.org/wiki/Jharia_coalfield.
[5] https://en.wikipedia.org/wiki/List_of_countries_by_oil_production.
[6] https://en.wikipedia.org/wiki/List_of_countries_by_natural_gas_production.
[7] https://en.wikipedia.org/wiki/Deepwater_Horizon_explosion.

[8] https://en.wikipedia.org/wiki/Deepwater_Horizon_oil_spill_response.
[9] NASA, https://en.wikipedia.org/wiki/Deepwater_Horizon_oil_spill.
[10] Additional literature about BP Oil Spill: https://en.wikipedia.org/wiki/Deepwater_Horizon_oil_spill; A. M. Kanso, R. A. Nelson and P. J. Kitchen, BP and the Deepwater Horizon oil spill: A case study of how company management employed public relations to restore a damaged brand, *J. Mark. Commun.* **26**(7), 703–731 (2020), DOI: 10.1080/13527266.2018.1559218; R. Pallardy, https://www.britannica.com/event/Deepwater-Horizon-oil-spill; W. Burggren, B. Dubansky, A. Roberts and M. Alloy, Deepwater Horizon Oil Spill as a case study for interdisciplinary cooperation within developmental biology, environmental sciences and physiology, *World J. Eng. Technol.* **3**, 7–23 (2015), DOI: 10.4236/wjet.2015.34C002; Deepwater: The Gulf Oil Disaster and Future of Offshore Drilling, Report to the President, https://www.govinfo.gov/content/pkg/GPO-OILCOMMISSION/pdf/GPO-OILCOMMISSION.pdf.
[11] https://www.history.com/this-day-in-history/natural-gas-explosion-kills-schoolchildren-in-texas.
[12] damfailures.org, https://www.icold-cigb.org.
[13] https://en.wikipedia.org/wiki/1979_Machchhu_dam_failure.
[14] https://www.indiatoday.in/magazine/special-report/story/19790915-after-devastating-floods-morvi-looks-like-a-ghost-town-facing-resurrection-after-death-822549-2014-02-22.
[15] https://en.wikipedia.org/wiki/Vajont_Dam.
[16] I. Eckerman, *The Bhopal Saga — Causes and Consequences of the World's Largest Industrial Disaster*. University Press, Hyderabad, India (2004).
[17] https://en.wikipedia.org/wiki/Bhopal_disaster.
[18] E. Broughton, The Bhopal disaster and its aftermath: a review, *Environ. Health* **4**, 6 (2005), doi: 10.1186/1476-069X-4-6 and references therein.
[19] https://en.wikipedia.org/wiki/Bhopal_disaster.
[20] See e.g., https://en.wikipedia.org/wiki/Biomagnification.
[21] R. Carson, *Silent Spring*. Houghton Muffin Boston, USA (1962).
[22] See, D. K. Srivastava and V. S. Ramamurthy, *Climate Change and Energy Options for a Sustainable Future*. Singapore: World Scientific (2020).
[23] V. S. Ramamurthy and D. K. Srivastava, Seventy-five years after Hiroshima, *Sci. Cult.* **87**, 4–9 (2021).

Chapter 5

New and Emerging Technologies

We are living in an era of rapidly evolving science and technologies. While the eighteenth century industrial revolution is often identified as the beginning of this era, it is the twentieth century that saw several path-breaking scientific discoveries and new technologies arising out of them in quick succession. In a matter of a few decades, we have seen the emergence of nuclear technology, space technology, computer and communication technologies, genetic engineering, and several others. These technologies in turn have led to several new products and services that have really changed the way in which we live. In fact, one can say that today there is no aspect of human life that has been left untouched by these new technology products and services in some form or another.

In general, any new product or service that arises out of new technology starts off as the "luxury of the rich" — exclusive and overpriced. However, their penetration into the marketplace depends on their socio-economic implications. Products and services that are not found economically viable or socially acceptable disappear from the market in course of time. Aluminium, for example, when first isolated in the 1820s, was more expensive than gold. It is believed that Napoleon-III had a prized set of aluminium cutleries for his special guests, while the others used gold knives and forks. In ancient times, initially, only the members of the royal family in China were allowed to wear silk. The privilege was extended to the noble classes later, but only royals could wear 'royal yellow silk'. Over a period, both aluminium and silk lost their exclusivity and became part of the market.

Telephones are one of the technological marvels of the industrialized world and have shrunk the world into a global village. The first telephone exchange came into existence in 1877–1878 in the US though the idea for a telephone had come almost two decades earlier. By the mid-twentieth century, more than 100 million telephone subscriber lines were functional across the globe. Telephones entered India with telephone exchanges in Mumbai (Bombay), Chennai (Madras), and Kolkata (Calcutta) within a few years of its invention and all the major cities and towns in the country were linked with telephones during the British period itself before India became independent. However, telephones were always seen as a luxury in India — limited to the Government, the business establishments, and the creamy layers of society. While the total number of telephones in 1948 numbered around 80,000 post-independence, the growth remained slow because the telephone continued to be seen more as a status symbol, a luxury of the rich, rather than being an instrument of utility and development. The number of telephones grew leisurely to a few million in the late eighties when, under Prime Minister Rajiv Gandhi, focussed efforts were launched not only to increase the number of lines but also to reach out into rural India. The Rural Telephone Exchange initiative in the eighties was perhaps the first effort to take telephony to the people in India. However, before the initiative could mature, it was overtaken by mobile phone technology. Mobile phones entered India in the mid-nineties when a telephonic conversation took place between the erstwhile Union Telecom Minister, Mr Sukh Ram, and the Chief Minister of West Bengal, Mr Jyoti Basu, on July 31, 1995. The perception that the telephone is a luxury of the rich continued in the mobile era also. There was indeed a government directive that no mobile phones were to be made available to Government servants at any level without explicit approval by a very high-level committee. However, within a very short time, the advantages of mobile phones were realized by everyone, rich or poor, urban, or rural, and both the networks and the clientele expanded at unprecedented rates.

The rural penetration even surpassed the urban penetration. Today, India's telecommunication network is the second largest in the world by the number of telephone users with more than a billion subscribers and the world's second largest internet user base. The mobile network forms the backbone of the e-revolution that is taking place in all sectors in the country from education to employment to entertainment.

The telephone story in India is a classic example of new technology penetration — Accessible, Affordable, and Acceptable — the three "A"-s of successful technologies. Twentieth century and beyond are full of new technologies and technology-based products and services. However, not all products that appear in the market display the kind of dramatic acceptability of mobile phones. We have seen products that are available in one part of the world but are not accessible to the public in another part of the world, the so-called dual technology products. We have seen products that are readily available but not affordable to most people. Even products that are Accessible and Affordable may not be Acceptable, for example, for reasons of perceived risks associated with the widespread use of the product. Such products disappear from the market in due course of time. Even in the seventeenth and eighteenth centuries, the nobles in Europe used Venetian ceruse, a paint obtained by mixing lead, water, and vinegar to paint their faces and skin white. In course of time, it was realized that this practice caused lead poisoning which in turn affected their skins and caused loss of hair and even death, and the practice disappeared. At the individual level, one always carries out a cost–benefit–risk analysis and accepts or rejects the product. When it is a question of public risks, the government is expected to put in place measures that balance public costs, public good, and public risks through fiscal, regulatory or any other measures. Often, the full potential of the new technology products and the risks associated with them are rarely understood in full right in the beginning. They may be still emerging.

It is illustrative to look at some historical examples of how human society has handled new technology products that carried some public risks.

5.1 X-Ray Radiography

One of the earliest examples of new technology applications is X-ray radiography. The potential of X-rays for radiography became apparent almost simultaneously with its discovery in 1895. However, the hazards associated with overexposure to radiation became known only over a course of time. In the beginning, patients were given very long exposures to locate fractures, bullets, foetuses, etc. The doctors also were not taking precautions and were exposing themselves to high levels of radiation [1].

The medical journal *The Lancet* published an article in 1896, proposing radiation exposure as an alternative to beard shaving, and special salons were set up around the turn of the century which were also frequented by women to get rid of their body hair. At one time, more than 75 such salons operated in the United States. It is estimated that tens of thousands of women across the USA and Canada may have taken X-ray treatments and many of them may have developed cancer. The American Medical Institute condemned the practice in 1929 and these salons were shut down in 1930. X-rays were also used from the 1920s to about the 1950s to determine properly fitting shapes for shoes for individuals, providing enough space to move toes inside the shoes and to avoid putting undue pressure on fingers.

While the early discussions did centre on a ban on the use of X-rays for radiography of any kind, it was soon realized that the balance of advantage lay in the sensible use of the technology for the public good. This was the beginning of the evolution of radiation safety standards, and today the regulatory system for implementing radiation protection standards is one of the most advanced and forms the backbone of the nuclear industry.

5.2 The Thalidomide Tragedy

Another historical example of our learning from experience is the thalidomide tragedy. Thalidomide is an immunomodulatory drug that was developed and first sold in West Germany in 1957. Primarily prescribed as a sedative to cure anxiety, insomnia, etc., it was also used against nausea and morning sickness in pregnant women. During this period, the use of medications during pregnancy was not strictly controlled, and drugs were not thoroughly tested for potential harm to the foetus. Thousands of pregnant women took the drug to relieve their symptoms. There soon appeared reports of findings of abnormalities in children being born, which were traced back to the use of the drug thalidomide. It was estimated that the drug led to the death of approximately 2,000 children and serious birth defects in more than 10,000 children. Thalidomide was taken off the market soon after due to massive pressure from the public and the press. The thalidomide experience globally led to more rigorous drug approval procedures. Thalidomide continues to be used even today but mainly to treat certain cancers.

5.3 Airbus A-320

The story of Airbus A-320, the first fly-by-wire aircraft for civilian travel, is interestingly different. When India introduced the A-320 in the early nineties, we opened our account with an air crash on the outskirts of Bengaluru. Another earlier A-320 crash in 1988 in Habsheim, France, in the prestigious air show was still fresh in our memory. India grounded the entire fleet of A-320s for quite some time but fortunately resumed after convincing itself that there were no unresolved safety issues with the aircraft. It has since then emerged as a very safe aircraft for civilian travel. In contrast, the story of Concorde, the supersonic passenger aircraft, is interesting. After more than 25 years of routine commercial operation, the aircraft went out of use for both commercial and safety reasons.

In all the above cases, the domineering role of the government cannot be missed.

5.4 Airships

There have also been examples of panic responses to public risks associated with an emerging technology product. Let us take the case of airships. Considered to be intrinsically safer and less expensive, the development of airships for diverse applications was at the forefront during the early decades of the twentieth century. A few accidents in the early days of airship development led to the complete denial of this technology for public use. Every time we hear the news of a helicopter crash in the northeastern regions of India, it pains us to think that the airship could have provided a safer option.

5.5 Mobile Phone Tower Radiations

We have already mentioned that mobile phones are a gift of modern technology to humanity. It converted the world into a global village with unprecedented connectivity. As with any other high-technology product, mobile phones entered the market as a luxury of the rich. However, within a short span of time, it emerged as a fundamental game changer by eliminating the need for laying phone lines to individual customers and taking a quantum leap in reducing cost and effort to provide connectivity. Today, mobile technology has become the backbone of every human activity — information technology, commerce, education, entertainment, etc. Even in a developing country like India, the subscriber base has exceeded a billion with more than half of them in the rural areas.

It should, however, be pointed out that mobile technology is not free of risks, some known and some only speculative. Following are some examples:

- The use of mobile phones is distracting during any activity that requires concentration, such as driving a car.
- Mobile phone use can interfere with sensitive electronic systems like medical devices.
- Excessive mobile phone use could be a health hazard to the users. The microwave frequencies used by mobile networks are non-ionizing. However, microwaves are known to heat the material in the vicinity, particularly water. There have been thermal photographs of people which suggests that body parts in the vicinity of the phone do get heated up after prolonged use. Media reports add to the confusion by suggesting that radiation from mobile phones and mobile phone towers can cause cancer. As mobile phone use is widespread, even a small increase in the risk

of cancer from mobile phones would be a cause of concern. If true, brain and nervous system cancers would be of particular concern as hand-held phones are held next to the head. The 2G, 3G, and 4G mobile phones use the frequency range of 0.7–2.7 GHz, while 5G will use the frequency spectrum up to 80 GHz. All these frequencies are still in the non-ionizing range of the spectrum, unlike X-rays, radiations from radioactive sources like cobalt-60 or radon-222, or cosmic rays, which are ionizing and can damage DNA and result in cancer.
- Mobile tower radiation could be a public health hazard.
- Mobile tower radiation could be an environmental hazard.

A decrease in the population of bees, butterflies, and sparrows has also been reported and often been blamed on the increasing penetration of mobile phone technology, though it could also be due to the increasing use of pesticides and insecticides. A decreasing bee and butterfly population is bad news for future agricultural production and food security. There have been very few serious studies in this regard.

None of the above has been conclusively proven. Neither have they been conclusively refuted.

While the above issues need to be conclusively resolved, countries across the world including India are taking steps to introduce the 5G mobile network, which promises lower latency, higher capacity, and increased bandwidth. In view of the far-reaching impact of technology on how people live, work, and entertain, one should recognize that there is a high level of public acceptance of mobile technology as a 'friendly' technology.

5.6 Internet

The internet is another technological development of the recent decades that has impacted sharing of information and knowledge by people across the world in unprecedented ways. It is one of the many technologies which emerged in pursuit of basic research. Sir Tim Berners-Lee, a scientist working in the European Centre for Nuclear Research (CERN) in Geneva, invented the World Wide Web

(WWW) in 1989 so that the enormous volume of data collected in the experiments could be accessed by researchers from their home institutions for analysis and the requirement for their travel to Geneva and stay at CERN could be avoided. CERN put the World Wide Web software in the public domain on April 30, 1993. Later, CERN made a release available with an open licence to maximize its dissemination. These actions allowed the web to flourish and transform the world. The internet has been the biggest boon during the days of long lockdown during the pandemic of COVID-19, which enabled people to remain connected to the world and each other, and activities like business, research, education, and communication to continue. Many more computer and internet-based technologies, such as internet telephony, video connectivity, video conferencing, grid computing, cloud computing, and techniques using artificial intelligence became possible. Over the years, the internet has become one of the most valuable tools for education, research, governance, and business.

5.6.1 *Impact of the internet on education and research*

We would like to make a special mention of the impact of the internet on education and research. Education and research have always been elitist and confined to "happening places". The internet has made scientific learning and communication a lot easier and increased the productivity of scientists in out of the way, isolated, and relatively smaller places. It makes the latest papers from leading institutes at Harvard, Princeton, or Cambridge available to everyone across the world instantly. The internet has given an opportunity to billions of people to rapidly become better informed, more learned, and to remain connected to each other. Self-education had never been so much easier and joyful. Now, students and even grown-ups are in control of their own education, and they have access to lectures being delivered at the best places in the world, which they can follow at their own pace. Scientists across the world have started utilizing video conferences to hold discussion meetings, collaboration meetings, seminars (now routinely called webinars), and even workshops and conferences, which can be attended by researchers from disadvantaged countries without having to travel to distant places. Education at most of the schools and universities has continued using the internet and it has saved valuable academic years for students, which they would have lost to COVID-19. Online tutorials for a variety of courses, including those for physical exercises and music and dance, have become extremely popular and have benefitted learners immensely.

At a personal level, the internet has provided a link to millions of children studying or working in faraway places to be able to remain connected to their ageing parents and families. Being connected on social media has helped a large number of people gain a sense of belonging and lifted them out of isolation and loneliness. The internet has also provided budding artists, writers, and poets with an open platform to share their creations and benefit from the feedback. Literary magazines, which had started dying due to the increasing cost of printing, have started flourishing again using the internet. Many organizations have taken initiatives to upload classics and other important literature on the internet and make them available to all.

5.6.2 *Is the internet risk-free?*

As audiences across the world rely on the internet and social media as primary sources of news and information, these can be used to manipulate our perception of the world, and we must devise means to counter it effectively. The internet has led to the emergence of cyber-crimes, such as purloining documents, identities, and money from bank accounts and credit cards of others. It is used to pedal drugs, prohibited substances, pornography, weapons, and surreptitiously advertise rave parties. Evidence has emerged that disgruntled elements have managed to make improvised explosive devices and carry out terrorist acts by collecting information on the internet. It has become possible for people to indulge in gambling and participate in illegal betting from the comfort of their homes. Several internet games challenge kids to harm themselves grievously and have led to severe distress. Kids have also been subjected to cyber-bullying and shaming. It is sometimes used to propagate hatred and fundamentalist views.

All this calls for enactment and enforcement of appropriate rules and regulations and vigilance at the level of authorities as well as parents.

5.7 Artificial Intelligence

Artificial intelligence (AI) is one of the most widely used technologies to emerge in recent times, even though it was being developed for over five decades and the visions of intelligent machines have been discussed from prehistoric times. The philosophers of antiquity are known to have mulled over the idea of artificial beings, mechanical men, and other automatons. Karel Čapek, a Czech playwright, explored the concept of factory-made artificial people whom he called robots. These robots have come a long way by now and can perform a variety of tasks requiring intelligent and informed decisions (see Fig. 5.1).

The wide applicability of AI emerged with the availability of very fast computers and their ability to store, exchange, and analyze vast amounts of data. Simply stated, AI is a simulation of human intelligence processes by machines, especially computer systems (see Fig. 5.2).

One of the first steps in this direction was the development of expert systems, which are fed information to build their knowledge base. The expert system then solves complex problems and provides decisions like a human expert. It performs this by extracting knowledge from its knowledge base using the reasoning and inference rules according to the user queries. These systems, however, do not have human capabilities of thinking and work only based on the knowledge base of the domain. The suggestion for spelling errors while typing in the search box of search engines is provided by one such simple system (see Fig. 5.2).

AI systems ingest large amounts of labelled training data, analyze the data for correlations and patterns, and use these patterns to

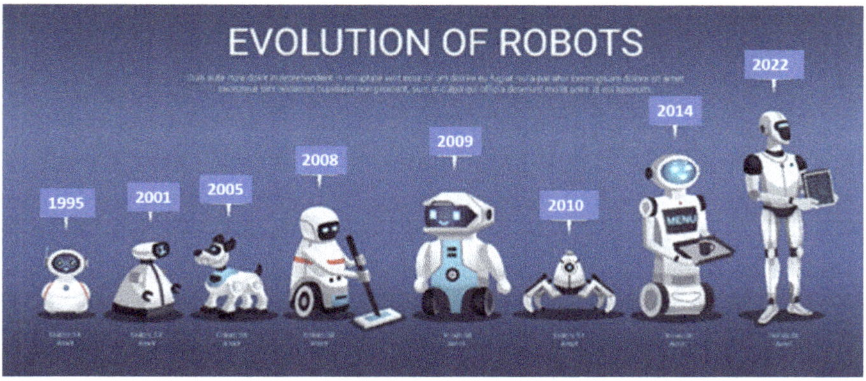

Fig. 5.1 Evolution of robots [2]

Fig. 5.2 Basic features of artificial intelligence (Adapted from [3])

make predictions about future states. Thus, for example, a chatbot (chatting robot) can be fed examples of text chats and can be trained to produce lifelike exchanges with people.

Similarly, an image recognition tool can be trained to identify and describe objects in images by reviewing millions of examples. The simplest example of the latter is a search engine, which can identify a particular person in a huge crowd. Some of the modern search engines can search over tens of billions of images in a fraction of a second and list the sites wherever a particular image appears. Several service sectors use chatbots for initial greetings to customers without their realizing that they are talking to a computer.

These are achieved by focusing on basically three cognitive skills of learning, reasoning, and self-correction. It is the development of the third skill which makes AI a very powerful technology.

In the learning process, AI programs focus on acquiring data and creating rules on turning the data into information that can be used to take an action. Algorithms are then used to give step-by-step instructions to the computer on how to complete a particular task. The reasoning process consists of choosing the right algorithm for the task on hand. And finally, the self-correction processes of AI programs continuously fine-tune algorithms and ensure that they provide the most accurate results possible.

Search engines, recommendation engines of shopping platforms, and global positioning system (GPS) route finders are some of the everyday examples of programs using algorithms of AI.

Using fast computers, AI can perform repetitive, detail-specific tasks much faster than humans, and reveal trends or patterns which humans may have missed due to the vastness of the data. The speed of communication coupled with the identification of trends using AI is used by taxi companies to connect passengers to taxi drivers, advise them to change routes due to traffic congestion, and be ready to receive a larger volume of passengers at a particular time or place. These advantages offered by AI have led to an exponential improvement of efficiency and opened many entirely new business opportunities for service providers. However, AI is still expensive as it requires good technical expertise to implement and at least so far knows only what it has been shown.

AI is being increasingly used in automation, analyzing images, natural language processing, such as translation, robotics, and self-driven cars. In years to come, it is likely to be used extensively in healthcare to make a better and faster diagnosis, in education, for example, by grading or tutoring students, in finances by looking at personal data collected from a large population and advising financial companies on issues such as buying housing, in legal practices by scanning through a large body of documents and assisting the attorneys, manufacturing, banking, transportation, security, etc.

Soon, it should be possible for us to develop AI robots that can overcome the physical limitations of humans and carry out risky jobs for us, like defusing a bomb, exploring the deepest parts of oceans, exploring the interiors of volcanoes, checking highly radioactive areas, mining for coal and oil, and helping and rescuing people during man-made or natural disasters, and even going to Mars. One would like to see the use of AI robots in the cleaning of drains and septic tanks and liberate workers engaged in these hazardous activities.

Another exciting possibility using AI arises in drug discovery, where an AI system can be trained to computationally sort through and compare various properties of millions of potential molecules, shortlist a few to synthesize, test and optimize in laboratory experiments before selecting the eventual drug candidate for clinical trials. Chemical space is believed to have more than 10^{60} molecules. AI could also help find new molecules with interesting properties or even new chemical or industrial processes by quickly sorting through them.

5.7.1 *Reasons for being on the guard*

AI gathers massive amounts of information, including data from mobile devices, messaging services, transportation services, hospitality services, expenditures using credit cards, web browsers, social media platforms, and entertainment services. This massive information about people can be used to target advertisements to suit an individual's tastes and paying capabilities. There is a concern that the medical history of people could be used by insurance companies to provide or deny insurance to them. The web browsing history could be used by authorities for profiling people, which may affect their employment opportunities. There are concerns that AI programs that use facial recognition for theft protection may discriminate against shoppers of certain races or ethnicities. Similar concerns have been raised when AI is used to locate potential terrorists in a crowd. All these acts seriously violate the privacy of people and as AI technology improves, effective regulations must evolve to protect it. The final decision should also be made by humans to avoid serious and costly mistakes. For example, unmanned aerial vehicles were used in Afghanistan to target terrorists using video footage, electronic signals, and some presumptions about suspicious behaviour. Not being fully aware of local customs and traditions, it was used to target a marriage party where people carry guns and indulge in a celebratory fire.

Fears have been expressed that the use of AI in social media platforms could hamper freedom of expression by 'silencing whole groups' or by deciding to allow only certain viewpoints to be circulated. There are also fears that AI could be used by computer-assisted writing software to generate and spread misleading, disruptive, or manipulative stories.

With their increasing use, there is now a call to formulate regulations to ensure that the use of AI does not violate the fundamental and human rights of individuals [4].

5.7.2 *More applications*

There have been suggestions as well as developments to use AI for analyzing weather forecasts and defects and deficiencies in crops and soils to help farmers take corrective measures. The weather forecast, especially the likely cloud cover and wind speeds and directions, could be used to estimate the production of renewable electricity and advise the baseline electricity providers like thermal, oil, gas, and nuclear power plants to plan their production (see Fig. 5.3).

The large body of scientific data which had to be analyzed for the discovery of quark–gluon plasma, Higgs Boson, and gravitational waves used several of these features and their use is increasing. NASA has been using AI-driven robots for carrying out difficult tasks in its space explorations for quite some time.

5.7.3 *Virtual reality and augmented reality*

Virtual reality is yet another wide application of AI. It involves a computer-generated simulation in which a person can interact within an artificial three-dimensional environment using electronic devices, such as special goggles with a screen or gloves fitted with sensors. It is

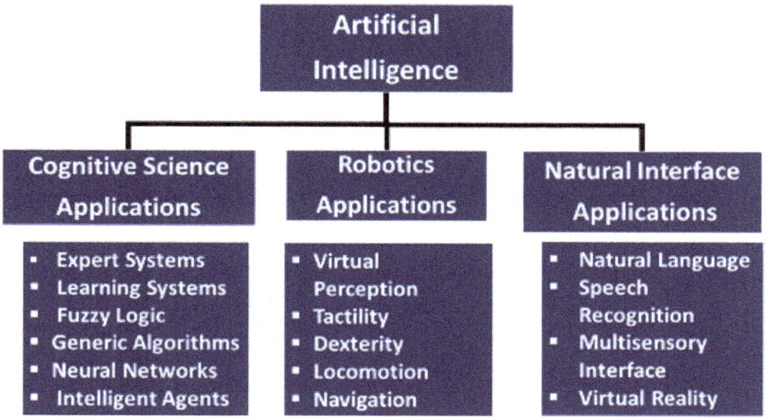

Fig. 5.3 Applications of artificial intelligence

very popular with video games and is used extensively in providing training to armed forces, sports personnel, medical students, and design students. Virtual field trips to museums, touristic places, coral reefs, and historical monuments or even laboratories can be taken, helping in teaching and learning.

This technology has been further refined as augmented reality, which is an enhanced version of the real physical world. It is achieved using digital visual elements, sounds, or some other stimuli, delivered using technology. It is being used by businesses to let one see how a particular piece of furniture would look in one's house, how a particular make-up or dress would suit him or her. It is being used extensively in higher levels of video games and training. It can revolutionize navigation by superimposing a route over the live view of the traffic or help explain and improve some games, e.g., cricket by tracing the actual ball and giving the exact possible picture of the path it would take, following a spin or fast bowling. It is being used extensively in reviewing decisions of "the leg before wicket (LBW)" as well as "run out" in cricket matches, given by the referee. This technology and its application are predicted to increase exponentially.

We have seen that AI makes processes more efficient by allowing a machine to take over some of the manual and low-level tasks that humans once controlled, such as assembly line work. It is likely to take up jobs like driving. These developments raise the concern of job losses and increased income disparities. On the other hand, the use of AI leads to economic growth and reduced prices for goods. Thus, this concern can be effectively addressed by retraining the workforce to perform jobs requiring higher levels of skills and providing better salaries.

A slightly different and interesting approach was proposed by Bertrand Russel in his famous essay, *In Praise of Idleness*, published in 1932 [5], where he had advocated shorter working hours or longer weekends for workers to give them an opportunity to follow academic or artistic pursuits as use of technology increases production.

It is also becoming evident that in the coming years, even the common people will need to acquire AI literacy. Many curricula have started taking steps to train their students in elements of AI from an early age. It is heartening to note that the National Education Policy of the Government of India acknowledges the importance of AI and emphasizes preparing everyone for an AI-driven economy.

AI is a rapidly evolving technology, with an enormous potential for the good of mankind if used with care. It also has a potential for misuse and requires us to be alert to this possibility.

5.8 Genetic Engineering

Genome stands for all the genetic material of living beings. From bacteria to bananas to elephants to humans, every living organism contains its own unique genome. Except for identical twins, the genome of every person is different from the genome of every other person on earth — in fact, it is different from that of every other person who has ever lived on earth. Genomes contain the complete set of instructions that helped us develop from a single cell into the person we are today. It guides our growth, helps our organs to do their jobs, and repairs itself when it is damaged. As our genome is unique to every one of us, the more we know about our genome and how it works, the more we will understand our own health and make informed decisions about our health (see Fig. 5.4).

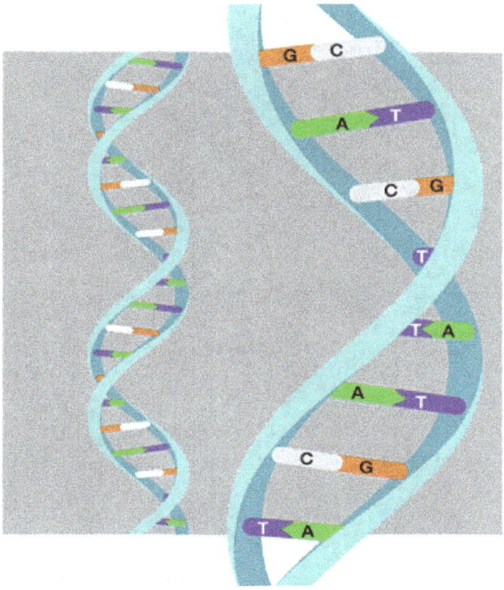

Fig. 5.4 The DNA double Helix [6]

Fig. 5.5 A typical sequence in one of the strands of DNA

Genomes are made of deoxyribonucleic acid (DNA), which constitutes extremely large molecules consisting of two strands, twisted around each other like a twisted ladder. DNA itself is a code. It is made up of four chemical building blocks, Adenine, Thymine, Cytosine, and Guanine, abbreviated with the letters A, T, C, and G on the backbone of alternating groups of sugar and phosphate groups (see Fig. 5.5).

The order of the letters in the code allows DNA to function in different ways and changes slightly from person to person to make each one unique. Bonds between the bases, adenine with thymine, and cytosine with guanine hold the strand together. Due to this unique bonding, sequencing of just one of the strands is enough to

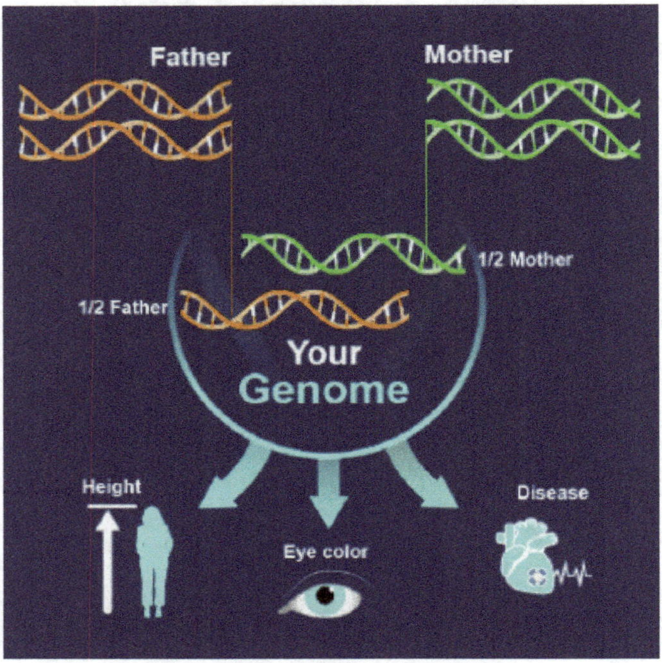

Fig. 5.6 Our genetic inheritance [6]

know the entire DNA. Each strand may consist of several billion of these units.

We get half of our genome from our mothers and the other half from our fathers (see Fig. 5.6). It makes us related to each, but identical to neither. Our parents' genes influence traits such as height, eye colour, and disease risk that make us unique. These, along with influences like our lifestyle and our environment, play a critical role in our ultimate development and health.

Changes in the DNA sequence produce a genetic variant. Most of the time, genetic variants have no noticeable effect at all. However, sometimes, just one missing letter or a changed letter may result in a damaged protein, extra protein, or no protein at all, which in turn may have a serious consequence for our health. As genetic variants are passed from one generation to the next, they may pass diseases like sickle cell or thalassemia. Haemophilia, for example, is mostly an inherited genetic disorder, which prevents the clotting of blood and leads to death by bleeding even from a minor injury. It was passed on to members of the royal families of Spain, Germany, and Russia by Queen Victoria of Great Britain through her two daughters. Some genetic diseases are caused by mutations that are inherited from the parents and are present in an individual at birth. Other genetic diseases are caused by acquired mutations in a gene or group of genes that occur during a person's life.

Genome sequencing, genome mapping, and identification of variations within genomes may help us to prevent and treat diseases more efficiently. The study of genomes could also open completely new possibilities, which we have not thought about so far. Many researchers believe that with the help of genomics, it will be possible to detect and cure cancer.

The most exciting possibility of the study of genomics is the likely emergence of precision medicine or the promise of therapies that are specifically selected to meet each patient's specific needs.

It is our ability to read genome sequences aided by the technologies that introduce new genes or gene changes that allow us to accelerate the process of selecting desirable traits in plants and animals or even create bacteria that can perform useful work such as the production of biofuels.

A related development is cloning, which is a process of making identical copies of an organism, cell, or DNA sequence. It is an asexual type of reproduction, used by many organisms, such as plants (e.g., water hyacinth), fungi, and bacteria. Propagation of plants from cuttings is an ancient form of cloning, and many vineyards have cultivars that have come down to us over several millennia.

In biotechnology, it stands for the process of creating clones of organisms or copies of cells or DNA fragments, when it is christened molecular cloning. There have been major advances in the field of cloning and scientists have successfully cloned sheep and cows. Potatoes and bananas have also been successfully cloned. There is a lot of debate about whether it is ethical to clone. The ethical concerns related to human cloning have prompted several nations to pass laws about it. Therapeutic cloning, where tissues or organs could be generated for humans or for treating the effects of ageing, is another exciting possibility.

5.9 The Bt Brinjal Story

Agriculture has always been vulnerable to pests and infections of various kinds. For example, potatoes were introduced in Ireland in the late sixteenth century, when it was realized that they could grow double the food in the same land. It soon developed into a staple food, especially for the poor during the winter months. Within a few decades, it spread to the rest of Europe. In the mid-nineteenth century, a fungus-like organism called "*Phytophthora infestans*" attacked the potato crops in Ireland, leading to the infamous Irish Potato Famine also called The Great Hunger, which killed 1 million men, women, and children over the next 7 years till it lasted and forced another million to emigrate to North America.

We discuss the story of Bt brinjal in the context of the above historical event. Brinjal (known also as eggplant or aubergine across the world) is one of the most common vegetable crops grown throughout India, accounting for about 7% of all the vegetables grown in India. It is believed that brinjal is native to India and has been cultivated in the country for over 4000 years. It is a popular vegetable, which can be cooked in many ways — boiled, roasted, or fried, along with other vegetables and meats and sauces, as well as pickled. In India, brinjal is grown in over 720,000 hectares across the country by about 1.4 million small and medium farmer families and has consistently had a yield of over 12 million tonnes during recent years [7].

While in West Bengal brinjal is harvested throughout the year, the peak harvesting is done in Odisha from November to February, in Madhya Pradesh during September and October, in Bihar during November and December, and in Gujarat from January to April and again from October to December. West Bengal, Odisha, Gujarat, Bihar, and Madhya Pradesh account for close to 70% of brinjal production in the country. These details are given to emphasize that India is blessed with a vast pool of genetic diversity suited to the soil and the climate conditions across the country, which provides it with a large biodiversity, which we know is critical for nutrition and sustainability, and insurance at a time of climate change.

Brinjal is very prone to damage by pests. The biggest threat for brinjal is fruit and shoot borer (FSB). It can damage up to 50–95% of the crop, especially during the rainy season. It is a tropical insect and is found in all brinjal growing states of India and is active throughout the year. It is essentially monophagous, i.e., it has no alternate hosts and predominantly eats only the shoots and fruits of brinjal. It is highly reproductive, and an average female lays 80–250 eggs. After hatching from the eggs, the young caterpillars bore into tender shoots, flower buds, or fruits. Their feeding leads to the destruction of the tissues of the fruit, and the feeding tunnel is clogged with their excreta, leaving the fruit unfit for marketing. A single larva often destroys four to six fruits. If the larva enters a shoot, it leads to wilting of the shoot (see Fig. 5.7).

Spraying insecticide is effective only if it is done before the larva bores into the fruit or the shoot. Thus, farmers often end up spraying insecticides 25–40 times during the life of the crop. Even 80–100 sprays have been reported from some places. The repeated spraying not only adds to the costs to the farmers but also leaves a large

Fig. 5.7 Brinjal fruit and shoot borer

insecticide residue in the ground as well as on the fruit, which is passed on to those who consume it. The farmers, while spraying the insecticides, are also exposed to the insecticide. The Bt technology came as a gift of the twentieth century to manage the brinjal fruit and borer infection.

5.9.1 *Bt technology*

To put our discussion in a proper perspective, we start with a brief history of the Bt technology. In 1901, Japanese biologist, Shigetane Ishiwatari, while investigating the cause of the sudden death of a large population of silkworms, first isolated the bacterium *Bacillus thuringiensis* (Bt) as the cause of the disease. He called it *Bacillus sotto*, as the disease of "sudden collapse of the population" was called the sotto disease. Ernst Berliner rediscovered Bt while investigating the death of Mediterranean flour moth in 1911 and named it *Bacillus thuringiensis* after the German town Thuringia where the moth was found. The name that Ishiwatari had used was later ruled invalid. In 1915, Berliner also reported the existence of a crystal within Bt, but its activity was not noted till much later.

Pesticides using Bt were used widely in Europe from the 1920s, but their use slowly decreased as it was found that these were easily washed away due to rain and were degraded by ultraviolet light. The spray also could not reach the insects which lived underground or inside the shoots and the fruits.

By then, the activity of Bt in killing the moths was traced to the parasporal crystal. This led to increased interest in the study of the crystal structure, biochemistry, and general mode of action of Bt. Several strains of Bt that targeted specific larvae were found and used in pesticides from the 1980s, as the pests were becoming resistant to the synthetic pesticides available at that time, which were also harming the environment.

By now, thousands of strains of Bt are known, and several of them have genes that encode unique toxic crystals in their DNA. They produce over 200 cry proteins that are active against an extensive range of insects and some other invertebrates. With the progress of molecular biology, it became possible to move the gene that encodes the toxic crystals into a plant. Bt is distributed in the soil sparsely but worldwide. Bt has been found in all types of terrain, including beaches, deserts, and tundra habitats.

Bt kills the insects upon ingestion. The Bt toxin dissolves in the high pH insect gut and becomes active. The toxins then attack the gut cells of the insect, punching holes in the lining. The Bt spores spill out of the gut and germinate in the insect, causing death within a couple of days. Treated plant parts are not damaged as the insect stops feeding within hours. Bt spores do not spread to other insects or cause disease outbreaks on their own [8].

However, different strains of Bt are specific to specific receptors in the gut of the insect, and therefore, each strain is specific to a particular insect.

Bt products are found to be safe for use in the environment and with mammals. The Environmental Protection Agency of the USA has not found any human health hazards related to using Bt. Humans have a pH level of 1.5–3.0 in their gut, where the Bt toxin does not dissolve. They also do not have receptors specific to Bt. Bt, when used near lakes, rivers, and living quarters, has not shown any effect on wildlife, such as mammals, birds, and fish [9].

In brief, the planting of Bt crops reduces the environmental impact of pesticides due to greatly reduced spraying. The Bt toxins kill specific insects and spare the beneficial insects.

5.9.2 *Genetic engineering*

Genetic engineering is the latest procedure to introduce a specific gene in any organism. A "genetically modified organism" or "transgenic" is an organism where a gene from one organism has been purposely moved to improve or change another organism to produce desirable traits. When this is done on crops, we call them genetically modified crops or GM crops. It is, in principle, possible to develop crops having desired properties by selective breeding and crossing. However, due to the probabilistic nature of these transitions, it may take a very long time to get the desired effect. The recent developments in the understanding of molecular biology make it quick and definite (see Fig. 5.8).

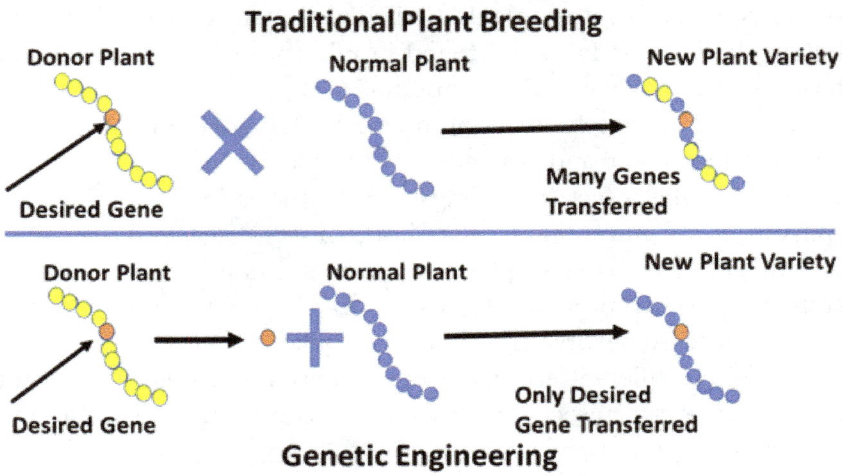

Fig. 5.8 Traditional and genetic engineering breeding of plants

Insulin is one such example of genetic engineering. To produce it, the insulin gene from the intestines of pigs or cows is inserted into bacteria, which then grow and produce insulin. This insulin is then purified and used for medical purposes. Thyroid hormone was until recently derived only from animals. Now, it is cultured from bacteria.

The first genetically engineered plant, corn, was registered with the Environment Protection Agency of the USA in 1995. Today, genetically modified (GM) crops including potato and cotton are planted throughout the world.

However, concerns have been raised that the genetic modifications make the organism (crop) become invasive, though no signs of that have yet been found. Additionally, there are concerns that GM crops could introduce new genes to native genes through cross-contamination. However, no evidence has been found for this either.

5.9.3 *Importance of refuse crops*

The biggest concern with using GM crops is that the insects may develop resistance to the introduced toxin. This requires special care and the use of refuse crops (see Fig. 5.9). To solve this, several strategies have been devised, which involve planting refuse crops

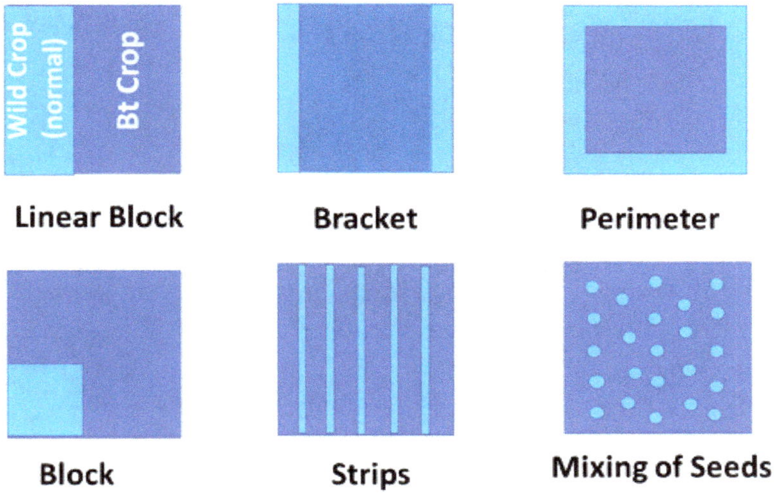

Fig. 5.9 Planting refuse crops along with Bt crop

(normal wild crop) along with the Bt crop. The refuse crop can be 5–20% of the Bt crop and planted as a block, as bracketing the Bt crop, along the perimeter, in strips in between, or by mixing the two seeds. This provides pests with a refuge where they could feed on plants lacking toxins, thereby maintaining Bt susceptible resistance alleles within the insect population.

Once this is done, the insects that have developed resistance to Bt have more chances of mating with an insect that has not developed resistance to Bt. By the laws of genetics discovered by Gregor Mendel in 1866, the progenies produced will be insects that are not resistant to Bt (see Fig. 5.10).

Currently, 64 countries, which include 28 countries of the European Union, require labelling of GM foods [10]. US and Canadian national policies require a label only giving significant composition differences or documented health impacts. Genetically Modified Organism (GMO) labels are not required. In the European Union, all food (including processed food) or feed that contains greater than 0.9% GMOs must be labelled. A list of the countries growing some of the Bt crops is given in Table 5.1.

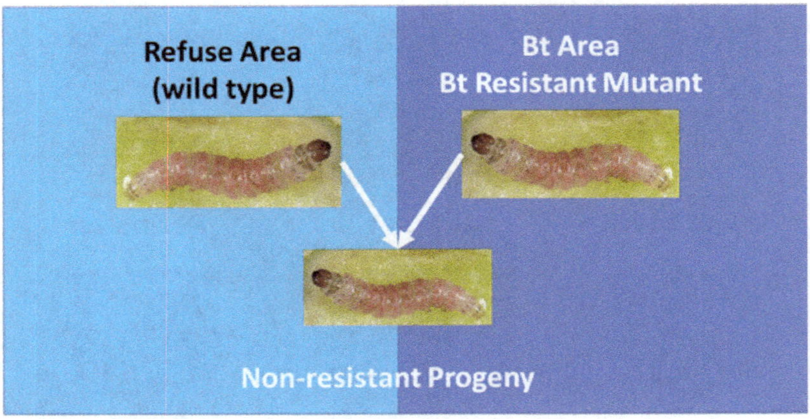

Fig. 5.10 Getting non-resistant insects

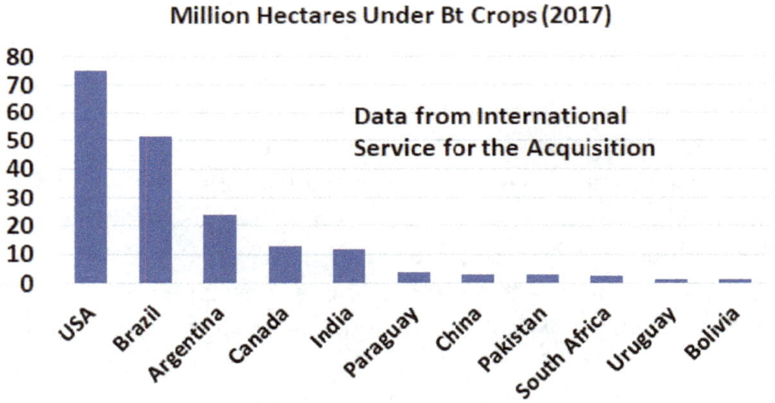

Fig. 5.11 Countries having more than 1 million hectares of farmlands under Bt crops

It is also worthwhile to see the countries which have more than 1 million hectares of land under cultivation of Bt crops (see Fig. 5.11).

We further note that, globally, the acreage of land under Bt crop cultivation has increased steadily over the last two decades (see Fig. 5.12).

Table 5.1 Countries growing different Bt crops

Cotton	Argentina, Australia, Brazil, Burkina Faso, Canada, China, Colombia, Costa Rica, European Union, India, Japan, Mexico, Myanmar, New Zealand, Pakistan, Paraguay, Philippines, Sine, South Africa, South Korea, Sudan, Taiwan, United States of America
Brinjal	Bangladesh
Maize	Argentina, Australia, Brazil, Canada, Chile, China, Colombia, Egypt, European Union, Honduras, Indonesia, Japan, Malaysia, Mexico, New Zealand, Panama, Paraguay, Philippines, Russian Federation, Singapore, South Africa, South Korea, Switzerland, Taiwan, Thailand, Turkey, USA, Uruguay, Vietnam
Poplar	China
Potato	Australia, Canada, Japan, Mexico, New Zealand, Philippines, Russian Federation, South Korea, USA
Rice	China, Iran
Soybean	Argentina, Australia, Brazil, Canada, China, Colombia, European Union, Japan, Mexico, New Zealand, Paraguay, Philippines, Russian Federation, South Africa, Taiwan, Thailand, Turkey, USA, Uruguay, Vietnam
Tomato	Canada, USA

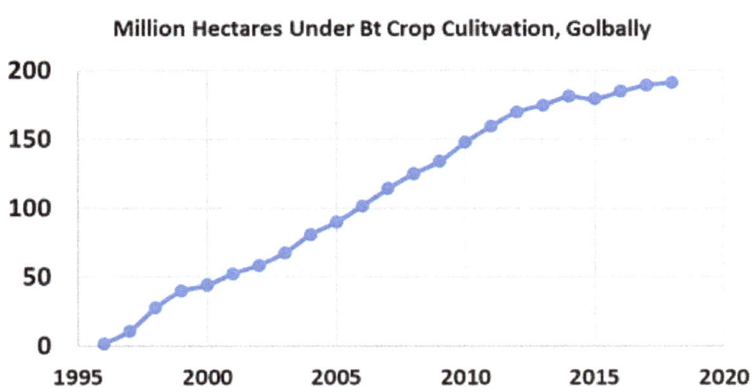

Fig. 5.12 Global rise of land area under Bt crop cultivation

It is also very instructive to see which Bt crops are being grown globally, which covered about 192 million hectares in 2018 (see Fig. 5.13).

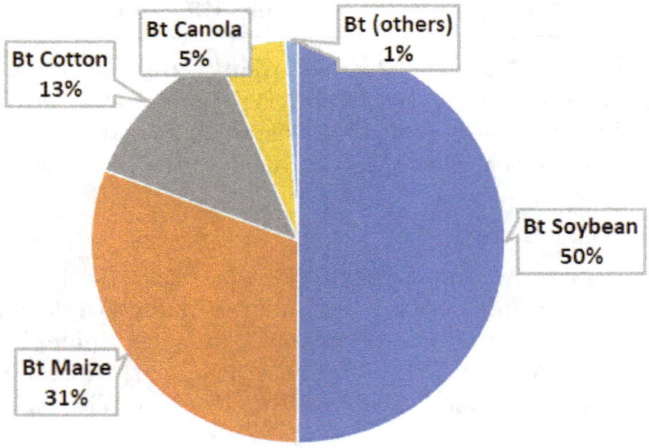

Fig. 5.13 Major Bt crops cultivated globally (2018)

5.9.4 *Bt brinjal in India*

The planting of Bt brinjal is expected to lead to the production of non-infested, undamaged, and high-quality fruits of brinjals with significantly reduced residues of pesticides on them. There is a reduction in the cost of production due to reduced expenditure on the pesticides and the labour involved in spraying and an increase in yield due to a reduction in damage to the crop. The other benefits include a reduction in the direct exposure to the insecticide during the process of spraying, as we discussed earlier, reduction in pesticide residues in the soil, water, and air, protection of useful insects, microflora, and invertebrates. The process of scientific validation of genetically modified crops is summarized in Fig. 5.14.

The so-called Event EE1 of Bt brinjal was developed by the Maharashtra Hybrid Seeds Company Limited (Mahyco), Mumbai, a subsidiary of Monsanto Company, the University of Agricultural Sciences, Dharwad, and the Tamil Nadu Agricultural University, Coimbatore. The results of tests carried out from 2000 to 2006 were presented in May 2006 by Mahyco with the conclusion that the targeted pest was controlled by Bt brinjal and no significant difference between Bt and non-Bt brinjal was found.

The Genetic Engineering Approval Committee for approval of activities involving large-scale use of hazardous microorganisms and

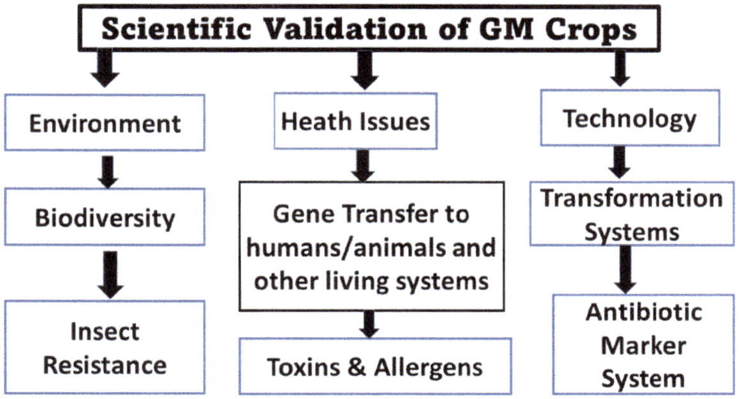

Fig. 5.14 **Scientific validation of genetically modified crops**

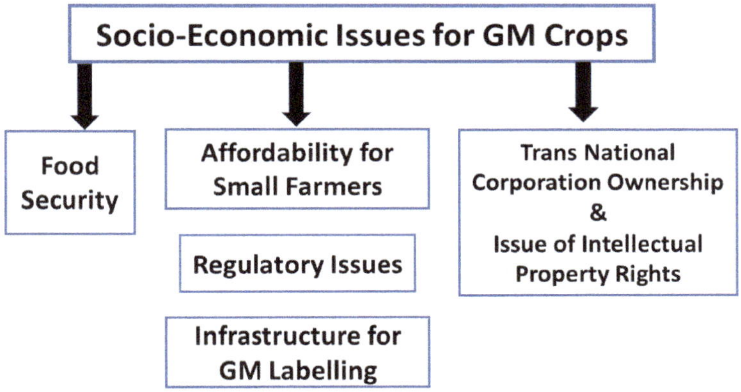

Fig. 5.15 **Socio-economic issues for GM crops**

recombinants in research and industrial production from the angle of environment, including field trials concluded that Bt brinjal was safe for environmental release. As the decision to produce Bt brinjal was likely to have major policy implications (see Fig. 5.15), these recommendations were forwarded to the Government of India for a formal view.

A wide-ranging consultation was held with farmers, farmer's organizations, scientists, state officials of the department of agriculture, non-government organizations, consumer groups, allopathic and ayurvedic doctors, students, housewives, *excluding the agricultural biotechnology companies.*

The Government of India decided on an indefinite moratorium on the commercialization of Bt brinjal in February 2010. The arguments given for this decision were as follows: no clear consensus within the scientific community, opposition from most of the states, including those which grow brinjal, unanswered questions from civil society and several scientists, fear among consumers and lack of global precedent, questions about the safety and testing process, no overriding need to go for Bt brinjal, etc.

One of the arguments against the introduction of Bt brinjals even contended that if the production of brinjal increased because of this, the prices would fall, which would benefit the consumers and harm the farmers. It was also suggested that the company may charge higher prices for the seeds, leading to further loss to the farmers. Fear of non-genuine or counterfeit seeds flooding the market and duping the farmers were other concerns. On the question of toxicity and nutrition, different scientists had different opinions.

Given this, the recommendation made in 2004 by Dr M.S. Swaminathan, eminent agricultural scientist, for the formation of an autonomous statutory body, such as a biotechnology regulatory authority, to be led by eminent professionals and with its own facilities for testing, independent of what the company or the breeder tells, assumes great significance. He had also suggested that the authority should have its own facilities to analyze long-term chronic effects and all biosafety aspects. He contended that people consume brinjal throughout their life, and it is necessary to know its chronic effect. Moreover, the country has a large variety of brinjals (more than 3000, to be precise), and growing just a few varieties of Bt brinjal puts that biodiversity at the risk, which can lead to serious consequences if the resistance of the Bt brinjal to the pests breaks down. It is also generally felt that genetically modified crops should not be introduced in the biological and agricultural hotspots of the country. One wonders if the issue of biodiversity can be addressed by developing FSB-resistant Bt brinjal for each one of the genetic varieties of brinjal prevalent in the country.

We add that Bangladesh imported seeds from Mahyco and developed some of its own Bt brinjal varieties and has been cultivating it since 2014. The brinjal production from these areas under cultivation is reported to have been doubled. In an interesting twist, it has been found that some farmers from Haryana somehow got the seeds of Bt brinjal and have started cultivating it in 2019.

5.10 GM Mustard

Understandably, the Bt brinjal story has also impacted the growth of modern biotechnology applications in the field of agriculture. Dhara Mustard Hybrid-11 (DMH-11) is a genetically modified mustard species, developed by the Centre for Genetic Manipulation of Crop Plants of the University of Delhi. Mustard is a self-pollinating plant, containing both male and female parts — no natural hybridization can take place in mustard to get improved seeds. These were created using transgenic technology, primarily involving the Bar, Barnase, and Barstar gene systems. The Barnase gene, derived from soil bacterium, confers male sterility to the plants, while the Barstar gene restores DMH-11's to produce fertile seeds. The third gene, Bar, derived from another soil bacterium, helped the plant produce an enzyme, which made it resistant to Glufosinate, a widely used herbicide, though there are conflicting reports about whether herbicides need to be used with these or not. Safety evaluations were ordered and performed by several agencies. The details of the results are however not yet made public. The Genetic Engineering Appraisal Committee issued the clearance in May 2017, but the Ministry of Environment and Forests did not give the final approval. Objections to the planned introduction of DMH-11 started almost immediately. Mustard is widely used to produce edible oil and a paste used in cooking. Its leaves are a popular leafy vegetable. It is used in many indigenous and ayurvedic medicines, and its oil cakes are fed to animals. The long-term impacts of DMH-11 on the health of people, the environment, the soil, the groundwater, or the food chain are not yet fully known. On the other hand, India presently imports 60% of its edible oil at a cost of 12 billion dollars per year. This bill is likely to increase with the increase in population and improvement in the standard of living of the population. The DMH-11 promises an increase of yield from 10% to 40% with a major impact on the economics of mustard production and use.

Another example is "Golden Rice", a rice strain that has small bits of corn and bacterial DNA added to its genome, which has not received a large-scale acceptance due to anxieties about genetically modified crops. These extra genes allow the rice to produce beta carotene (a vitamin A precursor). The lack of vitamin A affects millions in Africa and Asia, causing blindness and immune system deficiencies.

We know that the natural selection of organisms has been going on for millions of years, where the most suitably adapted organisms survive, multiply, propagate, and prosper. Selective breeding of plants and animals has been practised by humans for several thousand years to get good quality fruits, crops with higher yields, and more meat, milk, or wool production and friendly animals. Crossbreeding has also been practised by humans to improve the taste, size, yield, and quality of fruits, grains, and animals (see Fig. 5.16).

Merging human and animal forms brought terror to our ancestors in mythological stories across the world. In Greek mythology, the

Fig. 5.16 Chimera of Arezzo (Credit: Wikipedia)

Chimera is a monstrous fire-breathing creature, typically described as having the head of a lion, with a snake as a tail and the head of a goat emerging from its back. Disturbed by these thoughts, several countries have put a ban on research on these topics, especially if these involve human embryos [11].

Some useless and unnecessary efforts of crossbreeding in recent times included the crossing of tigers and lions, which resulted in sickly and short-lived progeny. Some crossbreeding efforts, like crossing horses and donkeys, have produced sterile but very useful mules for ages. An effort was made to breed sheep to produce more wool — it resulted in giving folds on their skin and made them sick due to excessive warming. One effort to create chicken yielding more meat resulted in chicken that could not stand on their legs and spent their entire life sitting. An effort to create cows yielding more milk resulted in getting cows that had very large udders, which made it difficult for them to walk and made them sick. Animals created to grow rapidly and yield more meat may have a reduced nutrition value for their meat. All these memories shape the perceptions of people to crops obtained by crossing or genetic modifications to the negative public perceptions of the Bt technology.

Our failure to analyze the benefits and the associated risks scientifically and reliably and to communicate these convincingly to the government and the public at large may be holding us back from taking full advantage of these developments in biotechnology.

5.11 Summary

As in the case of industrial disasters, our choice of technological developments that we take for discussion is neither complete nor exhaustive but is based on our perceptions of the lessons learnt.

During the last few decades, there has been a subtle change in the way in which society has been handling public good and public risks. The media and the internet have emerged as the primary sources of information to the public on all matters, including those relating to new and emerging technologies. It has also empowered them to influence public policy-making by the governments through democratic means or otherwise. We have also come across instances of deliberate misinformation by vested interests using the same media and internet. It has become a challenge to ensure that public perceptions are based on reliable information, particularly on matters of high and fast-changing technologies.

What is the way forward? With the increasing participation of the public in policy-making, including government policies on regulatory matters relating to high and emerging technologies, we do not see any alternative to taking the public into confidence and empowering them with reliable information. But communicating matters of high and emerging technologies to the public at large is complex and challenging. Often, genuine differences of opinion among experts erode the confidence of the public in the experts. Risk communication is even more of a challenge. Under- and overplaying risks are counterproductive and do not elicit a calibrated response in times of emergency. This is made even more complex in our country with multiple languages and poor scientific literacy. We will elaborate on these points in subsequent chapters.

References

[1] K. Sansare *et al.*, Early victims of X-rays: a tribute and current perception, *Dentomaxillofac. Radiol.* **40**(2), 123–125 (2011).

[2] https://www.freepik.com/free-vector/evolution-robots_7439098.htm; Designed by macrovector/Freepik.

[3] Adapted from *Future of Artificial Intelligence in Customer Experience* by R. Raza, https://medium.com/.

[4] *Unboxing Artificial Intelligence: 10 steps to protect Human Rights*, Council of Europe Commissioner for Human Rights, https://rm.coe.int/unboxing-artificial-intelligence-10-steps-to-protect-human-rights-reco/1680946e64.

[5] B. Russel, In Praise of Idleness, *Harper's Magazine* (October 1932). Reprinted, https://harpers.org/archive/1932/10/in-praise-of-idleness/.

[6] https://www.genome.gov/About-Genomics/Introduction-to-Genomics.

[7] Data from Statista and *Horticultural Statistics at a Glance 2018*, Government of India.

[8] http://www.bt.ucsd.edu/how_bt_work.html.

[9] T. R. Glare and M. O'Callaghan, *Bacillus thuringiensis: Biology, Ecology and Safety*. Wiley, Chicester, UK (2000).
[10] https://www.centerforfoodsafety.org/; https://www.isaaa.org/resources/publications/briefs/; https://royalsociety.org/topics-policy/projects/gm-plants/what-gm-crops-are-currently-being-grown-and-where/.
[11] https://www.bbc.com/future/article/20170222-the-uneasy-truth-about-human-animal-hybrids.

Chapter 6

Environmental Disasters

It is often said that human life on Earth is controlled by the "rule of three". An average human being can survive up to 3 weeks without food, 3 days without water, and 3 minute without oxygen. All three have come under tremendous stress during the last few centuries. The ever-increasing human population has been putting increasing pressure on the equitable availability of food and water. Industrial pollution has been leading to a dangerous deterioration of the quality of air that we breathe in. Even the water we drink and the food we eat have not remained untouched by pollution. Population pressure and callous use of resources have put undue pressure on our environment. Last but not the least, increasing use of hydrocarbons for satisfying our increasing energy needs is leading to an increase in the carbon dioxide fraction in the air, in turn leading to a warming of the atmosphere with disastrous consequences. In the following sections, we describe the risks posed by these changes with possible remedial measures.

6.1 Air Pollution

The air we breathe contains about 78% nitrogen, about 21% oxygen, the remaining being small amounts of several other gases like carbon dioxide, moisture, etc., and some particulate matter. It is the oxygen that sustains life. Humans and animals breathe in oxygen and breathe out carbon dioxide. Plants take in carbon dioxide and emit oxygen balancing the oxygen–carbon dioxide ratio. The level of carbon dioxide in the atmosphere had never exceeded 300 parts per million (ppm) during the last 800,000 years of Earth's history [1] till the onset of the Industrial Revolution. In 2021, it reached an unprecedented and alarming value of 419 ppm.

Unfortunately, over the last few centuries, the air around us has also been accumulating a variety of pollutants — pollutants that are detrimental to human health. The air, even though gaseous, also holds lots of tiny particles called aerosols. Some aerosols, such as dust, pollen, and spores from fungi, have natural origins. Other aerosols and polluting gases come from car and truck exhausts, factories, burning of wood, farm refuse, hydrocarbon, and even volcanoes and wildfires. Once there are too many particles in the air, it gets difficult for humans and animals to breathe and causes serious ailments. The World Health Organization has reported that air pollution is responsible for nearly 7 million premature deaths around the globe every year and has issued guideline limits for air pollutants. Unfortunately, 9 out of 10 human beings across the globe breathe air that exceeds the WHO's guideline limits for pollutants. However, there are suggestions as well as concerns that these guidelines does not take into account the presence of base-level natural aerosols in the atmosphere, especially in tropical countries (see Figs. 6.1 and 6.2).

Recent studies [4] have found that Delhi is the most polluted capital city in the world (see Fig. 6.3) and that 22 of the 30 most polluted cities in the world are in India. These studies are based on PM2.5, the amount of particulate matter in the air with an aerodynamic diameter equal to or smaller than 2.5 μm, for which a value of 0–10 $\mu g/m^3$ is considered ideal and safe. We add though a small amount of particulate matter may be good in countries near the equator as they help scatter and diffuse the strong sunlight, which could otherwise possibly burn our exposed skin. The numbers for many Indian cities is 50–100 $\mu g/m^3$, which points to the high level of pollution. Similarly, PM10 stands for particulate matter having a diameter of 10 μm or less, and a value less than 40 $\mu g/m^3$ is generally considered good for this. On occasions, this reaches a value which is 10 times or more in several parts of the country.

Fig. 6.1 Air pollution from use of coal [2]

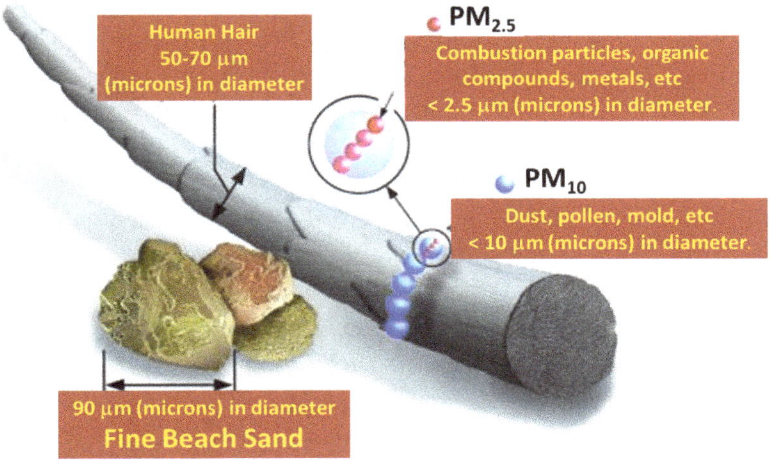

Fig. 6.2 Size of air pollutants [3]

Fig. 6.3 Smog in Delhi hides the Sun [5]

Different regions of the world have adopted slightly different measures called the Air Quality Index, which provides the extent of pollution. India has adopted a scheme that is based on the monitoring of PM10, PM2.5, NO2, SO2, CO, O3, NH3, and Pb in the air. A weighted index running from 0 to 500 then classifies the air quality as Good (0–50), Satisfactory (51–100), Moderately Polluted (101–200), Poor (201–300), Very Poor (301–400), and Severe (401–500). These limits are reviewed frequently. The health impacts of these are given in Table 6.1.

It is also important to keep in mind that air pollution affects young children most severely as their immune systems are not fully developed, their lungs are growing, and with every breath, children take in more air per unit of body weight than adults.

Reduction in the use of fossil fuels and emissions from industries is believed to be the most potent solution for getting over this crisis. This was confirmed by the observation that the air quality across the world improved enormously in recent months as extended lockdowns

Table 6.1 Categories of air quality index and their impacts adopted in India

Air Quality Index	Associated Health Impact
Good (0–50)	Minimal impact.
Satisfactory (51–100)	May cause minor breathing discomfort to sensitive people.
Moderately Polluted (101–200)	May cause breathing discomfort to people with lung disease, such as asthma, and discomfort to people with heart disease, children, and older adults.
Poor (201–300)	May cause breathing discomfort to people on prolonged exposure and discomfort to people with heart disease.
Very Poor (301–400)	May cause respiratory illness to the people on prolonged exposure. The effect may be more pronounced in people with lung and heart diseases.
Severe (401–500)	May cause respiratory impact even on healthy people and serious health impacts on people with lung/heart disease. The health impacts may be experienced even during light physical activity.

necessary to contain the spread of the recent pandemic COVID-19 also led to the closure of industries and a reduction in traffic. This observation was reinforced when the air quality deteriorated again as the lockdowns were relaxed and industrial and travel activities picked up again.

6.2 Water Pollution

Life on Earth depends critically on the availability of water. While nearly 70% of the Earth's surface is covered with water, less than 3% of it is fit for human consumption and for the survival of most animals and plants (Fig. 6.4). The bulk of the freshwater is frozen as ice sheets and snow on the Earth's surface. Some amount of it is stored in and moves slowly through geologic formations of soil, sand and rocks called aquifers. Less than 0.01% of the freshwater is in rivers and lakes (Fig. 6.5). This immediately suggests that we should take extreme care to "protect" freshwater, which is so essential for life.

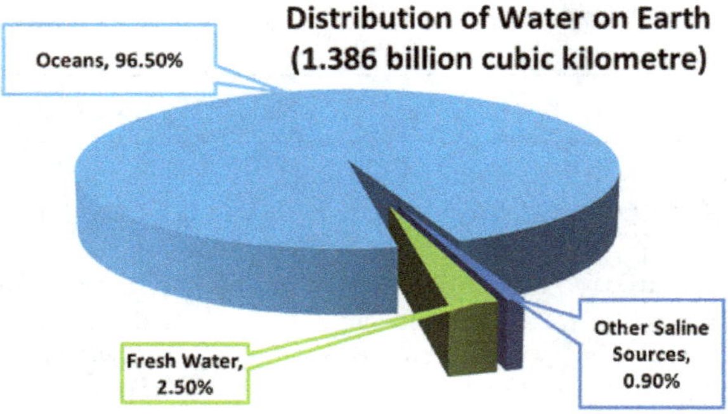

Fig. 6.4 Distribution of water on Earth

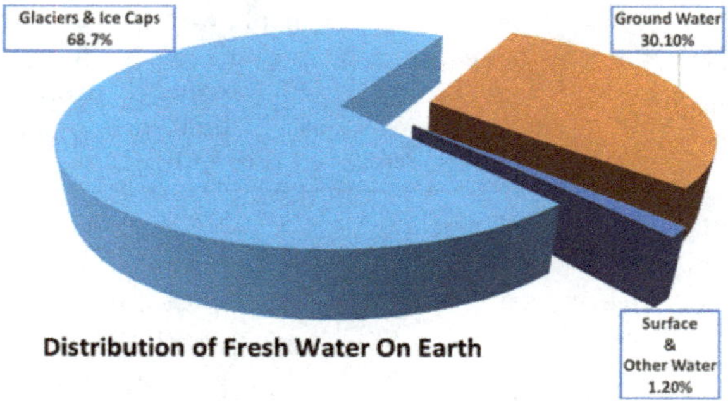

Fig. 6.5 Distribution of freshwater on Earth

Water is a finite resource — neither created nor annihilated. In a natural cycle called the hydrological cycle or simply the water cycle, sunlight evaporates ocean water and sends it up into the atmosphere as clouds; winds move the clouds across continents; when conditions are appropriate, the clouds condense as water droplets and come down as rain or snow — the only source of freshwater on Earth. The rivers carry the rainwater back into the oceans.

6.2.1 *The global water cycle*

Water on the Earth evaporates under the action of heat (mostly from the Sun) or it is released by plants by transpiration, and it condenses in the upper reaches of the atmosphere. It comes down to the Earth

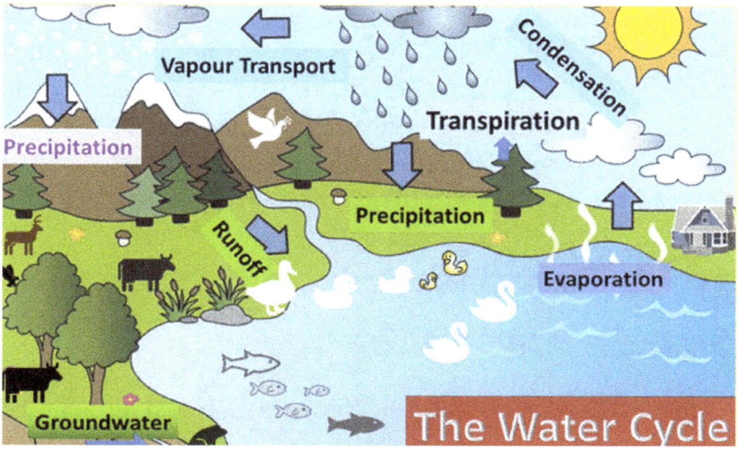

Fig. 6.6 The water cycle

as snow or rain as mentioned, and the cycle continues. The water cycles generally follow seasons specific to every place. Some amount of water is soaked by the Earth to charge its underground aquifers. Man has been drawing this water since the days of the Indus Valley Civilization when the first wells and stepwells are believed to have been dug (see Fig. 6.6).

Even though the seasons are well defined, the actual rainfall in different places can not only vary from year to year but can also be highly uneven within a season. We have seen that, while extremely heavy rainfall in a limited period results in a flood, prolonged failure of seasonal rainfall can result in droughts, having a serious impact on agricultural operations. Unseasonal rainfalls can destroy ready crops.

India is endowed with several perennial rivers in the north, fed by melting snow of the Himalayas, one of the major water towers of the world and rains, and seasonal rivers in the south primarily fed by seasonal rains. Ganga, Yamuna, Brahmaputra, and Sindhu are some of the perennial rivers of the north, which get their waters both from the melting snow and from rains, while Narmada, Krishna, Godavari, and Kaveri are basically rain-fed rivers. The Brahmaputra covers a part of its initial journey as the Yarlung Tsangpo River in Tibet and China. The Mekong, Salween, and Indus Rivers also originate in the Himalayas. The river basins of the Himalayas have an area of 2.75 million km^2, more than 20% of (577,000) square kilometres of which is irrigated. Rivers have always been the focal point of Indian civilizations since time immemorial. From ancient times, the literature of India is full of praise for these rivers. In one of the most important rituals people, across India, while taking bath, recite:

"गंगे च यमुने चैव गोदावरि सरस्वति ।

नर्मदे सिंधु कावेरि जलेऽस्मिन् सन्निधिं कुरु ।।"

("O Ganga, Yamuna, Godavari, Saraswati, Narmada, Sindhu and Kaveri, please enrich the water I am bathing with, with your presence." — Sri Bruhannardiya Puran)

The Vedas are full of praise for many of the rivers, including Saraswati, which has since dried up. In later times, poems of exquisite beauty were composed by Kalidas, Shankaracharya, Vidyapati, Punditraj Jagannath and many others in praise of Ganga. The starting points of rivers have remained important places of pilgrimage in Indian traditions and the presumed dates of their "descent on Earth" are celebrated as important festivals. It is known that Mughal rulers used to get their drinking water from Rishikesh, and it was carried in large pots on elephant back, wherever they went. There are also reports that the English used to carry water from Ganga to drink during their long journeys back to England.

In the following, we take the example of Ganga and discuss the extent of its pollution to illustrate the risks from the pollution of our water bodies. We will also discuss actions that can be taken to tackle this serious problem.

6.2.2 *The pollution of Ganga*

Ganga is a river of extreme importance for India. Originating in the Gangotri glacier at Gaumukh (Fig. 6.7) in The Himalaya as Bhagirathi, it meets Alaknanda at Devprayag (Fig. 6.8) and is called Ganga thereafter. Ganga enters the plains at Haridwar and flows to the Bay of Bengal. In the process, the river traverses a course of more

Fig. 6.7 Gaumukha

Fig. 6.8 Confluence of Alaknanda and Bhagirathi at Devprayag

than 2,500 km through the plains of north and eastern India. The Ganga basin, which also extends into parts of Nepal and Bangladesh, accounts for 26% of India's landmass. It also has about 400 million people depending on it.

Till 40 or 50 years ago, these rivers teemed with fish, river dolphins, gharials, crocodiles, tortoises, and shells. Our literature of yesteryears is full of references to river dolphins approaching boats and playing with the people to their utter delight. In fact, river dolphins could be seen even in very small rivers, which joined slightly bigger rivers, which in turn joined major rivers. Now, the river dolphins are so rare that their very occasional sighting even in a major river becomes news (Fig. 6.9). The pollution in the rivers has decimated them all. Crocodiles (the scavengers of the rivers) and gharials were also killed in large numbers for their skin. The decimation of the fish population has also deprived a large population of its protein-rich diet. The increasing pollution has put the water supply to people living along the river under extreme stress.

A famous Hindi proverb states, "*Bahataa paani nirmalaa*", which means "flowing water stays clean". The increasing number of dams and canals along the route of Ganga not only reduces the flow in the river at several places to a thin and swallow stream with very little flow leading to the silting but also leads to a deterioration of the quality of the water.

Fig. 6.9 A river dolphin sighted in Ganga near Meerut in April 2020

Numerous towns along its route empty almost 140 major drains into it, with industrial and municipal waste, amounting to more than 6,000 million litres per day of highly polluted water. The Sisamau Nala in Kanpur, often referred to as the "largest drain in Asia", was being used as a sewage conveyance channel since the 1890s, which emptied into the Ganga. To be specific, 66 of 97 towns along Ganga have at least one drain flowing into Ganga River. West Bengal has 41 towns along the river, followed by 21 in Uttar Pradesh, 18 in Bihar, 16 in Uttarakhand and 2 in Jharkhand (see also Fig. 6.10 based on data from Central Pollution Control Board, Government of India).

Untreated effluents from industries such as leather, textiles, and sugar mills release toxic chemicals into the water bodies. Inappropriate management of textile, industrial and municipal wastewater is one of the major causes of water pollution in the rivers. Textile effluents contain bio-resistant hazardous synthetic dye molecules and complex auxiliary chemicals.

Moreover, several pharmaceutical compounds (pain killers, beta blockers, cholesterol-lowering agents, antibiotics, and anaesthetics),

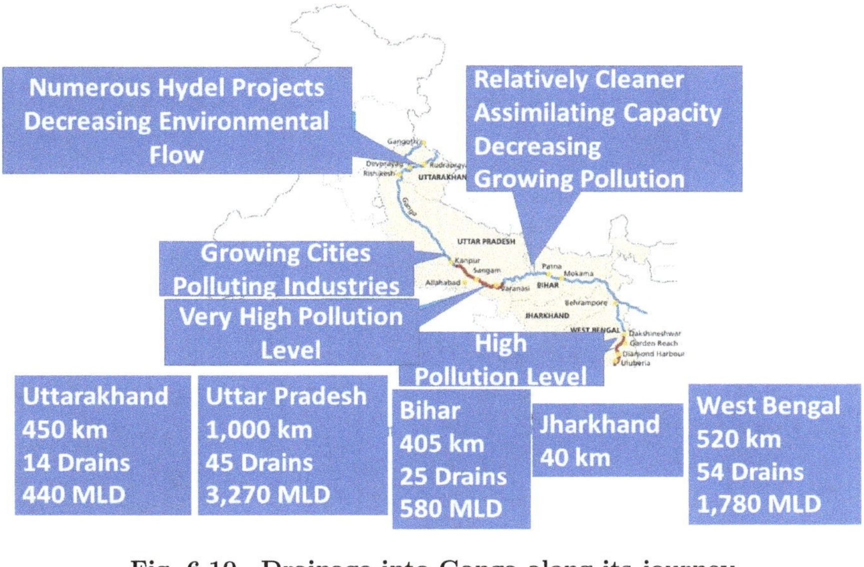

Fig. 6.10 Drainage into Ganga along its journey

coming from domestic, hospital, and drug manufacturing facilities, as well as fertilizers and pesticides from agricultural run-off, are also believed to be contributing significantly to the overall surface and groundwater pollution.

The authors of Ref. [1] have discussed some of these issues in detail. We quote them in the following:

> "There are persistent reports of these harmful chemicals polluting underground sources of water, which are also drying up due to excessive over-exploitation. It is estimated that 300–400 million tonnes of heavy metals, solvents, toxic sludge, and other wastes from industrial facilities are dumped annually into the world's waters. Fertilizers entering coastal ecosystems have produced more than 400 'dead zones' in the oceans, totalling more than 245,000 sq. km.
>
> The release of detergents containing phosphate salts is a big concern across the world. Phosphates inhibit the biodegradation of organic substances. They also cause the water bodies to get choked with algae and plants. The excessive richness of nutrients in a lake or other bodies of water, frequently due to run-off from the land (due to excessive use of fertilizers), causes a dense growth of plant life. This process is called eutrophication and deprives the water of available oxygen, causing the death of other organisms.
>
> Municipal sludge is often disposed of in an unorganized manner resulting in environmental pollution and a spread of diseases. The sludge produced carries a heavy microbiological load. Sludge also contains worms, ova, viruses, helminthic, weeds, etc. It also contains toxic heavy metals and organic pollutants like pesticides, poly-aromatic hydrocarbons, drugs, and other persistent pollutants. Sludge is a rich source of many macro (nitrogen, phosphorus, potassium), micronutrients (zinc, iron, copper, manganese) and organic carbon essential for soil."

It is not only important to take care of drains flowing into the Ganga. It is important that all the rivers which empty into the Ganga are also similarly cleaned.

As mentioned earlier, Ganga is used here only for an illustration (Fig. 6.11). The same fate is meted out to all the rivers in the country (see Fig. 6.12) and in most of the third world nations, which are reeling under the dual burden of water scarcity and water pollution.

Fig. 6.11 Polluted Ganga

Fig. 6.12 Yamuna: A major tributary to Ganga near Delhi

It requires a sustained effort both in treating the water flowing into the rivers and creating awareness among the public.

Every municipality is expected to provide drinking water to its inhabitants and clear the municipal waste. Most municipalities just dump the sewage in the nearest waterbody. Some have very primitive sewage treatment plants, which allow the sludge part of the sewage to settle down and release the water for irrigation or just let it flow into water bodies without any further treatment. The dry sludge is then sold to farmers to be used as fertilizer.

We have already seen that both the sludge and the remaining wastewater are quite toxic and contain extremely harmful pathogens, which get back into our food chain and create havoc. This toxic water is also contaminating our underground water sources.

It is a pity that, several thousand years ago, the cities of Indus Valley Civilization had a better water management system than what is operating in many third world cities today (Fig. 6.13).

"The most unique aspect of planning during the Indus Valley civilization was the system of underground drainage. The main sewer, 1.5-m deep and 91 cm across, was connected to many north-south and east-west sewers. It was made from bricks smoothened and joined seamlessly. The expert masonry kept the sewer watertight. Drops at regular intervals acted like an automatic cleaning device. A wooden screen at the end of the drains held back solid wastes. Liquids entered a cesspool made of radial bricks. Tunnels carried the waste liquids to the main channel connecting the dockyard with the river estuary. Commoner houses had baths and drain that emptied into underground soakage jars" [6].

6.2.3 *Sewage treatment plants*

Sewage treatment plants (Fig. 6.14) operate on a simple principle. The wastewater along with the sewage is put in a (primary) tank, where the sludge part settles down. The remaining liquid waste is then taken to a (secondary) biozone chamber. In the chamber, a pump airs the waste and encourages "friendly" bacteria to condense the organic matter. This breaks these down and purifies the water, which can then be used for irrigation or for flushing in toilets.

Fig. 6.13 Sanitary sewage at Lothal, Indus Valley Civilization [6]

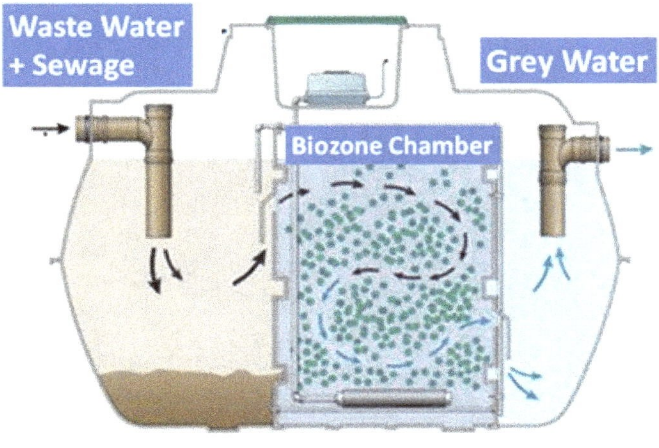

Fig. 6.14 The principle of a sewage treatment plant (Adapted from Wikipedia)

The sludge can be used as a fertilizer or even as fuel in a biogas plant, where the residue can again be used as fertilizer. In most developed countries, these are installed on a large scale and the water is reused several times for flushing before being finally discharged. Large-scale implementation of these facilities across cities will reduce the pressure on centralized large capacity sewage treatment plants. It will also minimize the need to regularly expand their capacities, which is not always easy.

A large capacity centralized sewage treatment plant (Fig. 6.15) of a major city will necessarily involve several steps before the sewage is finally treated. It normally has a mechanism to separate rainwater from the normal sewage by bypassing its passage through the process of treatment. It also has a pretreatment facility to remove garbage such as parts of trees, leaves and twigs, as well as sand, grit, and pieces of masonry, as these can damage pumps and remove fat from the wastewater.

Next, it goes through a primary treatment, where the sludge can settle down and get separated, followed by a secondary treatment

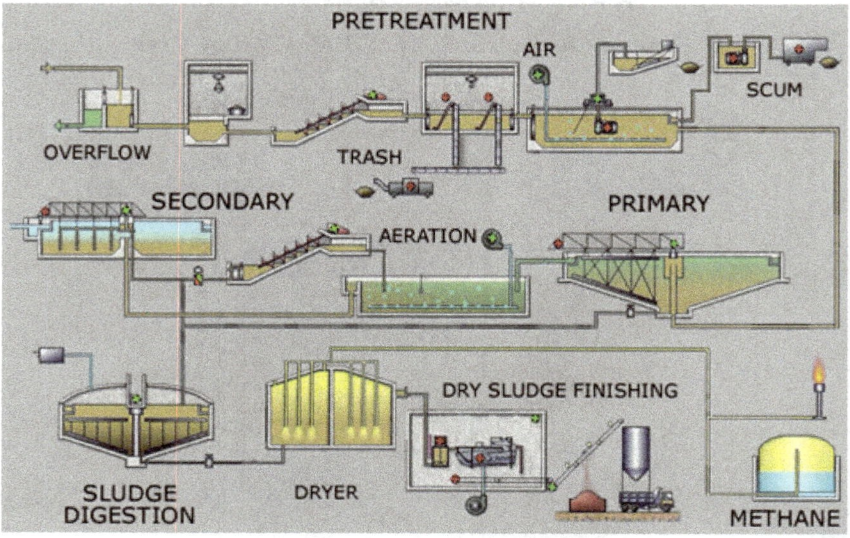

Fig. 6.15 Flow diagram for a typical large-scale treatment plant (Wikipedia)

using aerobic biological processes as before. The more sophisticated systems have a tertiary treatment to further clean the water for the removal of various chemicals by filtration, sedimentation, or chemical processes before the water is discharged in water bodies.

We have already seen that the sludge and the so-called "grey water" still have a very heavy load of harmful pathogens, antibiotics, and toxic chemicals, including dyes from the textile industry and metals like chromium from the leather industry. We reiterate that metal impurities from industries are best removed from the wastewater before it is discharged into drains. Several chemical methods, as well as special filters, are available for this, which must be implemented in all the industrial plants.

6.2.4 *Use of nuclear radiation to treat municipal sludge*

The sludge and the wastewater being released into water bodies can be more easily and most effectively treated to yield valuable and safe fertilizers and safe water for irrigation. Radiation (e.g., from Co-60) can be used to kill pathogens in municipal sludge, which can then be used as fertilizer. Bhabha Atomic Research Centre has set up a plant loaded with 150 kilo-Curie of Co-60 in collaboration with Amdavad Municipal Corporation, Ahmedabad. This "Sewage Sludge Hygienisation Plant" at Shahwadi, Ahmedabad (Fig. 6.16) was inaugurated in February 2019 and is in continuous operation since then.

Another liquid sludge irradiator, Sludge Hygienisation Research Irradiator (SHRI), is operating at Vadodara for radiation treatment of raw sludge containing 3–4% solids for the last 30 years. There is an urgent need to install these plants in all large cities of the country and convert the sludge to a valuable fertilizer instead of releasing this toxic waste into the farms.

This is an effective, economical, reproducible, scalable, and safe management process of sewage sludge treatment for agricultural applications. In addition to the radiation hygienization of the sewage sludge, a consortium of beneficial bacteria is added to it to make enriched organic manure for agricultural applications.

Fig. 6.16 The 100 tonnes per day sludge treatment plant in Ahmedabad

Wastewater generated from textile mills, paper mills and tanneries are often discharged directly to natural water bodies and pose great danger to the aquatic flora and fauna. Most of the dyes are not biodegradable and a layer of coloured water does not allow sunlight to penetrate beneath the surface, thus inhibiting photosynthesis for plants. It also uses up the valuable dissolved oxygen necessary to sustain aquatic life.

The wastewater and the sewage water can be treated with a 1-MeV-high current electron beam to kill bacteria and pathogens so that the water can be safely used for irrigation. The electron beam treatment breaks complex molecules of dyes and other chemicals into harmless simple molecules (Fig. 6.17).

Some plants have already been set up across the country using this phenomenon. Internationally, many experiments have been carried out on electron beam treatment of wastewater in countries such as Russia, Brazil, and South Korea with high-power electron accelerators. DC accelerators have been employed for this purpose

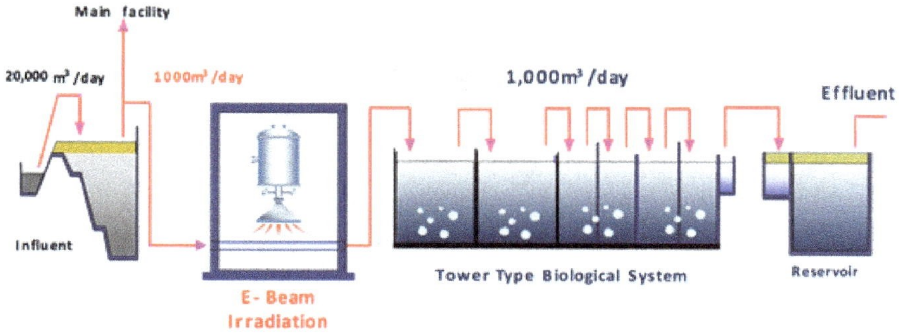

Fig. 6.17 Electron beam treatment of wastewater [7]

and a 1-MeV, 100-kW electron beam unit can treat up to 2 million litres of water per day, which can then be safely used for irrigation and industrial applications. One such unit is under construction for installation in Mumbai.

In many cities, like Bengaluru, sewage and municipal waste is often released into lakes and ponds, poisoning them forever. No marine animals survive in these waters. These water bodies are mostly covered with moss and water hyacinth, which harbours mosquitoes and other parasites and is not of much use. Gone are the days, when abundant water chestnut, lotus flowers and lotus seeds were routinely harvested from such water bodies across the country.

One has seen enough pictures of toxic foams forming in these lakes (Fig. 6.18) and many of the rivers, including the Yamuna River in Delhi, and even catching fire and blowing onto roads. Many water bodies, including even rivers, have been completely reclaimed in several parts of the country, leaving no place for the drain water to go, which leads to a collection of stinking water and causes severe flooding every year with the slightest rains, bringing diseases.

The sad story of neglect of Ganga is repeated with all the rivers in India and at most water bodies in all the third world countries.

It is painful to note that this very efficient modern treatment technique using radiation from Co-60 for treating the sludge and electron beam irradiation for the wastewater has been available in the country for decades and is not employed on a large scale. We hope

Fig. 6.18 Toxic foam from Varthur lake, Bengaluru

that the governments and municipal bodies take note of this very valuable development and employ it across the country to solve this problem once for all and secure the health of its citizens (see Fig. 6.19).

It can be adopted (Figs. 6.16 and 6.17) by all the third world nations and the International Atomic Energy Agency and United Nations Organization can provide necessary guidance and financial help for this. In absence of this, a large part of the world population is routinely exposed to disease and illness.

We must realize that pollution of water bodies such as rivers, lakes, ponds, and the oceans poses a serious risk for the health of the planet as well as its inhabitants. We have discussed the risk of several waterborne diseases like cholera which have haunted mankind from time immemorial. We share our water with all other creatures on the planet. Public awareness of our solemn duty to protect this natural source for the survival of our ecosystem will go a long way in tackling this problem. We have already indicated that the spectre of

Fig. 6.19 Citarum river in Bandung, West Java Province in Indonesia

water scarcity and even water wars are looming large over mankind, especially those in the countries near the equator, due to the ensuing global warming. There are even fears that it may lead to an enormous number of climate refugees.

We recall that sharing scarce resources of water from the Rohini River had led to a war-like condition between the nations of Shakya's and Koliya's during the life of Lord Buddha, and only a mediation by Him prevented the bloody war. We also recall that several civilizations in the past collapsed either because rivers dried up/changed course (Indus Valley Civilization) or because the salt from the river water used for irrigation, accumulated in the agricultural lands over centuries, turning them infertile (Sumerian Civilization). Recall that when the rainwater passes through soil and rocks it slowly dissolves bits of minerals, including sodium chloride (salt), which gets into rivers, making their water slightly salty. It is time that we wake up to the menace of pollution of our water bodies, which is putting our very survival at risk.

6.3 Land Degradation

Soil is among the most precious resources to humans as it sustains all vegetation on Earth. Every handful of soil has countless microbes that create a dynamic and complex ecosystem. Land degradation started when hunter and gatherer nomad humans started agriculture and animal husbandry by destroying natural vegetation to pave the way for the present-day agricultural and grazing lands. The increasing population has an increasing demand for food. This has encouraged or forced people to convert forests to farmlands and pastures. Agricultural crops do not bind and hold soil like natural vegetation, and this leads to land degradation. These along with unsustainable agricultural practices have resulted in the loss of half of the topsoil on the planet in the last 150 years. This includes compaction, loss of soil structure, nutrient degradation, and increased soil salinity. Recall again that the Sumerian Civilization collapsed due to the increasing salinity of its lands over centuries of irrigation by canals. This degradation of land has a cascading effect. Since degraded lands are not able to retain water, it leads to increased pollution and silting in streams and rivers. The runoff of the water causes floods and clogs rivers, which in turn leads to a decline in the population of fish and other marine animals.

In many cases, economic demand for agricultural land has led not only to land clearing but also to overcultivation, overgrazing, insufficient crop rotations and overuse of agrochemicals and pesticides. These practices provide short-term production and profitability to meet the demand of a growing population. Land degradation will get aggravated by climate change and it will adversely affect the living conditions of humans and wildlife as well as agricultural productivity and sustainable development. The extreme weather conditions that are expected to result from climate change will affect all aspects of food security by reducing production in many parts of the world, increasing prices and disrupting supply chains. These changes will be felt by low-income countries and harm rural communities the most. Already up to one-third of the land is degraded globally. It already affects 3 billion people, and it will get only worse as the population rises further, demand for food increases, and climate change results in prolonged droughts and heavy rains. This will affect countries around the equator most severely.

Indian Space Research Organization has recently released results of a detailed study of drylands, i.e., arid, semi-arid, and dry sub-humid areas of India, where any further degradation may lead to desertification. The study called Atlas [8] covered several of these aspects and concluded that about 30% of the land in India is getting degraded. This is a cause of concern as India supports 18% of the global population on only 2.4% of the world's landmass (see Fig. 6.20).

This study lists the processes of land degradation/desertification as: "vegetation degradation from deforestation, forest-blanks, shifting cultivation and grazing or grassland; water erosion resulting

Fig. 6.20 Desertification of land in Anantapur district of Andhra Pradesh, India (Photo by S. Dharumrajan)

in the loss of soil cover mainly due to rainfall and surface runoff water; wind erosion causing the spread of sand which can erode soil (the increased sand content makes it difficult for the soil to retain nutrients and water. The quartz crystals that make up sand are very fine, and they don't hold onto nutrients and water like regular soil does.); the salinity of soils in cultivated areas due to excess evapotranspiration, drought, excess irrigation, and overuse of fertilizers; waterlogging or the accumulation of standing water for long periods caused by floods, excess irrigation, and incorrect planning of drainage; frost shattering referring to the breakdown of rocks because of differences in temperature; frost heaving where ice lens forms under the soil; mass movement delineating the movement of masses of soil and rock due to gravity; and manmade causes such as mining, quarrying, brick kilns, industrial effluents, city waste, and urban agglomeration". Overexploitation of natural resources is considered the main reason for increasing land degradation in India.

The study has further prepared a detailed map of India (see Fig. 6.21) using satellites of the type of land cover, which includes forest or plantation, agriculture, grassland, scrubland, barren, rocky area, sandy area, glacial, periglacial, and others, for the country, which should be very handy in planning the measures for mitigation of land degradation. It concluded that the area under desertification (dryland areas) was 82.64 million hectares in 2011–2013, which rose by 1.16 million hectares from 2003 to 2005. While wind erosion was the main process leading to desertification in the arid regions, vegetation degradation and water erosion dominated in the semi-arid and dry sub-humid regions.

There is an urgent need to prevent soil loss by water erosion, which is the largest process leading to land degradation in India and to restore degraded lands. It is realized that systematic implementation of watershed interventions is needed to check soil erosion, improve soil moisture, increase recharge, stabilize river basins (catchments), which make agriculture and communities climate-resilient. Harvesting of rain/runoff water is an essential strategy to combat erosion by water. It will also help recharge the rapidly depleting groundwater.

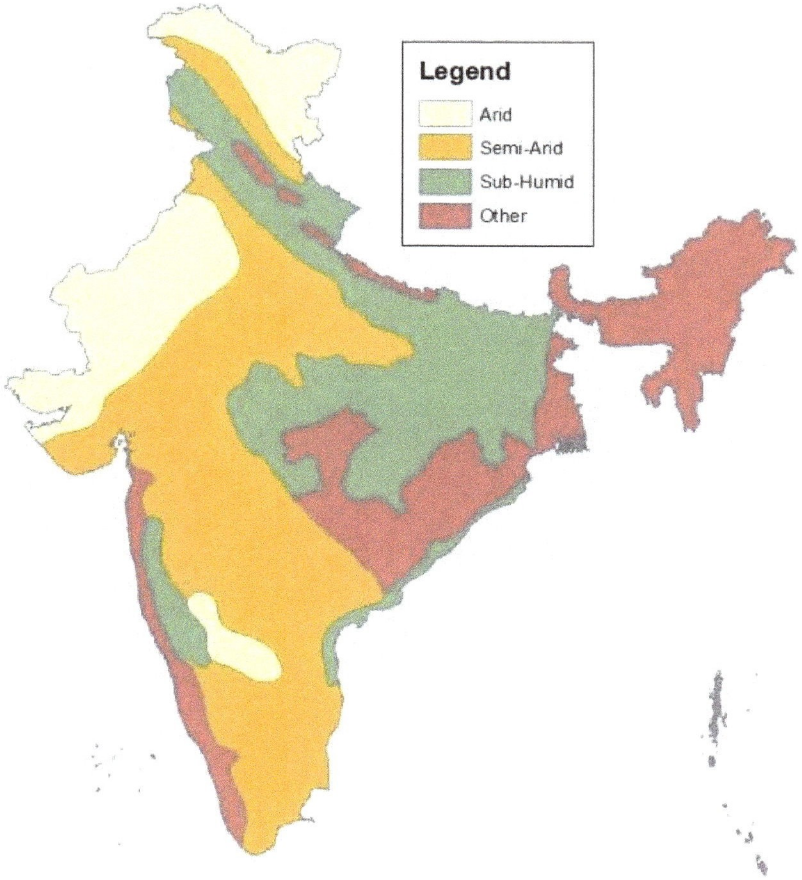

Fig. 6.21 Map of stages of land degradation of India [8]

Arresting land degradation can help slow the rate of climate change by assisting in carbon sequestration which is an important function of soil. It has been estimated that land degradation practices contribute around one-third of anthropogenic greenhouse gases. Conserving the capacity of carbon sinks, such as agricultural soils, provides an important pathway to reduce greenhouse gas emissions, in addition to helping sustainability, as discussed above.

It should be possible to reduce the pressure on India's agriculture to feed its population if good management practices can stop the current wastage of 30% of the food produced in India, which accrues during production, transport, and storage. Encouraging people to change their diets would further allow for a greater variety of crops, less water needed for production, and improved nutrition. It would reduce land degradation and food waste, and provide more equitable access to food. At the same time, there is a need to continuously improve seeds to have drought/flood/salt/pest/frost-resistant and high yielding crops.

It is known that the Green Revolution in India saw the widespread use of fertilizers that increased agricultural productivity at the cost of soil quality. The overuse of fertilizer is a major determinant of land degradation and reducing its use is likely to improve the situation. The use of shallow underground drip irrigation can also help reduce runoff and overexploitation of groundwater. It is felt that confidence in alternatives to the present excessive fertilizer, excessive irrigation, and excessive pesticide practices, which have provided the hard-earned food security for the country, will go a long way in solving the crisis before it hits us.

Moving to Africa, we note that countries in Africa face exceptional food shortages, and millions of people still face the threat of famine and starvation. Even without famine and starvation, malnutrition is widespread. Many of these countries suffer drought, desertification, and environmental degradation. Overgrazing, deforestation, removal of vegetation cover, agricultural activities in the vulnerable ecosystems of arid and semi-arid areas, which are thus strained beyond their capacity, and increasing population are believed to be responsible for this. Climate change, drought, and moisture loss on a global level also contribute to land degradation there.

Land degradation is taking place across the world. According to the World Atlas of Desertification prepared by the United Nations Environment Programme [9], the drylands across the world cover an area of about 1,035 million hectares, and about 40% of the population of Africa, about 39% of the population of Asia, and about 30% of the population of South America live in drylands (which are arid, semi-arid, and dry sub-humid areas). The reasons for the land degradation

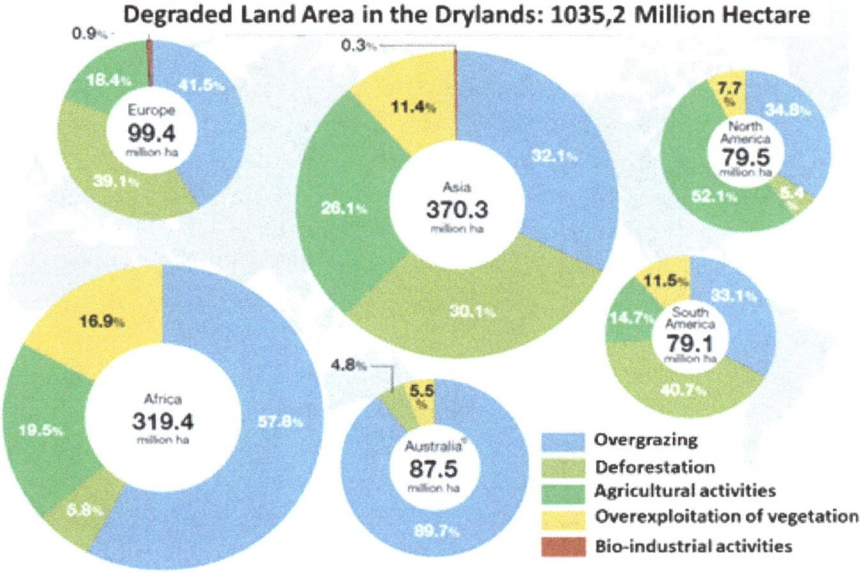

Fig. 6.22 Main causes of land degradation by region in susceptible drylands and other areas [9]

are given in Fig. 6.22. A coordinated action involving all the countries of the world is needed to tackle this crisis that the world faces.

India is a signatory to United Nations Convention to Combat Desertification, and its success in arresting land degradation will be keenly watched.

6.4 Municipal Waste

Cities, especially in developing countries, are groaning under mounting untreated municipal waste, which threatens to derail efforts at sustainable development and affect land, air, and water. The population of the world is close to 7.3 billion now, and it is expected to rise to 9 billion in coming decades and perhaps touch 11 billion towards the end of the twenty first century. There are suggestions that up to 80% of this population will live in cities, most of which are yet to be built! Presently, the world produces about 2 billion metric tonnes of waste per year, which varies from about 0.3 kg/day per person in poor countries to more than 4 kg/day per person in countries, such as New Zealand, Switzerland, and the USA. This puts an enormous strain on the environment of our planet, which is already under severe strain due to the unbridled exploitation of its sources and the resulting global warming. It has been realized for a long time that this can only be tackled effectively by adopting the so-called "circular development model". This would require that we reduce waste before it is produced and treat waste as a resource.

In this connection, a study by the United States Environmental Protection Agency [10] is very illustrative, which gives the composition of municipal waste (see Fig. 6.23). This study also immediately establishes the importance of recycling.

If waste is not treated properly, which is often the case, especially in the developing world, it poses a serious threat to the environment and public health. The United Nations advises that waste management should be considered a basic human need and should in fact be regarded as a "basic human right". It goes on to suggest that ensuring proper sanitation and solid waste management is as important as the provision of potable water, shelter, food, energy, transport, and communications, all being equally essential to the society and to the economy [11].

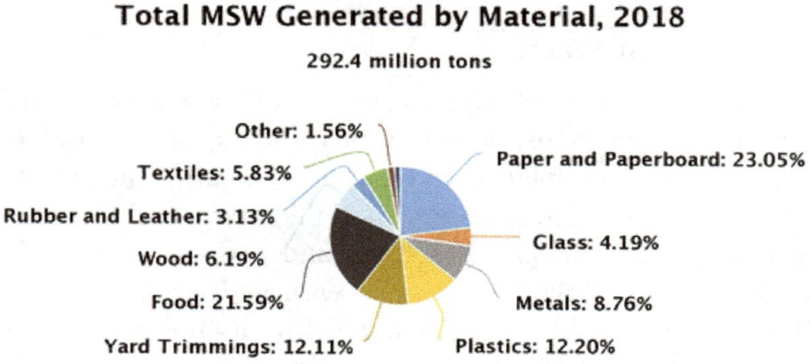

Fig. 6.23 Constituents of municipal waste in the USA [10]

In countries like India, it is not uncommon to see household solid waste dumped in the street, on the roadside, on vacant land, or into drains, streams, rivers, or other watercourses, or being burnt to lessen the nuisance of accumulated piles of waste, as at several places, one has a dysfunctional waste collection service. Needless to add that uncontrolled burning of waste leads to the production of particulate matter and emission of organic pollutants that are highly damaging locally and globally. The waste chokes the drain leading to the breeding of mosquitoes causing malaria and dengue. It also leads to cholera and other infectious diseases. It is a major source of flooding in cities and towns during monsoons in India, for example. The dumping of significant quantities of municipal or industrial solid waste in the open seriously affects the air (by emission of methane from the rotting of biodegradable parts), surface and groundwater, soil, and the coastal and marine environment.

We saw earlier that in 1994, the city of Surat in Gujarat suffered an outbreak of plague which was caused by major flooding because of uncollected waste blocking the drains and killing rats.

A very unfortunate incident occurred at Payatas, Quezon City, Philippines, in the year 2000. It had an 18-hectare municipal dump facility, which received an average of 1,500–1,800 tonnes of waste per day. It was home to waste pickers who constructed their houses up to and onto the waste slope. Heavy rain over 10 consecutive days in July 2000 led to a collapse of the dumpsite in the slum community, killing 300 and leaving hundreds of families homeless and without a source of livelihood.

One can see similar mountains of municipal waste around Mumbai, Kolkata, and Delhi, or for that matter close to all major cities. India produced about 147,613 tonnes of municipal waste per day in 2020. It is quite common to see ragpickers, including children, rummaging through these dumps, looking for anything of value, while animals muzzle through these for scraps of vegetables and food, surrounded by crows and vultures. It is well known that the vultures in India, who provide an important service as scavengers, have reached the verge of extinction by feeding on carcasses of animals, dumped at these sites, who were given diclofenac, a banned

Table 6.2 Regional annual waste generation [12]

Region	Waste Generation (Million Tonnes)
East Asia and The Pacific	468
Europe and Central Asia	392
South Asia	334
North America	289
Latin America and The Caribbean	231
Sub-Saharan Africa	174
The Middle East and North Africa	129

drug. It is also common to see these mounds of waste smouldering and giving out toxic smoke, as the green waste in these decays produces methane, which easily catches fire.

Table 6.2 provides the amount of waste collected annually in different parts of the world.

One of the largest dumpsites in the world is at Deh Jam Chakro near Karachi in Pakistan. It covers an area of more than 202 hectares. About 5,000 persons work there and the dumpsite seriously affects the lives of over 5 million people living within 10 km of the site. The Bantar Gebang dump in Bekasi, Indonesia adds 230,000 tonnes of municipal solid waste every year to its 40 million tonnes of already accumulated waste. The Vinca dumpsite in Belgrade, Serbia, receives 700,000 tonnes of waste annually, including medical waste and e-waste and is located just 2 km from the Danube River and the nearest settlement.

It is important to realize that municipal waste includes all the wastes generated in general at all households, offices, hotels, markets, and industry, and fall into the following general categories:

- *Biodegradable waste*: food and kitchen waste, green waste, paper (most can be recycled).
- *Recyclable materials*: paper, cardboard, glass, bottles, jars, tin cans, aluminium cans, aluminium foil, metals, certain plastics, textiles, clothing, tires, batteries, etc.
- *Inert waste*: construction and demolition waste, dirt, rocks, debris.

- *Electrical and electronic waste*: electrical appliances, light bulbs, washing machines, TVs, computers, screens, mobile phones, alarm clocks, watches, etc.
- *Composite waste*: waste clothing, Tetra Pack food and drink cartons, waste plastics such as toys and plastic garden furniture.
- *Hazardous waste*: most paints, chemicals, tires, batteries, light bulbs, electrical appliances, fluorescent lamps, aerosol spray cans, and fertilizers.
- *Toxic waste*: pesticides, herbicides, and fungicides.
- *Biomedical waste*: hospital waste, expired pharmaceutical drugs, etc.

We shall discuss hazardous waste, plastics, and e-waste separately (see Fig. 6.24).

We immediately realize that handling municipal waste can succeed, if and only if, everyone — including young children — participates in the process by separating the waste according to the category for the municipal authorities to collect it. Separating these, if all the waste is mixed, can be very difficult, time-consuming, labour-intensive, and expensive. The segregation reduces the cost of recycled products such as paper, metals, and glass, and ensures the success of the strategy. The strategy to treat municipal waste

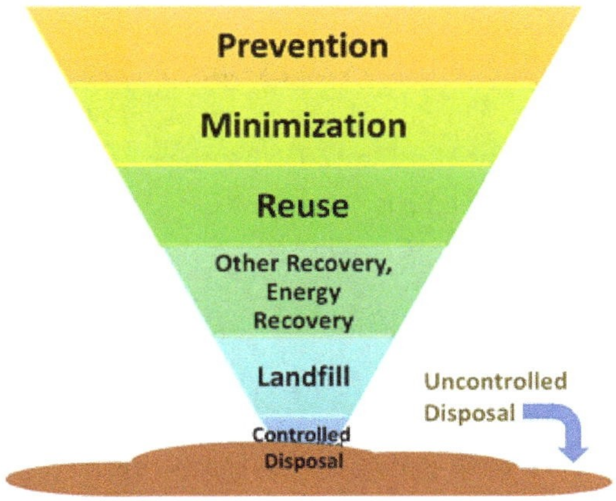

Fig. 6.24 Waste management hierarchy [11]

is often discussed in terms of waste management hierarchy. The so-called green or wet waste can be composted so that it is microbiologically degraded under aerobic conditions. This produces water, heat, carbon dioxide and manure, and leads to a large reduction in volume. The process requires agitating and aerating the waste for the completion of the process of composting and can be speeded up by doing these mechanically instead of leaving the waste in large and deep ditches.

The people assisted separation of the waste plays a very important role in recycling metals, paper, wood, glass, etc., and collecting green waste for composting, and as mentioned earlier is essential for the process to succeed.

6.5 E-waste

Revolution in information and electronic technology has led to an exponential rise in the use of new electronic equipment. At the same time, it has also produced growing volumes of obsolete products, which contribute to e-waste, one of the fastest-growing waste streams. Although e-waste contains complex combinations of highly toxic substances that pose danger to health and the environment, many of the products also contain recoverable precious materials, making it a different kind of waste compared with traditional municipal waste (see Fig. 6.25).

E-waste is an overlooked epidemic and a growing global challenge that poses a serious threat to the environment and human health worldwide. A study by the United Nations has revealed that around 50 million tonnes of electronic waste, or e-waste, is being thrown away each year, and this figure is projected to reach 75 million tonnes by 2030 and double further by 2050 [13]. This rapid increase is often called the tsunami of e-waste. E-waste may include computers, monitors, televisions, stereos, copiers, printers, fax machines, cellphones, DVD players, cameras, batteries, washing machines, refrigerators, air conditioners, microwave ovens, and many more electronic devices. Used electronic devices can be reused, resold, salvaged, recycled, or disposed of. And still, less than 20% of the e-waste is recycled

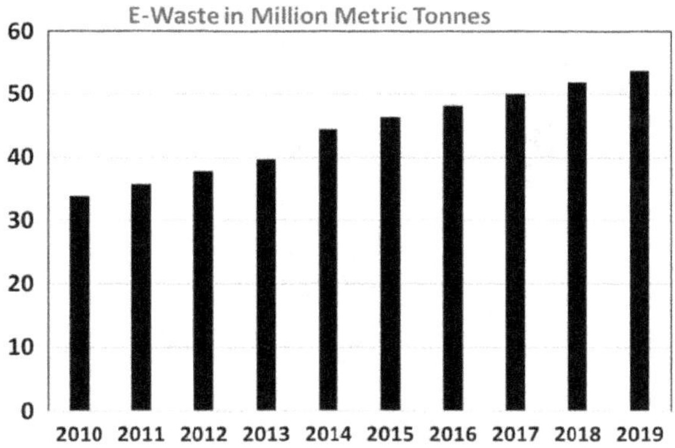

Fig. 6.25 Global E-waste production (Data from Statista.com)

appropriately, the rest ends up in landfills, or is disposed of by informal workers in poor conditions. This will explode into a global health crisis if it is not addressed.

The switch to renewables like solar energy, which is proceeding rapidly across the world, in order to combat global warming and climate change, will soon start producing a large bulk (several tens of millions of tonnes) of discarded solar panels every year. Solar panels degrade by about 1% every year and become uneconomical in about 15–20 years and must be replaced. The presence of hazardous materials in the end-of-life panels can result in significant pollution and health issues if released into the environment. The main contributor to the total weight of a typical crystalline silicon PV module is glass (75%), followed by polymer (10%), aluminium (8%), silicon (5%), copper (1%) and small amounts of silver, tin, lead, and other metals and components. Lead and tin, if leached into soil and groundwater, cause health and environmental concerns, while copper, silver, and silicon present a value opportunity *if recovered efficiently* (see Fig. 6.26).

When electronic waste is thrown away into landfills, its toxic materials, e.g., lead, barium, mercury, arsenic, and cadmium seep into groundwater. This groundwater contributes to most surface streams, ponds, and lakes, and is used by most animals who can get sick, thus leading to imbalances in the planetary ecosystem.

Fig. 6.26 E-waste (Credit: John Cameron, unsplash.com)

As these toxins leach into the soil, they influence the plants and trees that grow on this soil and finally enter the human food supply, leading to birth defects as well as several other health complications, such as damage to human blood, kidneys, and central and peripheral nervous systems. Unfortunately, this happens mostly in developing countries where most of the electronic waste is dumped. Several of these materials are also carcinogenic.

Developed countries have strict environmental regulatory regimes. This makes waste disposal rather expensive, and thus, many of them find exporting it to small traders in developing countries more profitable than recycling it in their own countries. There are also reports that e-waste reaches developing countries in the form of donations and charity from rich industrialized nations. At the same time, e-waste profiteers often make substantial profits due to lax environmental laws, corrupt officials, and poorly paid workers. Dismantling components, wet chemical processing, and incineration result in direct exposure and inhalation of harmful chemicals. Most of these workers have no access to safety equipment, such as gloves, face masks, or ventilation fans.

We have noted that computers and most electronics equipment contain toxic materials, such as lead, zinc, nickel, flame retardants, barium, chromium, and lithium. These also contain small quantities of precious metals. When e-waste is warmed up or burned to recover metal from wires and cables, it leads to emissions of brominated and chlorinated dioxins into the air, which damage the atmosphere. These can be carried for thousands of kilometres by air currents. The process of extraction and collection of tiny quantities of precious metals exposes the workers to poisonous chemicals and fumes of highly concentrated acids. Printed circuit boards and computer and television screens expose them to lead. Lead is known to cause irreversible brain damage to young children with their still-developing brains and lead to loss of appetite, weight loss, fatigue, stomach pain, vomiting, constipation and learning difficulties. Adults, when exposed to lead suffer from high blood pressure, a decline in mental functioning, pain/numbness of extremities, muscle weakness, headache, stomach pain, memory loss, mood disorders and fertility problems including a higher probability of miscarriages.

Guiyu, China, is the largest e-disposal site in China and quite possibly in the world and receives shipments of toxic e-waste from all over the world, amounting to 400,000 tonnes annually. It employed more than 60,000 workers in 2005. Here, many of the residents exhibit substantial digestive, neurological, respiratory and bone problems.

Up to 10,000 persons work at one of the world's largest destinations for used electronic goods, in Agbogbloshie dump, which receives 192,000 tonnes of e-waste annually. It is a wasteland with burning mounds of trash in Ghana's capital, Accra, where clouds of heavy, acidic gusts of smoke hang low. These workers suffer from burns, back problems, and infected wounds, as well as from respiratory problems, chronic nausea, and debilitating headaches, brought on by the hazardous working environment and toxic air pollution.

Vast amounts of e-waste are transported from the United States, Canada, Australia, Europe, Japan and the Republic of Korea to African, Asian, and South American countries. As e-waste dumps expand across the globe, so do the number of workers employed in the e-waste sector. It has been estimated [14] that at the moment, the waste management sector employs 64 million persons, and the number will increase by 70% by 2030 and employ another 45 million persons. Considering that e-waste is the world's fastest growing waste stream, many of these jobs, formal or informal, will be in e-waste processing.

It has also been estimated [14] that "as many as 12.9 million women are working in the informal waste sector, which potentially exposes them to toxic e-waste and puts them and their unborn children at risk. Moreover, more than 18 million children and adolescents, some as young as 5 years of age, are actively engaged in the informal industrial sector, of which waste processing is a sub-sector. Children are often engaged by parents or caregivers in e-waste recycling because their small hands are more dexterous than those of adults. Other children live, go to school, and play near e-waste recycling centres where high levels of toxic chemicals — mostly lead and mercury — can damage their intellectual abilities."

To avert child labour, better monitoring and tracking of the swelling numbers of waste workers in the informal labour force, and women and children e-waste workers are thus considered critical to protect those most at risk of exposure. It is hoped that the world rallies to protect our most valuable resource — the health of our children — from the growing threat of e-waste [14].

A very novel initiative was taken by Japan, where about 79,000 tonnes of e-waste (mostly mobile phones) was used to recover more than 32 kg of gold, 3,500 kg of silver, and 2,200 kg of bronze to prepare the medals for the 2020 Olympic Games, which were delayed due to COVID-19 and held in 2021.

This discussion will not be complete unless we recall two obnoxious events which led to the Basel Convention which tried to stop the practices of dumping e-waste in the countries of the third world. The Resource Conservation and Recovery Act was enacted in 1976 in the United States, which enforced strict adherence to laws governing the disposal of solid waste and hazardous waste. This led to a substantial increase in the cost of disposal of hazardous waste, which in turn led to dumping, export, and donation of this waste to less developed countries. And then two gruesome incidents took place in 1988.

A ship carrying about 14,000 tonnes of toxic incinerator ash from Pennsylvania sailed for New Jersey, which refused to accept it. Six other states also refused to accept the incinerator ash. It was decided to ship it to some other country with less stringent environmental laws. The ship sailed for 16 months, changed its name several times, and searched for a place to unload the waste and finally dumped it, calling it "topsoil fertilizer" near Gonaives in Haiti and in the Indian and Atlantic Oceans by November 1988. In the second incident, approximately 3,500 tonnes of toxic waste from Italy was dumped in the small town of Koko in Nigeria.

The enormity of these acts led to the Basel Convention in 1989, where an international treaty was formulated "to control transboundary movements of hazardous wastes and their disposal and to control the international trade in hazardous wastes between countries, and specifically to prevent the transfer of hazardous waste from developed to less developed countries", which was ratified by 187 countries and came into effect on May 5, 1992. India, officially, banned the import of e-waste for disposal into the country as per Hazardous and Other Wastes (Management and Transboundary) Rules, 2016 [15]. Its strict adherence, however, is not certain.

In the passing, we add that to maximize profits and to avoid strict laws for the disposal of excessive cow dung in a given area, a company from the Netherlands had entered into an arrangement with some Indian companies in 1994, under which the huge container ships carrying oil from Gulf countries to Europe, instead of returning empty, would have brought cow dung mixed with water to India, which by the way has among the largest animal stocks in the world. A huge protest, including one at the parliament, put an end to this scheme, which would have introduced vast quantities of toxic waste of animals fattened on hormones and steroids in India.

Even though ship breaking is also covered by the Basel Convention workers in Chittagong (Bangladesh), Alang–Sosiya (India), and Gadani (Pakistan) are exposed to the hazards of asbestos, the use of which was quite common till a few decades ago. These are taken out and sold for reuse, spreading the danger to larger areas.

6.6 Plastic Waste and Microplastics

Plastic is a man-made material that one can now find in the earth, in the air, and in the deepest ocean trenches. It is extremely durable, and thus, the majority of what has been created is still present in our ecosystem. It has made its way into the food chain and permeates our bodies. It flows from our blood into our organs and has even found its way into the human placenta [16]. The durability of plastic makes it most useful: cables stretching across ocean floors, water pipes under the ground, and packaging that keeps food fresh all rely on its durability. And it is cheap to produce. Its low cost has given rise to the culture of "use and throw", which has now inundated the land and the sea.

Plastic was invented in 1907. It is a material consisting of any of a wide range of synthetic or semi-synthetic organics that are malleable and can be moulded into solid objects of diverse shapes. This, coupled with the ease and low cost of producing them as well as several other properties to be discussed presently, makes them extremely popular. Plastics are typically organic polymers of high molecular mass, but they often contain other substances. They are usually synthetic, most are derived from petrochemicals, but many are partially natural. Most plastics are composed of polymers of carbon and hydrogen alone or with oxygen, nitrogen, chlorine, or sulphur in the backbone. Polythene, polyvinyl chloride, and polystyrene are largely used in the manufacture of plastics. Polythene (or polyethene), for example, is produced by the polymerization of ethene, at a temperature of 200°C and pressure of about 2,000 atmospheres, in the presence of a small quantity of oxygen:

$$n\,CH_2{=}CH_2(gas) \rightarrow [(-CH_2-CH_2-)_n]\ (solid)$$

Plastics that do not undergo chemical change during heating and cooling are called "thermoplastics". These are used for making plastic wraps, food containers, lighting panels, garden hoses, and ubiquitous plastic bags. Plastics that are permanently "set" once they are given a shape and cannot be remoulded are called "thermosets". These are used for making kitchen tools, glues, varnishes, electronic components, etc. (see Fig. 6.27).

The popularity of plastics stems from several useful properties:

- They are resistant to chemicals, water, and impact.
- They have excellent thermal and electrical insulation properties.
- They have good safety and hygiene properties, which is very useful for food packaging.
- They have a lighter weight than competing materials, which reduces fuel consumption during transportation.
- They are relatively inexpensive to produce.

Code No.	Code	Full Name	Uses
1	PETE	POLYETHYLENE TEREPHTHALATE	Aerated-drink bottles and oven-ready meal trays
2	HDPE	HIGH-DENSITY POLYETHYLENE	Bottles for milk and liquids for washing
3	PVC	POLYVINYL CHLORIDE	Food trays, cling films, and bottles for squash, mineral water, and shampoo
4	LDPE	LOW-DENSITY POLYETHYLENE	Carrier bags and bin liners
5	PP	POLYPROPYLENE	Microwaveable meal trays, margarine containers, and bottles for medicine
6	PS	POLYSTYRENE	Pots, fish trays, boxes and cartons, cups, plastic cutlery , packaging for electronic goods and toys
7	Others	MIX OF OTHER PLASTICS	Water drums, baby milk bottles, beverage bottles, melamine cups

Fig. 6.27 Types of plastics

Fig. 6.28 Plastic waste completely covering the Citarum river, Indonesia [17]

Finally, plastics are resistant to weather and chemicals. They are versatile, easy to clean, and can be recycled. Unfortunately, these very properties have created a situation where we produce up to 300 million tonnes of plastic every year, and a large part of it is discarded after a single use. The discarded plastic ends up either in municipal dumps or finds its way to water bodies (Fig. 6.28) and finally to oceans (Fig. 6.29). It may be noted that the waste plastic in a given year can be more than the production, as the discarded plastics may have been produced over a longer period.

6.6.1 *Pollutions due to plastics and microplastics*

This "use and throw" culture, associated with plastics (Fig. 6.30), mentioned earlier, has led to very unfortunate and damaging consequences, which if not addressed will cause serious harm to the health of the planet and its inhabitants. Plastic bags and plastic products are being regularly recovered from the guts of fish, animals,

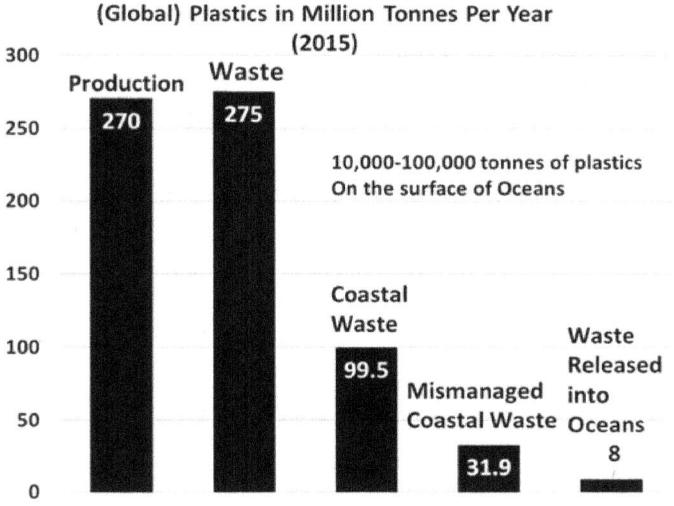

Fig. 6.29 Pathway of plastics to ocean [18]

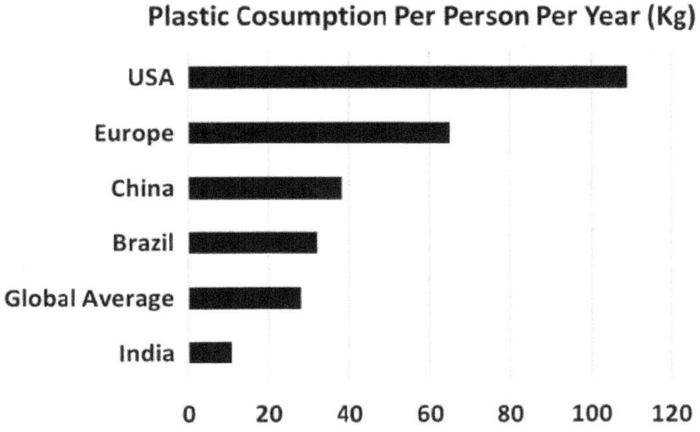

Fig. 6.30 Plastic consumption per head [19]

and birds. The seabirds, turtles, fish, and marine mammals, like dolphins and whales, are getting strangled in plastic debris. They are getting entangled in plastic debris. They are getting suffocated and asphyxiated by plastic debris. They are starving as plastic debris fills their stomach leaving no space for food. Additionally, careless disposal of plastic bags chokes drains, blocks the porosity of the soil, and causes problems for groundwater recharge.

Bigger pieces of plastic are broken into microplastics, under the action of the sun and seawater, and even into nanoplastics. Several cosmetics, special cleaning materials, synthetic clothes, paints, abrasion of tyres, ropes, nets, and all kinds of plastic objects release microplastics. These are now found in every corner of the globe from Mount Everest to Mariana Trench (Fig. 6.31). The ocean currents push plastics and microplastics to the coast, where many unique marine species such as marine turtles, sea birds, and sea lions come to rest and feed. There have been estimates that if we do not take steps to check this menace, by 2050 there will be more plastic than fish in the oceans.

Small organisms feed on the tiny bits of microplastic and absorb the chemicals from the plastic into their tissues. These have been detected in a range of marine species, including plankton and whales, which eat them. The small organisms that consume microplastics are eaten by larger animals. Thus, the toxic chemicals become part of their tissues. This journey up the food chain continues till it becomes part of the food that we eat. We have seen that microplastics have

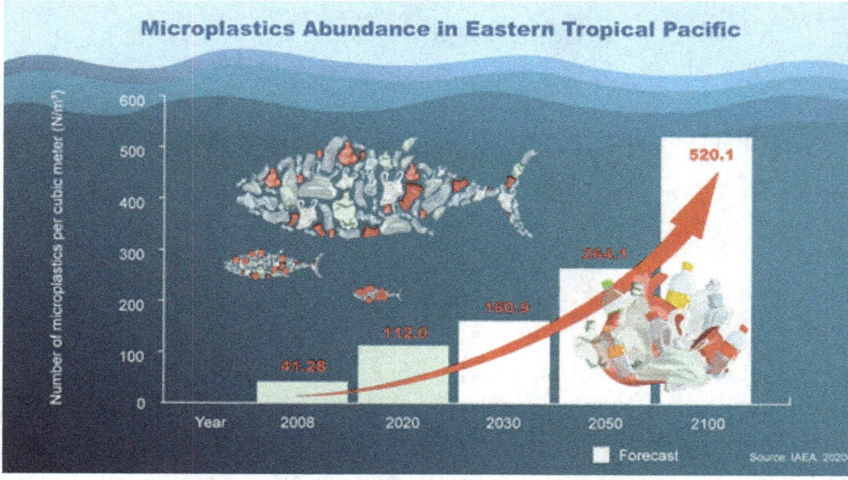

Fig. 6.31 Abundance of microplastics in eastern tropical pacific [19]

been detected in human blood and even the human placenta. Nearly every species of sea bird is known to eat plastics as it releases a chemical that makes it smell like their natural food.

Tests have also confirmed that microplastics cause liver and cell damage and disrupt the reproductive systems of oysters, making them lay fewer eggs. Research also finds that larval fish are eating nanofibers during the first days of life.

Plastic waste, thin single-use plastic bags, plastic wrappers, plastic bottles, plastic toys litter our land even in the remotest corners of the country. These fly around and are carried to the treetops by currents. Millions of animals are killed by plastics every year. In India, it is common to read about cows dying an excruciatingly painful death by choking on plastic bags. There are reports that plastics have been consumed by elephants, hyenas, zebras, tigers, and camels, often causing death.

The most unhappy situation is that our rivers, which were already polluted with untreated municipal and industrial waste, have become carriers of plastics, which is further choking them. Eight of the 10 most polluted rivers are from Asia and Africa (Table 6.3), but even rivers from developed nations are polluted.

We use plastics for our convenience and just throw them away, or if we are very kind and careful, we put them in a litter box and forget it. These are collected by municipal workers, loaded onto trucks

Table 6.3 Ten most polluted rivers of the world [20]

Rank (Most Polluted)	River	Country
1	Citarum	Indonesia
2	Yangtze	China
3	Indus	Pakistan
4	Yellow River	China
5	Marilao	Philippines
6	Sarno	Italy
7	Niger	Nigeria
8	Ganga	India
9	Buriganga	Bangladesh
10	Mississippi	USA

that proceed through the cities littering the streets and taken to a landfill. These landfills have now become mountains of garbage in metros, such as Mumbai, New Delhi, and Kolkata. The situation in smaller cities and towns is not much different, only the size of the garbage mountain differs.

In one of the most pathetic sights — repeated in most third world countries — young children and poor rummage through it and look for anything of value. They work in most unhygienic conditions without any protection and handle some of the most toxic waste produced by mankind. The rotting waste gives out methane gas. There are regular incidents of uncontrolled fires and acrid smoke. There is some hue and cry for a few days, the mountain runs out of gas, and all is forgotten.

We started using plastics made from fossil fuels, just about a century ago. Large-scale production of plastics started after the Second World War. Mass production of plastics began about six decades ago (Fig. 6.32). By now, about 8.5 billion tonnes of plastic have been produced. This is more than one tonne per head!

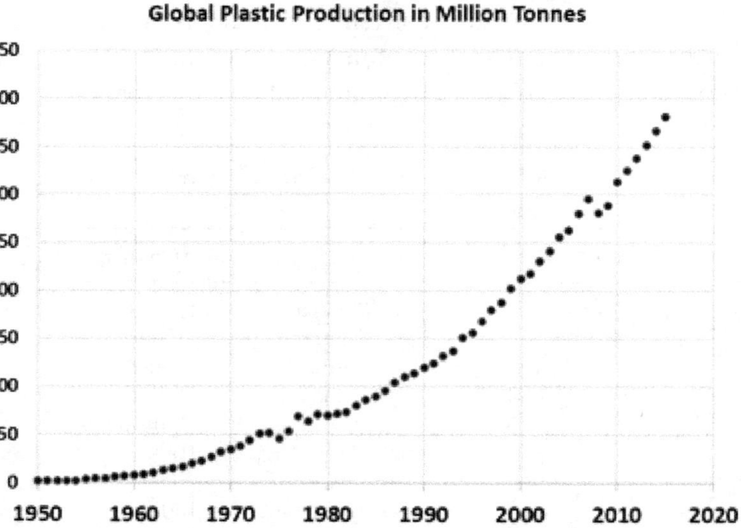

Fig. 6.32 Global plastic production [18]

We have seen that plastics have changed our lives. Plastics revolutionized medicine — both with life-saving devices and with packaging for its safe distribution. It played an important role in space travel; it reduced the weight of cars and planes, which in turn saved pollution-causing fuels. It gave us diapers, helmets, incubators, equipment for clean drinking water, and personal protection equipment, including gloves, coveralls, shoe covers, goggles, and surgical masks, to protect our medical practitioners and researchers (Fig. 6.33).

And it made life comfortable. However, as mentioned, the fact that it was convenient and yet cheap led to a culture of "use and throw". Most of the plastic is used for the packaging of commercial products and the plastic covers end up as trash. Only about 10–20% of it has either been recycled or incinerated. The rest has been dumped around in landfills or just garbage dumps. We have seen

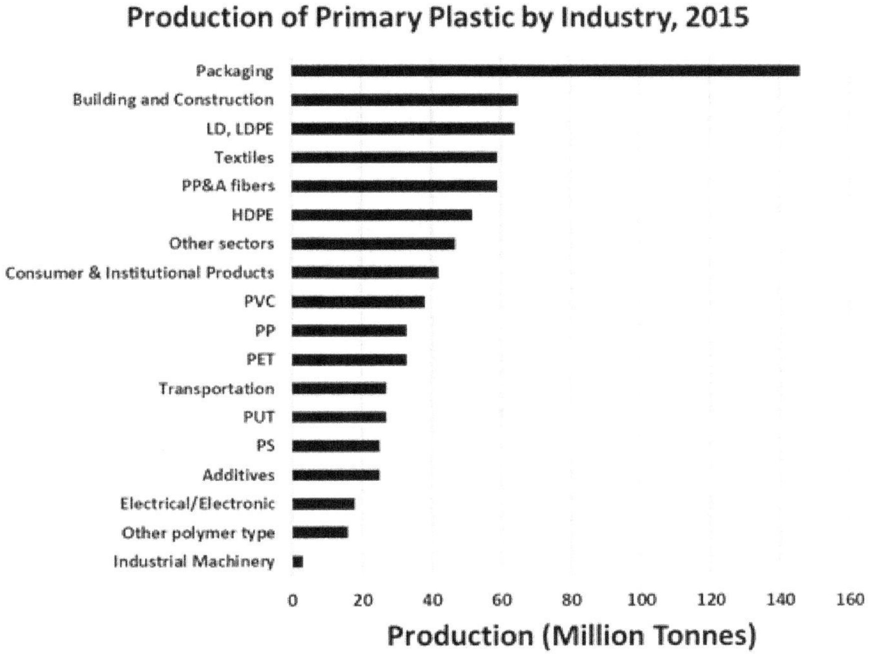

Fig. 6.33 Plastic production by industry [19]

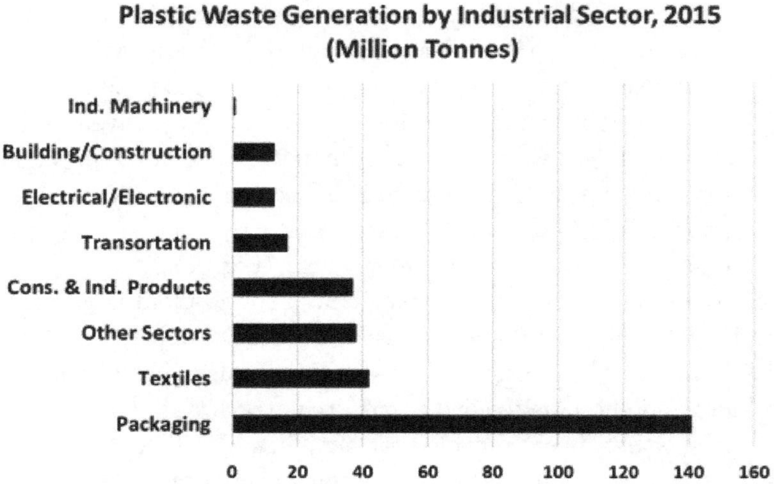

Fig. 6.34 Plastic generation by industrial sector [18]

that up to 8 million tonnes of these plastics find their way into oceans every year (see Fig. 6.34).

It is a pity that many of these products like plastic bags and food wrappers have a lifespan of a few minutes or a few hours, yet they persist in the environment for hundreds of years (Fig. 6.35). The serious hazard plastics pose is obvious.

The crisis arising out of waste disposal, especially in countries like India is a gigantic tragedy waiting to strike. The landfills, unlike in developed countries, are rarely, if ever, lined with leakproof linings and water bodies including underwater sources are being poisoned.

When plastic is burned in the air, it releases a host of poisonous chemicals into the air, including toxic chemicals like dioxins, which accumulate in the food chain mainly in the fatty tissue of animals. Styrofoam contains the chemical styrene, which can cause cancer and other diseases. When hot foods or liquids are consumed from Styrofoam plates and cups, the styrene leaches out of the Styrofoam and enters our bodies. Bisphenol-a (BPA), commonly found in a variety of consumer products, causes a higher risk of certain cancers, reduced fertility, birth defects and diabetes. BPA is the main

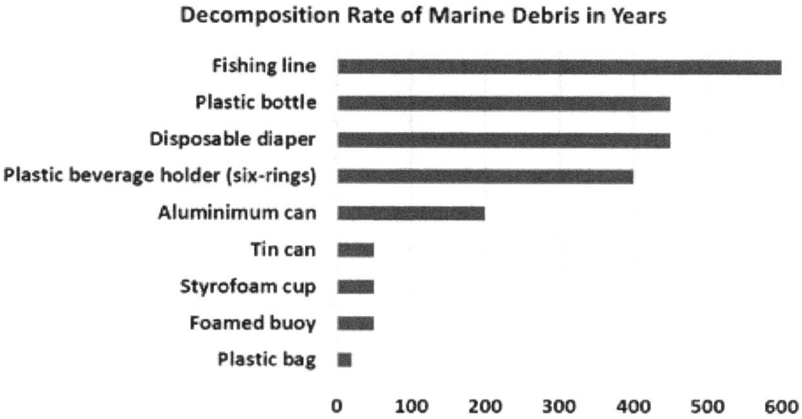

Fig. 6.35 Expected life of marine debris [19]

component of polycarbonate, the hard, clear plastic sometimes used to make water bottles, baby bottles, and food storage containers.

6.6.2 *Handling the plastic pollution*

It is known that the world generates about 2 billion tonnes of municipal solid waste annually. It has been estimated that it consists of metals (4%), glass (5%), plastic (12%), paper and cardboard (17%), and food and greens (44%) [21]. This is expected to increase to 3.4 billion tonnes annually by 2050. It is estimated that over 90% of the waste is mismanaged in poor countries, which increases emissions and risks of disaster, which affect the poor disproportionately. At least one-third of the solid waste is openly dumped or burned.

Before proceeding to discuss the possible methods for treating plastic waste, we look at the fate of plastic waste in the past and the future (Fig. 6.36). Geyer *et al.* [22] have estimated the extent of the problem of plastic waste by the middle of the twenty first century.

Having noted the enormity of the problem and its possible disastrous consequences, we proceed to discuss methods used for treating plastic waste (Fig. 6.37).

The conventional methods include recycling, incineration, and landfill. It should be realized that only some of the plastics can be

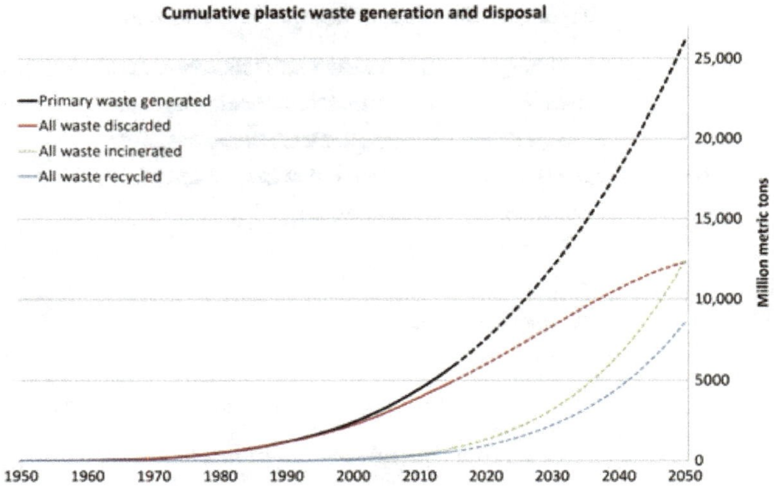

Fig. 6.36 Cumulative plastic generation and disposal [22]

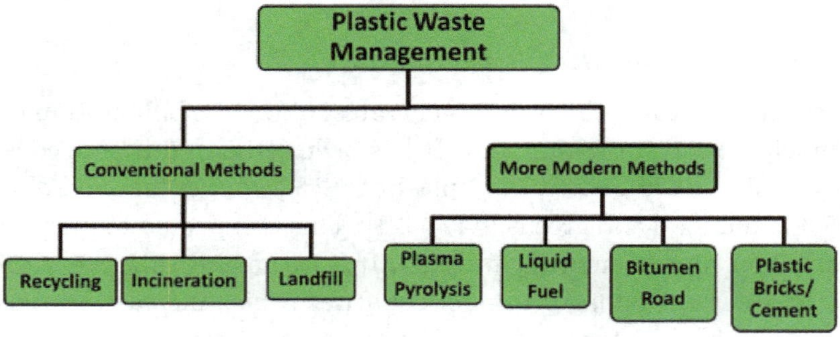

Fig. 6.37 Methods for treatment of plastic waste

easily recycled. There have been reports that many developed countries used to export their plastic waste by deliberately mislabelling them to China, Indonesia, Turkey, India, Malaysia, and Vietnam, which in turn struggled to separate these and try to recycle them. Most of these countries have now refused to accept plastic waste. We have already noted that open-air incineration releases toxic chemicals into the atmosphere, which can cause serious illnesses. Landfills are known to contaminate groundwater. Unfortunately, when the plastic

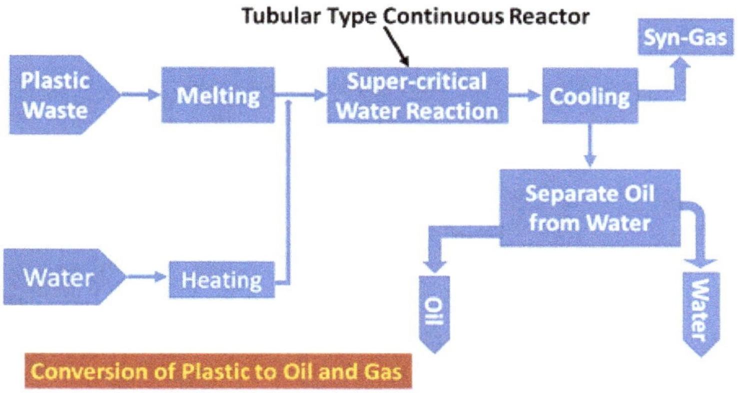

Fig. 6.38 Conversion of plastic to oil and fuel gas

is melted for the simplest process of recycling, the polymer chains are partially broken down. This decreases its tensile strength and viscosity, and makes it harder to process. The new, lower grade plastic often becomes unsuitable for use in food packaging and most plastic can be recycled only a very limited number of times before it is so degraded that it becomes unusable.

It is straightforward to convert waste plastic into oil and gas by heating it with water, and plants are available for this (Fig. 6.38). Plasma pyrolysis has been discussed in connection with the treatment of medical waste earlier. Pyrolysis differs from other processes like combustion and hydrolysis because it does not involve a reaction with oxygen. It can also be used to convert plastic into fuel gas. A cold plasma pyrolysis procedure has also been developed where the temperatures reached are about 400–500°C and convert waste plastics into hydrogen, methane, and ethylene. Hydrogen and methane can be used as clean fuels as they produce minimal amounts of harmful compounds, such as soot, unburnt hydrocarbons, and carbon dioxide. Ethylene is also the most abundant foundation for most plastics, and this could be recycled back into new plastic manufacturing.

A recent interesting development [16] involves a "hydrothermal process", where the shredded plastic is heated along with supercritical water. This process of heating, instead of heating the shredded plastics kept in a chamber, spreads the heat evenly, and thus, the procedure can be easily scaled. Next, this high-pressure system is depressurized. This causes most of the liquid to flash off as vapour, leaving unconverted waste behind. The vapour is cooled in a distillation column and the condensed liquids are separated on a boiling range to produce four hydrocarbon liquids and oils: naphtha, distillate gas oil, heavy gas oil and heavy waxy residue, akin to bitumen. These products can then be used directly by the petrochemical industry. The process does not involve any downcycling as the polymer bonds can be formed anew. Thus, the plastics can be *infinitely recycled.* The process has a conversion rate of more than 99% and holds out great hope as nearly all the plastic turns into a useful product.

A very powerful method for use of plastic waste to make roads has also been developed [23], which involves the following steps:

- Plastic waste is collected and segregated.
- Next, it is cleaned and dried.
- Then it is shredded into pieces measuring 2–4 mm.
- Subsequently, stone chips to be used are heated to about 160–170°C.
- The shredded plastic is added to the heated stone chips (5–10% by weight) and mixed thoroughly so that the chips get coated with (melted) plastic.
- These plastic-coated stone chips are mixed with hot bitumen at about 160–170°C.
- This composite is used to lay roads at a temperature of 110–130°C.

The construction of every kilometre of a road requires 9 tonnes of bitumen and 1 tonne of plastic waste. Considering that bitumen costs about 30,000 INR/tonne, this also leads to considerable savings. Roads thus made have been found to be very long-lasting and resistant to heavy rains compared to the normal bitumen roads. Already 100,000 km of roads have been made in India using this procedure.

It has also been suggested to use waste plastics as fuel in cement kilns.

Unfortunately, the fluctuating price of crude oil and the cost of collecting, segregating, cleaning, and shredding used plastic make recycling more expensive than making fresh plastics. A suggestion has been made that the producers of plastics may be levied a fee towards these steps. There have also been indications that some of the biggest users of plastics, viz., makers of aerated drinks, fashion products, and processed foods, etc., may have lobbied to stall legislation on reducing the use of plastics. If true, this is rather unfortunate.

There have been attempts to develop biodegradable alternatives for several plastic products. One interesting example involves replacing nylon ropes used in the fishing and shipping industry with those of sisal (*Agave sisalana*) fibres. Sisal is a native of southern Mexico and Brazil, and was introduced in India a long time ago (see Fig. 6.39). It can grow in poor land and does not require any special care. Ropes

Fig. 6.39 Sisal plants [24]

made of these fibres were quite common at one time till they were replaced with those of nylon.

Products made of coconut fibre or jute fibre can also be used in place of plastics in many applications. It may be helpful if required legislation is introduced for these practices. These will have the additional advantage of generating jobs in rural India. We recall with satisfaction the ban on single-use plastics in most of the states in India and a campaign to encourage people to use cloth shopping bags. There has also been considerable awareness on the issue of plastic waste by now, and we see active participation in this by a large number of young people.

There have also been encouraging reports of bacteria (*Ideonella sakaiensis*) that can digest plastics.

We thus note, that left untreated, plastic waste has choked our water bodies and is causing havoc with animals and marine life in addition to posing serious health hazards. Awareness of this risk has led to the formulation of the policy of "reduce, reuse, and recycle" for plastics. However, only a small part of the total plastic waste is recycled. A massive education programme to involve the public in this management is essential, and perhaps economic incentives may be given to promote plants for conversion of plastics to fuels and recover some of the cost. Finally, we should know that no cost is too small when it comes to protecting the life, health, and livelihood of people.

6.7 Biomedical Waste

Man has fought illnesses and injuries from the very beginning of his history. In fact, it is believed that caring for the sick and the injured marked the beginning of human civilization. This has led to an increased life expectancy of mankind over the last several hundred centuries. The earliest humans lived under unhygienic conditions with high burdens of infection and limited access to effective medicines. As these conditions improved, more and more people lived to be 60 or beyond. This has allowed the evolution of stable multigenerational support of the young, a uniquely human trait, and a great source of transmission of knowledge and experience.

Healthcare activities such as research, diagnostics, and medical care protect and restore health and protect lives. In this process, these generate a large variety of waste, a part of which can be infectious and hazardous and can lead to the spreading of disease in a susceptible population if not handled properly.

The major sources of healthcare wastes or biomedical wastes are as follows:

- laboratories and medical research centres,
- animal research and testing laboratories,
- blood banks and collection services,
- nursing homes for the elderly,
- hospitals and nursing homes,
- mortuary and autopsy centres.

This waste is of several types and handling each type of waste requires different procedures and protocols [25]:

- *Non-hazardous or general waste*: waste that does not pose any biological, chemical, radioactive, or physical hazard.
- *Radioactive waste*: products contaminated by radionuclides, including radioactive diagnostic material or radiotherapeutic materials.
- *Cytotoxic waste*: waste containing substances with genotoxic properties (i.e., highly hazardous substances that are mutagenic, teratogenic, or carcinogenic), such as cytotoxic drugs used in cancer treatment and their metabolites.
- *Pharmaceutical waste*: expired, unused, and contaminated drugs and vaccines.
- *Chemical waste*: solvents and reagents used for laboratory preparations, disinfectants, sterilant, and heavy metals contained in medical devices (e.g., mercury in broken thermometers) and batteries.
- *Sharp waste*: syringes, needles, disposable scalpels, blades, etc.
- *Pathological waste*: human tissues, organs or fluids, body parts and contaminated animal carcasses.

- *Infectious waste*: waste contaminated with blood and other bodily fluids (e.g., from discarded diagnostic samples), cultures, and stocks of infectious agents from laboratory work (e.g., waste from autopsies and infected animals from laboratories), or waste from patients with infections (e.g., swabs, bandages, and disposable medical devices), and personal protective equipment, such as masks, gloves, shoe cover, overalls, goggles.

Infectious waste contains pathogens (viruses, bacteria, parasites, or fungi) and can cause disease in susceptible hosts.

It is believed that biomedical waste is best treated at the place where it is generated to minimize exposure, accidental spillage, and problems of transportation. The first step in the treatment of this is segregation. Even though more detailed colour codes are available for different categories of waste, the ones commonly used are as shown in Fig. 6.40. The figure also shows the methods of treating these wastes.

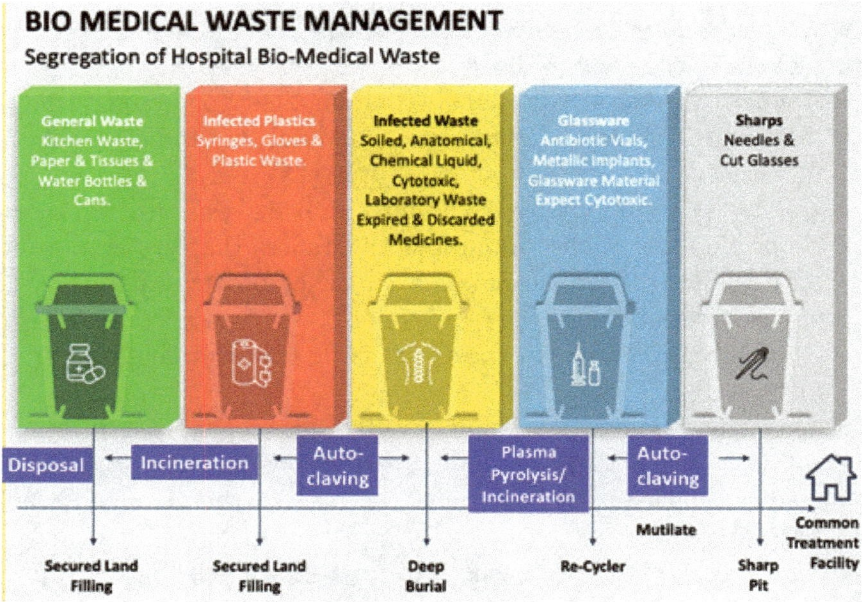

Fig. 6.40 Treatment of biomedical waste

The above does not include radioactive biomedical waste and we discuss it briefly in the following. Radioactive isotopes are being used increasingly for diagnostic and therapeutic applications. The main radioisotopes used in hospitals are Technetium-99m (Tc-99m), Iodine-131 (I-131), Iodine-125 (I-125), Iodine-123 (I-123), Fluorine-18 (F-18), Tritium (H-3), and Carbon-14 (C-14). The bulk of the radioactive waste gets generated in the department of nuclear medicine in hospitals.

There are about 300 nuclear medicine centres in India. India has about 250 functioning gamma camera (single-photon emission computed tomography and computed tomography) units. Most of the isotopes are generated in nuclear reactors, and about 20 medical cyclotrons operate in the country. Radioactive waste must be disposed of according to the Atomic Energy (safe disposal of radioactive waste) Rules of 1987 promulgated by the Atomic Energy Act 1962 of the Government of India.

The collected radioactive waste is disposed of using one of the following procedures:

- dilute and disperse;
- delay and decay;
- concentrate and contain (rarely used);
- incineration (rarely used).

The guidelines for disposal for medicines are prescribed by the World Health Organization and the United States Food and Drugs Administration. Some of the methods suggested to dispose of expired and unused medicines include landfill and waste immobilization: encapsulation and inertization, flushing it down the sewer and incineration.

Let us return to other biomedical wastes mentioned above. The general waste is best incinerated and sent to secure landfills. The sharp objects, like needles and pieces of glass, should be shredded, autoclaved (see later) and buried in secure pits meant for depositing these. The glassware and metallic objects need to be sanitized in autoclaves, after which these can be recycled.

The anatomical wastes are either buried or incinerated.

The infectious waste should either be autoclaved and incinerated, and sent for deep burial or incinerated using plasma pyrolysis at high temperatures.

6.7.1 *Handling of biomedical waste in India*

It is well known that most of the time, the medical waste is dumped in open space, enabling ragpickers to collect contaminated syringes, cotton, plastic, etc. In many hospitals, medical waste is burnt in the open atmosphere. It is known that poorly designed landfills contaminate groundwater. Some handlers use oil-fired and electric incinerators which work at low temperatures (~400–700°C) against the statutory secondary treatment of gases at 1,100°C. Many small hospitals and clinics provide a contract to private agencies for the disposal of their waste and do not even know whether it is destroyed properly or not. Microwave systems are available only at a very few places.

Incineration as normally practised is the burning of waste material in the presence of oxygen. Often, the incinerators used have no control over emissions. It is known that pathogens can survive if the incineration is incomplete or is done at a low temperature. Airflow that is more than the stoichiometric requirement for combustion is essential for the incinerator to enhance the combustion process. The demand for excess airflow limits the temperature that is achievable. Due to insufficient temperature generated in the process chamber, incinerators produce extremely toxic products, such as furans and dioxins (toxic carcinogenic molecules). This can cause air pollution, or the toxic pollutants can remain in the bottom ash, eventually finding their way into landfills.

Sometimes, a hydroclave is used to treat infectious waste. Hydroclaves (Fig. 6.41) have a double-walled vessel containing a powerful rotator. The rotator breaks the waste into small pieces and mixes it thoroughly. This increases the exposed surface area. The gap inside the double wall is then filled with high-temperature steam, which heats waste and makes it sterile in 20 min. After that, it can either be incinerated or put into a landfill.

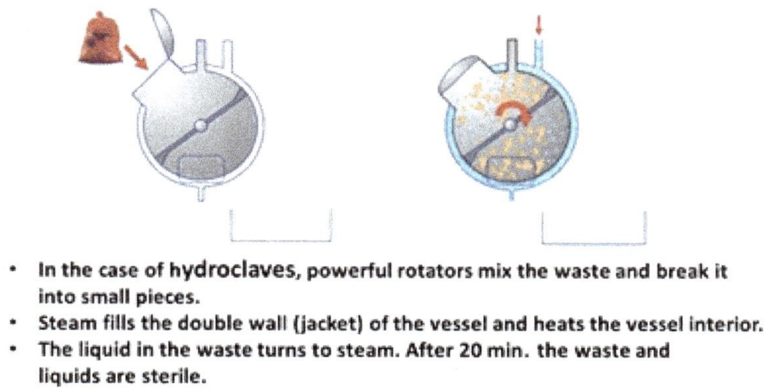

• In the case of hydroclaves, powerful rotators mix the waste and break it into small pieces.
• Steam fills the double wall (jacket) of the vessel and heats the vessel interior.
• The liquid in the waste turns to steam. After 20 min. the waste and liquids are sterile.

Fig. 6.41 Working principle of hydroclave

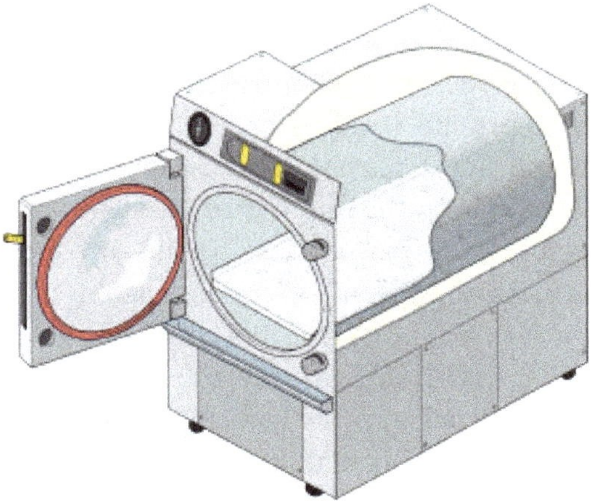

Fig. 6.42 An autoclave [26]

Autoclaves have been used to sterilize medical equipment since 1879 to sterilize syringes, surgical instruments, glassware used in medical research, and medical waste, e.g., personal protection equipment. It uses pressurized saturated steam at 121°C for about 20 min to sterilize the load (see Fig. 6.42).

Both methods, autoclave and hydroclave, require handling of the contaminated waste and subsequent use of an incinerator for complete disposal, which make these processes tedious.

All types of microorganisms can be destroyed by the application of a microwave frequency of about 2,450 MHz. Exposure to microwaves rapidly heats the water content of the medical waste and results in the destruction of the infectious components and compounds. This technique allows microbial inactivation of biomedical waste in 30–35 min. All types of biomedical waste (solids, liquids, glass, sharps, blades, etc.) can be treated with the system, which is first ground using powerful blades/shredders. The microwave oven converts biomedical waste into dry, inert material. This resulting material is like municipal waste and can also be used as secondary fuel with high energy output. It has two main disadvantages: (1) The microwave generator requires regular and intensive maintenance and the presence of even a trace of metal in the waste can damage it. High-power microwave generators also tend to be expensive. (2) It requires the handling of the medical waste for shredding and grinding.

A robust and powerful method to treat medical waste is plasma pyrolysis using a plasma torch (Fig. 6.43). The working of plasma torch is well established since the 1960s when it was used to study the conditions created during the re-entry of missiles and space crafts into the atmosphere of the Earth. Plasma torches are electrical discharge plasma sources with the plasma being extracted as a jet through an opening in the electrode and out of the confines of the cathode–anode space. The inherent thermal and electromagnetic instabilities of the arc column are stabilized by forced gas flow along the current path or by interaction with a guiding wall or by external magnetic fields. DC, RF, and microwave power sources can be used to produce the arc.

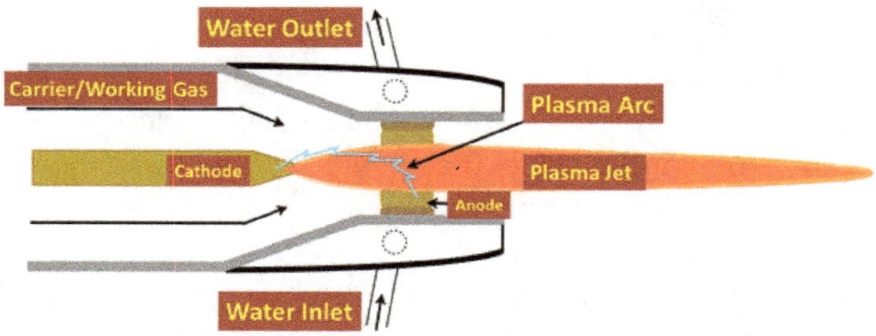

Fig. 6.43 Working principle of plasma torch

Plasma pyrolysis integrates the thermochemical properties of plasma with the pyrolysis process. It uses extremely high temperatures of plasma arc in an oxygen-starved environment to completely decompose waste material into simple molecules. Hot plasmas are particularly appropriate for the treatment of solid waste and can also be employed for the destruction of toxic molecules by thermal decomposition. Unlike incinerators, segregation of chlorinated waste is not essential in this process. Another advantage of plasma pyrolysis is the reduction in the volume of organic matter, which is more than 99%. Unlike their smoke-belching, conventional counterparts, plasma pyrolysis facilities burn the waste without producing any harmful residuals. The quantity of toxic residuals (dioxins and furans) is much below the accepted emission standards. The pathogens are completely killed and there is a possibility to recover energy. As the temperatures are very high, all the matter is converted into simple molecules, which are quenched from 500°C to 70°C, which ensures that complex molecules are not formed, leaving gases like CO, hydrogen, and methane, which can be harvested as fuel or burned to heat the waste.

The Facilitation Centre for Industrial Plasma Technologies of the Institute of Plasma Research, Gandhi Nagar has developed this technology and plants of various capacities, as high as 1–5 tonnes/day, are available in the country (see Fig. 6.44).

About 20 such plants have been installed at various places in the country and have been operating successfully. The plants are fully automated and do not require handling medical waste. It can also incinerate plastic and convert it to fuel gases.

6.7.2 *The quantum of medical waste*

It is estimated that the generation of medical waste can be 1–2 kg/patient per 8-h shift. In normal times, India generates 330,000 tonnes of medical waste every year.

In COVID-19 times, the generation of medical waste has increased several times. Just to give an example, the medical waste related to COVID-19 generated in India in 2021 was 53 tonnes/day in February, 75 tonnes/day in March, 139 tonnes/day in April and

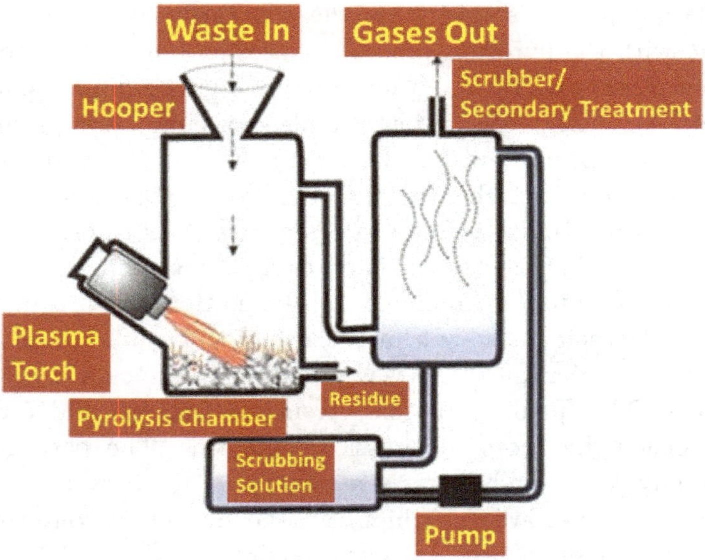

Fig. 6.44 Working principle of plasma pyrolysis [27]

203 tonnes/day in May. Globally, 65 billion gloves and 130 billion masks are being discarded every day. All these need to be destroyed. Images of birds, fish, sea lions, and animals finding these even in the remotest part of the seas, and forests are emerging. We are sitting on a ticking time bomb, and we need to solve this issue before it explodes with a massive force in the face of the nation and the world.

It is important to add that the World Health Organization has analyzed the reasons for the failure of waste management and attributed it to a lack of awareness about the health hazards related to healthcare waste, inadequate training in proper waste management, absence of waste management and disposal systems, insufficient financial and human resources and the low priority given to the topic, and absence of appropriate regulations or their enforcement.

It is important that the entire world wakes up to risks associated with unmanaged medical waste.

6.8 The Challenge of Global Climate Change

Carbon dioxide occupies a special place in the changing composition of the atmosphere. Its level has been rising continuously since the Industrial Revolution due to the burning of fossil fuels and has reached a concentration of about 419 ppm already and continues to increase. Global climate models have shown that such an increase in carbon dioxide concentration is resulting in an unacceptable rise in global temperature with disastrous consequences on global climate [1]. The World has resolved to limit the level of carbon dioxide to 450 ppm, by rapidly eliminating the use of fossil fuels, so that global warming can be limited to less than 1.5–2.0°C, and we can avert danger to our very survival.

Tropospheric ozone (close to the surface of the Earth) is also a major pollutant. It is created by chemical reactions between oxides of nitrogen and volatile organic compounds emitted by cars, power plants, industrial boilers, refineries, chemical plants, etc., in the presence of sunlight. Recall that our planet is enveloped in an atmosphere that extends to 10,000 km, or even beyond, from its surface. The troposphere is the densest part of the atmosphere. It extends to a height of about 8–14.5 km from the surface of the Earth. Just beyond it lies the stratosphere, which extends to about 50 km. It contains the ozone layer which protects us from ultraviolet radiation and is called "good ozone" (see Fig. 6.45).

When particles in the air combine with ozone, they create smog. Regions of North India, including Delhi are regularly covered with dense smog during winter, as farmers burn stubbles to prepare their fields for sowing. These cause breathlessness, chest constriction, irritation in the eyes, asthma, and allergy, as well as problems for traffic, including air traffic. The Great Smog of December 1952 over London killed more than 4,000 persons within 6 days. Recent estimates have revised the number of deaths to 12,000. The primary reason for this was believed to be the burning of coal in its thermal power plants and at homes.

We have deliberately discussed the case of ozone here, as it holds a major lesson in handling global crises and stands out as a symbol

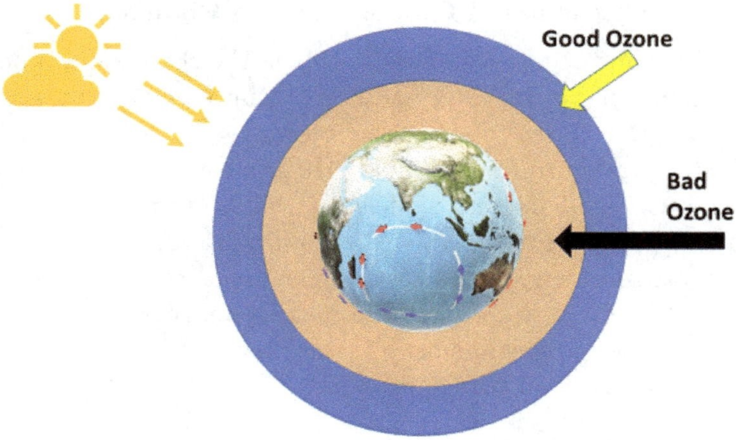

Fig. 6.45 The good and the bad ozone

of hope. The first evidence for the degradation of the ozone layer over Antarctica emerged in 1985. It led to the international adoption of the Montreal Protocol on Substances that Deplete the Ozone Layer in 1987. Thirty years later, the ozone layer has shown a great recovery. We have no doubt that an international concerted and coordinated science-driven effort can avert this crisis if we act immediately.

6.8.1 *Global climate changes*

The most serious natural disaster that the entire mankind is facing now is climate change and global warming, spurred by the increasing emission of greenhouse gases since the beginning of the Industrial Revolution, anchored on the increasing use of fossil fuels [1]. The report on "State of the Global Climate" by the World Meteorological Organization [28] has recently summarized the grim situation (see Fig. 6.46).

This has been brought about by the dangerous and alarming rise in the concentrations of carbon dioxide, nitrous oxide, and methane due to the use of fossil fuels. Each of the apprehensions and concerns has been confirmed and re-emphasized in the 2021 report of the Intergovernmental Panel on Climate Change [29], which

Fig. 6.46 State of global climate, 2020 [28]

most strongly suggests that we have no time to lose (see Figs. 6.47 and 6.48).

It has been reported that the globally averaged mole fractions of carbon dioxide (CO_2) have already exceeded 419 ppm. The mean temperature is already more than 1.1°C above the pre-industrial level. Climate change is continuing relentlessly, leading to an increasing occurrence and intensification of high-impact events and severe

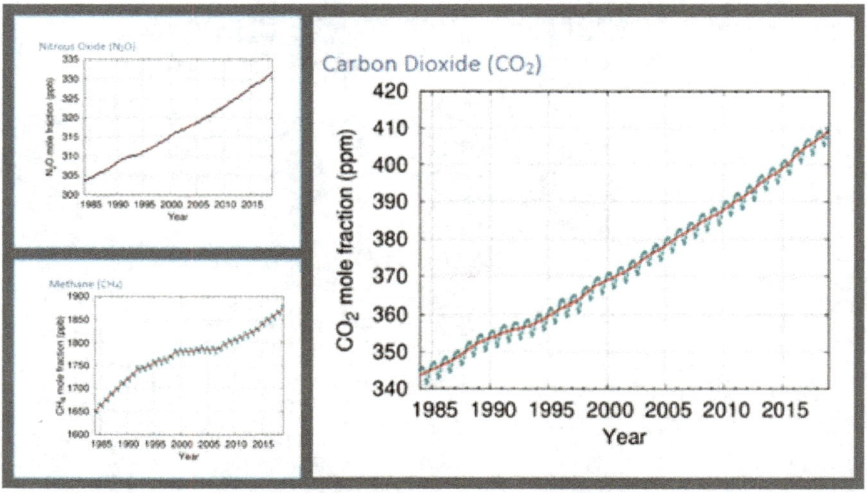

Fig. 6.47 Rising concentration of greenhouse gases (Extracted from [28])

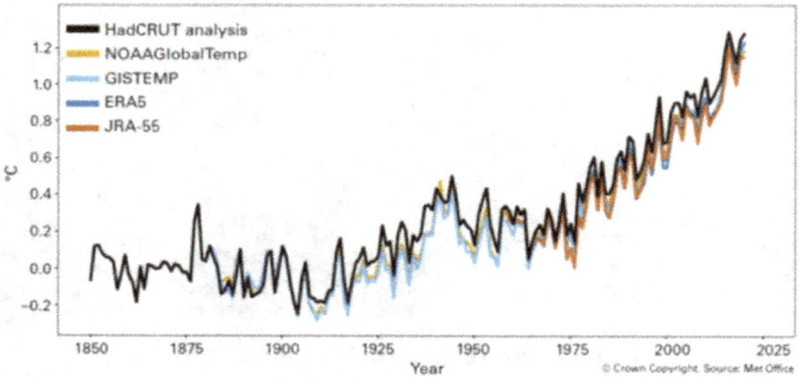

Fig. 6.48 Rising temperature of the planet [28]

losses and damages affecting people, societies, and economies. It further concludes that stabilizing global mean temperature at 1.5°C (better) to 2°C (at least) above pre-industrial levels by the end of this century will require an ambitious reduction of greenhouse gas emissions, which must begin to occur during this decade. This means reducing global greenhouse gas emissions by 45% from 2010 levels by

2030 and reaching net-zero emissions by 2050, which is a tall order, but achievable, if the entire world makes a determined effort.

6.8.2 *Deforestation: The shrinking carbon dioxide sink*

The area covered by forests across the world is about 4.06 billion hectares, which is about 31% of the land area of our planet. Forests of the world purify water and air, and play a crucial role in mitigating climate change as they act as a carbon sink. At least 80% of land-based species, e.g., elephants, rhinoceros, monkeys, antelopes, and gorillas, live in the forest. Forests serve as the lungs of our planet (see Fig. 6.49).

Forests, across the world, are being cleared for agriculture, cattle ranching, palm-oil plantations, coffee plantations, pulps, timber, infrastructure development, and mining. They are also being lost to illegal logging and burning. Deforestation in tropical rainforests is seriously impacting biodiversity. It is often not realized that rainforests have several layers of greenery, viz., trees, sub-trees, canopy, and shrubs, with each one of these contributing to the absorption of carbon. The Amazon lost around 17% of the forest in the last 50 years, mostly around more populated areas, roads, and rivers. It has been found that roads into the Amazon bring in illegal

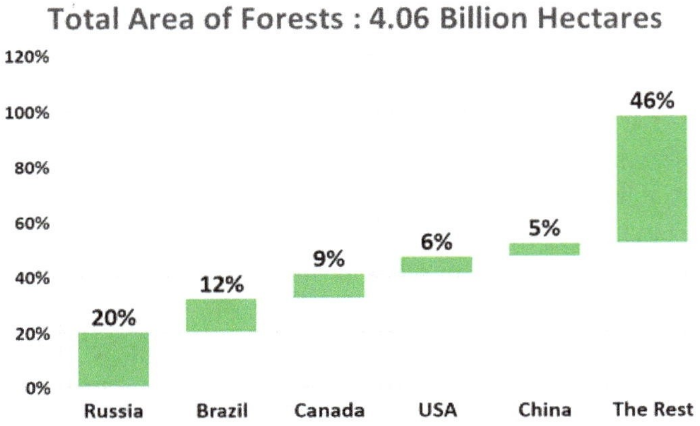

Fig. 6.49 Distribution of forests across the world

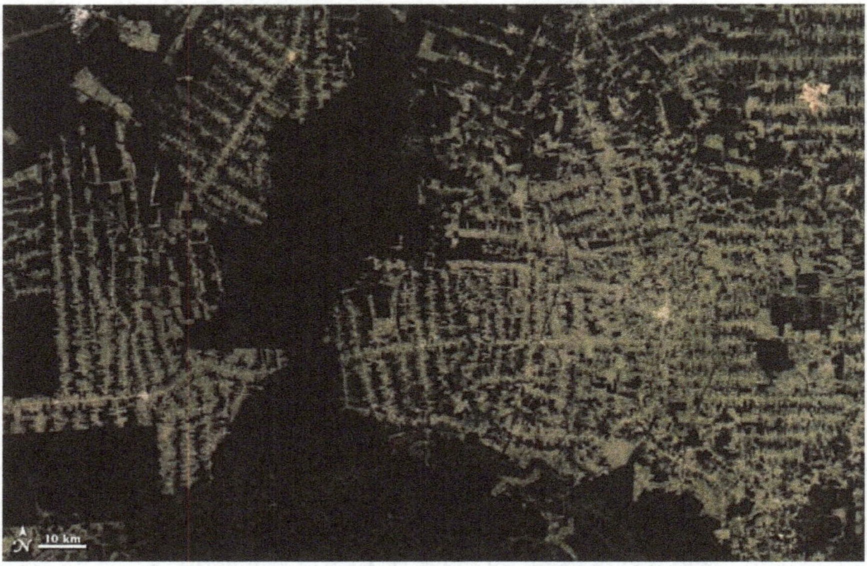

Fig. 6.50 Deforestation in Amazon (Courtesy NASA)

loggers, then cattle ranchers, and then soy farmers. This vicious cycle ravages the tropical rainforest along with its biodiversity. This is leading to a possible catastrophic collapse of the rainforest to a degraded savanna. Even remote areas are being encroached upon as mahogany, gold, and oil are discovered. The Brazilian Amazon, in particular, lost close to 1 million hectares of forest in 2019, and the rate of destruction is only accelerating (see Fig. 6.50).

Indonesia has one the most biologically diverse forests in the world, and its forests covered close to 84% of the total land area of the country in 1900 AD. This forest cover amounting to 170 million hectares at the beginning of the twentieth century had decreased to 100 million hectares towards its close. As the pace of deforestation has continued to increase, there are apprehensions that its unique tropical rain forests may soon be completely lost to mostly illegal logging and burning of the forests. Some part of the forests is also cleared for the primitive slash-and-burn agricultural practices (see Fig. 6.51).

Fig. 6.51 Clearing of forests in Sumatra [30]

One of the biggest casualties of deforestation has been the orangutans and within just over 15 years, from 1999 to 2015, as many as 100,000 of the critically endangered orangutans perished in Borneo, which is governed by Indonesia, Malaysia, and Brunei. If the present rate of deforestation continues, experts fear that within a few decades they may no longer survive in the wild.

Africa loses up to 4 million hectares of forests every year, out of which the Democratic Republic of Congo alone accounts for more than 300,000 hectares of lost forests per year, threatening the survival of rare species like mountain gorillas and okapi.

We have seen that deforestation in the catchment areas of rivers and natural and manmade reservoirs leads to unabated soil erosion by water and causes mudslides and landslides. It decreases soil's capacity to hold water and is one of the main reasons behind flooding. Deforestation-induced landslides in the Himalayas and other parts of India lead to serious damage to road and rail transport every year. With no large trees to hold the rainwater, the mountain springs across the Himalayan range are rapidly drying up.

The Western Ghats covers an area of 140,000 km^2 in a stretch of 1,600 km parallel to the western coast spread across Kerala, Tamil Nadu, Karnataka, Goa, Maharashtra, and Gujarat. It is one of the hotspots of biodiversity in India, with unique flora and fauna, e.g., Nilgiri Tahr, Lion-Tailed Macaque, and Indian Gaur. It is reported to have lost 20,000 hectares of its area over the last 17 years because of deforestation.

Deforestation increases encounter between man and animals, which the latter invariably lose. It is no longer uncommon to see panthers or elephants entering towns and villages. It also exposes humans to animal viruses and at least according to some experts, every pandemic in the history of mankind may have had its origin in these encounters, which led to zoonotic viruses and diseases, such as the Zika virus, Ebola virus, avian flu, SARS, MERS, West Nile virus, Lyme disease, and yellow fever. COVID-19 is the latest addition to this list.

The imminent danger to mankind can be understood if we recall that the Mayan civilization which had attained great heights possibly collapsed due to deforestation of the surrounding areas. The deforestation and the vanishing of large mammals from the forests of Europe are rarely, if ever, raised. The forests in the USA and Canada are also diminishing rapidly, or they are being converted to industrial forests, which are not a very effective carbon sink, nor do they support biodiversity, including bird and animal life. The Siberian forests are also being destroyed rapidly.

6.9 Planetary Boundaries

To combine issues of rising greenhouse gas concentration, rising ozone concentration in the troposphere and decreasing ozone in the stratosphere, rapidly depleting biodiversity, ocean acidification, etc. in a single illustration, the concept of Planetary Boundaries was introduced by Rockstrom *et al.* [31], which identified the safe operating zones for various measures for our planet in a sustainable manner. These have been recently revised and upgraded [32] and include climate change, change in biosphere integrity, stratospheric

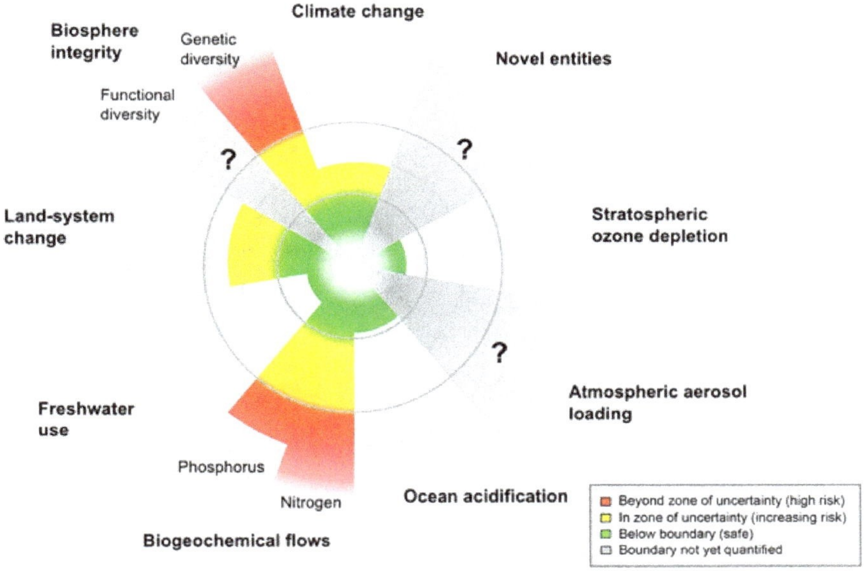

Fig. 6.52 Current status of the control variables for seven of the planetary boundaries (Credit: J. Lokrantz/Azote based on Steffen *et al.* [32])

ozone depletion, ocean acidification, biogeochemical flows (P and N cycles), land-system change, freshwater use, atmospheric aerosol loading, and introduction of novel entities (not yet fully defined). The latest findings are given in Fig. 6.52. In these, the green zone is the safe operating space, the yellow represents the zone of uncertainty (increasing risk), and the red is a high-risk zone. The planetary boundary itself lies at the intersection of the green and yellow zones. Processes for which global-level boundaries cannot yet be quantified are represented by grey wedges; these are atmospheric aerosol loading, novel entities, and the functional role of biosphere integrity.

The authors [31] conclude that these "Planetary Boundaries are scientifically based levels of human perturbation of the Earth System beyond which Earth System functioning may be substantially altered. Transgression of the Planetary Boundaries thus creates a

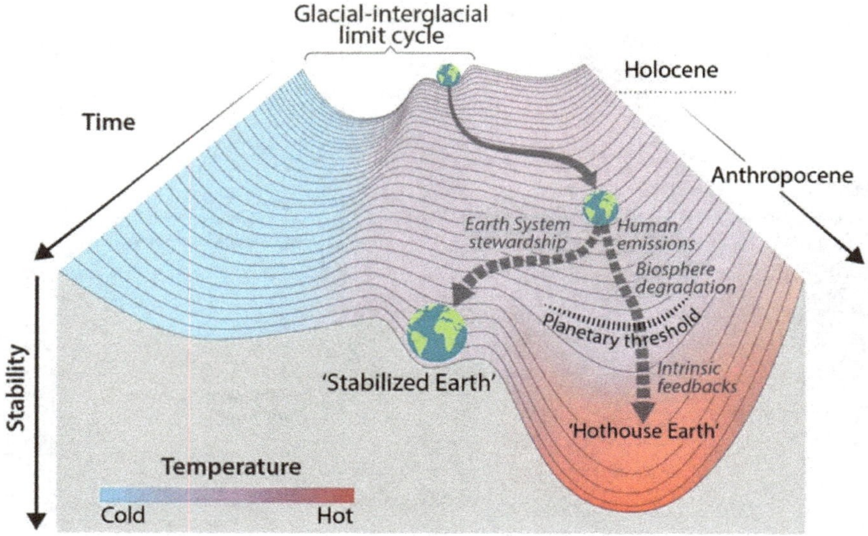

Fig. 6.53 The fate of Earth [32]

substantial risk of destabilizing the Holocene state of the Earth System in which modern societies have evolved."

Thus, for example, the safe atmospheric concentration of carbon dioxide is 350 ppm (with uncertainties ranging from 350 to 450 ppm) and we have already touched a value that is greater than 410 ppm. The change in biosphere integrity measured in extinctions per million years (E/MSY) should have been less than 10 E/MSY (with uncertainties ranging from 10 to 100 E/MSY) — though ideally less than 1 E/MSY, it has touched 100–1,000 E/MSY.

The biogeochemical cycles of nitrogen and phosphorus are severely altered beyond the self-adjusting healing or the carrying capacity of Earth, due to industrial agriculture, which depends on chemical fertilizers. These provide nitrogen, phosphorus, and other nutrients to the soil to increase production. A large part of the applied fertilizers is, however, not taken up by the plants and it returns to air and water. These pollute air, water bodies as well as groundwater. These extra nutrients in the water bodies give rise to an explosion of algae, which soaks up oxygen in the water, leading to dead zones and killing the fish and marine life in a process called eutrophication.

Similar pressures on other boundaries like land usage change and ocean acidification are seen, which cry out for a concerted and dedicated effort by all the nations on an emergency basis.

Steffen *et al.* [32] have further argued that if we do not take immediate and effective corrective measures, our planet could fall (Fig. 6.53) into the trap of a "Hothouse Earth", with serious consequences for our survival.

6.10 Summary

Human lifestyles during the last two centuries have severely compromised the quality of the three essential resources that sustain human life on earth: air, water, and food. While population pressure is a major contributor to this, it is our lifestyles that have compromised the quality of even the limited resources available to us. It is amply clear that only with suitable lifestyle changes and technological interventions, it is possible to get out of this trap, but it must be done before it is too late.

We already know that continuing global warming and climate change can push millions into an abyss of hunger, drought, and disease. It will have cascading effects with falling values in the nutrition of common foods and simultaneous crop failures which will affect the world's poor most severely. Global warming will cause serious disruptions in the rain cycle which will, in turn, affect rain-fed crops, especially in sub-Saharan Africa. For the same reason, the rice-producing regions in India may see a decrease in their rice yields. Even the production of the so-called coarse grains such as maize, millet, and sorghum are likely to be affected. The high levels of carbon dioxide are believed to disrupt plants' internal chemistry, reducing their capacity to produce protein and other vitamins. If that happens, the protein content of rice, wheat, barley, and potato is likely to decrease, affecting people's health. Unfortunately, all this will mostly happen in the regions where people are already at disadvantage and who are least equipped to deal with these burdens.

However, the worst problem, which is likely to get aggravated, is the scarcity of safe drinking water; this is already a matter of serious concern as up to half of the world faces serious water scarcity. The groundwater in many parts of the world is already getting depleted. The rising sea level is likely to drown coastal regions across the world; these, along with the inhabitants of island nations, will add to the swelling population of climate refugees. The situation is not helped by the poisoning of rivers by the runoff of agricultural pesticides and fertilizers, and municipal and industrial pollution, as well as overexploitation. Rising temperatures will lead to the rapid melting of glaciers and it will ultimately seriously jeopardize the water supply of several billion people across the world.

As the warm regions expand to cover higher latitudes due to global warming, there are fears that vector-borne pathogens such as dengue, yellow fever, malaria, Lyme fever, and Zika virus may find newer regions to spread. The rising temperatures will cause a rise in the concentration of ozone in the troposphere, and that coupled with poor quality of air will give rise to an increase in lung- and heart-related diseases. It is imperative that we immediately thoroughly revamp and considerably upgrade our health systems across the world to meet the challenges arising from the above and many more which we have not listed.

References

[1] D. K. Srivastava and V. S. Ramamurthy, *Climate Change and Energy Options for a Sustainable Future.* World Scientific Publishing Company, Singapore (2020).
[2] https://en.wikipedia.org/wiki/Air_pollution.
[3] See also https://www.epa.gov/pm-pollution/particulate-matter-pm-basics.
[4] 2020: World Air Quality Report.
[5] https://en.wikipedia.org/wiki/Air_pollution_in_Delhi.
[6] https://www.harappa.com/lothal/14.html.
[7] http://www.etrontechnologies.com/water.
[8] Desertification and Land Degradation Atlas of India (Based on IRS AWiFS data of 2011–13 and 2003–05), (2016), Space Applications Centre, ISRO, Ahmedabad, India, 219 pages.

[9] World Atlas of Desertification: Second Edition; United Nations Environment Programme (1997).
[10] https://www.epa.gov/facts-and-figures-about-materials-waste-and-recycling/national-overview-facts-and-figures-materials.
[11] *Global Waste Management Outlook*, United Nations Environment Programme, https://www.unep.org/resources/report/global-waste-management-outlook.
[12] Satpal Singh, *Solid Waste Management in Urban India: Imperatives for Improvement*, ORF Occasional Paper No. 283, November 2020, Observer Research Foundation.
[13] *Children and digital dumpsites: E-waste exposure and child health*, World Health Organization, https://www.who.int/publications/i/item/9789240023901.
[14] https://www.who.int/news/item/15-06-2021-soaring-e-waste-affects-the-health-of-millions-of-children-who-warns.
[15] P. K. Dutta, Electronic waste, *Sci. Cult.* **87**, 115–119 (2021).
[16] K. Latham, Future Planet, BBC, https://www.bbc.com/future/article/20210510-how-to-recycle-any-plastic.
[17] https://commons.wikimedia.org/wiki/File:Citarum_River_pollution,_2009.jpg.
[18] https://ourworldindata.org/plastic-pollution.
[19] https://www.iaea.org/newscenter/news/world-oceans-day-2020-new-iaea-research-records-dramatic-increase-in-microplastic-pollution-in-eastern-tropical-pacific-ocean.
[20] https://ibanplastic.com/top-10-most-polluted-rivers-in-the-world/.
[21] https://www.worldbank.org/en/news/infographic/2018/09/20/what-a-waste-20-a-global-snapshot-of-solid-waste-management-to-2050.
[22] R. Geyer, J. R. Jambeck and K. L. Law, Production, use, and fate of all plastics ever made, *Sci. Adv.* **3**, e1700782 (2017).
[23] https://en.wikipedia.org/wiki/Rajagopalan_Vasudevan.
[24] S. Sarkar and A. K. Jha, Research for Sisal (Agave Sp.) Fibre Production in India, *Int. J. Curr. Res.* **9**, 61136–61146 (2017), https://commons.wikimedia.org/wiki/File:Plantsisal.jpg.
[25] https://www.who.int/news-room/fact-sheets/detail/health-care-waste.
[26] https://en.wikipedia.org/wiki/Autoclave.
[27] S. K. Nema and K. S. Ganeshprasad, Plasma pyrolysis of medical waste, *Curr. Sci.* **83**, 271–278 (2002); S. K. Nema, V. Jain, K. S. Ganeshprasad, A. Sanghariyat, S. Soni, C. Patil, V. Chauhan and P. I. John, Plasma Pyrolysis Technology and its Evolution at FCIPT, Institute for Plasma Research, India, Report number: IPR/TR-364/2016, DOI: 10.13140/RG.2.1.3435.6880.

[28] *State of the Global Climate*, World Meteorological Organization, WMO-No. 1264.
[29] *Climate Change 2021: The Physical Science Basis*, Intergovernmental Panel for Climate Change. https://www.ipcc.ch/report/ar6/wg1/downloads/report/IPCC_AR6_WGI_Full_Report.pdf.
[30] https://en.wikipedia.org/wiki/Deforestation_in_Indonesia.
[31] J. Rockström *et al.*, Planetary boundaries: Exploring the safe operating space for humanity, *Ecol. Soc.* **14**, 32 (2009); J. Rockstrom *et al.*, A safe operating space for humanity, *Nature* **461**, 472–475 (2009).
[32] W. Steffen *et al.*, Planetary boundaries: Guiding human development on a changing planet, *Science* **347**, 1259855 (2015).

Chapter 7

Managing Public Risks

There is an old saying: good times divide people; it is bad times that bring people together. The discussions in the previous chapters have demonstrated that humanity has always been vulnerable to natural disasters such as cyclones, earthquakes and infectious diseases. Humanity has been looking at these as "Acts of God" and learning to live with them for a long time. During the last two centuries, advances in science and technology have given us not only a better understanding of these hazards and the associated risks but also strategies to combat these risks. For example, our understanding of global weather phenomena has enabled us to predict extreme weather events like cyclones and prepare ourselves to minimize loss of life and property. Similarly, the development of drugs and vaccines for many infectious diseases has enabled us to either eradicate them for good or limit their impact.

We have also seen many industrial disasters like coal mine fires, oil spills and poisonous gas leaks following the Industrial Revolution. New and emerging technologies of the recent decades have also brought with them new risks. Last but not the least, the ever-increasing energy demand and burning of hydrocarbons to satisfy our increasing energy demands have opened the whole world to environmental disasters of the kind that humanity has never witnessed in the past.

We have already pointed out that public risks of the kind described above can only be managed by collective actions by the people, and people across the world look at governments as the custodians of public good and therefore expect them to put in place mechanisms to manage public risks and eliminate or minimize loss of life, livelihood, or property of the citizens. Unfortunately, the governance systems across the world are highly diverse and therefore public risk preparedness and management of disasters are also highly diverse.

The examples we have chosen to describe in the following sections are limited to India mainly because of the professional experiences of the authors.

7.1 Natural Disasters

Natural disasters are in general location-specific. A population that is aware of its vulnerabilities to risks associated with the natural events specific to that region is in a better position to combat these risks. It is often said that it is not the natural events that kill people, but it is the ignorance of the people and institutional apathy that converts extreme natural events into disasters.

7.1.1 *Extreme weather events*

Extreme weather events are something that humanity has been facing regularly. Lack of adequate precipitation, either rain or snow, can not only cause a prolonged water shortage but also lead to reduced groundwater and soil moisture, ultimately resulting in drought and extensive crop damage. A drought can last for weeks, months, or even years. Throughout history, humans have always looked at droughts as "disasters" due to their impact on food and water availability. At the other extreme, precipitation much more than normal results in flooding. It could be the result of the flow rate of water exceeding the capacity of a waterway like a river or the overflow of water from water bodies like a lake or a dam. Floods often not only cause damage to homes and other infrastructure but also result in the loss of lives. Across the world, more people are affected by floods than by any other type of natural disaster. Occasionally, heavy precipitation and flow of water also result in landslides in hilly areas.

Land areas at elevations less than 10 m above sea level are also at risk of seasonal flooding. While countries like India, Bangladesh, and China account for the largest number of citizens exposed to river floods, the situation is even more precarious for island states like the Maldives (just 1.6 m above sea level with the highest natural point at just 5.1 m). These island communities indeed face the prospect of mass relocation before long if we do not stop the emission of greenhouse gases immediately and arrest global warming since the rising level of the seas may take several hundred years to reverse.

India is a peninsular country with a long coastline on the east and the west and the Himalayas on the north. Coastal cities like Chennai and Mumbai are vulnerable to floods triggered by heavy rains and cloud bursts, especially when these coincide with high tides.

The Indian sub-continent is also vulnerable to seasonal cyclones from the Bay of Bengal and the Arabian Sea and has witnessed some of the most devastating cyclones in history. Coastal regions in Tamil Nadu, Andhra Pradesh, Odisha, and West Bengal are vulnerable to the Bay of Bengal cyclones, whereas coastal regions in Kerala, Karnataka, Goa, Maharashtra, and Gujarat are vulnerable to the Arabian Sea cyclones.

During the last few decades, there have been considerable developments in our scientific understanding of the Earth system enabling us to even predict atmospheric conditions for a given region for a specific period. The formal practice of weather forecasting started in the nineteenth century. These are made by collecting quantitative data on the state of the atmosphere and oceans through a set of instruments (weather monitoring) and using an understanding of meteorological processes to project how the atmospheric conditions will change in a given time (weather modelling and prediction). The invention of the electric telegraph in 1835 allowed one to collect reports of weather conditions from a wide area simultaneously while the invention of photography in 1845 allowed one to record variations in meteorological observations. Francis Beaufort and Robert FitzRoy of the Royal Navy laid the foundation of scientific forecasting, and their forecasts were used by both the Royal Navy and the mariners.

The first daily weather forecast was published in *The Times* on August 1, 1861.

India is one of the few countries in the world that put in place a formal system of meteorological observations very early, more than 200 years ago. The British East India Company established the Calcutta Meteorological Observatory in 1785. The Asiatic Society of Bengal founded in 1784 initiated scientific studies in meteorology. Following a disastrous tropical cyclone that struck Calcutta in 1864, the then Government of India established the India Meteorological Department (IMD), bringing all meteorological work in the country under a central authority. IMD today operates as a dedicated agency of the Government of India under the Ministry of Earth Sciences for weather and climate monitoring, weather forecast and extreme weather warning services. IMD has also set up a network of state meteorological centres to facilitate better coordination with the state and district level administrative agencies. IMD also represents India in the World Meteorological Organization and has access to global meteorological data.

Over the years, IMD has not only been continuously expanding its infrastructure for meteorological observations but also achieved considerable expertise in weather modelling, weather forecasting and delivering weather services. Today, India is one of the few countries in this part of the globe to have its own weather satellites, Doppler weather radars, supercomputers for weather modelling, etc. IMD has been issuing a bouquet of weather reports and forecasts daily for use by different user groups. We would like to highlight two forecasts that have a direct bearing on public risks.

The first one is the seasonal rainfall forecasts. Agriculture plays an important role in feeding India's 1.3 billion population and driving the Indian economy. Monsoons play an important role in satisfying the water requirements of Indian farmers. Vagaries of the monsoon, too much rain or too little rain or unseasonal rains, have always played a significant role in India's fortunes. IMD has been issuing short-term (a few days) rainfall forecasts for a long time. In the last few years, IMD has made considerable progress not only in weather monitoring but also in medium-term and seasonal monsoon forecasts based on advanced numerical weather prediction models. Not only have these forecasts substantially decreased surprises like more-than-normal rains or droughts but they have also enabled planned agricultural operations.

In recent years, apart from riverine floods, urban flooding has also become a recurrent and serious issue in several major cities. The urban floods are mainly due to inadequate drainage and unscientific planning when heavy rains occur. Some of these floods are also caused by human actions like callous choking of drains and mindless building over water bodies by reclaiming them. Forecasting urban floods is not just a necessity to save lives but also a challenge. For example, the Chennai floods in December 2015 affected four million people; more than 500 lives were lost and property worth INR 200 billion was damaged. Irrespective of whether the Chennai flood was a natural disaster or a man-made disaster, could it have been prevented or forecast? As we write this, Chennai is again facing a large-scale inundation of its residential areas.

An expert system has recently been developed by Ghosh *et al.* [1] to forecast urban floods. In this system, outputs of regional weather models, tide, overland flow, and stormwater drainage information etc. were integrated. The model also used a high-resolution digital terrain model and high-resolution bathymetry and provided information on areas under inundation and likely periods of flooding for each municipal ward. It allows visualization of inundated areas by administrators to respond in near real time. This near-real-time flood warning system is operational in Chennai and Mumbai.

Another area where IMD has made significant progress is in cyclone forecasts. As has already been mentioned, cyclones are one of the deadliest natural hazards affecting the coastal population, infrastructure, and agriculture. The East Coast of India is more vulnerable to cyclones as many more cyclones originate in the Bay of Bengal than in the Arabian Sea. It has been observed that the intensity, as well as the frequency of cyclones, has increased, during the last couple of decades, due to the warming of the seas. The increase in intensity has resulted in stronger winds, higher waves and storm surges and deeper inundation of inland areas. Thus, coastal regions are increasingly becoming vulnerable to cyclones. On the one hand, we have no alternative to living with the hazards of cyclones. On the other hand, an ability to detect early and monitor the cyclones, forecast their tracks and the likely risks, and communicate in near real time to all stakeholders by way of early warnings will go a long way in reducing loss of life and property and mitigating the risks.

The first information on the formation of a cyclone — its location, intensity, areal extension, and movement — is essentially based on satellite data. The assimilation of satellite data in numerical weather prediction models provides a reasonably accurate prediction of its track, landfall, and a reasonably accurate intensity a few days in advance. The average landfall-point errors have been now only 32, 62 and 92 km for the 24, 48 and 72 hour lead periods of forecasts, respectively. This provides adequate advance warning to the local authorities well in time to "prepare" [2].

With very specific and accurate advisories, the response of the local disaster management agencies and the communities has been extremely positive. For example, during the 1999 Super Cyclone in Orissa, about 10,000 people lost their lives apart from billions of INR in damages to properties and infrastructure. In contrast, the loss of lives during a more recent 2019 extremely severe cyclone, Fani, was less than 100. Prior to Fani's landfall, authorities in India and Bangladesh could move at least a million people each from areas within Fani's projected path onto higher ground and into cyclone shelters thanks to timely warnings and emergency plans for evacuation, relief and rescue. *More importantly, over a period, the trust of local communities in the overall disaster management plans has also increased substantially.*

7.2 Earthquakes and Tsunamis

We have already pointed out that the entire Indian subcontinent is vulnerable to earthquakes of varying magnitudes. It is often said, and rightly so, that earthquakes don't kill people, but it is the buildings that do. The need to construct buildings considering vulnerabilities to earthquakes has therefore gained importance in recent years. It is often said that Japan and Taiwan are the "most prepared nations in the world" for an earthquake. In the absence of reliable earthquake prediction methods, their preparedness consists essentially of earthquake-resistant structures and disaster management strategies. Their expertise needs to be adopted in all earthquake-prone areas.

In India, towns and villages located in the foothills of the Himalayas and the North-Eastern part of the country are known to be vulnerable to high magnitude earthquakes. Peninsular India is relatively free of large magnitude earthquakes, but there are specific zones that are vulnerable to powerful earthquakes. Based on historical data, an earthquake hazard zonation map of the country has been prepared. Several urban centres including some metropolitan cities fall under "moderate" to "severe" seismic hazard zones. Building codes exist for different zones (see Chapter 2).

Densely populated areas like metropolitan cities call for further subdivision of a region with respect to soil and ground motion characteristics. Seismic microzonation is the accepted tool in seismic hazard assessment and risk evaluation in densely populated areas. The concept of seismic microzonation is based on the fact that the intensity of ground shaking in certain frequency bands gets modified by the pile of unconsolidated sediments, or in a larger sense, local geological conditions alter the characteristics of ground motions. The damage pattern of many recent earthquakes in India such as the 1997 Jabalpur, 1999 Chamoli, and 2001 Bhuj earthquakes have demonstrated that the soil conditions at a site can have a major effect on the level of ground shaking. The Chamoli earthquake caused moderate damage to some buildings in Delhi built on soft alluvium although the epicentre was 250 km away. The 2001 Bhuj earthquake caused severe damage not only in the epicentre region but even in Ahmedabad, 350 km away from the epicentre due to increased shaking of the soft alluvium. The microzonation maps can be used not only to plan new structures but also to assess vulnerability to earthquakes of existing structures, such as schools and public utility buildings, to allow ranking of priority areas or structures in terms of seismic vulnerability, thus providing a rational basis for upgrading, retrofitting, and other remediation efforts.

In addition, seismic microzonation information could be incorporated into building codes to improve the seismic design of new structures in terms of local site effects. The seismic microzonation maps for a few urban areas such as Delhi (see Fig. 7.1), Lucknow, Kolkata, Bangalore, Ahmedabad, Chennai, Dehradun, Jammu, Chandigarh, Sikkim, and Guwahati have been carried out. However, they are yet to be integrated with the urban planning maps. An enactment of risk legislations being adopted in most countries to face these and other risks needs to be examined.

7.2.1 *Earthquake early-warning systems*

An earthquake is caused by the release of stored elastic strain energy during rapid sliding along a fault. The sliding will start at some location and progress away from this hypocentre in each direction along the fault surface. The energy is transmitted by seismic waves whose speed is around 7 km/s. These are called primary or P-waves and are the first to arrive at seismographs. Shaking is caused by the shear (or surface) waves, called S-waves, which arrive a little later as they travel at a speed of about 4.5 km/s (see Fig. 7.2).

A large earthquake can be located within seconds using data from nearby stations. Immediately, a warning can be issued to other urban/industrial centres for an impending earthquake. The seconds to minutes of advance warning, depending on the location, can allow people and systems to take actions to protect life and property from destructive shaking. Even a few seconds of warning can enable citizens to move to safer places, an emergency shutdown of sensitive installations like nuclear power plants, stoppage of metro trains, and disaster alert to emergency response teams. Earthquake Early Warning (EEW) systems of this kind are already operational in several countries, such as Japan, Taiwan. Mexico, Romania, and the USA. Japan has been successfully using this system to stop the movement of bullet trains in time and avert accidents.

A pilot project for the development of the EEW system in India has been undertaken in the state of Uttarakhand. In this project, 100 sensors connected to a central recording station in Roorkee have been installed in Uttarakhand. These sensors detect the ground motion

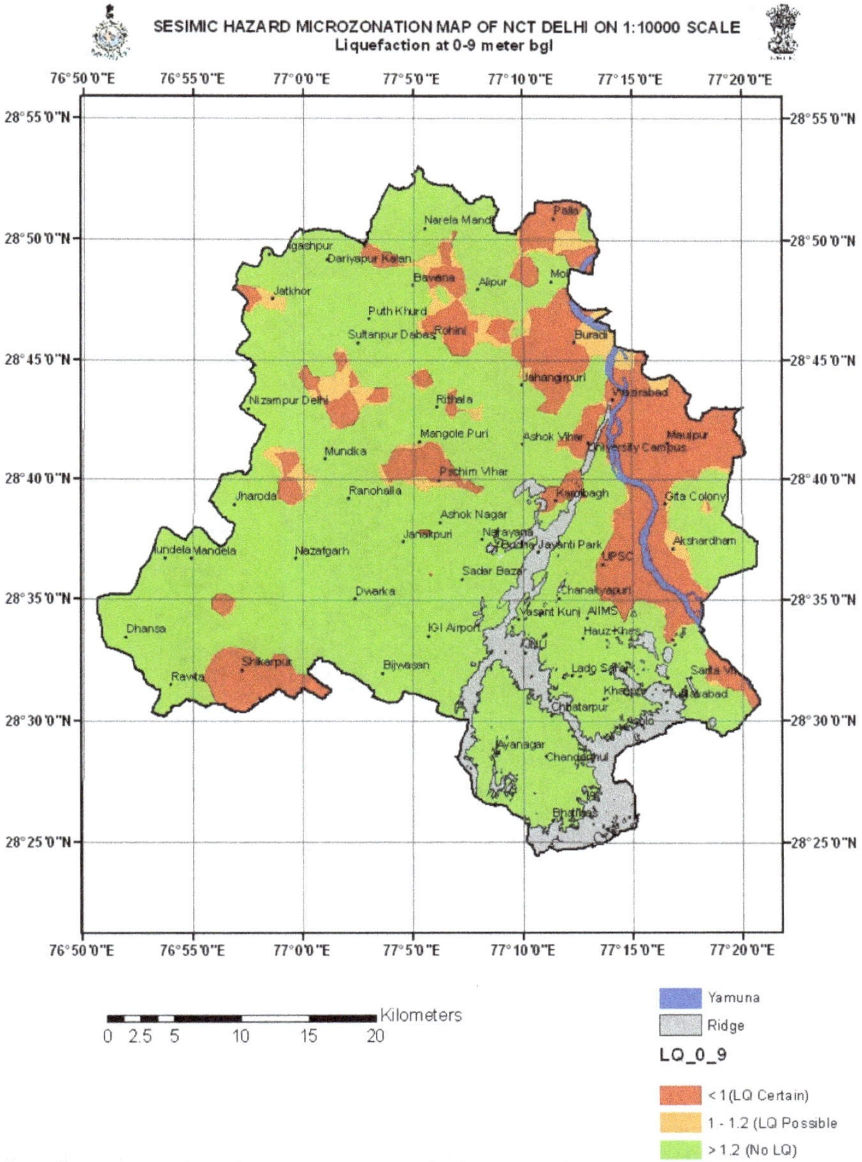

Fig. 7.1 Seismic hazard microzonation map of Delhi (Courtesy: Government of India)

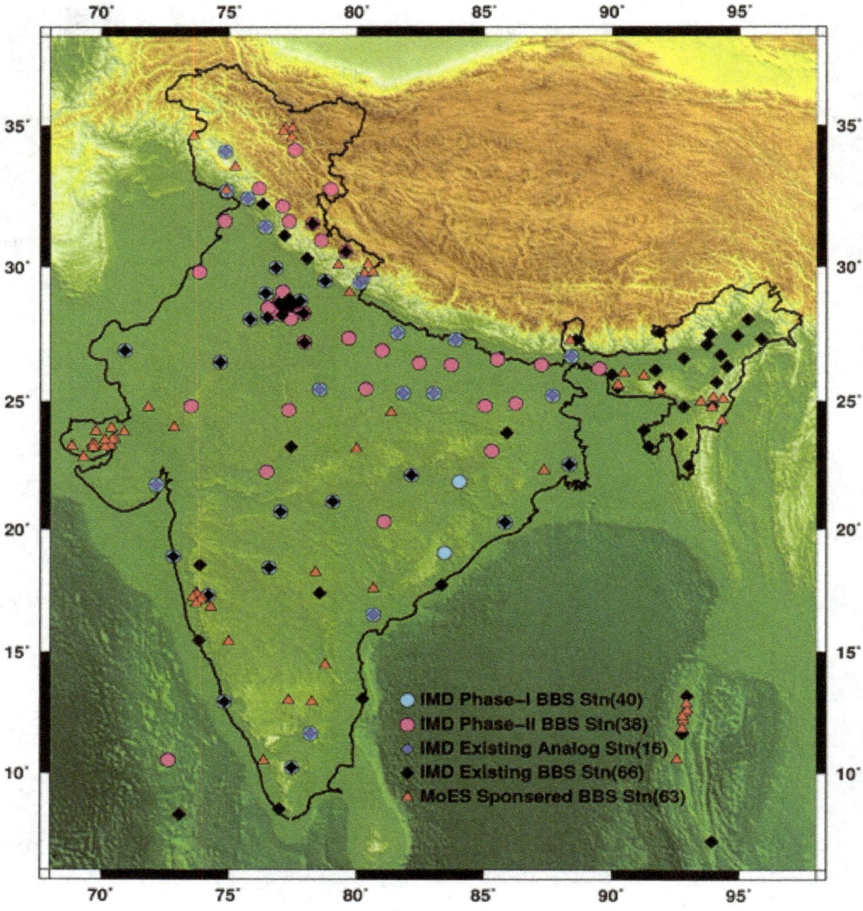

Fig. 7.2 Seismograph network India

radiating from an earthquake rupture and estimate the resulting ground shaking that will occur later in time either at the same location or some other location. The warning time will range from a few seconds to a little more than a minute and will primarily be a function of the distance of the location from the epicentre. For example, a successful EEW system can provide a lead time of about 60–90 seconds to Delhi in case of a big earthquake occurring in the Himalayas.

7.2.2 *Triggered earthquakes*

An earthquake essentially represents the release of elastic strain energy stored in the rocks in the form of seismic waves. Earthquakes can also be triggered when anthropogenic engineering activities bring about the release of pre-existing stress of tectonic origin. Such earthquakes also have significant social and economic impacts. Some of the activities that can trigger earthquakes are impounding water in artificial reservoirs, large-scale surface and deep underground mining, fluid injection under high pressure/fracking for extraction of hydrocarbons, and large underground explosions. A recent example of a triggered earthquake event is the Koyna earthquake of M 6.3 that occurred in 1967. As mentioned earlier, about 200 lives were lost and the Koyna township was severely damaged. The Koyna–Warna region in western India is known for reservoir triggered seismicity. More than 200 earthquakes have been reported during the last 50 years in a very small region covering an area of about 30 km × 20 km. Most of these earthquakes have a hypocentre at a depth of fewer than 10 km and have a strong association with the annual loading and unloading cycles of the Koyna and Warna reservoirs [3].

7.2.3 *Tsunami*

As was discussed in Chapter 2, powerful underwater earthquakes can cause large-amplitude ocean waves that can travel long distances and create havoc even in faraway coastal areas. Since the Tsunami waves take time to reach faraway coasts, the population in the vulnerable areas can be warned in advance to move away from the shores or to higher elevations. Such warning systems [4] will require the following components: identification of hazard-prone areas, a network of sensors (seismic and sea level) to detect earthquakes and evaluate its potential for tsunamis, tsunami modelling capability [5] (generation, propagation, and inundation models), high-resolution database on bathymetry and coastal topography, and communication infrastructure to issue appropriate warnings to the vulnerable population. For this, space-based platforms are valuable for providing inundation mapping, damage assessment on a detailed scale, identification of safer places for rehabilitation, and providing communication links for relief, telemedicine, and counselling via satellites.

Across the world, there are four major tsunami warning systems operational today. They are Pacific Tsunami Warning Mitigating System (PTWS), Indian Ocean Tsunami Early Warning and Mitigation System (IOTWMS), Tsunami Early Warning and Mitigation System in the North-Eastern Atlantic, Mediterranean and Connected Seas (NEAMTWS), and Tsunami and Other Coastal Hazards Warning System for the Caribbean and Adjacent Regions (CARIBE-EWS).

The Pacific Ocean Tsunami Warning System consists of a network of seismographic stations and sea-level monitoring stations around the Pacific basin that can send all the information via satellite to tsunami warning centres located in vulnerable states. The moment an earthquake takes place somewhere in the region, the centre analyzes the data from the seismographs and the tidal stations to look for potential signs of a tsunami. The tsunami warning system also has the necessary modelling capabilities to predict the progress of the tsunami and databases on bathymetry and coastal topography to predict likely inundation. If the emergence of a tsunami is confirmed, warnings are issued to all the vulnerable states.

In the aftermath of the 2004 Indian Ocean tsunami, the Intergovernmental Oceanographic Commission (IOC) of the United Nations Educational, Scientific and Cultural Organization (UNESCO) coordinated the establishment of regional tsunami early warning systems in the Indian Ocean, the Caribbean and Mediterranean Seas. These regional systems, along with the Pacific Tsunami Warning System (PTWS), form a globally integrated system built on three pillars: tsunami risk assessment and mitigation; tsunami detection, warning, and dissemination; and tsunami awareness and response.

In the following, we discuss, in little more detail, the Indian Tsunami Early Warning Centre (ITEWC), one of the tsunami services providers in the Indian Ocean Tsunami Warning and Mitigation System, with similar centres located in Australia and Indonesia.

Formed in 2007, the Indian Tsunami Early Warning Centre is housed in the ESSO-Indian National Centre for Ocean Information Services (INCOIS), Hyderabad and functions in collaboration with other scientific agencies and disaster management organizations in India [2, 4]. In addition to data from the national seismic network set up by India, ITEWC also accesses data from the global seismic networks such as Incorporated Research Institutions for Seismology (IRIS), Global Seismographic Network (GSN), Comprehensive Nuclear Test Ban Treaty Organization (CTBTO), and German Research Centre for Geosciences (GFZ), Geofon Extended Virtual Network, which are also used to detect and assess the magnitudes of earthquakes in the region in real time. Data from such diverse sources are crucial to monitor the tsunamis in the Indian Ocean region as the two known earthquake sources of the region, the Andaman-Sumatra Arc and Makran coast, are at very close distances and very short tsunami transit times. Sea-level data obtained in real time from tide stations, bottom pressure recorders and Coastal Ocean Dynamics Applications Radar (CODAR) are also used to confirm the generation of the tsunami and its likely magnitude. Numerical models are used to predict the propagation of the tsunami wave, travel time, run-up height and likely inundation. Advisories are provided at every coastal forecast point (each separated by 50 km). For the Indian Ocean, there are 1800 coastal forecast points. Detailed bathymetry and coastal topography data are required for the accurate prediction of inundation. Topographic details were extracted using stereo satellite (CARTOSAT) and airborne Light Detection and Ranging (LIDAR). The information about the inundation zone is critical for planning evacuation and assessing likely damage to properties. These data were also used for generating a coastal vulnerability index and multi-hazard vulnerability maps were generated for the entire Indian coast. 3D modelling and visualization of inundation areas have also been carried out for the most vulnerable locations. As the advisories have to be communicated to all stakeholders in less than 15 min, a standard operating procedure and decision support system (DSS) have been designed.

Depending upon the risk involved, the advisories are classified as a *watch*, an *alert*, or a *warning*. The advisory is also issued after the threat has passed. Each type of advisory provides definite action to be taken. *Warning* advisory is issued when a tsunami wave is likely to inundate coastal regions and evacuation of people is required. *Alert* advisory is issued for preparing officials to make arrangements for evacuation if required. *Watch* advisories provide information about the earthquake and no immediate action is required. Each of these advisories is continuously upgraded, continued, or cancelled depending upon tsunami updates as available. Depending upon the details provided in advisories, they are classified as Service Levels I, II and III. Service level I provides information about the earthquake and qualitative estimation of the tsunami. Service Level II provides information about estimated wave height and expected travel time and areas under threat. Service Level III provides information about likely inundation also. Though the services have matured considerably during the last 10 years, constant efforts are being made to further improve them.

There have been criticisms of whether India should have invested in such a tsunami warning system when the event is so rare. No one can predict when the next tsunami will hit the Indian coast. But the risk is real and probability theory tells us that even a rare event has the maximum probability of happening NOW. The Indian investment ensures that not only India will not be caught unaware as and when the next tsunami strikes the Indian coast, but also together with the other tsunami warning systems around the globe, no part of the world will be caught unaware when the next tsunami strikes anywhere in the globe.

In summary, India has built over a period a robust capability not only in understanding and modelling natural disasters but also in the dissemination of timely and appropriate warnings to the public. As will be discussed a little later, the Government of India has also put in place structures that take care of post-disaster rescue and relief. These capabilities have reduced not only the loss of lives and property but also the trauma associated with such disasters in recent times.

7.3 Infectious Diseases

Natural disasters like floods, earthquakes, or tsunamis are geographically localized disrupting normal life for a few hours or days, though a complete recovery and rehabilitation may take time, depending on the extent of the damage. In contrast, a public health emergency like an epidemic is neither space-limited nor time-limited. An epidemic can last several months, even years. Physical evacuation of people from an affected area to safer zones is not an option because that would only increase the possibility of further spread of the infection. The strategies across the world to combat infectious diseases have been very diverse.

India's response to health emergencies has so far been governed primarily by the Epidemic Disease Act, 1897 and implemented by the Ministry of Health. As was mentioned earlier, the eradication of smallpox and polio are outstanding examples of the effectiveness of this system. On the other hand, even after decades of efforts in eliminating tuberculosis, India is still far away from achieving this goal. It is believed that one of the reasons for this failure is the inadequate public health infrastructure in the country. Figure 7.3 shows the number of hospital beds and number of doctors per 1000 persons in India.

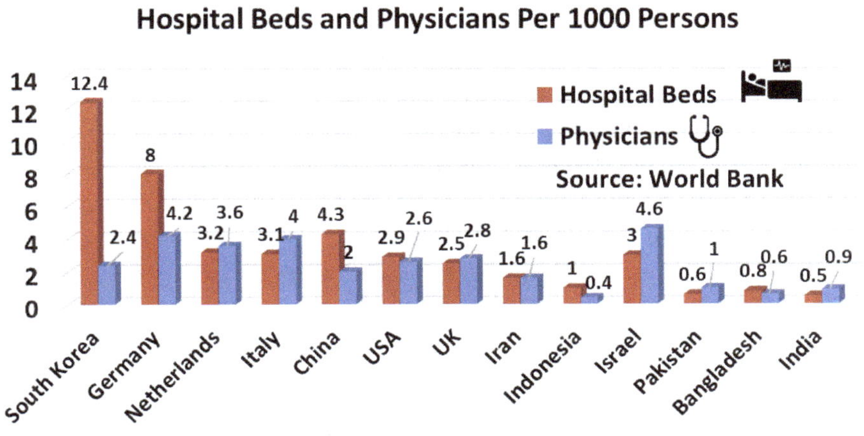

Fig. 7.3 Hospital beds and physicians per 1000 persons [6]

The World Health Organization prescribes a minimum of one general physician per 1000 persons. India is definitely wanting on both counts. The situation is aggravated further as these numbers are not evenly distributed and are mostly concentrated in bigger cities, leaving the vast countryside in the hands of fate.

We have already mentioned in Chapter 3 that India has not only eradicated smallpox and polio but has also been controlling several infectious diseases like cholera and vector-borne diseases like malaria and dengue. In recent decades, India has also emerged as a major manufacturer of vaccines as in the case of hepatitis-B and rotavirus.

7.4 The COVID-19 Crisis

The recent COVID-19 crisis is yet another test of our disaster preparedness. India was facing, like the rest of the world, an unknown, highly infectious virus, with no vaccines or drugs to combat the infection. It took some time for the country to repurpose its systems to face the pandemic by which time precious lives and livelihoods were lost.

The outbreak of the COVID-19 pandemic exposed not only the inadequacies of India's healthcare system but also the inadequacies of the country's preparedness to manage health disasters. The unprecedented death toll and trauma experienced by the people during the tsunami of 2004 prompted India to set up a Tsunami Warning System and even more importantly set up a National Disaster Response Force, which has repeatedly demonstrated its effectiveness in rescue and relief in all kinds of disasters. *We hope that the present COVID-19 crisis will prompt the country not only to strengthen the public healthcare infrastructure but also to put in place a similar mechanism specifically to handle public health emergencies.*

7.4.1 *Social security*

Besides the health crisis, the pandemic has inflicted one of the worst economic turmoils all over the world due to prolonged lockdowns. In India, the unorganized labour of the informal economy has been the worst hit due to joblessness and social insecurity during the

Fig. 7.4 Migrant workers walking to their villages following lockdown (Credit: PTI)

crisis. A large section of unorganized labour who work as migrants in cities couldn't return to their families residing in their native places due to the sudden declaration of the national lockdown. Caught in between economic hardship, health crisis and absence of family support, millions of them were compelled to walk on foot to their native homes several hundred kilometres away, as transport facilities were halted (see Fig. 7.4). This also led to the loss of several lives due to accidents, illness, and exhaustion. Many were also forced to stay back in cities in the government shelters which had limited facilities. Even when they were allowed to travel home, they faced social stigma from the administration and community back in their native states as they were suspected of carrying the virus. Clearly, India has a long way to go in offering adequate social security to the citizens across all social and economic strata in times of emergencies like a pandemic.

7.4.2 *India in the global war against infectious diseases: Development of vaccines*

Vaccines play an important role in combating any infectious disease. India has always had vaccine production capabilities for many infectious diseases as and when they were available. During the recent decades, India has also developed capabilities to design and manufacture new vaccines. It took almost a year for the world to come out with a vaccine for COVID-19. Immunization of a critical mass of the world's population is crucial for getting the pandemic under control. Even internationally, the accelerated development of multiple vaccines in less than a year is unprecedented in history, as the process typically takes 8–15 years. India is one of the first countries in the developing part of the world to come out not only with major vaccine manufacturing capabilities but also develop a vaccine of its own. As we write this, Cuba is another country in the developing part of the world that has come out with a vaccine for COVID-19, though it remains to be recognized by the World Health Organization. But the world is now pitted against a new set of challenges — production challenges, global competition over a limited supply of doses, vaccine nationalism, new virus strains and above all vaccine hesitancy — which are all presenting hurdles in universal vaccination. Even within the country, the absence of a centralized agency to coordinate mass immunization was quite apparent.

7.5 Industrial Disasters

Industrial disasters, by definition, are industry-specific. There are well-established regulatory mechanisms for industrial safety. Accidents within the perimeters of the industry are handled by the industries themselves. If and when the impact of the accidents spills out of the confines of the industry, the local disaster management authorities step in to assist the industries. However, if the magnitude of the disaster is large, it can overwhelm the healthcare system, as we saw in the case of the Bhopal Gas Tragedy.

In the case of specialized industries like the nuclear industry, there are dedicated agencies like the Atomic Energy Regulatory Board (AERB) in India that look after all safety aspects of the industry. AERB also works in close tandem with international agencies like the International Atomic Energy Agency, Vienna. However, for other industries, similar coordinated systems do not exist.

Emerging technologies bring new public risks, and we are still learning how to combat them. For example, emerging technologies like genetically modified organisms (GMOs) are regulated under the "Rules for the manufacture, use, import & storage of hazardous microorganisms, genetically engineered organisms or cells, 1989", notified under the Environment Protection Act, 1986. New technologies like artificial intelligence can bring new public risks and we are still learning how to face them if and when they emerge. Management of public risks associated with such technologies can't be entrusted to routine administrative mechanisms. The scientific community has a major role to play in evolving suitable regulatory mechanisms.

7.6 Fire Safety

Before we conclude this chapter, we would like to focus on one hazard that cuts across industries. Fire accidents across the country not only claim several thousand lives every year but also threaten business continuity when they take place in industrial hubs. There is also a direct correlation between deaths due to fire accidents and population density associated with urbanization. Fire service is a state subject. Municipal corporations and local bodies are responsible for providing fire services in many states. Budget constraints and inadequate firefighting infrastructure are common. Implementation of fire safety norms is generally below par. A common perception is that the budgets allocated to fire safety (buying firefighting equipment, etc.), if unused, are a waste of precious resources rather than efficient use of the resources. Willful negligence is yet another cause of fire accidents.

A glaring example of system failure is the Uphaar Cinema fire tragedy in an upscale area of New Delhi in 1997, which caused the death of 59 persons and seriously injured 103. The event is remembered for a determined legal fight put up by the families of victims to compel the owners of the cinema halls to not only pay compensation but also undergo punishment for wanton negligence.

In a similar incident in 2014, a major fire engulfed a school in Kumbakonam in the state of Tamil Nadu. Ninety four children below the age of 10 died in the fire. More children were injured in the stampede. The cause of the accident was a thatched roof that caught fire. Although the fire service personnel arrived in a few minutes, they were unprepared for such a large-scale fire. It was not an accident of fate but an accident on account of utter disregard of existing fire safety rules. It was an accident waiting to happen.

Couldn't the accidents have been prevented? We would like to narrate an anecdote as an answer.

This is a story of a small town in rural India. Most of the houses had a thatched roof. Fire accidents were quite common. The town had no fire station of its own and fire engines and firefighting staff from an adjacent town had to attend to the fire accidents in this town. With a lot of effort, the town managed to get a fire station sanctioned with basic necessities and a skeleton crew including a young officer. This being his first posting, the officer was quite enthusiastic, but the low workload was quite boring. He started talking to the public, the young students, about fire safety, the lists of "dos and don'ts", how to prevent a fire accident, how to fight a fire, etc. In a short period of time, public awareness of fire safety improved considerably, and the number of fire accidents came down substantially. It was then time for the annual audit. The audit team saw that the number of fire accidents was quite low, and the fire station was not being "used" often enough to justify a dedicated station. On their recommendation, the station was closed, and the young officer was transferred to a busier station. In the town, public interest in fire safety waned and the number of fire accidents started increasing. The demand for a fire station resurfaced. What is the moral of the story?

In matters of public risk, risk communication can make a big difference. Unfortunately, you are your own enemy. A job well done will make you redundant.

7.7 Post-Disaster Rescue and Relief

How to combat a disaster if a risk actually turns into a disaster? Again, historical data on the past disasters allow the disaster management agencies and the vulnerable population to prioritize their efforts and resources in risk mitigation — minimization of loss of lives and property and the associated trauma. For example, Indian villages were known to practice very strict social isolation in case of infectious diseases like smallpox in the house for millennia.

The Armed Forces have always been seen as the last resort not only in the rescue and relief operations in times of disasters but also in the maintenance of essential services in times of emergencies. Following a series of natural calamities, such as the 1999 Orissa Super Cyclone, the 2001 Bhuj earthquake, and the 2004 Indian Ocean Tsunami, an urgent need for a comprehensive national disaster management strategy was recognized by the Government of India, which led to the enactment of the Disaster Management Act on December 26, 2005. The Act led to the creation of two apex bodies: the *National Disaster Management Authority (NDMA) and the National Disaster Response Force (NDRF)*. The NDMA is mandated to lay down the policies, plans and guidelines for disaster management, while the NDRF is mandated to provide a specialized response to the disasters and minimize public trauma. In addition to dedicated manpower, NDRF also has access to several high-technology disaster management tools. *Pre-positioning and proactive availability are the two declared objectives of NDRF.* The state governments have also been encouraged to put in place their own disaster relief forces (SDRFs) and disaster management strategies.

NDMA has also been implementing a scheme, Aapda Mitra, for training community volunteers in disaster response. The scheme aims to provide the community volunteers with the necessary skills that would enable them to respond to the community's immediate needs in the aftermath of a disaster, enabling them to undertake basic relief and rescue tasks. It has been reported that the services of these trained community volunteers have been very critical in offering immediate services in the cases of several natural disasters like floods and cyclones. Even during the ongoing pandemic, these volunteers have been providing commendable services, such as home delivery of essential items to women-headed households, senior citizens, and disabled people, in addition to dissemination of information and

Fig. 7.5 NDRF providing rescue and relief during floods [7]

awareness creation. The scheme has received positive feedback from both the disaster management agencies and the public.

The first major test for NDRF in disaster management was the 2008 Kosi floods in Bihar. NDRF resources were moved to Bihar on a war footing after the breach in the Kosi barrage on 19th August 2008. About 150 high-speed motorized boats were airlifted and about 780 trained personnel were sent to the flood-affected areas. Over 100,000 affected people were rescued during the initial stage itself.

NDRF has continued to win the hearts of millions of countrymen, demonstrating its expertise and effectiveness in handling disaster situations (see Fig. 7.5).

A very valuable and comprehensive document, describing "Dos and Don'ts" for all, including those preparing to deal with various public disasters, has been published by the National Disaster Management Authority [8]. Extensive dissemination of this information will go a long way in our efforts to manage disasters. In fact, we would strongly recommend that relevant portions for every region are included in the school curricula.

7.7.1 *Public participation in managing public risks*

"Each One, Teach One" is an African proverb that originated in the United States during centuries of slavery when Africans were denied education. When someone learned how to read or write, it became their responsibility to teach someone else. The idea is to spread knowledge for the betterment of your community. Illiteracy and ignorance, as we know, are some of the most abominable scourges of mankind. It has since been adopted by various organizations and countries to spread public awareness. It was again made popular by Mahatma Gandhi during the freedom struggle and has since been invoked from time to time in India. It exemplifies the role of an enlightened citizenry in spreading knowledge and combating ignorance, superstition, and obscurantism. Taken one step further, it signifies the momentous unleashing of the enormous potential of public participation in managing risks and disasters.

On the occasion of any disaster, people all over the world step forward to help. The help could be at the individual level or joining a volunteer force or as monetary contributions to various relief funds. Schemes such as the National Cadet Corps, National Service Scheme, Scouts and Guides, Red Cross, and a large number of non-government organizations have always stepped forward to help people in distress during disasters. With their rudimentary training about first aid and a disciplined volunteer workforce, they are often the first ones to reach any site where help is needed till more competent and better-equipped forces arrive. If they also happen to be locals, their in-depth knowledge of the terrain, language, local sentiments, and sensitivities prove valuable. They also assist in relief and rehabilitation efforts. Another important group are amateur ham radio operators, who have provided emergency communication networks during natural calamities, such as floods, cyclones, storms, earthquakes, and tsunamis. Their help was especially valuable during the dam failure in Morbi, earthquakes in Uttarkashi and Latur, cyclone in Odisha, and tsunami in southern India. After the event, these volunteers also provide evidence of damage and assist in providing compensation to affected people. Such citizen-science-centric initiatives can also be beneficial in recovery programmes. Such people should not only be trained to carry out their functions but also be equipped with a few essential tools.

We note that every disaster brings with it innumerable narratives of hope, inspiration and resilience of the public at large speaking volumes of human will. For example, in the case of the 2018 Kerala floods, in addition to the government machinery, the role of fishermen and a massive network of volunteers played leading roles in the rescue operations. They are reasonably well informed about possible dangers from the disasters specific to that location. It has been observed that many villages have volunteers who inform people about potential dangers as well as assist the administration in directing people to safe places and providing necessary relief.

The recent COVID-19 pandemic has brought into focus another group of people who played a critical role in managing the public health disaster, the COVID warriors — healthcare professionals such as doctors, nurses, sanitation workers, the law-and-order personnel and many others like transport workers who continued to function during the disaster, putting their own lives at stake in the interest of the public. At the same time, various NGOs across the country provided food, water, medicines, oxygen, ambulance services, and even help with cremations and burials. This altruism is one of the most endearing, ennobling, and redeeming features of mankind and the most important confirmation that together we can face any disaster.

Rescue, relief, and rehabilitation are vast exercises. The rehabilitation, depending on the nature of the disaster, may take from weeks to months to years of sustained efforts and flow of funds to be completed. Climate change will take decades of sustained effort for mitigation. During disasters, people lose their loved ones, their homes, their documents, and their livelihood. In disasters like floods, agrarian communities lose their dwellings, crops, cattle, seeds, and equipment. Floods can even change the topology of the terrain and destroy the sources of drinking water; vast areas may be swallowed by overflowing rivers, which may even change their course. Rivers changing their course is also seen during severe earthquakes. These leave people traumatized and emotionally weak. The need to provide them counselling along with food, water, shelter, and medicines, for diseases that must follow, becomes paramount.

The purpose of relief is to provide immediate sustenance to the affected, while rehabilitation should ensure that the affected communities bounce back strongly and, as far as possible, do not face the same trauma again, following a careful damage assessment to evaluate the quantum of loss. Almost all governments as well as the United Nations have well chalked out strategies for this, and we shall not dwell further on this point.

We have discussed the very active role played by the National Disaster Response Force in meeting these challenges. It is felt, though, that rehabilitation and reconstruction may require a more sustained and prolonged effort than what such a force specifically equipped for a rapid deployment can handle.

7.7.2 *Equity in managing public risks*

It is often said that being poor is a great sin. Poor people are less able to get out of harm's way as low-income groups live in unsafe, crowded spaces and are more vulnerable to the risks of natural disasters and disease. They also struggle most to recover, as they often lack the safety net of insurance and savings. Incidents of inequity lead to a severe distrust of the authorities and their efforts and alienate the masses. It has to be remembered that the affluent sections can easily relocate to safer places or get access to the best and most expensive medical facilities, when sick or hurt, while the poor are solely dependent on the government during times of disasters.

We have seen that migrant workers in India were forced to walk home when a very harsh and strictly implemented lockdown was suddenly enforced in India, without making adequate provisions for them, during COVID-19, which led to their undergoing extreme suffering. This will remain among the saddest episodes in recent times in handling a disaster. The only saving grace was the help extended to them along the tedious journey by individuals and charitable organizations.

Equity in the management of public risks, where everyone has access to what they need to face the risk, will go a long way in instilling confidence among the public that everyone would be cared for. Pandemics like COVID-19 bring out this realization much more clearly. Equity in public risk management is not only a humanitarian task; it is also the only workable strategy as *No One is Safe Unless Everyone is Safe.*

Natural disasters and pandemics are few and far in between. Are there lessons to be learnt from such events? There is no doubt that everyone is vulnerable to the risk, and everyone is responsible for containing the risk. Who is responsible for protecting the public from the risk? As we have already seen, it is usually the government that is seen as responsible for the public good. The government must balance public costs and public good while charting out a strategy to fight the disasters while putting in place the necessary support systems. Some of the weaknesses of the government system are also well known. For example, there are always resource constraints. The government systems are in general slow and any indecision by the government is a risk in itself. We have also seen that the three wings of the Government, the Legislative, the Executive and the Judiciary, do not often see eye to eye. The legislative wing is often constrained by electoral compulsions. Bureaucracy goes largely by rules, regulations, and precedents even if they are outdated. The judiciary goes by the rule of law, some of which could again be outdated. For many public risks, there may not even be a precedent as in the case of first-time epidemics and new and emerging technologies and the Government is charting an unknown trajectory as much as the public. Interference of vested interests cannot be ruled out.

It is interesting to recall the story of the introduction of Euro-II emission standards for cars and compressed natural gas (CNG) for buses and auto-rickshaws in Delhi in the mid-nineties. We now know that these two interventions not only brought substantial improvement in the quality of air in the Delhi region but also paved the way for the introduction of emission standards across the country. However, one cannot forget that both these decisions were not based on well-thought-out legislative or executive decisions of the Government but were judicial interventions. The legislators were obviously apprehensive of the adverse public reactions to such an intervention.

In yet another instance of Government indecision in the face of perceived public opposition, the Government has not been able to either convince the farmers in Western Uttar Pradesh, Haryana, and Punjab to stop the practice of burning stubbles of Kharif (rainy season) crops or enforce an administrative decision on this issue despite clear evidence of severe deterioration of quality of air and visibility in the region during winter.

Despite all the above, we have no alternative but to look to the government to manage public risks. As will be discussed in the following chapter, with more and more countries opting for a democratic form of governance, communication of public good and public risks to the public at large becomes central to any policy-making by the governments.

7.8 Outlook

Before we conclude this chapter on managing public risks, we would like to focus on one highly disappointing response of the governments across the world to a well-known public risk that is round the corner: Global Climate Change. As has already been pointed out, continued burning of fossil fuels like coal, oil, and natural gas to satisfy the increasing energy needs of the population and industry is bound to increase the accumulation of greenhouse gases and a steady warming of the atmosphere, which has changed the global climate and will continue to do so for tens of decades or beyond. Scientists from across the world have been issuing warnings about it for decades. Many of the warnings such as rising sea levels, retreating glaciers, melting of polar ice, increased frequency and ferocity of droughts, floods, storm surges, cyclones, forest fires, and extinction of species are coming true. Another major concern is that the melting of ice in the Antarctic regions and Greenland as well as numerous glaciers across the world is threatening to release unknown viruses buried there for millions of years. The risk is very real and some of the dangers are even unknown. If left unattended, this is likely to push our planet into a "Hothouse Earth" trap, from which it will be difficult, if not impossible, to get out. It is now well recognized that the world has no alternative but to drastically decrease the use of fossil fuels, increase the use of renewable and green sources of energy, end deforestation, conserve freshwater, end pollution of all kinds, and increase investments in research and development (R&D) in cleaner and greener technologies. While countries across the world have set targets for themselves, the action plans at the ground level have been very diverse and often disappointing. It is even more sad to note that the major polluters are also the major defaulters in implementing the control measures. We still believe that if the entire world decides and swiftly acts together, this impending calamity can be averted. India, despite its population, is only a small contributor to greenhouse gas emissions and is aggressively pursuing the path of renewable and green energy resources. Many of the developed countries are not only dragging their feet in fulfilling their past commitments but also actually changing the goalposts despite being major polluters. Our only hope is to increase public awareness about risks relating to global climate change so that they can put enough pressure on their respective governments to take immediate action.

References

[1] S. Ghosh *et al.*, Development of India's first integrated expert urban flooding forecasting system for Chennai, *Curr. Sci.* **117**, 741–745 (2019).

[2] Cyclone warning in India — Standard operation procedure. India Meteorological Department, March 2021.

[3] A. K. Sutar, S. Roy and V. M. Tiwari, Revisiting the Koyna-Warna seismic zone: strain budget, present-day potential and associated hazard, *J. Seismol.* **25**, 1265–1279 (2021). https://doi.org/10/10007/s10950-021-10024-1.

[4] S. Nayak, T. Srinivasa Kumar and E. P. Rama Rao, *Tsunami Watch and Warning Centers.* Encyclopedia of Solid Earth Geophysics (H. K. Gupta, ed.), *Encycl. Earth Sci. Ser.* (2020), https://doi.org/10.1007/978-3-030-10475-7_230-1.

[5] F. Imamura, TUNAMI-N2 (Tohoku University's numerical analysis model for investigation of near field tsunamis version 2 Manual draft) (2006). Available at: http://www.tsunami.civil.tohoku.ac.jp/hokusai3/J/projects/manual-ver-3.1.pdf; V. V. Titov and F. I. Gonzalez, *Implementation and testing of the Method of Splitting Tsunami (MOST) model.* NOAA Technical Memorandum ERL PMEL-112. Contribution No.1927 from NOAA/Pacific Marine Environmental Laboratory (1997).

[6] https://data.worldbank.org/indicator/SH.MED.PHYS.ZS.
[7] http://www.ndrf.gov.in/.
[8] *Be Smart Be Prepared: Disaster Survival Guide*, National Disaster Management Authority, Government of India, https://ndma.gov.in/sites/default/files/PDF/pocketbook-do-dont.pdf.

Chapter 8

The Way Forward

"And ye shall know the truth and the truth shall make you free."
— *John 8:32*

Forests across India have one inhabitant, Grey langur (*Semnopithecus entellus*), which has alerted the wild animals of the forest of one particular risk, a predator they all fear, the Tiger, for millennia. Perched on the highest point of the tallest tree in the forest, they keep a vigil. Their eyes continuously scan the forest. They notice everything, including the tiger moving stealthily in the shadows — even though its black stripes provide him with a perfect camouflage! When they give out a call, "Khyak..., khayak..., khakarrrr khak", one can be sure that a tiger or a leopard or a pack of wild dogs is on the move. This is a signal to spotted deer and other antelopes to stand still and to get fully alert to flee away at their top speed in a fleeting moment if necessary. Herds of wild buffaloes and elephants with babies organize themselves in a formation, keeping the babies in the middle. The smaller animals hurriedly take cover. Mynahs, the sentinels of the forest since eternity, take up the alarm and keep it up; the nature of the danger coded into it, till it persists. Animals like spotted deer and wild boars have survived in our forests because they have learned to avoid predators and the risk they pose by paying heed to the alarms raised by the langurs and the mynahs. (Vervet monkeys of African forests are known to give varying alert calls in a similar manner.) Many of the tribal communities living on the periphery of

Fig. 8.1 Grey Langur (Credit: Wikipedia)

forests keep an ear for the warnings from the langurs even today (see Fig. 8.1).

This is an archetypal example of unambiguous risk communication and the appropriate response, of which one can be justly proud. It has evolved and it has been perfected over thousands of years in the struggle for survival by animals in the wild. The langurs also take immediate steps to protect themselves as well as their babies. Thus, it has been noted that they move to higher branches if they see a panther. They are known to move down to denser foliage if they notice a hawk overhead, which can hurt their smaller babies. The mynah keeps the alarm till the danger exists, much like an air-raid siren. The elephants and wild buffaloes take steps to face the danger head-on while keeping the babies under protection.

8.1 Perceptions of Public Risks

We have already seen that humans during their long and perilous journey from ape-like hominids to *Homo sapiens* of today have been facing public risks of one kind or another and have survived by pitting their wits against nature and by organizing themselves into a vibrant society, continuously learning from their successes and failures and continuously communicating the risks to others in the community, often leaving detailed accounts of their experiences for the benefit of the future generations, using a variety of means such as oral histories, songs, proverbs, and finally, writing. For example, the Charak and Sushrut Samhitas — compendiums of diseases, medicines, and surgical procedures — are from a period several hundred years before Christ.

Public perception is a belief or a sentiment, which is shared by most people; it is also termed the voice of the people (*vox populi)*. The evolution of a vibrant society of humans has transformed public perceptions of all public risks into a complex yet rich social phenomenon, where the psychology of individuals and the society as a whole play significant roles. Unfortunately, the voice of the people is often guided more by discussions among people than by learned discourses. The majority view may even be guided by the so-called herd mentality. Sometimes, a desire to be different from others can also shape one's perception. One's past experiences, education, social and economic backgrounds, and even individual attitudes go into shaping the perception. We also realize that public perceptions, not always based on facts and not necessarily rational, can easily overestimate or underestimate risks, both of which make risk management a difficult task. It is also known that public perceptions can be "influenced" by vested interests who are not easily distinguishable from objective scholarly commentators.

We have already mentioned that the spectrum of public risks has considerably broadened during the last few centuries. At the same time, the recent developments in science and technology (S&T) have given us many new tools to manage the risks we face. For example, soon after the man started mining coal, he was exposed to the deadly, colourless, and odourless carbon monoxide. He learnt to get an alert about its presence by carrying canaries with him while descending into the depths of the mines. Now, very powerful and elaborate sensors are available for this. Our scientific understanding of several natural disasters has enabled us to issue timely warnings to the public to minimize the loss of lives and property. Drugs and vaccines have enabled us to contain, treat, and even eradicate several infectious diseases. There have also been substantial improvements in disaster management tools such as satellite imaging and emergency medical facilities including diagnostic instruments. Man has also built shelters and gears that can provide him protection even under the most adverse conditions. Emerging risks such as those associated with long-term climate change are not fully understood even by experts. Managing public perceptions of the public risks associated with these require new and focussed efforts.

Most of the public risks are generally location-specific. Even public risks like global warming or pandemics like COVID-19 that are not location-specific affect different regions of the world differently. While the first step in any public risk management strategy is the identification of risks based on experience and historical data and preparing the population to face the risks, one must recognize that some risks may be completely new with consequences not fully known. For example, we do not even know whether there are risks associated with emerging technologies like artificial intelligence and human cloning and, if yes, what are the risks and how to handle them (black cats in a dark room!).

It is also important to remember that the risk environment can change or evolve with time. Thus, identification and mapping of risks and preparedness for a disaster, if and when these strike, are not one-time exercises but need to be carried out on a regular basis. A classic example is the "risk map of malaria" in India. Malaria is usually associated with stagnant water bodies. One would have thought that malaria would not be a threat in the arid deserts of Rajasthan. This was indeed so till several canals were dug to take water there about two decades ago. The canals provided breeding space for mosquitoes, leading to the appearance and spread of malaria. It has also been suggested that diseases, which are normally prevalent in tropical, hot zones of the Earth, would shift further north and south of the tropical regions, as global warming gets aggravated and becomes more severe.

Risk maps also exist for several other hazards, such as dengue, hookworms, yellow fever, kala-azar, arsenic, or fluoride in groundwater. Similarly, large-scale deforestation and construction in the Himalayas have altered the patterns of landslide risks. Urban flood maps undergo continuous change as more and more water bodies and low-lying areas are built over, blocking the natural flow of water. Unfortunately, public perceptions of the public risks are often more "rigid" and do not necessarily follow the ground realities. In view of such scenarios, the understanding and managing the perception of any public risk is very complex.

8.2 Managing Perceptions of Public Risks

Community awareness of past disasters (or tribal memory) plays an important role in public risk perceptions and risk preparedness. For example, it has been reported that the Sentinelese, Jarwa and Onge tribes in the Andaman and Nicobar Islands survived the 2004 Indian Ocean tsunami despite its heavy impact on their islands. On seeing the sea recede, they *knew* to move to higher ground. We have already mentioned in Chapter 2 how a farmer, noticing rapidly retreating sea waters, following an earthquake earlier on that day in the region, warned his entire village about an oncoming tsunami by setting his harvest to fire to attract their attention and lead the villagers to the safety of a hill, from where they saw their village getting destroyed by the tsunami. We also saw in Chapter 2, how a 10-year-old student and a teacher recognized the signs of the tsunami on the beaches of Thailand and saved numerous lives by alerting people to move to higher ground.

What if the public perceptions underestimate or overestimate a risk? A dramatic demonstration of the diversity of Public Perceptions of Risks was witnessed during the recent COVID-19 pandemic:

1. Resistance to COVID Appropriate Behaviour

There is ample evidence that simple steps such as wearing a mask, observing social distance, washing hands frequently and not touching the nose, the mouth, and the eyes unnecessarily slow down the spread of the COVID infection considerably. Governments across the world have been trying hard to convince the public to follow such COVID Appropriate Behaviours. However, a small but vocal group of people across the world refused to follow these behavioural norms since they considered these as an infringement of their personal freedom.

2. Vaccine hesitancy

Vaccines offer the first level of protection against any infectious disease. Vaccine hesitancy refers to a reluctance to get vaccinated or even refusal to get vaccinated despite the availability of vaccines. Reasons for the hesitancy range from concerns about the safety of vaccination to a misplaced "confidence" that nothing will happen to "me".

3. Narrow cultural, religious, and political dialogues

We already mentioned in Chapter 3 that cultural and religious sentiments against vaccinations played a major role in our failure to eradicate some of the dreadful diseases like polio from the face of the earth. It was strange that similar objections were raised in the case of COVID-19 vaccinations also. Similarly, vaccine hoarding by nations can compromise the safety of the global population, as the non-availability of the vaccine in poorer nations gives it a free run and time to mutate.

It is quite apparent that the simple message that "**No one is safe unless everyone is safe**" in the case of a public risk like COVID-19 was being missed.

8.2.1 *Frustratingly inadequate public response to climate change*

There are also instances where public perceptions of risks are not strong enough to force government action. Let us take the example of *global warming and long-term climate change* arising from the indiscriminate burning of hydrocarbons for energy. It is now known that the public risk arising out of this could be more devastating than any of the past natural disasters or pandemics. For more than two centuries following the Industrial Revolution, we have been burning hydrocarbons to satisfy our increasing energy needs. It is well established that the burning of hydrocarbons for energy results in an increase in atmospheric carbon dioxide, leading to global warming with several disastrous consequences. The warning signs are already around us — the summers are getting hotter everywhere, heavy rains and prolonged droughts are recurring more frequently, forest fires are getting more severe, tropical storms and cyclones are more frequent and fiercer, the polar ice caps are melting, sea levels are rising, glaciers are receding, and coral reefs are bleaching. Even more worrying is the fact that the poorer countries, which contributed least to global warming and are least equipped to face these calamities, are hit the most [1].

Climate scientists are clear that we are very close to the tipping point of irreversible climate change and the only option available to us is to migrate to green energy technologies before it gets too late. Even if we completely stop the emission of carbon dioxide due to fossil fuel burning today, the Earth will continue to get hotter for decades before it starts the process of recovery as carbon dioxide stays in the atmosphere for hundreds of years.

It was (only!) in 1992, that countries across the world formally recognized the need to control greenhouse gas emissions that cause global warming and long-term climate change and agreed to an international convention, the United Nations Framework Convention on Climate Change (UNFCCC), setting the expectations and ground rules for global cooperation on combating climate change. In 2015, the nations signed the Paris Climate Agreement that set the goal of limiting global warming to "well below" 2°C and preferably 1.5°C to avoid catastrophic climate change.

The twenty sixth session of the Conference of the Parties (COP26) of the UNFCCC took place in Glasgow, UK recently (October 31 to November 12, 2021). The Sixth Assessment Report (AR6) of The Intergovernmental Panel on Climate Change, released on August 9, 2021, has indeed confirmed the warnings that we are almost at the irreversible tipping point. We are still nowhere near firm commitments towards a time-bound migration to green technologies despite several decades of negotiations. Countries across the world have repeatedly made commitments on time-bound reduction on hydrocarbon burning for energy, but these commitments have rarely been fulfilled. On the contrary, there is a continuous shifting of the goalposts.

On the technology side, it has always been recognized that renewable energy technologies like hydro, solar, and wind offer options that can help us in getting away from hydrocarbon burning for energy. But there are several challenges in making a full transition to renewables. Time variations and land and material requirements are the biggest drawbacks of solar and wind energies. Large hydel power stations have limitations of site availability and environmental impact. Large-scale energy storage technologies are still on the anvil, and high-capacity batteries have their own problems such as costs and the need for special materials. Lithium, one of the most frequently used ingredients of batteries, requires 2.3 million litres of freshwater per tonne for its extraction. The use of hydrogen requires platinum, both for hydrolysis and for fuel cells, which is among the scarcest materials on the Earth with a finite supply. The silicon used in the manufacture of solar panels uses up to 1.5 billion litres of freshwater for dust control for a 500 MW power plant and releases silicon tetrachloride and hydrochloric acid into the environment. Such a plant would additionally need more than 25 million litres of water annually to wash the panels. Solar PV is slated to produce millions of tonnes of E-waste per year, as the efficiency of solar panels deteriorates by about 1% every year, and their utility goes down considerably after 15–20 years. It is usually the conventional power stations running on coal or natural gas that stabilize the electricity grid [1].

8.2.2 *The promise of nuclear power*

It has always been recognized that nuclear energy, though not strictly renewable, offers another clean energy (carbon-free) option for electricity. Nearly 450 nuclear reactors are in operation across the world today delivering nearly 10% of the global electricity demands. Most of the nuclear power plants are of course located in the developed part of the world. Recognizing that nuclear energy has distinct advantages over renewable energy resources from the point of view of land requirements, material requirements and duty factors, there have been suggestions that a judicious mix of hydrocarbons, nuclear and renewable energy resources would satisfy the global energy requirements while addressing the global climate change concerns [2, 3].

Unfortunately, despite several reactor years of accident-free operations across the world, three reactor accidents, the 1979 Three Mile accident, the 1986 Chernobyl disaster and the 2011 Fukushima Daiichi disaster, created considerable negative vibes towards nuclear energy across the world. *It is not surprising that public perceptions of the safety of electricity from nuclear reactors also underwent a strong negative swing*. For example, in the 32 years before the Chernobyl accident, 409 nuclear reactors were commissioned for electricity generation, but in the three decades following the accident, only 194 have been added. One may also recall several public agitations against nuclear power projects across the world, presumably in the backdrop of the three reactor accidents. Repeated assurances by the experts did not convince the agitators. That the world can't afford to say NO to nuclear power was also not convincing to the agitators.

What was the response of Japan itself to the Fukushima accident? Before the Fukushima accident, the share of nuclear energy in the total energy basket in Japan was about 25%. Immediately after the accident, Japan shut down all their nuclear reactors and carried out a detailed safety review. Based on the safety reviews, while several reactors were permanently shut down, many reactors were also restarted, recognizing that Japan's geographical constraints do not allow the country to fully make a transition to renewable energies. Already in 2019, nuclear reactors were providing 7.5% of Japan's electricity needs. By 2030, Japan aspires to achieve 22–24% of its energy from renewables, 20–22% from nuclear and the remaining from fossil fuels. Substantial emphasis is also being laid on energy efficiency.

Many other countries like India, Russia, China, and South Korea have also recognized that nuclear power will remain an essential part of the energy mix of the coming decades and are moving forward with their nuclear energy programmes while strengthening their safety and security infrastructures.

Responses of some countries like Germany with a strong anti-nuclear lobby, both in and outside the government, were almost panic reactions. Within a few days after the Fukushima disaster, Germany embarked on an "exit" plan from nuclear energy. Having already committed to an exit plan from hydrocarbons in the next few years, this is not going to come without a cost [4]. It is rather ironic that Germany continues to buy power from France, most of which comes from nuclear power plants.

There is no doubt that we can't afford to have accidents like Chernobyl and Fukushima. But one can't also ignore the fact that these accidents may not have taken place if internationally accepted safety standards had been followed strictly.

8.2.3 *International electricity grid*

It has also been suggested that the intermittency inherent in the power generated by renewable sources can be mitigated to a great extent by having an international grid, e.g., One Sun, One World, One Grid proposed by India in 2015, which now includes about 140 countries across Asia, the Middle East, and Africa, as well as Germany, UK, and the USA. If this grid can be expanded to include nuclear power plants, it would not only stabilize the grid but also give us an option to locate the nuclear plants in more suitable locations following international safety guidelines. This grid could also address the power needs of the poorer countries without resorting to polluting sources of power [1, 5].

The world is now facing three competing public perceptions vis-a-vis global energy needs and long-term climate change:

1. **Weak public perceptions** of the risks of global warming and long-term climate change that is not enough to put pressure on the

governments to implement policies to reduce hydrocarbon burning for energy in a time-bound manner.

2. **Widespread public enthusiasm** for renewable energy technologies (driven by attractive subsidies and media coverage). The public however is generally unaware of their drawbacks like land and material requirements, and complexities of energy storage technologies.
3. A **negative public perception** of the safety of nuclear energy.

There is no doubt that on matters of public risk, governments across the world would like to be guided by public perceptions. Unfortunately, public perceptions on global climate change and energy options are strongly influenced by pockets of activism — some well-informed and some ill-informed. *The net result is that there are literally no public pressures on the governments on time-bound reduction of CO_2 emissions despite nearly three decades of negotiations.* Managing Perceptions of Public Risks associated with long-term climate change is clearly the challenge of the hour and can only be managed by effective communication of the public risk.

8.3 Public Risk Communication

How does one manage public perceptions of public risks particularly when there are no historical precedents? With more and more countries opting for democratic forms of Governance, there is no alternative but to manage public perceptions through effective risk communication.

Recall that the physical phenomenon, nuclear magnetic resonance (NMR), was discovered in 1952. It was then recognized in 1973 that it could produce detailed images of a patient's internal organs in a non-invasive fashion. NMR was soon cleared for routine clinical use. Though this technology had nothing to do with radioactivity or ionizing radiation, negative perceptions associated with the word "nuclear" during the Cold War years compelled NMR practitioners to change the name from NMR to MRI, magnetic resonance imaging, to ensure everyone was feeling safe. Unfortunately, managing public perceptions is not always as simple as that.

Traditionally, the pursuit of knowledge was considered the exclusive domain of academics. The twentieth century and beyond saw major developments in S&T that not only pushed the limits of knowledge beyond known frontiers but also led to several products and services that are of use to the common man. In fact, it is said that there is no aspect of our lives today untouched by S&T in some form or another. This has necessitated a greater familiarity of S&T to the citizens at large which could be made possible only by more and more S&T communication. S&T communication is however a one-way process between an expert and the public at large. Considering that most scientists are not experts in science communication, professional science communicators usually take the message of science to the public at large using a variety of communication tools, such as books, newspapers, radio, television, and the internet. Traditional communication forms such as music, drama and folk arts are also used for S&T communication. The multiplicity of languages across the world, across even one country like India, is an additional barrier for S&T communication.

8.3.1 *Communication of science and technology*

Prior to independence, science communication in India was largely limited to individual scientists or individuals committed to a scientific way of thinking. For example, Ruchi Ram Sahni was a well-known teacher, physicist, and meteorologist. Prof. Sahni was also a well-known science communicator. Mahendra Lal Sircar was a famous medical doctor. He was also a social reformer and propagator of scientific studies in nineteenth-century India. He founded the Indian Association for Cultivation of Science (IACS) in 1876 in Calcutta with the primary objective of science communication and research. It was in IACS that the only Indian Nobel Laureate in Physics, Sir C V Raman, carried out his research. Today, IACS is one of the leading research universities in India. Sir J. C. Bose, Prof. S. N. Bose, and Prof. M. N. Saha also worked extensively for the popularization of science.

Just after independence, India had a large rural population: illiterate, highly superstitious and lacking a scientific temper. Thus, the immediate goal of science popularization was basically to create a scientific temper among the masses. The level of missing scientific temper is best illustrated by the following example. A total solar eclipse was to occur across India in 1980. A frenzy was created in the country about how harmful it could be for the people and their eyes and how it "presaged" catastrophic events for the country. The authorities bowed down to public pressure and declared the closure of offices and schools at several places along the path of the total eclipse. The sole television channel of the country broadcasted popular movies to encourage people to stay indoors.

A total solar eclipse was to occur again in 1995. Professor Yash Pal (1926–2017), a highly respected scientist, was by then hosting a science popularization programme, *Turning Point*, on Indian television. He discussed the occurrence of the solar eclipse and its progression, the spectacle of advancing eclipse, the return of birds to their nests, the sickle shape images of the Sun, formed by the pin-hole camera action by leaves of trees, the corona, the "celestial diamond ring" (see Fig. 8.2), Bailey's beads, and return to normalcy. He encouraged people to take necessary precautions, make

Fig. 8.2 Celestial diamond ring: Nature's gift to humanity (Credit: NASA)

goggles of exposed photographic films and come out and enjoy the most beautiful celestial display put up by the Sun and the Moon. It created a vibrant mood across schools and colleges, and science clubs arranged visits to the most favourable sites and explained the advancing stages of the eclipse to the people. The Indian Air Force joined the celebration and took out a sortie of its fighter jets at Mach 2.5 at an altitude of 25,000 m, chasing the shadow of the Sun, and filming the corona, to the delight of all!

It is important to recall that India is perhaps the only country in the world that has enshrined the objective of nurturing scientific temper among the citizens in its constitution.

Yet, almost as an exception, during "The Green Revolution" in the seventies, modern agricultural practices were readily adopted by the Indian farmers, which not only made India achieve self-sufficiency in food production but also made it a leading producer of fruits and vegetables. However, there are concerns that excessive use of fertilizers and pesticides are affecting the environment, while excessive irrigation is depleting underground sources of water.

In general, there is almost always a resistance to the introduction of new technologies, which are generally seen as luxuries of the rich. It is not easy to forget the widespread agitations against computerization in government offices because of the perceived fears of job loss. We do have agitations against automation across the world every now and then.

However, 75 years after Independence, we see the emergence of a more mature India. This required (and requires) the creation of awareness for S&T to draw full benefits of emerging technologies in agriculture, computers, ICT, and biotechnology/genetic engineering. This is an ongoing process and must continue to transfer the knowledge, understanding, and benefits of the latest developments in S&T, and a willing embracement of the progress.

Scientists in general (and government functionaries) are not known to be good communicators of S&T. Quite often, journalists and science fiction writers have succeeded in giving much wider publicity to a scientific idea than the scientists themselves. Of course, there have been rare exceptions.

George Gamow, one of the well-known theoretical physicists, was perhaps one of the earliest and most successful science communicators, who ignited the minds of millions of young people and got them interested in the study of sciences and developing a scientific outlook. Much later, Carl Sagan was to do that, now aided with modern means of communication. Carl Sagan once lamented [6]: "We live in a society exquisitely dependent on science and technology, in which hardly anyone knows anything about science and technology." He further added: "Ignorance of science threatens our economic well-being, our national security, and the democratic process." For the last several decades, Sir David Attenborough has been creating very informed awareness about natural ecosystems, biodiversity, and climate change using the medium of talks, articles, books, documentaries, and films about animals, birds, marine life, and forests from across the world. His recent documentary, *Breaking Boundaries: The Science of Our Planet*, is a cry of despair and pain and an eye-opener, with the devastating ecological damage of the wildfires and coral reef bleaching to the importance of tree planting for sustainable development and survival. The documentary is packed with scientific data and leaves audiences in tears at the unfolding tragedy of climate change.

8.3.2 *Communication of public risks*

Public Risk Communication is however more complex than S&T communication. At the outset, risk perception by the experts and risk perception by the public at large are very different. Experts judge risks in terms of quantitative assessments of mortality, morbidity, financial losses, and other quantifiable losses. The public at large however sees risk as a disruption in their normal lives. Differences in educational, economic, and social backgrounds are some of the other well-known factors that influence their risk perceptions. Risk communication, therefore, involves people with very different risk perceptions. Recent developments in information and communication technologies including the World Wide Web have indeed made information on anything to anyone, anywhere, at any time a reality. It has also made risk communication risky by spreading unvalidated information, some of which could have even been spread with ulterior motives. But we have no option but to communicate. As in the case of science communication, a multiplicity of languages across the country and the world is an additional barrier for risk communication.

The inherent uncertainties in estimating risks make risk communication even more difficult. Let us elaborate on this point a little more by taking the example of weather forecasts. Meteorological agencies across the world operate fairly robust systems to monitor weather, in particular extreme weather events, and issue appropriate warnings. It should however be remembered that weather forecasts are attempts to predict the behaviour of a complex system, which is inherently chaotic. A small change in the state of the atmosphere in one location can lead to remarkable consequences over time elsewhere. Despite this, there is no doubt that the recent developments in weather forecasting have been reasonably accurate and have had a positive impact on forecasting events, such as extreme rainfall, droughts, and cyclones.

The India Meteorological Department has been issuing warnings of extreme weather events for a long time. Do these warnings always elicit appropriate responses? If not, why not?

As was mentioned earlier, while the disaster forecasting agencies like the IMD are well identified, the "public" is large in number and highly "diffuse", with widely diverse social, educational, and financial backgrounds. Often, the information and warnings that reach the man on the street is not only cloaked in technical and official jargon but is also not very focused. This often distorts public perception of the risks and plays a very important role in the public response to the warnings.

8.3.3 *Cyclones*

We discussed in Chapter 2 the 1999 Super Cyclone in Odisha that caused enormous loss of lives and property. Looking back, it is generally accepted that these heavy losses of life could have been avoided. Considering that the India Meteorological Department (IMD) had a robust system for the detection and tracking of cyclones even at that time and had been issuing warnings about the event for several days preceding the Super Cyclone, it is unfortunate that the vulnerable population did not take appropriate precautions and move to safer locations beyond the reach of the tidal waves. Why didn't it happen?

Cyclones are not new to the Odisha coast. The IMD "saw" the 1999 Super Cyclone forming and gathering itself, 4 days before it hit the coast and it was regularly issuing alerts and advisories. Public warnings for the cyclone were broadcast in the print and electronic media for more than 2 days before the event, reaching even the remotest villages. Evacuation of certain low-lying areas was also advised. If only Odisha had an adequate number of cyclone shelters like their neighbouring state, Andhra Pradesh, if only the population from low lying areas had been shifted to these cyclone centres, Odisha would not have seen the loss of lives at such a large scale, as was witnessed in 1999.

Why didn't the population respond appropriately to the IMD warnings? By an unfortunate coincidence, a lower intensity cyclone had also hit the Odisha coast (Ganjam district) 10 days before the Super Cyclone. The warnings for the Ganjam cyclones were very similar to the Super Cyclone — strong gale, widespread rain, 2–3-m-high tidal waves, damage to houses, uprooting of trees, and travel and communication disruptions. The people "assumed" that the two cyclones would be similar. Since the onus of making decisions to shift to safer grounds was left to the people themselves, a majority of the population decided to stay indoors in their mud-walled houses on the flat low-land coast in 1999, only to be swept away by the tidal waves. The absence of timely and clear risk communication to the public undoubtedly contributed to the scale of the disaster.

It is worthwhile recalling that 20 years after the 1999 Super Cyclone, when an extremely severe cyclonic storm, Fani (2019), struck the Odisha coast, the loss of human lives was less than 100. This has been ascribed to the fact that prior to Fani's landfall, the authorities had not only issued appropriate warnings but also issued clear instructions to move away from areas within Fani's projected path onto higher ground and into cyclone shelters.

Looking back, one could confidently state that the 1999 Super Cyclone triggered not only the evolution of disaster management structures in India during the following years, including the formation of the National Disaster Management Authority, the National Disaster Response Force, and other enabling structures at the state level, but also better and effective risk communication.

8.3.4 *Earthquakes and tsunamis*

However, such forecasting capabilities do not exist for all kinds of disasters. For example, no scientifically validated method exists for predicting earthquakes and issuing appropriate warnings. As mentioned earlier, earthquake zonation and microzonation maps do give some indication of earthquake vulnerability of any region. For example, the entire Himalayan belt is more likely to face strong earthquakes. We have also seen that for big cities with a high density of population and constructions, even microzonation maps exist. Risk communications in such cases are mainly focused on making the population familiar with the hazards and the possible measures that one could take to minimize the damages. This includes, among other things, instructions on building earthquake-safe dwellings. Recall that most deaths during earthquakes occur as people get trapped under collapsing buildings.

Earthquake precursors such as radon emission and sudden change in subsoil water levels have been discussed in the scientific literature for a long time. However, these signals neither point to specific locations nor indicate the likely magnitude and time of the occurrence of the event. We have a long way to go before reliable warnings can be issued prior to a major earthquake. At the same time, the importance of such signals cannot be underestimated. How does one keep public interest alive in such disaster-related precursors? Again, risk communication alone can help.

Tsunamis belong to another class of public risks. Though tsunamis are caused by earthquakes that are not predictable, they take time to reach distant shores where they can cause severe damage. Therefore, it has become possible to put tsunami warning systems in place, and in cases where there is enough time, one can issue timely warnings and minimize loss of life. It is however important to highlight the importance of public awareness creation to prepare the communities to act decisively and without panic when such alerts reach them from any source.

On 12 January 2010, when a devastating earthquake occurred in Haiti, it claimed more than 200,000 lives and the damage exceeded 11 billion USD. Till then, Haiti neither had an in-country seismologist nor a seismic network; there was no active fault map, no seismic hazard map, no microzonation, no building codes, nothing that could have either forewarned the public or made them ready to face the disaster. The tragedy prompted the introduction of affordable seismographs all over the country, including at schools and private homes. This simple step led people to ask questions. They wanted to be informed and they wanted to know how to prepare themselves either in case of an earthquake or a tsunami. It has even created a population that would like to be able to help improve knowledge about earthquakes. We have already pointed out how a similar educational programme in the state of Uttarakhand has been modified to create awareness about earthquakes among students. We also recall that during the 2004 tsunami, the Pichavaram mangrove forest saved the Cuddalore district of Tamil Nadu. This was also achieved in the historic town of Pondicherry, which was protected from the same tsunami by a combination of mangroves and a massive stone sea wall built and reinforced earlier by the French during the three centuries of their occupation of the area. The mangrove forests also support the marine ecosystem and its diversity. We must strive to raise awareness in protecting and nurturing mangrove forests in areas vulnerable to tsunamis. To keep public interest alive on such disaster events, October 19 is observed as International Shakeout Day. Similarly, November 5 is observed as World Tsunami Awareness Day in memory of a tsunami that hit the village of Hiromura in Japan on November 5, 1854.

8.3.5 *Infectious diseases*

Communicable diseases belong to another unique class of public risks. Risk communication [7] in the case of a known epidemic involves informing people of the onset, spread, necessary precautions to contain the spread, availability of drugs and vaccines, availability of hospitals and other support systems, as well as necessary measures for timely relief. The public also looks forward to assurances from the government that their welfare is being taken care of.

The problem gets complicated in the case of first-time epidemics like COVID-19. The governments have no alternative but to function with incomplete information on various aspects of the infection. As in the case of COVID-19, there may not even be a drug or a vaccine. Initially, for close to 1 year, we had no vaccines. Now, we have several vaccines, though we still do not have any effective drugs at the time of writing this. In the absence of drugs, the treatment necessarily involves only treating the symptoms (palliative care) and this needs to be communicated to people in clear terms. The efforts of scientists developing vaccines and drugs need to be publicized to instil hope among the people. The advisories need to be continuously updated in the face of emerging evidence and clearly stated since any flip-flop in policies only creates confusion and panic. Some epidemics and pandemics linger on for a long time, occasionally due to mutations of the pathogen. Sustaining the discipline of the masses for maintaining appropriate behaviours such as social distancing, wearing masks, and frequent sanitizations for a prolonged period becomes a challenge. These forced lifestyle changes often have severe economic consequences, which also need to be addressed.

8.3.6 *Unknown risks in case of new and emerging technologies*

We have repeatedly emphasized that the twentieth century marks the beginning of a new era in the history of human civilization, an era dominated by S&T. Every new technology has also brought with it new risks, some of which are not even fully understood at present. Communication of such risks to the public at large is a challenge. We have already mentioned that risk perception even on a familiar day-to-day matter varies from person to person and from time to time for the same person. In matters of new and emerging technologies, perceptions of the associated risks are not based solely on technical grounds. They often involve emotional, social, cultural, or simply psychological perceptions as well, as we have pointed out repeatedly.

As mentioned earlier, the Green Revolution in the seventies made a dramatic difference in food production in the country and India today is a food surplus country *despite almost a four-fold increase in population.* How did this happen? Over and above the technological inputs such as the seeds, fertilizers, and pesticides, effective communication with the farmers played a crucial role in this transformation. It involved the psychological process of convincing farmers to adopt the new varieties and to follow the recommendations for growing them. They had to change their practice of farming, perfected over millennia, to adapt to the new seeds, developed by Norman Borlaug (1914–2009). It was not achieved by dictating but by demonstrations of plots of the new varieties right alongside traditional ones.

There are concerns that the Green Revolution has plateaued out and we need to take recourse to new technologies to not only increase food production, with lesser inputs, but also increase their nutrition values, shelf lives, and resistance to pests and to the vagaries of weather. One such example is the GM technology. For example, nearly two decades ago, Bt brinjal was developed to give resistance against the brinjal fruit and shoot borer pests. It was approved for commercialization in India in 2009. But a series of public agitations against the introduction of Bt brinjal led the Government to impose a moratorium [8] on its release for widespread use. The resistance to GM technology has also impacted the introduction of another genetically modified seed variety, mustard with better nutritional qualities and higher yield. Clearly, risk communication to the public on these developments has been inadequate.

The rapidly advancing climate change and the worsening global warming make it imperative that we develop seed varieties that provide crops resistant to drought, rust, pest, salinity, flood, and heat with greatly increased yield and nutrition. Developing them through natural selection is fraught with uncertainties, unpredictabilities and inordinate delays. Radiation-induced transmutation and genetic modification can greatly accelerate the process, but we have to convince our farmers and the general public to adopt these, of course after their safety and efficacies have been scientifically established.

Yet another case of poor risk communication involves food irradiation, which is known to increase shelf lives of agricultural products by delaying sprouting and spoiling. It has also been shown to control insects and invasive pests. This technology has been available in India for several decades. Yet, either because of ignorance or because of "perceived concerns", it is not practised widely, resulting in an unfortunate loss of up to 40% of the fruits, vegetables, and grains. Different standards for doses and a differing list of products that can be irradiated by different countries have only added to the confusion.

Are the long-term interests of the country being compromised by these hesitancies?

In this context, it is interesting to recall a court case in Geneva that demanded denial of permission to the commissioning of the Large Hadron Collider — the largest and the most powerful particle accelerator in the world, conceived, designed, and built at CERN, Geneva, due to a perceived fear that it could produce microscopic black holes, which could swallow the Earth! The case was not entertained by the courts. Still, the CERN authorities appointed an international committee to examine the objection as a confidence-building measure. The committee ruled out any threat to the Earth since even if microscopic black holes are indeed created in the collision of protons, they would evaporate almost instantaneously before interacting with any other particle.

Public risks associated with some of the emerging technologies like human cloning and artificial intelligence are not even fully understood.

How does one translate complex technical assessments into public perceptions? How does the public risk perception shape public risk acceptance? How does one thwart vested interests from derailing some of the well-intentioned initiatives? These are complex issues that warrant interdisciplinary research and dialogue [9–12].

When the World Health Organization embarked on the effort to eradicate smallpox, volunteers and health professionals travelled to even remotest villages of Asia, Latin America, and Africa, visiting marketplaces, village fairs, and other meeting places with photographs and posters explaining the symptoms of smallpox, locating infections, and then vaccinating all those living within a distance of 2.5 km. This awareness drive was to prove most valuable in this effort. A similar awareness drive about polio and tuberculosis has also proved to be quite effective. The awareness drive about COVID-19 is too recent and was discussed earlier in detail.

Similar awareness drives are needed for almost all the risks that we face. Underplaying or overplaying risks are counterproductive and do not elicit a calibrated response from the public. Public trust in risk communicators is central to risk communication. Unfortunately, much of the information on public risks come to the public from disaster management agencies through electronic and print media on which public trust is the least. We have also seen that due to the recent developments in information and communication technologies, there are multiple sources of information, even though not all of these are necessarily unbiased, unmotivated, and even correct, on any public risk resulting in expert opinions and public perceptions. Therefore, public reactions to risks often have a "rationality" of their own. Literature is also flooded with a great deal of pseudoscience, which can easily confuse untrained individuals. All these necessitate that risk communication is not a one-way process of transferring information but a dialogue, two-way communication of the risk perceptions, the "expert" perception and the "layman" perception.

8.3.7 *Dialogues in place of discourses and debates in risk communication*

We have already mentioned that science communication is a discourse — an expert talking to the layman to create familiarity and to remove superstition, the threat of the unknown. Unfortunately, discourses do not fulfil the objective of instilling the right perceptions. Sometimes, debates between groups having different perceptions are resorted to. Unfortunately, in a debate, both sides are very combative, acrimoniously oppose each other and try to prove each other wrong, with an aim to win. Thus, during a debate, one listens to the other side, with the sole purpose of finding flaws and countering the proffered arguments. Debating parties assert, affirm, and reaffirm their own points of view and defend their own assumptions as "the truth". Debates are intended to demolish the position taken by the other side and to assert that the solution offered by the "home side" is the only correct solution to the exclusion of the other side. Thus, the two sides end up criticizing each other's arguments. Once again, a debate is based on the firm belief that one's own point of view is the only truth and requires one to defend it against challenges. Debates look for differences and, as mentioned earlier, flaws and weaknesses of the other side's arguments. In the process, the participants suspend their "feeling of relationship" and end up belittling, deprecating, and ridiculing each other. Debates invariably rule out the possibility of the emergence of a "new" solution, as both sides tend to believe that they already have it. Thus, debates often end in a stalemate, where both sides continue with their stated views and continue to claim "victory".

There is yet another aspect to risk communication by way of debates that we would like to mention here. In many of these debates, scientists are often pitted against social activists. Social activists, by their training in dealing with people and their emotions, tend to be ebullient, eloquent, and voluble. Scientists, on the other hand, trained to deal with difficult observations, careful measurements, and analysis of data, tend to be cautious and men of a few words. To an uninformed onlooker, this hesitation to comment without examination on the part of the scientists appears as a sign of weakness and can be counter-productive.

We would like to emphasize that in dealing with public perceptions of public risks, dialogues can be far more effective than discourses and debates. These have been used for millennia for the resolution of conflicts even among warring sides, with great success [13]. Dialogues, unlike discourses and debates, envisage collaboration between two (or more) sides. Thus, the two sides look to find a common ground and a common understanding. To achieve this, the two sides listen to each other to be able to understand each other, find meaning, and find agreement. In the process, the worldview of both sides is enlarged and admits a possibility of undergoing change. During dialogues, people put forth their assumptions for scrutiny and allow for introspection of their position. This opens the possibility of even a far better solution than what either side had originally proposed. Dialogues signify an open-minded attitude, a willingness to accept that one could be wrong, and a readiness to change. One's own positions are freely discussed during dialogues, with a belief that the other side will ponder over it and will even help improve upon it rather than ridicule it or destroy it. This allows one to be open to discussing one's own beliefs. Unlike during a debate, in a dialogue one searches for basic agreements and for strengths in the arguments of the other side, with a willingness to find a solution and even co-opt it. Most importantly, dialogues are based and built upon a real and genuine concern for each other and do not seek to alienate, offend, or ridicule the other side. This then provides that a part of the solution could be held by both sides and together, they can arrive at a better and workable solution. Thus, dialogues open a pathway to discovery and remain open-ended, improving the solutions as one proceeds.

8.4 Information and Communication Technologies: New Challenges and Opportunities

We have talked about it before and would like to reemphasize that another major shift that is taking place in recent times in risk communication is that government sources and experts are no longer seen as the only "trusted" sources of information. Information and communication technologies (ICT) are going through revolutionary and fast-paced changes for the last few decades. The ubiquitous mobile phone links anyone to anyone, anywhere, at any time. Communication media like television provide visual news almost on a 24×7 basis. The World Wide Web has emerged as a very potent source of information on anything, at any time, anywhere. People have an inherent tendency to "trust" the information passed on to them by someone whom they know. Opinions of public figures, the public at large, and social media contents compete with information from the government and the experts. Even genuine differences of opinion among experts are seen as an indication of a lack of reliability. It is worth remembering that during the polio vaccination drive, the government had taken extensive help from such groups of people as popular actors, singers, and sports personalities to improve the effectiveness of the government channels with great success. A similar exercise is being used for educating people about COVID Appropriate Behaviours. Professional and social networks are emerging not only as major sources of information but also as sources of advice on anything. Unfortunately, this channel of information is also vulnerable to "misinformation" with ulterior motives. "Deepfake" is the latest weapon in the hands of unscrupulous persons to spread doctored information with ulterior motives using audio visuals which are very difficult to distinguish from undoctored information.

Scientists across the world are treated with trust. While this increases their responsibility, neither public outreach is a priority in our scientific institutions nor every scientist is an effective communicator. In a democratic setup, we can only proceed if we reach a majority consensus. On the other hand, scientists are often seen as intimidating specialists living in their ivory towers. Quite often, their attempts at outreach are taken up too late and are the only occasions when common people get to meet high officials or scientists. This deep "chasm" or "divide" needs to be bridged before we even begin to embark on the task of risk communication. The idea should be to familiarize the public with the risks and convince them about the measures being undertaken and prepare them to welcome the measures so that there is no need to justify them. It is also important that persons engaged in the exercise of outreach have cultural competence and linguistic skills appropriate for the audience.

Political and socio-religious leaders, celebrities and media can play a major role in carrying the message from the specialists to the public. The role of professional bodies, such as science and engineering academies, science clubs, and voluntary agencies, such as the Red Cross, Ramakrishna Mission, and even Rotary International, cannot be underestimated.

As mentioned earlier, public perceptions of public risks are not always logical and are highly influenced by the views of others, in particular, enlightened religious, political, and social leaders.

Fig. 8.3 Birsa Munda (1875–1900)

We are reminded of a very powerful and historical example of risk communication by a social leader. Birsa Munda was a very popular and influential tribal leader of Munda tribes inhabiting the forests in what we now call Jharkhand (see Fig. 8.3). He had a good elementary education. The tribals living in the forests used to drink water from streams and ponds, which were often stagnant and which they shared with domestic and wild animals. During the late nineteenth century, an epidemic of cholera started and spread rapidly in his area of influence. He asked people to boil water before drinking. His immense popularity and near-cult status helped in the wide dissemination of this information and saved thousands from miserable death [14]. It is a pity that he himself died in the prison of Ranchi, supposedly of cholera at the young age of 25, though no symptoms of cholera were found in his remains. It is heartening to note that the Government of India has decided to observe his birth anniversary (November 15) as Janjatiya Gaurav Divas (Tribal Glory Day) to celebrate the contribution of tribes of India to its history and culture, and preserve their cultural heritage.

It is also illustrative to recall another historical anecdote. When a severe earthquake hit Bihar in India (see Chapter 2), Mahatma Gandhi called it "a divine chastisement for the great sin we have committed against those whom we describe as Harijans". Another well-known intellectual of that time, the Nobel-Laureate Rabindranath Tagore, who had earlier bestowed the title Mahatma (Great Soul) on him, took a serious offence to the irrationality in the statement, even though he was totally in agreement with the issue on hand and wrote: "I find it difficult to believe it. But if this be your real view on the matter, I do not think it should go unchallenged." He also drafted a long rejoinder and sent it to Mahatma Gandhi, with a request to print it in a newspaper he was publishing. The opening paragraph of the letter stated: "It has caused me painful surprise to find Mahatma Gandhi accusing those who blindly follow their own social custom of untouchability of having brought down God's vengeance upon certain parts of Bihar, evidently specially selected for His desolating displeasure. It is all the more unfortunate because this kind of unscientific view of things is too readily accepted by a large section of our countrymen..." The letter also argued that one should not "associate ethical principles with cosmic phenomena". However, even though the letter was published, a rejoinder was also published by Mahatma Gandhi, essentially reconfirming the earlier position. We can only speculate that a rational view propagated and supported by leaders with such vast influence could have greatly helped inculcate a scientific temper among his followers without compromising the crusade against untouchability in any way.

Also recall the articles of Lokmanya Bal Gangadhar Tilak (see Chapter 3), which are believed to have incited the Chapekar brothers to assassinate the commissioner of Poona during the Poona Plague. Once again, we can only speculate that the traumas and the tragedies of Poona could have been minimized had the authorities taken the help of Tilak and utilized his vast influence to spread awareness about the plague and precautions to be taken.

More and more countries across the world are moving towards democratic forms of governance. With the increasing participation of the public in government policy-making, there is no alternative to taking the public into confidence and empowering them with reliable information on all matters including management of public risks. But communicating public risks to the public at large, especially if it involves matters of new and emerging technologies, is complex and challenging. This is made even more complex in a country like India with large social and economic differences and multiple languages of communication. In the absence of authentic and scientifically validated information, rumours, superstitions, and unverified claims flood social media and inundate the public discourse, often giving a false sense of security and causing irreparable harm. Often, genuine differences of opinion among experts erode the confidence of the public in the experts. Communication of public risks will always remain a challenge, which also makes its execution more interesting and even satisfying. And a continuing dialogue with the public plays a pivotal role in this endeavour.

8.4.1 *Engaging the young*

It is also known that grown-ups generally tend to cling to known concepts. It is the young who are open to new ideas and new opportunities. They are also more willing to take a chance. We need to engage with them.

We recall that the European Organization for Nuclear Research (CERN) in Geneva regularly invites students as well as citizens of all ages to visit CERN, see the facilities, and interact with the scientists. CERN also runs an extensive summer intern programme, which gives an opportunity to young students to work in frontier areas of S&T. At the end of their visits, they return as ambassadors of CERN and its programmes. National Aeronautics and Space Administration conducts similar programmes for students and is easily the most recognized science organization across the world, igniting the minds of young students.

It is high time that Climate Change and its root causes, as well as its mitigation scenarios, become a standard and compulsory subject in the syllabus for young students to involve them and prepare them to face this crisis and to engage them in its solution.

Opposition to the establishment of nuclear plants has often been found to diminish after the public, in particular, young students are taken to existing sites. In France, communities vie with each other to host nuclear programmes, contrary to the "not in my backyard" syndrome witnessed in most countries regarding new nuclear-related initiatives.

We will take two well-known examples of public response to two infrastructure projects in India: the Singrauli resettlements and the Sriharikota resettlements.

The area in the eastern part of Madhya Pradesh and the adjoining southern part of Sonbhadra district in Uttar Pradesh is collectively known as Singrauli. Due to the rich coal districts in the area, Singrauli is often referred to as India's energy capital. A cluster of thermal coal plants, both government and privately owned, dot the area with a declared potential for 35,000 MW of generation capacity. The history of displacement in this area is indeed revealing. The entire area of Singrauli was originally covered by a dense forest. The river, Rihand, was dammed in the late 1950s to create an artificial lake called the Rihand reservoir (Rihand Dam or Govind Ballabh Pant Sagar). The building of the dam displaced around 200,000 people. However, due to a misjudgement of the catchment area, people had to move again as the reservoir area expanded in the early 1960s. In 1975, people were again displaced for the National Thermal Power Corporation, Shaktinagar thermal project. Not only the tribals were disproportionately affected, but also the so-called compensatory development had little to talk about — no schools, no health centres, no roads, not even electricity and clean drinking water. Very high unemployment among the displaced communities has also been noted. It is not surprising that, in 1993, a proposal to expand the Rihand Ash Dike through World Bank financing met with stiff resistance from the villagers. The pattern is replicated across India, souring relations between the government, corporates, NGOs, and the public.

In contrast, there are important lessons to be learnt in another case — the relocation of Yenadi (or Yanadi) tribes in Sriharikota, the hub of India's space launch programme. By a conscious decision, the strategy was to cohabilitate rather than rehabilitate the locals which made them partners. The island has seen no conflicts during the last few decades.

In the case of new and emerging technologies, when neither the costs nor the risks can fully be enumerated, a hope to arrive at a consensus through truly democratic means is indeed a utopia.

8.5 Summary

Humanity has always been vulnerable to a wide spectrum of public risks, such as natural disasters and infectious diseases. The recent developments in S&T, while providing tools to manage public risks of different kinds, have also broadened the spectrum of public risks that we have to face. Across the world, the governments, as the custodians of public good, are expected to also hold the responsibility of managing public risks. With more and more countries across the world opting for democratic forms of governance, we also see that formulation of government policies on the management of public risks are highly vulnerable to public perceptions. Overestimation and underestimation of the risks by the public often inundate policy-making by the governments.

Risk perceptions are highly individualistic. Consequently, risk communication between people could be complex because their risk perceptions may not coincide. The traditional form of risk communication by persons in authority and experts is often inadequate and ineffective because of the differences in their risk perceptions. We argue that risk communication has to be a dialogue with ample opportunities for both parties to share their perceptions and strive towards a consensus.

Recent developments in information and communication technologies (ICT) have certainly enhanced our ability not only to disseminate information on the possible risks to the public but also to manage the risks by effectively disseminating timely warnings and coordinating disaster relief and rescue operations. Unfortunately, ICT has also made it easier to spread unsubstantiated and often incorrect information, sometimes even with ulterior motives.

With increasing public participation in government policy-making, there is no alternative to taking the public into confidence and empowering them with reliable information on all matters related to public risks and the steps being taken to combat the risks.

We would like to conclude our discussions by recalling the Indian tradition of "वसुधैव कुटुम्बकम्", i.e., the world is a family. No one is safe unless everyone is safe. This concept is most relevant in the case of public risks and at times of disasters. We would also like to recall the Hawaiian Greeting "Aloha" at this juncture, which stands for love, affection, peace, compassion, and mercy, and signifies a force that holds existence together.

References

[1] D. K. Srivastava and V. S. Ramamurthy, *Climate Change and Energy Options for a Sustainable Future.* World Scientific, Singapore (2021).

[2] *Nuclear Energy for a net-zero world*, International Atomic Energy Agency, Vienna, Report 62/2021'.

[3] R. B. Grover, Managing transition to a low-carbon electricity mix in India, *Econ. Polit. Wkly* **LVI**(39), 29 (2021).

[4] V. S. Ramamurthy and D. K. Srivastava, *Fukushima, A Decade After: An energy mix of renewables and nuclear is the most viable option*, CWA # 462, April 27, 2021; http://globalpolitics.in/view_cir_articles .php?url=Fukushima:%20A%20Decade%20After&recordNo=554.

[5] D. K. Srivastava, *Shades of Green Energy*, Invited talk at BRICS Young Scientists Conclave on Affordable Healthcare, Energy Solutions and Cyber-Physical Systems, The World Academy of Sciences, September 2021.

[6] C. Sagan, Why we need to understand science, *Sceptical Enquirer* **4**(3), 263–269 (1990).

[7] V. S. Ramamurthy and D. K. Srivastava, Communication and management of public risks (with specific reference to the COVID-19 global pandemic), *Curr. Sci.* **118**, 1878–1884 (2020).

[8] J. Ramesh, Responsibilities of science, responsive to society: A new dialogue, in P. Bagala and V. V. Binoy (Eds.) *Bridging the Communication Gap in Science and Technology — Lessons from India.* Springer, Singapore (2017).

[9] D. B. McCallum and L. Anderson, Communicating about pesticides in drinking water, in R. E. Kasperson and P. J. M. Stallen (Eds.) *Communicating Risks to the Public. Technology, Risk, and Society*

(An International Series in Risk Analysis), Vol 4, Dordrecht: Springer (1991); S. Lang, L. Fewtrell and J. Bartram, Risk Communication, https://www.who.int/water_sanitation_health/dwq/iwachap14.pdf?ua=1.

[10] *Health Emergency and Disaster Risk Management Framework*, World Health Organization; https://www.who.int/hac/techguidance/preparedness/health-emergency-and-disaster-risk-management-framework-eng.pdf.

[11] O. Renn and D. Levine, Credibility and trust in risk communication, in R. E. Kasperson and P. J. M. Stallen (Eds.) *Communicating Risks to the Public. Technology, Risk, and Society (An International Series in Risk Analysis)*, Vol 4, Springer, Dordrecht (1991).

[12] D. C. Glik, Risk communication for public health emergencies, *Annu. Rev. Public Health* **28**, 33–54 (2007).

[13] D. Yankelovich, *The Magic of Dialogue: Transforming Conflict into Cooperation*. Touchstone, New York (1999); United States Institute of Peace, www.usipglobalcampus.org.

[14] M. Devi, *Aranyer Adhikar* (The Rights Over the Forest) (1977).

Chapter 9

Epilogue

Whatever their business let politicians take up
My message is just love; far, far, let it reach

— Jigar Moradabadi,
Guldasta Dar Guldasta,
vol. 3, p. 160.
(English translation by Syeda Hameed).

Wolf Larsen, the enigmatic sea captain in Jack London's famous novel *Sea Wolf*, declares in his usual blunt manner: "..., life is the cheapest thing in the world. There is only so much water, so much earth, so much air; but the life that is demanding to be born is limitless. Nature is a spendthrift. Look at the fish and their millions of eggs.... Could we but find time and opportunity and utilize the last bit and every bit of the unborn life that is in us, we could become the fathers of nations and populate continents.... Nature spills it out with a lavish hand. Where there is room for one life, she sows a thousand lives,..."

What the sea captain does not elaborate upon is the fact that life faces life-threatening and life-extinguishing risks at every step. It starts from the very moment life starts its journey. Just imagine billions of seeds produced by a banyan tree every year. If each of them were to grow into a tree, the Earth would be covered with banyan trees very quickly. Yet, it does not happen, and we may get just one or two banyan trees growing out of their seeds during their lifetime. Just to overcome this large-scale destruction of its seeds, the banyan tree developed a capacity to drop aerial roots, which grow into trees.

Considering nature's fury and the wanton destruction, which life faces at every step of its journey, right from its "inception", it should be our endeavour and bounden duty to treasure life and protect it to the best of our ability and ingenuity. After all, ours is the only planet in the Universe we know so far, which harbours life in all its wondrous diversity!

The famous dictum:

"चरैवेति, चरैवेति ।।"

i.e., "keep moving, keep moving" from the Aitareya Brahmana (Chapter 3, Part 3) was interpreted by Swami Vivekananda as follows: "Life lives under a constant threat of Death at every moment, and yet Life lives, and it lives by challenging Death with every step it takes and every moment it lives." Our life is a testimony to this vitality of Life.

Our early human ancestors, starting their journey as hominins, stumbled through various risks, and most of them vanished, leaving behind only a faint trail, to emerge as the *Homo sapiens*. With their improved vocalization, *Homo sapiens* evolved into large groups, and with control of fire faced predators, ate healthier food, made better weapons, and spread to occupy the entire globe. And they have faced risks all along — for getting food and water and for their very survival. This constantly evolving ability to face risks has defined mankind, his accumulation of a wealth of knowledge, and his civilization. *Homo sapiens*, in the process, have conquered land, sea, and airspace and started venturing beyond our planet. They have learnt to live under the harshest conditions even in the remotest parts of the world. And they have multiplied, starting perhaps from a few tens of thousands to more than 7 billion now. This number is likely to touch 10 or 11 billion by 2050.

But our planet has paid a very heavy price for it. Millions of plant and animal species have gone extinct. The land, the water, and the air have become polluted. The use of fossil fuels is depositing tens of billions of tonnes of carbon dioxide and other greenhouse gases in the atmosphere every year, which is threatening to push Earth into a hot bath. Deforestation is changing the patterns of the weather and even rainfalls, which have supported agriculture for millennia. Even more tragically, it is bringing man into conflict with wild animals, and he is contracting zoonotic diseases. And the requirement of providing a decent life and making profits have caused and continue to cause industrial disasters.

One unambiguous message that the recent COVID-19 pandemic has left us with is that we continue to live in a fragile world despite thousands of years of continuous existence on the face of the Earth and unprecedented advances in science and technology over the last few centuries. Humanity has faced the wrath of extreme natural disasters and learnt to face them and live with them. Epidemics and pandemics have also been part of human history. Multiple civilizations have been erased by these disasters. Following the Industrial Revolution of the eighteenth century, we have also learnt to live with industrial disasters of various kinds. The twenty first century is dominated by several new and emerging technologies, each of them carrying its own known and unknown risks. Humanity is also learning to live with them. Recent developments in science and technology have enabled us to face the risks with a lot more confidence. Our understanding of extreme natural events like cyclones and earthquakes has increased considerably in recent years. With appropriate and timely warnings, we have been able to minimize the loss of lives to a great extent. Economic losses however continue to be high because of the increasing economic activities. The modern development of drugs and vaccines has changed the way in which humanity now faces infectious diseases. *Yet*, COVID-19 has sent us a grim reminder that managing public risks will remain a challenge to humanity.

Governments across the world have a major role in managing public risks. With an increasing number of countries opting for democratic forms of government, public perceptions and public acceptance of public risks also play important roles in managing public risks. Unfortunately, in electoral politics, long-term strategies are distinctly at a disadvantage and public perceptions can easily be swayed by vested interests. Consensus is a utopia. In matters of new and emerging technologies, the government is as ignorant as the public at large.

Risk communication plays a crucial role in moulding public perceptions and public acceptance of public risks. In particular, the ever-increasing bouquet of communication channels like mobile phones and the World Wide Web in addition to the traditional radio and television make risk communication extremely easy and complex at the same time.

Countries across the world are always in competition — for political, strategic, or economic reasons. However, in managing public risks, international "coopetition" (cooperate while competing or compete while cooperating) has proven again and again as a far better strategy for all. Understanding weather and weather-related disasters have benefited a lot from international cooperation. The development of affordable vaccines is yet another case in favour of international coopetition. *Last but not the least*, one must not forget the critical role played by science and technology in combating public risks.

It is known by now that 2020 has been the hottest year on record. This has been attributed to the atmospheric carbon dioxide levels, which are the highest they have been over at least the past 3.5 million years. It is also known that the world has about 2.2 billion children, out of which about 2 billion live in developing countries. People everywhere, but more so in the developing countries, are facing multiple climate-related and pollution-related issues, such as severe drought and flooding, extreme temperatures and other extreme weather events, air pollution, water scarcity and water pollution, crop failures, and decreasing fish catches. It leaves their children vulnerable to hunger, malnutrition, and disease. Almost every child on the Earth is exposed to at least one of these climate and environmental hazards. Children are more vulnerable to air pollution as their immune systems are still developing and their lungs are still growing. In fact, as we mentioned earlier, a child takes in more air per unit of body weight than an adult. Continued burning of fossil fuels and numerous environmental pollutants cause an increased risk of respiratory diseases, including asthma and pneumonia. It is known that pneumonia is the biggest single killer of children, especially in developing countries, and we lose 800,000 children under the age of 5 years every year to pneumonia. There is absolutely no reason why we can't stop this cruel fate to which our most helpless citizens are exposed.

Natural disasters, infectious diseases, industrial disasters, and unknown dangers of emerging technologies expose our children to danger, suffering, and even premature death. In the developing world, these issues are further compounded by political, economic, social, cultural, ethnic, or religious issues that compromise children's basic rights. UNICEF has estimated that 149.2 million children under the age of 5 years were stunted and 45.4 million children were wasted in 2020. One-third of stunted children of the world are from India. Children of the developing world carry a bigger burden since they (or their parents) do not have the financial cushion available to the people of the developed nations. We owe it to our children and future generations to initiate urgent action, else the number of those suffering will continue to rise.

As Lord Gautam Buddha lay dying, his disciples, including his cousin Anand, were worried about who would guide them in his absence. His famous advice was, "Appa Deepo Bhava" — (Be a light unto yourself). We have seen that the research and development in sciences are the lights that have guided mankind through all the risks that it faced in the past to safety. It is our firm conviction that it will continue to do so in the future.

Science playing the role of saviour of mankind in the face of disasters has a very endearing parallel in Indian tradition.

Govardhan Lila (see Fig. 9.1) is one of the celebrated events in the life of Lord Krishna. According to Shrimad Bhagwat, Vraja (now called Brij), where he lived with his foster parents, had a tradition of offering sacrifices to Indra, the God of rains and thunder for bountiful rains. Krishna argued with them to instead offer their gratitude to Govardhan, the hillock with its verdant forest, fruit-bearing trees, green pastures, and lakes and streams with crystal clear waters, which sustained them, their cows, and their agriculture. Indra, annoyed by

Fig. 9.1 Krishna lifting Govardhan Hill to protect people from torrential rains and flood

this "denial" of offerings, "ordered" torrential rains, which flooded the village. To protect the villagers, Krishna lifted the Govardhan and asked the villagers to take shelter under it:

"इत्युक्त्वैकेन हस्तेन कृत्वा गोवर्धनाचलम् । दधार लीलया विष्णुश्छत्राकमिव बालकः ॥ १९ ॥

अथाह भगवान् गोपान्हेऽम्ब तात व्रजौकसः । यथोपजोषं विशत गिरिगर्तं सगोधनाः ॥ २० ॥

Having said this, Kṛishṇa picked up Govardhana Hill with one hand and held it aloft, just as easily as a child holds up a mushroom. The Lord then addressed the cowherd community: O Mother, O Father, O residents of Vraja, you may now come under this hill along with your cows.

— Shrimad Bhagwat, 10.25.19-20"

Krishna returns to the importance of knowledge again and again during his teachings and declares as follows:

"न हि ज्ञानेन सदृशं पवित्रमिह विद्यते ।

In this world, there is nothing as purifying as knowledge.

— Gita 3.48"

Truly, scientific knowledge has been the "Govardhan", which has provided protection and succour on several occasions when mankind has faced disasters. It is also the only protection we have against future disasters such as the ferocious onslaught of climate change and its attendant woes which threaten our very existence on the Earth. We trust that mankind can face this crisis as well, with a sensible and equitable application of science.

Index